PRAISE FOR *THE YOUNG LORDS SPEAK*

"*The Young Lords Speak* delivers an in-depth exploration of the Young Lords Organization from its origins as a street gang in Chicago to its transformation into a powerful revolutionary force. Professor Lazú expertly curates the first collection of primary sources, filling a critical gap in the historical narrative of the Young Lords. The anthology illuminates the ideals and actions that ignited a radical social justice movement within the Puerto Rican diaspora in the late 1960s and continues to inspire the ongoing struggle for Puerto Rican liberation."

—**Iris Morales**, activist, educator, former Young Lord in New York, and author of *Revisiting Herstories: The Young Lords Party*

"This dazzling collection—part archive, part memoir and ethnography, part the everyday poetry of the street—hits like a hammer and then settles like an abiding life lesson. Its authenticity—meaning its contradictions, disagreements, ambiguities, paradoxes, and uncertainties—illuminates the movement muddle in full. There's no attempt here to present the fragmented, dynamic, and contested reality of revolutionary struggle as linear or coherent, but rather as it truly is: achingly human, deeply aspirational, trembling, and real. I left my encounter with *The Young Lords Speak* energized, refreshed, and with my radical imagination unleashed and my courage renewed."

—**Bill Ayers**, author of *Demand the Impossible!* and *When Freedom Is the Question Abolition Is the Answer*

"Through memoir, speeches, oral histories, primary sources, and incisive framing, this reader ushers in a long-awaited compendium of the history of the Chicago Young Lords Organization. Attending to how the history of the Young Lords has often been told through the works of their counterparts and comrades, Lazú carefully lays out an archive of political thought and action that remain ever salient."

—**Yomaira C. Figueroa-Vásquez**, professor and director of the Center for Puerto Rican Studies (CENTRO)

"*The Young Lords Speak* brings to life the origins and history of the Young Lords Organization. In the late 1960s, the Young Lords took a stand refusing to accept the repetitive forced removal of their families and friends from yet another Chicago community. With one foot in Chicago, another in the Puerto Rican diaspora, they demanded better. They organized breakfast programs for hungry children, a health center for the sick, daycare for mothers struggling to support their families, and they organized their community to envision, hope for, and demand a better future. Their efforts were embraced by the community but targeted with repression and reaction from the powers that be. This is their story, the perspectives and lived experiences of members of the Young Lords Organization.

"Each of us engaged in the struggle for a more just society do so standing on the shoulders of those who went before. Knowing that history and sharing it is our path to building the sea for future changemakers to swim in and be successful. For an important piece of that history, this book is a must-read."

—**Helen Shiller**, former Chicago City Council member and author of *Daring to Struggle Daring to Win: Five Decades of Resistance in Chicago's Uptown Community*

"This reader offers an essential collection of primary sources on the Chicago Young Lords Organization. Covering various aspects of the group's history, the documents provide critical evidence of the activities, motivations, political ideologies, and achievements of the YLO."

—**Lilia Fernandez**, historian and author of *Brown in the Windy City: Mexicans and Puerto Ricans in Postwar Chicago*

THE YOUNG LORDS SPEAK

BUILDING REVOLUTION ON THE STREETS OF CHICAGO

EDITED BY JACQUELINE LAZÚ

FOREWORD BY CHAIRMAN JOSÉ "CHA CHA" JIMÉNEZ

Haymarket Books
Chicago, IL

Published in 2026 by
Haymarket Books
P.O. Box 180165
Chicago, IL 60618
www.haymarketbooks.org

ISBN: 979-8-88890-454-1

Distributed to the trade in the US through Consortium Book Sales and Distribution (www.cbsd.com) and internationally through Ingram Publisher Services International (www.ingramcontent.com).

This book was published with the generous support of Lannan Foundation, Wallace Action Fund, and Marguerite Casey Foundation.

Special discounts are available for bulk purchases by organizations and institutions. Please email info@haymarketbooks.org for more information.

Cover design by Shane Ramos.

Printed in Canada by union labor.

Library of Congress Cataloging-in-Publication data is available. Library of Congress Control Number: 2025943415.

10 9 8 7 6 5 4 3 2 1

Contents

7. Alliances and Coalitions

8. Counterintelligence, Infiltration, and Indictment

9. A New Era

Foreword

The turbulent 1960s were a period of worldwide revolutionary thought and action. The Vietnam War was happening, and many were going off to fight. Some never came back. Others returned only to find they weren't treated like heroes. At the same time, external forces were shaping the world around us. After the assassination of Martin Luther King Jr. in April of 1968, riots erupted, primarily on the West Side, as well as across the South Side and near the Cabrini-Green projects close to Lincoln Park. Later that summer, the Democratic National Convention saw hippies and reporters bloodied by Mayor Richard J. Daley's police, and those images played out on national TV. These events occurred in Lincoln Park, the park bordering Chicago's Lincoln Park neighborhood.

Meanwhile, powerful liberation struggles were unfolding across the globe. We watched with surprise and admiration as the Black Panther Party carried out their work in California, which resonated deeply with us because of our own experiences with police brutality. We learned about the efforts of the Black and Brown Berets, Corky Gonzales, Cesar Chavez and the United Farm Workers, the American Indian Movement, among others. Many of these groups eventually became part of our network of allies, forming a coalition that posed one of the greatest challenges to the government.

Lincoln Park, much like Greenwich Village, New York, and Berkeley, California, became a haven for peace and change. Intelligentsia thrived here, reading and quoting theories from existentialism to those of Marx, Lenin, Mao, Che Guevara, Zapata, Malcolm X, and Huey Newton, ideas they hoped would ignite revolutionary change beyond the classroom and into the streets of US cities. The Young Lords, identifiable by our distinctive purple berets, brought these radical ideas to life by naming the modern-day land question and organizing the community against the forces of gentrification, including Old Town redevelopment, one-way streets, slum conditions, sheriff evictions, and police brutality.

We chose September 23, 1968, as our official founding date. This aligned us with the symbol of El Grito de Lares, the 1868 Puerto Rican uprising against Spanish rule, and it recognized an important moment in our efforts for working-class solidarity. Our actions got the attention of the media, the police, and the city. From that point on, the police made me the leader of the Young Lords, constantly arresting me and targeting the group, which only further mobilized members who were on the fence about becoming political. Soon, we started organizing community actions and programs, including demonstrations for welfare rights, women's rights, against police brutality, and for self-determination for Puerto Rico and other Latin American nations.

A major political turning point for the Young Lords came after the killing of Manuel Ramos by an off-duty cop on May 4, 1969. His death mobilized many more of our members and others in the community. Two weeks later, we occupied the McCormick Theological Seminary. This occupation highlighted the various oppressions our communities faced, from displacement to police violence, and the complicity of institutions claiming Christian values. Shortly after, we established the Young Lords' National Headquarters at the People's Church and joined William "Preacherman" Fesperman of the Young Patriots and Deputy Chairman Fred Hampton of the Illinois chapter of the Black Panther Party to form the Rainbow Coalition. Daycare centers, breakfast programs for children, health clinics, institutional takeovers, demonstrations for self-determination, and voter education and registration stood as powerful examples of weapons to mobilize power to the people.

The Young Lords not only joined a revolution but expanded upon it, leading efforts in Lincoln Park and barrios across the country. But it's important to recognize that this is a people's struggle, rooted in self-development and directed at the neighborhood level. It is also a protracted struggle, still in its initial stages during the late sixties. For this reason, we view our historical data as part of a developmental process rather than as an end result and understand the Young Lords as an inseparable vanguard entity within a larger mass movement. Anything less would stunt the growth of our people.

It is true that we experienced moments of retreat amid the height of our activity, but these were never passive periods where we ceased to function altogether. Instead, they were strategic retreats, when we took on different forms to prepare for new battles. This is a fight for people's control over their nations and neighborhoods. We are not alone. We stand for self-determination—neighborhood-driven self-development, self-determination for Puerto Rico, Latin America, and all nations of the world. This remains as true today as it was in 1969. We cannot afford the luxury of giving up this fight or functioning separately from the community that gave us our roots.

Our target audience has always been the US barrios. These are the spaces where the unskilled and underemployed, *the lumpenproletariat*, workers, and minorities live, not as a market audience but as the most exploited members of this society. This exploitation places them in direct opposition to the superpower, "policemen of the world" ideology. There is no need to spend much time educating them about slave-like conditions because they are already trapped and chained by them. What they need are role models and leadership to guide them out of this bondage, and this is why they followed the Young Lords.

Education has been our most effective weapon. Done right, it makes people independent, united, strong, and resistant to co-optation. Inspired by Frantz Fanon, we understood that poverty and instability in our families and barrios were imposed conditions. Today, cities still deny these systemic issues. Private real estate speculation and City Hall–sponsored land grabs create a tax base but displace families, destabilize neighborhoods, and expand slums. This is a crime, not a solution to crime. Real solutions lie in education, employment, cultural diversity, empowered role models, and self-development.

The Young Lords also believed in direct action. Theories can only be truly understood and internalized through the everyday practice of working in programs, participating in demonstrations, and engaging in other educational events. While book learning is essential, shaping a future through action is far more impactful. This is what the Young Lords were accomplishing and why our history stands as a testament to revolutionary practice. While others talked about revolution in the '60s, we were creating change.

We never stood for violence. Violence is a disease that already exists in our neighborhoods, one we aim to eliminate. We stand for peace. But this vision is constantly threatened by the beneficiaries of the status quo, whose response to ghetto violence is to focus on property development rather than human development. We protected ourselves by uniting Lincoln Park against developers and Latinos against their nations' oppressors. While we may have lost property and prime land, we won the hearts and minds of the people. That was our goal: to unite our barrios to defeat the oppressors.

When the Young Lords and Latinos were racially targeted by Daley's police repression, we used it as a rallying point, and the community responded by demonstrating nonviolently, both inside and outside the Chicago Avenue police station. When the Young Lords were forced underground by the courts in 1969, our most powerful weapon was education, not guns. Our struggle was never about machismo; it was about courage and perseverance. We feared no one, and the police can attest to this. At the same time, we were not suicidal. As Mao said, "Preserve ourselves in order to defeat our enemy," and this has always been our objective.

We responded by forging coalitions with the Black Panthers and Young Patriots Organization (YPO), a mostly white Appalachian group from Uptown. We traveled to the West Coast to establish ourselves and ties with the Chicano-Mexicano and Native American movements. We organized Young Lords chapters that included both Puerto Ricans and Chicanos in Los Angeles and Hayward, California. While operating underground, we opened a Young Lords branch in Milwaukee and published our newspaper. Later, on a farm near Tomah, Wisconsin, we established and ran a training school focused on armed self-defense, organizing techniques, and revolutionary thought. Over twenty individuals participated, and the school lasted two years. We referred to this as an *active retreat*.

We didn't just take action. We built a political foundation. Our early platform was influenced by the Chinese Communist Party, but more directly by the Black Panther Party's Ten-Point Program. In Chicago, we started with the Three-Point Platform focused on Puerto Rican self-determination, liberation for all oppressed peoples, and neighborhood empowerment. As the struggle grew, we created a twelve-point and later a ten-point program to meet our communities' changing needs. My connection to the Panthers was both personal and political. I worked closely with Fred Hampton and stayed in touch with his family and members of both the Illinois and national chapters after his assassination. We learned from the Panthers' discipline and community programs, and they recognized us as comrades in the same fight. That bond shaped our vision and taught us that real power comes through solidarity across movements.

In New York City, Young Lords chapters echoed our call for power to the people. They launched garbage protests, established free clinics and breakfast programs by taking over a church, fought police brutality with funeral marches, and advocated for women's rights and Puerto Rican independence. While we acknowledged the separation of our groups, there was no division in philosophy or commitment to the people. This unity strengthened our organizing, with New York focusing on the East Coast and Chicago building a base in the Midwest. By then, no Puerto Rican could ignore the Young Lords. Authorities in both cities tried to discredit us, sow division, and incarcerate leaders, forcing us underground and out of the People's Church.

In December 1972, the Young Lords brought the training school back to Chicago and Milwaukee. On December 4, I turned myself in on trumped-up charges, using the moment to highlight Fred Hampton's murder and continue our struggle. Despite subzero temperatures, five hundred community members gathered outside the Town Hall District police station. After two years out of the media spotlight, the crowd's size forced police to hand me a microphone, allowing me to speak. Unbeknownst to them, this demonstration also set the stage for our aldermanic campaign in the 46th Ward, marking another chapter in our fight.

While I was serving that year, my father died from alcoholism, and it hurt deeply that I was not permitted to attend his funeral. He had told me he was tired of people speaking badly about his son, and that stayed with me. My children, like the children of so many others in US jails and movement politics, grew up without the warmth of their father's love. My only consolation was knowing I was not alone in that pain. It is true I had already spent a good part of my life locked up for being in a gang. Now I was serving more time for standing up for justice than I ever did for anything I did in the street. Through it all, I thought a lot about my mother. She carried the weight of our family through some of the hardest times, and I know my choices and absence broke her heart. It also affected how my sisters and I related to each other. We each had our own pain and ways of dealing with it, and for a long time, we struggled to find common ground. Like many in the movement, I learned that fighting for liberation often meant sacrificing the very people we loved most.

One month after my release, we addressed a packed congregation of Latinos in a Lakeview church, where I officially announced my bid for alderman in a ward that included Wrigley Field, the Gold Coast lakefront, working-class neighborhoods, and segregated minority communities, many of them Latinos displaced by urban renewal and facing arson for profit. While I became the first Puerto Rican to run a major organized campaign in Chicago, our focus was not on that milestone. With only 1,100 Latinos registered to vote in the 46th Ward, our campaign was framed as a fight between the neighborhoods and City Hall. Our theme song captured the spirit: "People, have you heard the news? City Hall has got the blues. People dancing in the streets, united to a mighty beat. Together, we can change it, turn it around and rearrange it. Hand in hand, hand in hand, there's a new day dawning in our land."

The 46th Ward campaign was an extension of the Young Lords' fight for neighborhood-driven self-determination and a direct response to repression by Daley's patronage machine, the Chicago police, and the Cook County courts. Promoted as an "organized vehicle for change," the campaign also aimed to transform the Young Lords' image, as the media persistently labeled me the "former leader of the Young Lords street gang." Our voter registration efforts expanded beyond Chicago into other Latino neighborhoods, and one of our earliest rallies took place outside Pontiac Correctional Center. Three campaign managers led the effort: Slim Coleman, representing the Black Panthers' Intercommunal Survival Committees; Jim Chapman, from the Independent Precinct Organization (IPO), which had run William Singer for mayor and Dick Simpson for alderman; and myself, as both a campaign manager and the head of the Young Lords. We held daily strategy meetings at my home office, which also served as the Young Lords' headquarters. Located at Wilton and Grace Streets, the office featured our name, logo, and signature purple and black colors prominently above the doors, reflecting the movement's presence and purpose.

Our aldermanic crusade echoed the Black Panthers' electoral strategy in Oakland, challenging critics who dismissed it as petty bourgeois reformism. In the early '70s, how many Latino politicians existed, or even belonged to the petty bourgeoisie? We believed revolutions are made by the people, not for them, and it was our role to facilitate that process. Some argued that elections in Puerto Rico were a farce perpetuating poverty, and we agreed they were not the solution. In Puerto Rico, we supported leadership and self-determination, and in the US, we fought for neighborhood-directed self-development, human rights, and civil rights equal to all others living within US borders. Like the Panthers, we saw local elections as a way to protect and empower our people and as part of the larger fight against colonialism in Puerto Rico and for civil rights in the United States.

We were fortunate that others, like Helen Shiller, who had organized alongside us and later also ran for alderman, took up our banner for the neighborhoods and emphasized gentrification in areas like La Clark, La Madison, Lincoln Park, Lakeview, and Uptown, the very same issues we had fought for. In 1982, a few Young Lords came together to support the election of Chicago's first Black mayor, the honorable Harold Washington. His campaign theme was "Neighborhoods First," and I became the first Hispanic citywide precinct coordinator. I also served as the North Side Hispanic precinct leader for his campaign. After Washington's victory, the Young Lords, as the Puerto Rican Diaspora Coalition, became the first Latino group to host a victory rally, drawing 100,000 Puerto Ricans to Chicago. In collaboration with the Puerto Rican Parade Committee, we distributed 10,000 "Tengo Puerto Rico en mi corazón" buttons. Washington's campaign paved the way for Hispanics from our area to win seats in City Council, the Illinois State Congress, and the US Congress.

This history showcases the Young Lords' organizing success, but its value diminishes if revolutionary goals remain unmet and those alive today choose not to continue the fight. Our struggle is a protracted one, a process of development that will continue with or without us. It is a struggle of action, not one of armchair theorizing. Education has always been central to this work, not just as a means of learning but as a revolutionary tool for empowerment and collective action. Through popular education initiatives and community workshops, we created spaces where knowledge and awareness fueled transformation, directly challenging systemic oppression and pushing the movement into the twenty-first century.

While the Young Lords were always of diverse cultural backgrounds, many Puerto Rican leaders were directly affiliated with the Young Lords Organization in Chicago. These included Sexto and Ruben Aviles, Tony Baez, Orlando Dávila, Edwin Diaz, Luis Figueroa, Carlos Flores, Carmen and Mirna Flores, José "Pancho" Lind, Yolanda Lucas, Raul Lugo, Adrian Luna, Alfredo Matías, the Matos brothers, Cano Miller, David Mojica, Edwin and Carmen Nieves, Joe and Chabela Nieves, Andres Nuñez, Hilda Ortiz, Beata Perez, Benny Perez, Fermin Perez, Eddie Ramírez, Marta Ramos, Margaret Resto, Miguel Ríos, Cisco Rivera, David Rivera, Modesto Rivera, Ralph and Luis Rivera, Danny and Juan Rodríguez, María Romero, Hector Salgado, Beatrice Santiago, Joe "Cosmo" Torres, and many others. Some held clear leadership roles within the organization and the Central Committee. Others were what we called Rally Lords, the rank-and-file members who showed up at a moment's notice, working tirelessly to support our survival programs. They are all Young Lords.

Prominent Mexican American organizers included Omar López Zacarias, minister of information for the YLO; Angel "Sal" del Rivero, head of security; Hilda Ignatin, a leader in the women's movement; Luis Chavez, who led the People's Church takeover alongside David Rivera; and Alberto and Marta Chavira, directors of the Betances Health Center. Cuban Americans Luis Cuza and Juan Montenegro were among our most effective strategists. Angie Lind (Navedo), an Italian American who had been with us since the gang days and later served as communications secretary, was one of our most dedicated members throughout every stage of the movement. Faith Schumacher, a Jewish American ally, was also among our most committed members during the Young Lords' protracted struggle. Marion Stamps, one of the many Black leaders we collaborated with, integrated the Young Lords into her efforts to organize Cabrini-Green residents, standing together against displacement.

White supporters included Mike James and Rising Up Angry, Mike Klonsky, Walter "Slim" Coleman, and other former Students for a Democratic Society leaders who stood with the poor and Latinos in Lincoln Park. Dick Vision and Pat Devine of the Concerned Citizens of Lincoln Park were the first non-Latinos to organize Puerto Ricans against the land grab. Father Hoffman and Reverend James Reed of the Church of the Three Crosses mobilized clergy against gentrification, while business owner Buddy and his Tab Root Pub led a courageous fight against eviction. Helen Shiller and the Intercommunal Survival Committee in Uptown played key roles in my aldermanic campaign, as we did in her successful 1987 run for 46th Ward alderman. Angie Shansky also took on a leadership role in my campaign.

The Young Lords built strong partnerships with other Latinos fighting for change in Chicago. In Wicker Park, we worked alongside the Latin American Defense Organization (LADO) to support welfare caseworkers' unions and recipient rights. In Lakeview, Hilda Frontany's Lakeview Citizens Council and David Hernández's La Gente organization played pivotal roles in the fight against gentrification. Leaders like Reverend Jorge Morales, Marilou Porrata, and Mecca Sorrentini of the Puerto Rican Socialist Party and the Segundo Ruiz Belvis Cultural Center organized rallies, marches, and trained new youth leaders. In Humboldt Park, the Spanish Action Committee (SAC), the Puerto Rican Organization for Political Action (PROPA), and Allies for a Better Community were key collaborators. By the mid-1970s, the West Town Concerned Citizens Coalition united groups to address police brutality, school reform, and low-income housing. While not all can be named, every partner was vital to our collective struggle.

Finally, this work has flourished through years of collaboration with many colleagues and institutional partners at DePaul University and Grand Valley State University. In particular, Dr. Jacqueline Lazú, a sister from the East Coast whose passion for Young Lords history stems from her deep understanding of inner-city struggles, human rights, and Puerto Rican independence. Her belief in the transformative power of culture and education shaped this project, inspiring us to uncover untold stories and forge pathways that once seemed impossible. I am deeply grateful for her unwavering commitment and camaraderie.

I dedicated most of my life to preserving the history of Puerto Ricans in Lincoln Park and the Young Lords while continuing the movement that began over fifty years ago. Lincoln Park, the birthplace of the Young Lords, became central to the fight for Puerto Rican self-determination, a struggle tied to resisting colonialism and human rights violations all over the world. We hope this book inspires others to share their stories, strengthening our collective memory and ensuring the Young Lords' legacy of resistance continues to inspire future generations of change makers.

José "Cha Cha" Jiménez
Founder and Chairman
Young Lords Organization
December 2024, Chicago

Introduction

Toward a Reparative History of the Young Lords and the Origins of the Movement

Cada guaraguao tiene su pitirre.
—Puerto Ricans

The Puerto Rican saying "cada guaraguao tiene su pitirre" (every hawk has its kingbird) expresses a deep cultural logic: the small and unrelenting *pitirre* (kingbird) defends its home by attacking the powerful *guaraguao* (hawk). This image of bold resistance in the face of overwhelming force has long been a symbol of Puerto Rican defiance. Poet José de Diego adopted it in his early-twentieth-century *Cantos de pitirre*, depicting the actions of the United States:

La cruz se alargaba
sobre los brazos batientes y, encesa
de lumbres de oro la pupila brava,
el guaraguao inquiría en las sombras del monte su presa . . .

The cross stretched out
over its flapping wings, and, ablaze
with golden lights, its fierce gaze,
the hawk searched in the shadows of the forest for its prey . . .

While the small but mighty bird, symbolizing Puerto Rico, protects its forest home:

"¡Pitirre!" resuena su grito,
cada vez que el audaz pajarito
como una rígida flecha al cuello del monstruo acomete.

"Pitirre!" resounds its cry,
each time the bold little bird,
like a rigid arrow, strikes at the monster's neck.[1]

The metaphor resonates not only with Puerto Rico's political condition under US colonialism but also with a broader spirit of survival and dignity in the struggles of the diaspora. *The Young Lords Speak: Building Revolution on the Streets of Chicago* offers a documentary history of the Young Lords Organization (YLO) in Chicago by returning to the people, places, and ideas that gave the movement its form and by inviting a critical examination of the narratives that have overshadowed them. The Young Lords embodied the defiant spirit of the pitirre. Their newspaper *Y.L.O.* was briefly renamed *Pitirre* by their minister of education, Tony Baez. In fact, Baez worked on three publications as an organizer, all titled *Pitirre*, produced in Puerto Rico, Chicago, and Milwaukee. For the YLO, the newspaper was a vital tool for empowering marginalized communities and linking self-determination to global struggles for liberation. From its beginnings in Chicago, the YLO forged the political, aesthetic, and ideological foundation for one of the most influential and enduring Latinx social justice organizations in the United States, sparking a movement within the Puerto Rican diaspora.

Reframing the Origins

Yet, more than fifty-five years later, the history of the Young Lords in Chicago is still too often reduced to a few familiar leaders, obscuring the group's collective vision, political depth, and deep community roots. Their influence did not disappear in the early 1970s; it lived on in the activism and public work of former members and in the memories of the communities they served. People still remember the Betances Clinic, the marches, the park cleanups, and the everyday rhythms of life in Boricua Lincoln Park.

A growing body of scholarly essays, case studies, dissertations, artistic projects, and journalistic work has begun to open the door to more expansive and nuanced research on the Young Lords. This book begins with the premise that history lives not only in the documents we preserve but also in what people remember, feel, and claim. The most meaningful part of this work is witnessing people taking pride in their stories, challenging dominant narratives, and affirming the value of grassroots knowledge in shaping how we understand the past.

Founded in 1959 as a street gang in Lincoln Park, the mostly Puerto Rican group emerged from a multiracial, working-class community shaped by postwar migration, poverty, and the need for protection from systemic violence. Inspired by the era's social movements, they shifted from street survival to organized resistance under the leadership of Chairman José "Cha Cha" Jiménez. They cast their work as self-defense against police brutality, discrimination, and the urban renewal projects of the 1950s and 1960s, which displaced low-income residents and communities of color to make way for wealthier newcomers.

As sociologist Arnold R. Hirsch notes in *Making the Second Ghetto: Race and Housing in Chicago, 1940–1960*, Chicago pioneered models of segregation through these redevelopment programs.[2] Neighborhood associations like the Lincoln Park Conservation Association (LPCA) advanced preservation measures that simultaneously excluded longtime residents. The Young Lords understood these policies as part of a larger system of colonial and racial domination, linking local displacement to the broader struggle for Puerto Rican independence and global anti-imperialist movements. By late 1968, they were putting this analysis into practice through community alliances and direct action.

While some Young Lords leaned into activism and others straddled the street life, it was precisely this tension that shaped the group's radical political direction. From the beginning, they built alliances across a wide political spectrum. They collaborated with progressive religious organizations like the Concerned Citizens of Lincoln Park (CCLP) and the North Side Cooperative Ministry, working with Pat Devine, Reverend James Reed, Reverend Bruce Johnson, and Eugenia Johnson to resist displacement and challenge city development plans. They also formed ties with more militant groups such as the Latin American Defense Organization (LADO), led by Obed Lopez, and the Black Panther Party (BPP). Even as they radicalized, the Lords maintained ties to street organizations. They worked with groups like the Latin Kings, the Young

Comancheros, the Latin Eagles, and the Blackstone Rangers, alliances that grounded their politics in the everyday realities of urban youth.

These coalitions, especially with the Black Panther Party, not only were strategic but reshaped how the Young Lords understood politics. The Panthers influenced their work through political education, direct action, and a structural analysis centered on class solidarity. Rejecting cultural nationalism, the YLO embraced a Puerto Rican identity grounded in the material needs of working-class people, where cultural expression took shape through demands for health care, housing, education, and liberation. Gina Pérez's work shows how Puerto Ricans in Chicago were first framed as a model minority before being recast as a racialized threat amid anxieties over neighborhood change.[3] Historian and Young Lord Martha Arguello extends this analysis by tracing a diasporic identity shaped by racialization and colonialism yet forged through coalition and struggle.[4] Cultural identity thus became a political tool that invited Black, Mexican, and white working-class youth to see their own conditions reflected in the Puerto Rican fight for liberation. The Young Lords' inclusive strategies located Puerto Rican self-determination within a broader movement rooted in material conditions, racial consciousness, and solidarity across oppressed communities.

The Young Lords chose September 23, 1968, as the date marking their emergence as a political organization, linking their movement to El Grito de Lares and its anticolonial legacy. They named their free health clinic after Ramón Emeterio Betances, the nineteenth-century abolitionist, doctor, and independence leader who embodied the struggle for freedom and justice. As cultural studies scholar Wilson Valentín-Escobar notes in the closing chapter of this book, Betances and other early independence leaders understood Puerto Rican liberation as transnational in scope. The Young Lords extended this legacy by tying their demands to global movements, invoking the slogan "Tengo Puerto Rico en mi corazón," later expanded to "Tengo Aztlán en mi corazón" in solidarity with Chicanx and other Third World struggles. Their organizing reflected a grounded yet expansive vision that connected diasporic self-determination to internationalist revolution, developing alongside a growing class analysis rooted in their experiences as poor and marginalized urban youth.

It is important to remember that the Young Lords began as a gang in Chicago. Their political outlook was shaped by life within the so-called lumpenproletariat, a category Marx and Engels dismissed as politically unreliable and that encompassed the poor, the unemployed, welfare-dependent families, and street organizations living at the margins of the economy.[5] The Black Panther Party reframed this group as a potential revolutionary force when politicized through education and action.[6] This reframing resonated with the Young Lords' own experiences and affirmed their relationships with street organizations as part of their political strategy. This approach was visible in November 1968 when they cohosted the Month of Soul Dances with the Blackstone Rangers at St. Michael's gym, creating early spaces of Black–Puerto Rican unity and Afro–Puerto Rican cultural visibility in a community where it had long been neglected.

At the same time, the Young Lords' political commitments were taking shape through the everyday struggles of marginalized Puerto Rican and Mexican welfare mothers, tenants, and service workers in Lincoln Park. Their early work with the Latin American Defense Organization (LADO) supported efforts to secure representation, defend welfare rights, and organize workers excluded from formal unions. Standing with welfare mothers, the Young Lords came to understand women and urban poor families as central to revolutionary struggle. These early connections formed the political foundation for their later participation in the Rainbow Coalition founded by Deputy Chairman Fred Hampton, which brought together the Black Panther Party, the Young Lords, the Young Patriots Organization, and other groups organizing poor and working-class communities, across racial lines.

1968 was a period of intense political upheaval. Cha Cha often described his arrest that year as an early awakening. He also pointed to a meeting of the Lincoln Park Community Conservation Council, where he was struck by the absence of Puerto Rican residents, as a pivotal moment in the Young Lords' political shift. In the months that followed, he and other members organized protests, confronted urban renewal offices, and built alliances that strengthened the Young Lords' political resolve.

The killing of Manuel Ramos by an off-duty police officer in May 1969 became the deeper turning point for many in the organization. Manuel, admired within the group, and Ralph Rivera, who was also wounded, were among its most politically engaged members. The shooting brought profound grief and exposed the reach of police violence, and in later years some reflected on how differently members experienced the shift that followed. The officer was never arrested, yet four Young Lords, later known as Los Cuatro Lords, were taken into custody. In response, members organized a major protest march and joined the Poor People's Coalition, which included seminarians, LADO, the BPP, the YPO, and the CCLP, to lead the takeover of McCormick Theological Seminary. For nearly a week they occupied the Stone Administration Building and renamed it the Manuel Ramos Memorial Building. As historian Felipe Hinojosa explains, the takeover forced a white religious institution to confront its role in gentrification and opened new possibilities for solidarity.[7]

Two months later the Young Lords took over the Armitage Avenue Methodist Church, renamed it the People's Church, and made it their national headquarters. With support from Reverend Bruce Johnson and his wife Eugenia, they launched the Betances Health Clinic, opened a free daycare, held rallies, helped build the People's Park, and collaborated with the Neighborhood Development Corporation, the Poor People's Coalition, and architect Howard Alan on a low-income housing plan rooted in community needs. These initiatives formed the foundation of the Young Lords' survival programs. They also carried forward the Black Panther Party's emphasis on political education, grounding their work in the slogan "educate to liberate." The People's Church era marked the consolidation of the Young Lords' political vision. Over roughly a year and a half, the organization became its most cohesive and widely supported. Women played essential roles in shaping and sustaining the survival programs, particularly through Mothers and Others, which made community care central to their understanding of liberation. From their headquarters the Young Lords strengthened coalitions with national and transnational movements including Students for a Democratic Society, Revolutionary Youth Movement II (RYM II), the Puerto Rican Socialist Party, and the Third World Committee for Solidarity with Vietnam. Their revolutionary platform attracted working-class youth, students, gang members, and artists who saw themselves reflected in the movement.

As the Young Lords expanded their reach, they became targets of escalating state and local repression. City Hall and the media painted them as violent criminals, while police and federal agents actively worked to destabilize the organization. The Chicago Police Department's Gang Intelligence Unit and Red Squad monitored their activities, and the FBI's COINTELPRO targeted their connections to Puerto Rican independence and other radical groups. Senate hearings labeled them subversive, and city departments such as Human Resources circulated hostile propaganda. At the neighborhood level, groups like UPTIGHT (United People to Inform Good-doers Here and There), organized by 43rd Ward Alderman George Barr McCutcheon, and the We Love America Committee became the Young Lords' fiercest local adversaries. They operated a hyperlocal surveillance network that sent flyers and even the group's discarded trash to the FBI. The murders of key allies including the Reverends Bruce and Eugenia Johnson, Fred Hampton, Mark Clark, Pancho Lind, and Manuel Ramos reflected the violent conditions in which these movements operated.

In this climate, and facing another excessive charge, Cha Cha went underground in 1970 for his own safety. While he was underground, others stepped into leadership at the People's Church and continued the group's work. During this period, Minister of Education Tony Baez helped establish a Milwaukee chapter of the YLO where *El Young Lord* was published, further strengthening connections to the Chicanx movement and the Puerto Rican nationalist struggle. Cha Cha emerged from underground in December 1972 to serve a one-year jail sentence. After his release, his allies began organizing his historic 1975 aldermanic run. Though he lost, winning 39 percent of the vote in Chicago's 46th Ward was a major achievement for a formerly criminalized radical. As Marisol V. Rivera and Judson L. Jeffries note in their case study of the campaign, it marked a turning point in Puerto Rican and Latinx political participation.[8] Even as they faced the full force of state surveillance and political hostility, deep internal strains, and a civic landscape determined to erase them, the organization refused to disappear. That persistence continued into the 1980s, when Jiménez and the Young Lords helped mobilize Latinx support for Harold Washington through rallies and grassroots outreach under the name Puerto Rican Diaspora Coalition. On June 5, 1983, he introduced Washington at a Puerto Rican festival in Humboldt Park that drew an estimated one hundred thousand people.

In the decades that followed, former Young Lords remained active, building institutions in education, housing, labor, and health. Although many did not describe this work as a direct continuation of their time in the YLO, the political formation they experienced shaped their commitments and the fields they entered, from social services and public health to union organizing, community development, and cultural work. By the 1990s, a smaller core group who continued to see their activism as linked to their Young Lords experience began preserving their history through archives and oral histories, reconnecting their professional and political trajectories to the movements that had shaped them. This book brings together those memories, recollections, and materials not as a nostalgic tribute but as a reminder that understanding this history is essential for confronting the unfinished struggles that shape our present.

Hidden Histories and Changing Stories

In July 1969, the Young Lords in Chicago inspired the opening of a YLO chapter in New York. By mid-1970, the organizations parted ways, with the New York group assuming the name *Young Lords Party*. Despite broad public interest, the published record on the Young Lords' history as a whole is limited, and much recovery work remains. Popular understandings of the Young Lords follow a dominant narrative centered on the New York group that emerged after the national split. Their early activities were documented in 1971 by the cinema verité film *El Pueblo Se Levanta*, produced by Third World Newsreel, and the book *Pa'lante: The Young Lords Party*. Visibility deepened as many New York members took on roles in the media as journalists, editors, political commentators, and activists. Former member Miguel "Mickey" Meléndez published an early memoir, *We Took to the Streets*, in 2005, and Felipe Luciano released *Flesh and Spirit* in 2025. Darrel Enck-Wanzer's *The Young Lords: A Reader* (2010) gathered key documents in a project aligned with what *The Young Lords Speak* seeks to achieve, and Johanna Fernández's *The Young Lords: A Radical History* (2020) offered the first comprehensive, scholarly study of their politics. Within this landscape, former member Iris Morales's work stands apart. Her documentary *Pa'lante, Siempre Pa'lante* (1996) and her books *Through the Eyes of Rebel Women* (2016) and *Revisiting Herstories* (2025) bring a feminist perspective that connects the histories of New York and Chicago and foregrounds voices long overlooked. Her commitment to recovering women's experiences underscores the unevenness of the archival record and helped me approach the history of the Chicago Young Lords with a recognition that gaps continue to exist.

Books, articles, and oral histories have helped preserve the Young Lords' legacy but often blur the line between the Young Lords Organization and the Young Lords Party, making it difficult to trace the movement's full trajectory. After the 1970 split, the New York group rebranded as the YLP, adopted a new platform, and shifted its focus to Puerto Rico, diverging from the YLO's commitment to local empowerment. Although they moved in new political directions, they kept the Young Lords' name and logo, which shaped how the movement came to be publicly understood. In *Flesh and Spirit: Confessions of a Young Lord*, Felipe Luciano reflects on the importance of names. Drawing on his experience as a member of the Last Poets, the seminal Black Arts group whose breakup preceded the Young Lords' split, Luciano recalls that rupture with an acute awareness of how identity and recognition are shaped through names. Although the YLP moved away from the YLO's gang roots and decentralized structure, these elements remained central to how many young activists understood and identified with the movement. When the YLP became the Puerto Rican Revolutionary Workers Organization in 1972, the Young Lords' name disappeared from their political work, but the dominant narrative had already taken hold.

This dominance shapes not only public memory but also scholarly interpretation. In *The Young Lords: A Radical History*, Johanna Fernández acknowledges important distinctions between the Chicago and New York chapters, including Chicago's more sophisticated newspaper and its grounded political formation rooted in local community struggle. Ultimately, the analysis presents Chicago's resistance to the 1970 split as futile, citing its supposed weakness and marginality within the national structure.[9] This framing suggests that once ties to New York were severed, Chicago no longer carried national weight. The view is shaped by a geographic logic that understandably centers New York and the East Coast because of their larger Puerto Rican populations, but it obscures the enduring significance of the political work that emerged from the Midwest and continued to shape regional coalitions as well as national politics well beyond the split. It also fails to fully consider the structural tensions, government surveillance, and ideological rifts that shaped the break. As Cha Cha Jiménez has argued, scholarship that centers New York or treats Chicago as merely local erases the working-class, barrio-based leadership and strategic solidarity that sustained the movement beyond its peak visibility.

The Chicago Young Lords were not weak—they were targeted, repressed, and excluded from the archives of visibility. Their political trajectory was shaped by Chicago's own conditions, including the stark racial segregation that led Martin Luther King Jr. to call the city one of the most hostile places he ever confronted. In this landscape, the power of solidarity work carried a different weight. The Young Lords built coalitions across Latinx, Black, and white working-class communities in ways that challenged the city's entrenched racial order. Their confrontations with Mayor Richard J. Daley and the political machine reflected this reality. Daley himself had been a member and president of the Hamburg Athletic Club, a notorious white ethnic gang on Chicago's South Side that fed directly into Democratic Party power.[10] The Young Lords understood both the dangers and the possibilities of mobilizing their own street-based networks. Their coalition-oriented, class-conscious politics linked local fights against displacement and policing to broader decolonial movements in a form of organizing that grew directly from Chicago's political landscape.

In Chicago, the Young Lords built strong alliances that left an organizing legacy still felt today. Yet the stories of the internal ruptures, including those within the chapter and the local base, were rarely shared, which contributed to the perception that the breaks were smooth or ideologically aligned. Jiménez attributed the breakdowns to both internal division and government interference, explaining that COINTELPRO infiltration, state redirection of the movement's goals, and divide and conquer tactics intensified existing tensions. He also acknowledged the role of members who spread rumors or pursued personal interests at the expense of collective ones. Out of loyalty to the larger struggle and a political commitment to protect the organization from further harm, Jiménez seldom spoke about these conflicts in public, even though his views were clear within the organization.[11]

The consequences of the historical silences in Chicago were felt as a familiar form of displacement, a quiet erasure of the resistance and everyday struggles of inner-city Puerto Rican youth and the informally educated, poor, and working-class residents of old Lincoln Park. These stories were essential to the birth of the Young Lords, yet the movement's history increasingly came to be narrated from elsewhere. This invites reflection on the role of narrative in cultural and activist spaces. Narratives give meaning to struggle and shape collective memory, yet they can also flatten complexity and reproduce the hierarchies they claim to challenge. Reading primary materials such as letters, manifestos, speeches, and photographs alongside the dominant accounts that have come to define movements like the Young Lords reveals how history is negotiated and never settled. Storytelling becomes an act of preservation as well as a political practice that reveals what power makes visible and what it conceals.

Across the decades of doing this work, that dynamic resurfaced again and again in the struggle to tell the story of the Young Lords. The desire to control how the story is told, who becomes the hero or the villain, and at times the fear of it being told at all, speaks to the pain of that neglect. For Jiménez, it strengthened his determination to ensure the story existed, that his story and the story of Chicago would not disappear. To document was itself a form of resistance, an act against the silences and distortions. As early as 1968, he began recording the Young Lords' formation, cowriting an early history of the gang with Ralph Rivera as it was evolving into a political organization for the local newspaper *Lincoln Park Press*. In 1972, while serving a one-year sentence at Cook County Jail, he wrote the manifesto *Que Viva el Pueblo*, elaborating on his role in the movement and reflecting on his family's migration to Lincoln Park and the group's transformation from a gang into a radical political organization. His writings, in English and Spanish, moved between personal and collective voices, sometimes attributed to him and at other times to the YLO or Central Committee.

This narrative approach aligns with what Yarimar Bonilla and Marisol LeBrón describe in *Aftershocks of Disaster*, where post-María testimonies confront both material vulnerability and the solitude that comes from realizing one has been unseen.[12] In the diaspora, that solitude is shaped by the experience of living in the United States as a racialized community whose political status remains unresolved. Puerto Ricans navigate unstable forms of belonging that reflect both the pressures that have pushed generations to migrate and the limits of the citizenship we hold. Attending to these lived conditions makes clear why the stories people tell about their own lives matter. This book follows that understanding by tracing the history of the Chicago Young Lords through the voices, memories, and experiences of the people who built it.

Cha Cha quickly became the Young Lords' most visible figure in its early months, especially after repeated arrests and growing media attention. People followed him for his charisma, candor, and deep roots in the community. He was organizing alongside friends from the neighborhood. He and a few others urged the group to adopt the Black Panther Party's ministerial structure, but not all members embraced that hierarchy. What developed instead was a decentralized leadership model that, although uneven at times, encouraged shared agency and grassroots creativity and allowed the organization to endure beyond any one individual. Even so, Cha Cha remained its emotional and political center. He was also polemical and complex. Over time, he spoke openly about his struggles with addiction and wove those experiences into his organizing. Leadership weighed heavily on him, and his intensity sometimes set him apart. Omar López Zacarias recalls him once leaving a meeting in the middle of a debate, saying, "Nobody understands me." His political identity took shape in that tension, in the solitude of carrying a vision others did not always share, and in the persistence required to remain the movement's only chairman. The same conditions that had once marked him as disposable ultimately made him the leader of a movement of the dismissed—of those who are erased from history.

While both the dominant narrative and Cha Cha's counternarrative have limitations, each helped preserve the Young Lords' legacy within movement histories and community memory. In Chicago, the movement grew out of the political terrain shaped by the 1966 Division Street Uprising, which sparked a wave of activism that challenged city institutions and demanded recognition for Puerto Ricans. As community groups expanded their reach, gained visibility, and secured institutional support, they helped establish a more formal Puerto Rican civic presence in the city. Ironically, this growth also contributed to the gradual marginalization of the Young Lords' history. The official accounts produced by cultural centers, service agencies, and local political organizations often emphasized stability, continuity, and community uplift, approaches that tended to privilege more established sectors of the community and left little room for the radical, street-based activism that defined the YLO. Over time, the Young Lords became peripheral to the story Chicago told about itself, even as the broader Puerto Rican community became more firmly rooted in the city's political and cultural landscape.

The shift toward institutionally grounded activism in Chicago is reflected in the evolution of the Puerto Rican Cultural Center (PRCC), co-founded in 1973 by Oscar López Rivera and led primarily by his brother José E. López. Oscar was also associated with the Fuerzas Armadas de Liberación Nacional (FALN), the US-based, clandestine group that emerged in the early 1970s from a broader transnational push for Puerto Rican independence and had a strong organizational base in Chicago. He helped establish several key community institutions, including La Escuelita Puertorriqueña, now Dr. Pedro Albizu Campos High School, before his 1981 arrest on federal seditious conspiracy charges. After Oscar's imprisonment, José guided the PRCC's expansion. Today the PRCC stands as a cornerstone of Puerto Rican resistance, blending cultural programming, community services, and political advocacy. It became a national voice in the campaign for the release of the Puerto Rican political prisoners and carried forward the political tradition of the Puerto Rican Nationalist Party while emphasizing education and human rights. Through projects such as Flags of Steel, murals, and public festivals, the PRCC reshaped the neighborhood landscape, resisted gentrification, and helped define how Puerto Rican activism in Chicago has been remembered and retold.

The Young Lords Organization played a formative role in shaping Puerto Rican political life in Chicago, yet their contributions have not been woven as visibly into the city's cultural landscape as those of their counterparts in New York. Even so, the YLO's influence endures in institutions such as the People's Law Office, Segundo Ruiz Belvis Cultural Center, and San Lucas United Church of Christ, all of which carry forward the grassroots vision the Young Lords helped forge. Chicago's history is often narrated in fragments, with the YLO, the Puerto Rican Cultural Center, and the FALN treated as separate or competing projects. A closer look shows how deeply interconnected they were and how each emerged from the same community conditions. The public conversation between Cha Cha Jiménez and Oscar López Rivera at DePaul's 2018 Young Lords symposium underscored this continuity, highlighting how their paths diverged in form but not in purpose. The YLO's coalition-based organizing and the FALN's underground resistance both advanced expansive visions of liberation. Read together, these histories reveal that Chicago, despite its smaller Puerto Rican population, generated a remarkably powerful political imagination. Understanding them in relation to one another illuminates a unified struggle and affirms Chicago as a central site of Puerto Rican liberation.

The inspiration for this collection's title comes from the 1970 book *The Black Panthers Speak*, edited by Philip S. Foner. It opens with a quote from economist Paul R. Brissenden, who describes widespread misconceptions about the Industrial Workers of the World.

> The public still knows but little about the organization and its members. . . . The public has not been told the truth about the things the IWW has done or the doctrines in which it believes. The papers have printed so much fiction about this organization and maintained such a nationwide conspiracy of silence as to its real philosophy—especially to the constructive items of its philosophy—that the popular conception of this labor group is a weird unreality.[13]

Foner saw these distortions reflected in public portrayals of the Black Panther Party, and these distortions have echoes in how the Young Lords Organization in Chicago has been remembered. The "weird unreality" has gradually shifted over the last half-century, particularly as movements like Black Lives Matter, much like the Civil Rights Movement, brought ideas once seen as radical into mainstream liberal awareness. The reissue of Foner's book by Haymarket Books, with new contributions by Barbara Ransby, Clayborne Carson, and Julian Bond, reframes the Panthers as visionary thinkers committed to community power and liberation. As Ransby reminds us, what the Panthers truly represented was political imagination, which remains more vital than ever.

The Young Lords Speak invites us to revisit these histories with care, recognizing the full complexity and connections among these movements.

Method and Memory

We began talking seriously about a book like this when I joined the Lincoln Park Project in 2002. Cha Cha had first approached the Center for Latino Research (CLR) around 1993, when poet David Hernández was serving as artist in residence at DePaul, to document the Young Lords' history and Puerto Rican displacement from Lincoln Park. With CLR staff, archivists at DePaul's John T. Richardson Library Special Collections and Archives and Young Lords members, including Tony Baez, Omar López Zacarias,

Sal del Rivero, Angela Lind (née Rizzo), and Carlos Flores, we built a collective effort around oral histories, preservation, and public memory.

A project of this scope requires sustained engagement and a range of methods, including community-based research, archival reconstruction, and oral history. It demands working through uneven documentation, conflicting accounts, and the effects of time, loss, and institutional neglect. The work also raises questions about voice, representation, and historical authority, especially when recovering narratives shaped by surveillance, displacement, and marginalization. Over time, the project has grown to include exhibitions, symposia, curricular collaborations, and partnerships across institutions, all grounded in a shared commitment to historical recovery, collective memory, and ongoing advocacy.

My approach to organizing this book is grounded in the understanding that archives are not fixed repositories but living sites of memory shaped by power, performance, and participation. This perspective is deeply informed by Diana Taylor's *The Archive and the Repertoire*, a work that shaped my early scholarly development and my understanding of embodied memory as a source of knowledge.[14] Growing up in Hartford, Connecticut, I experienced firsthand the poverty and segregation that defined Puerto Rican life in a state otherwise known for wealth and whiteness, an experience that showed how even a large and long-standing community could remain outside narratives of visibility and belonging. Years later, I learned that former Young Lords Minister of Education Tony Baez had been brought in to support the *Sheff v. O'Neill* desegregation case at my own high school, revealing an unexpected link between my personal history and the political networks I would later study.[15] I came to the Young Lords project as a Puerto Rican diaspora scholar, inspired by the movement yet unaware of its Chicago origins. My first contribution, *The Block/El Bloque: A Young Lords Story*, a play developed from newly gathered archival materials, invited public engagement and modeled how performance can function as a space for historical reclamation and community memory.

This work would not have been possible without the dedication of people who worked together to expand our funds of knowledge about the Chicago Young Lords. In Humboldt Park, San Lucas United Church of Christ, led by Carmen Flores, became a vital space for intergenerational education and community building. Chicago Public Schools teachers, including those at Lincoln Park High School, helped make this history visible in classrooms despite institutional resistance. The Honeycomb Network, a grassroots coworking space on Division Street's Barrio Borinquen, copresented *Encendidas: Women of the Young Lords, 1965 to Present* in 2023, the first community-based public history exhibition we organized. The Chicago Grassroots Curriculum Taskforce has also developed educational tools inspired by the coalition politics of the Young Lords and the Black Panther Party, among other collaborations that gave this project momentum. Family members of the Young Lords played a vital role, contributing time, memory, and perspective. Long before institutions took notice, visual artists, poets, and musicians carried these stories through their work. Photographers captured the spirit of the movement, while many others shared memories, memorabilia, and insight that shaped a more inclusive historical record. I remain deeply grateful to all who helped bring this history to life and continue to affirm its relevance.

Finally, among the influences shaping my engagement with archival gaps, Saidiya Hartman's "Venus in Two Acts" is especially important.[16] Her idea of "critical fabulation" grounds my choice to privilege storytelling to confront and reimagine what history has erased. In this spirit, our work embraces participation and collective authorship as both method and critique, unsettling conventional boundaries between subject, storyteller, and historian. From Richardson Library's meticulous archival team to the artists, educators, and family members who preserved memories, this history has always been a communal endeavor. Through performances, exhibitions, curricula, and coalition building, we continue the Young Lords' legacy by making memory a living, participatory process that speaks directly to present struggles.

Structure of the Book

This book unfolds across nine chapters and a curated set of archival documents that highlight the varied forms and media the Young Lords Organization used to build power, communicate, and preserve their history. The first two chapters focus on political frameworks and revolutionary print culture. Chapter one presents foundational materials, internal memos, guiding principles, and timelines tracing the YLO's evolving ideology from its Three-Point Platform to its later ten- and twelve-point programs.

Chapter two examines the group's bilingual newspapers (*Y.L.O.*, *Pitirre*, and *El Young Lord: Latin Liberation News Service*) as tools of grassroots education and cultural resistance. Their bilingual format reflected the linguistic reality of Puerto Rican and Latinx communities in the diaspora, where Spanish and English coexist within raciolinguistic hierarchies.

Raciolinguistics studies how language and race shape one another, revealing how ways of speaking become tied to ideas about racial identity and power. As anthropologist Jonathan Rosa notes, raciolinguistic ideologies mark racialized speakers as improper—even when they follow dominant norms—reinforcing colonial structures that devalue everyday speech.[17] In this context, the Young Lords' use of nonstandard Spanish was a radical affirmation of identity. The slogan "Tengo Puerto Rico en mi corazón" captured this spirit, asserting love for the homeland in the people's own words. Editing their language for correctness would erase its power. Preserving it affirms both its cultural integrity and political intent.

Chapters three through six deepen this portrait through first-person essays, protest literature, visual culture, and spatial storytelling, all produced or led by YLO members. Chapter three presents autobiographical and political essays that capture pivotal shifts in the organization's development, from its street gang origins to its transformation into a revolutionary force. While not centrally focused on gender, these texts begin to gesture toward questions of voice and visibility, particularly around whose accounts were preserved and whose remain absent. The small group represented here reflects the core members who remained engaged through the decades and eventually formed the foundation for our collaboration on the Lincoln Park Project. Chapter four features flyers; newsletters; project plans and campaign materials tied to direct actions, such as the occupations of hospitals, schools, and churches, and the creation of People's Park; housing plans; and documents from Cha Cha Jiménez's aldermanic campaign. These materials show how everyday tools of communication became instruments of disruption and community control. Chapter five highlights the creative and cultural production of the Young Lords and affiliated artists—poetry, mural sketches, theater pieces, sculptures, and photographs brought aesthetic vision and urgency to their politics. These works were rooted in barrio experience and gave shape to the movement's imagination. Many remain only as images in old photographs or fragments of memory tucked into personal collections. Chapter six focuses on a single but significant contribution to public memory: the Young Lords neighborhood tour created by DePaul archivist Derek Potts in collaboration with YLO members, students, and community organizers. Building on José "Cha Cha" Jiménez's original Latino Civil Rights Tour, this walking tour reclaims the built environment of Lincoln Park as a site of displacement, resistance, and political awakening.

The final three chapters examine the YLO's revolutionary alliances, state repression, and lasting legacy through editorial commentary, oral histories, public testimony, and declassified surveillance materials. Chapter seven focuses on solidarity work, especially the Lords' coalition building with the Black Panther Party, the Rainbow Coalition, and other radical movements. It opens with a keynote essay by former Black Panther Party chairman and activist Elaine Brown on Black–Puerto Rican unity and concludes with a conversation between José "Cha Cha" Jiménez and Oscar López Rivera reflecting on shared visions and long-term struggle. Chapter eight presents government and civilian surveillance efforts, including excerpts from the House Internal Security Committee hearings and files gathered by the We Love America Committee. These documents are paired with internal YLO materials that reveal the group's strategies and resilience in the face of political targeting. The final chapter centers voice and testimony. It features a speech by Wilson Valentín-Escobar on memory as resistance delivered during the fiftieth anniversary of the YLO event and an essay by Paul Mireles, a graduate student at DePaul and leader of the New Era Young Lords, one of several groups inspired by or carrying the name of the original Young Lords Organization. The book closes with a conversation between Mireles and original member Omar López Zacarias, an intergenerational exchange that affirms the YLO's values as a living tradition carried forward by young activists.

The Enduring Call for Resistance and Justice

On September 18, 2023, DePaul University in Chicago hosted *¡Todo el poder pa' la gente!: 55 Years of the Young Lords in Lincoln Park* to commemorate the movement's local legacy. The event brought together core members like Omar López Zacarias and journalist Juan González, co-founder of the New York chapter. Paul Mireles represented the power and vision of a new generation. Melissa Jiménez, daughter of Young Lords founder José "Cha Cha" Jiménez, spoke on behalf of her father, who, after more than fifty years of advocating for the Chicago roots of the Young Lords and passionately championing what he saw as an enduring movement, requested not to speak. That day, the university announced plans to install a historical marker honoring the 1969 takeover of the Stone Building, now part of DePaul's School of Music.

A striking coincidence unfolded. The marker was installed the same day a pro-Palestinian encampment began on campus, Chicago's longest occupation protest until it was dismantled by police at the end of the academic year. In solidarity, the YLO marker committee composed of faculty, students, staff, community members, and Young Lords canceled all formalities with the administration. This decision recalled the historic alignment between the YLO, its student and community solidarity networks, Puerto Rican independence movement, and Palestinian liberation struggles. While the marker offered symbolic recognition, the protest made clear that the legacy of the Young Lords is not confined to the past. Their history continues to resonate, and today's institutional responses reveal the contradictions that accompany commemoration.

In 2023, Cha Cha Jiménez also received the Public Scholar Award from DePaul University's Center for Latino Research, where early efforts to document the Young Lords first took shape. The archives developed there have become vital resources for scholars, educators, activists, and community members, inspiring projects across disciplines. Jiménez also helped establish an extensive Young Lords archive at Grand Valley State University, including the most comprehensive oral history of the organization. Over decades, he and his collaborators gathered photos, videos, newspapers, artifacts, and propaganda that document the Young Lords' formative years, their impact on Lincoln Park, the Rainbow Coalition, and their continued activism. More than fifty years later, these collective efforts continue to illuminate why the Young Lords emerged in Chicago and why their legacy still resonates.

That legacy was the result of sustained and careful labor. As I was completing the first full draft of this book, Cha Cha passed away on January 10, 2025. Our collaboration had grown from an urgent need to preserve and tell this history on our own terms and in our own voices. Over time, our work deepened into a relationship grounded in trust, shared purpose, and mutual respect. Even as his health declined, Cha Cha continued to offer guidance, insisting that this story be told with honesty and collective vision. I was honored by his confidence in me and took seriously the responsibility of shaping a book that could hold the complexity this history deserves. What began as a working relationship became a friendship, and it was a privilege to contribute to a movement that long preceded me. These pages aim to honor not only the work he helped lead but the urgency with which he pursued justice until the very end.

In 2024, while US media focused on Latinx voters in swing states during the presidential election, Puerto Rico held a historic election. Since then, questions of political status have intensified alongside the island's accelerated remilitarization as a US outpost for imperial projects in Latin America, making the conditions of colonial subordination across the Caribbean and the diaspora more urgent and visible. Yet Puerto Rican struggles remain largely absent from US political discourse, reduced to data points or cultural shorthand. Across communities, divisions over status and belonging expose the deeper contradictions of colonial dependency, where migration, precarity, and US citizenship blur the lines between survival and consent. The Young Lords understood these tensions and built coalitions across racial and class lines while navigating their own internal struggles. Even now, the histories most often told leave out the women, queer, and trans organizers who made that struggle possible, repeating the exclusions that sustain colonial and patriarchal power. Their stories are central to understanding the movement's true scope and unfinished work.

What made the Young Lords revolutionary was their political clarity and their insistence on reading struggle through the logic of material conditions, continually adapting that analysis to the demands of the moment. They rejected capitalist individualism and grounded their work in collective power, informed by Maoism and the realities of Puerto Rican life in the barrio. Cha Cha Jiménez captured this when he said, "Ours was a community-wide movement that staunchly rejected capitalist individualism. We read every day in our training school in Tomah, WI, Mao Tse Tung's *Red Book*, which states that 'petty individuals' do not make change. The grassroots people, united, make change."[18] The Young Lords understood that liberation emerges from contradiction, that power reveals itself through the conflicts between people and the institutions that dominate them, and that resistance must be sustained with discipline and love for the people. Their politics challenged every system that tried to contain them, and their example remains a touchstone for young people imagining freedom today. Like the pitirre facing the guaraguao, their struggle reminds us that courage grows in the face of overwhelming force, and their call cannot be silenced.

PITIRRE

YOUNG LORDS ORGANIZATION

TENGO PUERTO RICO EN MI CORAZON

YLO

SUMMER 1970

VOL. 2 NO. 7

Ministry of Information

834 W. Armitage

25¢

"THEY CAN JAIL US;
THEY CAN BRUTALIZE US;
THEY CAN EVEN KILL US,
BUT THE MOTHERFUCKERS CAN'T STOP US!"

José "Cha Cha" Jimenez

GUILTY OR INNOCENT?

(story inside)

1.

SYMBOLS, PROGRAMS, AND STRUCTURE OF THE YLO

YLO Symbol and Logo (1969)
Designed by Cha Cha Jiménez and Ralph Rivera
Photograph by Carlos Flores. Courtesy of the photographer

People's Church Symbol (1969)
Y.L.O. vol. 1, no. 4, October 10, 1969, p. 3
Young Lords Newspapers Digital Collection
Special Collections and Archives
DePaul University Library, Chicago, Illinois

Original YLO Mission: Three-Point Platform

(ca. 1969–1970)
Young Lords Organization
Courtesy of José "Cha Cha" Jiménez personal collection

THREE POINT PLATFORM
YOUNG LORDS ORGANIZATION

1. Self-determination for Puerto Rico
2. Self-determination for all Latino Nations and all oppressed nations of the world
3. Neighborhood empowerment

Platform and Twelve-Point Program

(1972–1973)
Young Lords Organization
Printed in *Que Viva el Pueblo*, 1973
Courtesy of José "Cha Cha" Jiménez personal collection

TWELVE POINT PROGRAM
YOUNG LORDS ORGANIZATION—(1973)

1. We want Independence and self-determination for the People of Aztlán and Puerto Rico.
2. We want an end to all imperialist wars—economic and military.
3. We want an end to the mercenary nature of the U.S. military system and an end to oppression of Latinos and other poor and oppressed people by threats of imprisonment or by economically

depriving them of their basic needs then forcing them to volunteer or allowing them to be drafted into unjust, imperialist wars.

4. We want equality for the sexes.
5. We want an end to the inner-city removal of Latinos and other poor and oppressed people. We want Latinos and all poor and oppressed people to control the housing to be built in their respective communities so that they can be sure it is fit for human beings and economically reasonable. We also want all existing housing brought up to comply with the codes.
6. We want a guaranteed income and full employment for Latinos and all poor and oppressed people.
7. We want bi-lingual education for Latinos. An education that teaches Latinos and all poor and oppressed people the true history of their past and exposes the true nature of this decadent society.
8. We want an end to the robbing of Latinos and all poor and oppressed people by GREEDY YANQUI BUSINESSMEN in the Latino community.
9. We want an end to the enormous drug problem caused by this decadent society. We want the drug pushers, the rich perpetrators of this society, arrested and tried by their victims. We want all those now in jail for crimes related to drugs discharged to community-controlled rehabilitation centers and provided with good and efficient medical care. We want research begun immediately so that the use of methadone on heroin addicts can be discontinued.
10. We want the same good and efficient health care that is given to the rich to be given to Latinos and other poor and oppressed people. We want it to be free to Latinos and all poor and oppressed people. HEALTH CARE IS A HUMAN RIGHT.
11. We want an end to the brutalization and cold-blooded murder of Latinos and all poor and oppressed people by Yanqui police in this country. We want police in Latino communities to be Latinos and under the control of the Latino community.
12. We want all Latinos released from federal, state, county, and city jails, because they have not had fair trials nor have been tried by a jury of their peers as defined by the U.S. Constitution. They have been tried by Yanqui courts and jurors who have no basic

understanding of Latinos nor of the conditions to which Latinos are subjected.

Cha Cha Jimenez, General Secretary
Young Lords Organization
Cook County Jail
December 31, 1972

Ten-Point Program

(1993)
Young Lords Organization
Courtesy of José "Cha Cha" Jiménez personal collection

TEN POINT PROGRAM
YOUNG LORDS ORGANIZATION—1993

1. We stand for self-determination for Puerto Rico, all Latin American nations, and all nations of the world.
2. Bilingual, Bicultural education.
3. End discrimination and abuse of women/children. Pro-choice but against the Malthusian theory of over-population as it relates to Puerto Rico.
4. End police brutality, harassment, and repression of the people.
5. A just and humane criminal justice system that focuses on rehabilitation of offenders vs. punishment.
6. Free health care for all.
7. Neighborhood self-development.
8. Full employment or guaranteed income.
9. Peace
10. Consumer protection, worker's rights, and corporate social responsibility.

Central Committee Structure: Roles and Responsibilities

(n.d.)
Young Lords Organization
Courtesy of José "Cha Cha" Jiménez personal collection

CENTRAL COMMITTEE STRUCTURE

ROLES AND RESPONSIBILITIES

Chairman

Communications Secretary	Ministry of Education	Ministry of Defense	Ministry of Information	Chief of Staff	Ministry of Finance
Mailing	Political Education	Field Marshall ——— Head of Security	Media Commercial and Movement	Office Management	Fund Raising
	Cadres	Recruitment	Organization Newspaper Graphic Work		Bail Fund
	Community	Community			Other funds Breakfast Clinic
		Gangs			
		Professionals			

YLO Direct Action Timeline

(ca. 2002, rev. 2008)
Cha Cha Jiménez, Chairman, Young Lords Organization
From "Brief Notes: The Young Lords"
Courtesy of José "Cha Cha" Jiménez personal collection

1945–1950

- WWII ended and massive unemployment forced many Puerto Rican jibaros to emigrate as "tomateros" or tomato pickers to US migrant camps.
- FOMENTO replaces the sugarcane industry and other agriculture with industry and tourism in Puerto Rico.
- US and Mexico in conflict with immigration concerns, related to the Bracero Program.
- Jibaro "tomateros" continue to move from Puerto Rico, East Coast cities, and migrant camps into steel mills near Chicago, factories, as downtown housing maids and hotel workers.
- Luis Muñoz Marin begins campaigning and becomes the first popularly elected Puerto Rican governor.

1950–1955

- Luis Muñoz Marin pushes for a neocolonial type of Commonwealth status, acceptable to the US interests, and promotes more massive immigration to the US hoping to alleviate 60 percent unemployment in Puerto Rico.
- Massive migration increases, and in Chicago, the first Puerto Rican barrios or communities: La Madison and La Clark are formed. La Madison (Halsted to Kedzie via Madison, with pockets from Roosevelt to Chicago Ave.) and La Clark (Ohio to Armitage via State, Clark, La Salle, Wells, Halsted, including pockets near and buildings within the Cabrini-Green housing complexes).

1955–1960

- The construction of the Carl Sandburg Village and University of Illinois Circle Campus destroys completely the Puerto Rican communities of La Madison and La Clark, displacing tens of thousands of (census undocumented and politically powerless) Puerto Ricans and other poor.

- Lincoln Park and Wicker Park have now been transformed rapidly from white ethnic minorities into primarily Puerto Rican neighborhoods.
- The Caballeros de San Juan and Damas de Maria form church councils or concilios in numerous churches throughout Chicago, starting at a Latino enclave in Woodlawn and including Puerto Rican enclaves in Lakeview, Uptown, La Madison, La Clark; and now within the two main barrios of Wicker Park-West Town-Humboldt Park (La Division) and Lincoln Park (including La North Ave. and La Armitage).

1960–1965

- Poverty, lack of supervised youth programs, and the destabilization of Latino neighborhood support networks, via city-sponsored urban renewal displacement, turn YMCA youth athletic clubs into hardcore street gangs.
- White flight also uproots the ethnics from Lincoln Park and La Division and leaves behind blighted, unstable neighborhoods, ruled by absentee "politicos" and absentee landlords.

1966

- Right after the first Puerto Rican parade, organized first as El Dia de San Juan, by the Caballeros de San Juan and Damas de Maria at St. Michael's Church in Lincoln Park; Puerto Ricans rioted over a police shooting of an unarmed youth, at Damen and Division streets, in La Division.

Young Lords Origins

September 23, 1968

- Reorganized by the founder/chairman José "Cha-Cha" Jiménez, the Young Lords are restructured into a human rights movement for self-determination for Puerto Rico and other nations, and for neighborhood-controlled development and empowerment.
- Young Lords take over a Community Conservation Council meeting and completely thrash the Department of Urban Renewal Office.
- Local mafia-owned real estate offices on Armitage Avenue are picketed by the Young Lords, while one real estate owner points a submachine gun at protestors.
- All windows of Anglo businesses on Armitage Avenue, between Larabee and Sheffield streets are busted and boarded up, in a replanned riot, organized by Young Lords, including members from all the gangs in Lincoln Park.

January 1969

- Wicker Park welfare office is stormed by Young Lords and Latinos.
- Young Lords began setting up a formal organizational structure, patterned after the Black Panther Party's ministerial structure. They conduct political education classes in homes.
- Films and literature of Corky Gonzales, Reies Lopez Tijerina, Cesar Chavez, the Brown Berets, Black Berets, and Black Panthers are shown for the first time to the Young Lords and the community of Lincoln Park.
- Two hundred people picketed Commander Braasch and the 18th district police after the arrest of Cha Cha Jiménez for disorderly conduct and mob action resulting from the urban renewal office destruction. He is forced to be released on his own personal recognizance bond.

February–March 1969

- Young Lords take two busloads to Corky Gonzales's Crusade for Justice Conference on Youth in Denver, Colorado.

- Young Lords, LADO, Black Panthers, caseworkers, and other activists together hold a sit-in at the Wicker Park public aid office to demand dignified treatment for clients; and a union for the employees.
- Cha Cha Jiménez is indicted by Hanrahan's grand jury eighteen times within six weeks. Charges range from alleged possession of marijuana to aggravated battery against police and numerous mob actions.
- Ralph Rivera and Cha Cha Jiménez designed the "Tengo Puerto Rico en mi corazon" button, which became the symbol or logo of the Young Lords.
- Young Lords take over the 18th District Chicago Avenue police workshop meeting held inside the police station. They inform a jam-pack audience that the Young Lords and their programs have been instituted to protect and serve the community and that the police have harassed and perpetrated violence against Lincoln Park residents.
- Meetings begin with Armitage Avenue Methodist Church for space for more Young Lords' programs: a free daily breakfast for children program, Emeterio Betances Free Health Center, Puerto Rican Cultural Center, and a free community daycare co-op.
- Cha Cha is in the audience at the University of Puerto Rico that is rendering an homage to Puerto Rican singer Daniel Santos who asks him to say a few words about the Young Lords. The same day, students protesting Puerto Ricans being forced to fight in Vietnam burned down the ROTC building on campus.

April 1969

- Chairman Fred Hampton of the Black Panther Party asks Bill "Preacherman" Fesperman of the Young Patriots and José "Cha Cha" Jiménez of the Young Lords to join together to form the Rainbow Coalition. The initial organizing work predating the coalition was carried out on behalf of the Black Panther Party in Uptown and Lincoln Park by Field Marshal Bobby Lee and his staff.
- Mayor Daley, State's Attorney Edward Hanrahan, Superintendent of Schools James Redman, Police Superintendent James Conlisk, and Human Resource Director Deton Brooks, in a highly publicized press conference, called for a "War on Gangs." They specifically name the Black Panthers, Young Patriots, and Young Lords along with

some established street gangs like Black Gangster Disciples, Latin Kings, Latin Disciples, and Blackstone Rangers, as their targets.

May 1969

- Manuel Ramos is shot outside birthday party for Orlando Dávila (founder in 1959, with Cha Cha and five others, of the Young Lords street gang), by off-duty policeman James Lamb. Four Young Lords, the Cuatro Lords, are arrested after making a citizen's arrest for aggravated battery, against James Lamb. Charges against the Young Lords were later dropped. James Lamb was never charged nor reprimanded for shooting and killing an unarmed Latino, Manuel Ramos.
- One thousand community persons joined the Young Lords, dressed in black with purple berets and their buttons at St. Teresa's Catholic Church, for a funeral procession for Manuel Ramos. In front of the procession are about one hundred members of the Sons of the Devil Motorcycle Club, led by David Rivera, a Young Lord field marshal and also the president. Prominent Puerto Rican leaders also side with Young Lords against police abuse related to the Manuel Ramos death.
- Young Lords and 350 primarily Latino community residents, take over and sit in at the McCormick Theological Seminary Stone Administration Building for one full week, renaming it the Manuel Ramos Memorial Building, until their demands are completely met:
    - $650,000 to be invested in low-income housing in Lincoln Park
    - $25,000 to open another free clinic, to be run by LADO for La Division (Wicker Park-West Town-Humboldt Park)
    - $25,000 to open up the People's Law Office in Lincoln Park
    - $25,000 was committed (but never received) for a Puerto Rican Cultural Center within the People's Church

June 1969

- Urban renewal land to be used for a $1,000-a-year tennis court club is seized to prevent its construction. This site was once, several four-story structures connected, that housed about thirty-five Puerto

Rican families. Over four hundred persons camped out for one week in a tent city, from Armitage to Dickens on Halsted Street, until the tennis club (later constructed at Fullerton and Damen streets in Wicker Park) removed its bid. Later, the Young Lords and the community convert the land into a People's Park, and playground equipment is constructed or donated by local merchants.

- Police harass visitors and attempt to incite a riot in People's Park. While attempting to calm the crowd, several Young Lords are arrested and charged with mob action.
- Young Lords march with ten thousand people several miles, from Halsted and Armitage through La Division and into Humboldt Park to honor Don Pedro Albizu Campos and the Puerto Rican Nationalist Party.
- Plans formalized for chapter of Young Lords to be started in New York City.
- Young Lords visit California and other West Coast cities to hold various meetings, to strengthen unity with several organizations, including the Black Panthers, SDS, new left groups, Crusade for Justice, Black Berets, Alurista, and the Aztlan Movement, and the Brown Berets.
- Chapter of the Young Lords opens up in Hayward, California.
- Young Lords march in solidarity with the Industrial Workers of the World (IWW) in Chicago.

July 1969

- Young Lords take over Armitage Avenue United Methodist Church (led by Mexican American Luis Chavez and others) and later the congregation renames the church, People's Church.
- The Young Lords set up a daycare center, a clinic, a cultural center, and their national headquarters offices.
- Gang Intelligence Unit and the Chicago Red Squad station a police car, parked twenty-four hours a day, photographing anyone entering or leaving the Young Lords People's Church (later it was also discovered that COINTELPRO among other acts was also involved in inciting riots at demonstrations, infiltration, door to door rumor or discrediting campaigns and creating divisions within

the new left, Latino and African American movements.

- Felícitas Nuñez, also of proud Mexican heritage, along with activist Ron Clark, paints murals of Adelita, Emiliano Zapata, Lolita Lebrón, Don Pedro Albizu Campos, and the national Young Lords logo (reading, "Tengo Puerto Rico en mi corazon") on the outside church walls.

September 1969

- Young Lords are asked by Deputy Chairman Fred Hampton and the Illinois Black Panthers to help mobilize demonstrators to protest at the downtown Chicago federal building, during the Chicago 8 Conspiracy Trial, in support of Chairman Bobby Seale.
- Several Young Lords from Chicago travel with Cha Cha Jiménez and Manuel Rabago of the Nationalist Party, to march at the annual Grito de Lares demonstration in Jayuya, Puerto Rico.
- The Catholic Caballeros de San Juan and Damas de Maria are urged by Don Jesus Rodriguez and vote unanimously to volunteer and support the Young Lords and their neighborhood programs.
- UPTIGHT (United People to Inform Good-doers Here and There) was formed by Alderman McCutcheon to collect data, including going through the Young Lords People's Church garbage cans. This information is then prepared into letters and flyers to discredit the Young Lords leadership and to remove the pastor of People's Church, Rev. Bruce Johnson. The flyers are passed at suburban Methodist Churches, and the letters are sent to the bishop of the United Methodist Church asking him to remove Rev. Bruce Johnson and the Young Lords from People's Church.
- Alderman McCutheon's press conference is taken over by Young Lords. The media is reminded by Young Lords that the alderman had been arrested for soliciting prostitutes in Old Town, is harassing Young Lords with UPTIGHT, and is part of the old Alderman Paddy Bauer's organization, well known for their mafia ties.
- Puerto Rican Bishop Antulio Parrilla Bonilla celebrates Mass for Young Lords in Chicago.
- Cha Cha Jiménez and Deputy Chairman Fred Hampton are arrested together, for an alleged assault and battery on police, at the Wicker

Park welfare office. Obed Lopez is brutally beaten up by police. Maria de Lourdes Porrata is also assaulted by a welfare caseworker.
- Young Lords visit Alcatraz during an Indigenous people's takeover led by Native American Richard Oakes. The Young Lords witness Richard Oakes's newborn baby, allegedly being dropped accidentally from a ferry and drowning in San Francisco Bay.
- Police attempt to disrupt Young Lords Block Party. Young Lords are arrested by community protests, and they are released.
- Pastor of Young Lords People's Church, the Methodist Rev. Bruce W. Johnson is found by a postal worker, stabbed to death alongside his wife, Marjorie Eugenia Johnson. The Young Lords open up the church and cooperated, but the case has never been solved, nor investigated fully by the police.

October 1969

- The Emeterio Betances Free Health Center screens people door to door for lead poisoning.

November 1969

- Fred Hampton filed an appeal for a previous court ruling against him on charges of stealing $71 worth of ice cream from a Good Humor ice cream truck driver and distributing it to children. His appeal attacks the sufficiency of the complaining witness's identification, alleging numerous trial errors which he claims operated to deny him a fair trial, and addressing the egregious sentence.

December 1969

- Fred Hampton is set up and drugged by police informant William O'Neal and murdered in a predawn raid organized by State's Attorney Edward Hanrahan and a special police team.
- Young Lords attend Hampton's funeral and vigil
- Cha Cha is told by attorneys not to sleep in the same house two days in a row.

1970

- The New York chapter breaks away from the Young Lords Organization to form the Young Lords Party.
- Young Lords organize the Lincoln Park Poor People's Coalition, hire architect Howard Alan and draw up plans for a low-income housing development at Larrabee and Armitage Streets. It is endorsed by the community, a coalition of churches, renowned architect Buckminster Fuller, and the former head of the Department of Urban Renewal, Ira Bach. However, it was still rejected by Mayor Daley's housing committee of the city council. They claimed that the Lincoln Park Poor People's Coalition lacked experience in housing construction.
- After pleading guilty to a misdemeanor and receiving a one-year sentence for the infamous $23 lumber case, Cha Cha Jiménez requests personal time from the court, before being jailed, and goes underground. An underground training school is set up to train Young Lords leadership, to take over the organization.

1971

- Young Lords Communications Secretary Angela Lind meets with Vietnamese women at a Canada conference.
- José "Pancho" Lind is beat to death by an all-white street gang. One of the killers is the brother of one of the first policemen at the scene. Important evidence is compromised and no one is ever convicted, even though there are court-filled rooms and plenty of protest marches outside the courthouse.

1972

- On December 4, 1972, exactly three years after Fred Hampton's murder, Cha Cha Jiménez turned himself in at the Town Hall District police station after two years underground. He was greeted by five hundred supporters and members of the Young Lords.
- Angie Lind becomes acting chairman while Cha Cha Jiménez serves out his sentence.

1973

- The Young Lords posted a $75,000 cash bond for the ten remaining felony charges, and Cha Cha Jiménez was released.
- Soon after Cha Cha's release, the Intercommunal Survival Committee led by Walter "Slim" Coleman, the local United Farm Workers led by Marcos Muñoz, the American Indian Movement, and some remaining members of the Black Panthers (others were disbanded or in Oakland for concentration and training and/or to work on Bobby Seale's mayoral campaign) joined the Young Lords for a press conference announcing the José "Cha Cha" Jiménez bid for 46th Ward alderman.

1975

- The Young Lords came in second and garnered 39 percent of the votes, in an area now being gentrified, with only one thousand Latino registered voters.

1980

- The Puerto Rican FALN group is arrested in Evanston, Illinois. The same week Cha Cha Jiménez is also arrested and charged with an alleged kidnapping of a United States Census supervisor, in support of the arrested FALN freedom fighters. He demanded a trial since there was no kidnapping, and constitutionally anyone has a right to support any cause within the United States. After misplaced records and after nine months in Cook County Jail, awaiting trial, Cha Cha Jiménez is released, when the time expires on the four-month speedy trial law. There are no witnesses or accusers voluntarily brought into court by the state's attorney's office.

1983

- Young Lords, including a new generation of Young Lords (to avoid being labeled as a gang) work under the name of the Puerto Rican Diaspora Coalition, and become the first Latino group to hold a public rally for the mayoral campaign of Harold Washington.
- Right after the victorious election of Harold Washington, the

Young Lords organized together with the Puerto Rican Parade Committee of Chicago and the new mayor's Office of Special Events and Cha Cha Jiménez introduced Harold Washington, before a crowd of one hundred thousand Puerto Ricans in Humboldt Park.

1995

- In the fall of 1995, Young Lords' Tony Baez from Milwaukee, Omar López Zacarias, Carlos Flores, Angel del Rivero, and Angie Lind are brought together by Cha Cha Jiménez to form the Lincoln Park Project, which will begin to archive and document Young Lord history and the history of the complete displacement of Puerto Ricans, Latinos, and the poor of Lincoln Park. They approach DePaul University and begin working closely with Dr. Felix Masud-Piloto and the Center for Latino Research. A collection is being housed at DePaul's Richardson Library.

2002

- The Young Lords show support for the protesters at Vieques, Puerto Rico, and also to continue the fight for stable neighborhoods and to end Latino and poor people's displacement, by celebrating Puerto Rican Independence Day or El Grito de Lares, with the opening of Lincoln Park Camp, near Grand Rapids, Michigan. This becomes an annual event for supporters.

2.

Y.L.O., PITIRRE, EL YOUNG LORD: LATIN LIBERATION NEWS SERVICE

VOICES OF THE MOVEMENT

Why a Young Lords Newspaper?

Y.L.O. vol. 1, no. 1, March 19, 1969, pp. 1, 9, 11
Young Lords Newspapers Digital Collection
Special Collections and Archives
DePaul University Library, Chicago, Illinois

A Latin American movement is developing in Chicago for the purpose of putting an end to the injustices, suffering and exploitation which is forced upon our people.

Y.L.O. considers itself as part of that movement; a movement that wants a new society in which all people are treated as equal; a society whose wealth is controlled and shared by all its members, and not a few; A society in which men and women view other members as brothers and sisters and not as people to be exploited and hated.

Y.L.O. stands for an end to police brutality and mistreatment; adequate housing for all; decent jobs and living wages for all; community control of the schools, the police, and all other institutions in our country; an end to the colonization of Puerto Rico and all other third world countries which are politically, economically, or militarily controlled by the US and the USSR.

The Latin American movement has not yet decided on the path it needs to follow. That is, some want reform in the system like more Latin American cops (pigs), teachers, politicians, caseworkers, social workers, etc. And believe that little by little L.A. will be able to win (somewhat peacefully) control; others are not sure what is needed, so they work diligently, often militantly, to achieve reform measures, but never developing clear understanding of the American system and its complexities.

Others see the need to follow the road to basic social change: destroying the rich and its tools and setting up a society where "human needs" rather than "profits" are the primary goals of the society. But the conscious majority is a confused combination of two or more of the above. Since the path to be taken is not in front of all, we need to make a case for our goals (clarifying them), and develop a strategy that will win the people over to our side.

In order to develop a Movement, we shall have to develop militancy and consciousness among our people. The goal is the most difficult one and will require constant clarification. We need to understand and be able to explain our goals, and how our strategies bring us closer to those goals.

In the last few years there has been a rise in consciousness among Hispanos, particularly the youth, that has created an entirely new political climate in Chicago. In the past various organizations were formed that were essentially single-issue oriented: education, welfare, the police, urban renewal, etcetera. These organizations have a life of their own internal organizational activity, with lots or a few people doing concrete work against these institutions. But they could not sustain themselves, they would fall apart or barely sustain themselves. Their main weakness was the lack of a clear, complete philosophy which they can communicate.

Single-issue organizations led by organizers that do not understand or cannot explain to the people how the system works, how all the institutions are used to ensure the interests of the rich, die or are co-opted. They generate temporary militancy, but not the consciousness necessary to build a force that see present struggles as scrimmages that prepare us for the big battles to come. The job of a revolutionary is to "educate the masses," and to build a revolutionary force that clearly sees the enemy (the rich) and understands how it will ultimately have to be destroyed in order to put power in the hands of the people.

Since even when the goals are clear, conflict will exist as to the best way to get there, strategies need to be discussed fully among us and corrected.

Our task now is to 1) define revolutionary goals; 2) recruit individuals to our cause and train them as educators and protectors of the people; 3) develop the correct strategy for educating the masses and enlarging our fighting organization; and 4) connect ourselves with or develop fighting groups in the different areas of the city. The role of the newspaper is not confined solely to the spreading of information, the political education, and to winning movement allies. A newspaper is not merely a collective educator and collective agitator; it is also a collective organizer. In that respect it can be compared to the scaffolding erected around the building in construction; It marks the contours of the structure, and facilitates communication between the builders, permitting them to distribute the work and to view the common results achieved by their organized labor.

With the aid of a newspaper there will develop an organization that will be concerned not only with local activities, but also with regular, general work; It will teach its members carefully to watch political events, to discuss and collectively estimate their importance and their influence on the various sections of the population.

A newspaper can be the focus of a permanent organization; It could provide a bridge between the peaks of activity. It creates an organization and organizes the division of labor among activists. It creates the kind of division of labor needed not just for the newspaper, but also the guidelines for action and study of an organization interested in radical change. And it develops a necessary network throughout the city. Groups who are clarifying their strategies, and developing goals must be constantly aware of their actions and motives and develop forums for discussion and criticism of their strategies and goals.

The YLO newspaper exists for the benefit of the Latin American community. We welcome all news items and suggestions as to how to make YLO serve more effectively.

Y.L.O.

affiliated, with the Young Lords Organization

PUBLISHED MONTHLY

VOL. 1, NO. 1

Ministry of Information
2512 N. Lincoln Avenue
Chicago, Illinois 60614

Latinos Demandan Nuevo Director de Welfare

—La policia ataco y golpeo a varios Hispanos en una demostracionen contra del Departamento de Asistencia Publica en Wicker Park.

Mas de 300 personas demostraron en una Coalicion de la Comunidad en la cual varias organizaciones participaron: LADO, Spanish Action Committee, las agencias del United Christian Community Services, Women Mobilized for Action, the Black Panther Party, y los Young Lords Organization

En la marcha tambien se vieron miembros de muchos grupos del area como los Latin Kings, y otros.

Las demandas de la Coalicion eran 1) que despidan al Director de la oficina de Welfare en la Milwaukee y North; 2)que un nuevo Director sea nombrado con el apruebo de miembros de la comunidad; 3)que la comunidad tenga el derecho de aprobar o rechazar cualquier regla que tenga dicha oficina.

En frente de la Oficina, la poli-θia provoco un incidente cuando los policias empezaron a empujar

(cont. pag. 11)

YLO takes over POLICE STATION

"Who are all these people? Is this planned?" asked Sgt, Harrington, second in command at the 18th District Police Station, on Tuesday, February 11. It was 7:30 p.m. and masses of people were pouring into the station for what was scheduled to be a routing police-community workshop.

For weeks the pigs of the 18th District had been harrassing Cha-Cha Jimenez, Chairman of the Young Lords Organization, and the rest of the Young Lords. Cha Cha had four charges on him as he went into the meeting.

The situation had become intolerable. Meetings attended by the Young Lords Organization were surrounded by pigs. At one meeting of the school-community planning committee (EDUC 7) of which Cha Cha is vice-president, there were 14 plainclothesmen and two uniformed police inside and 8 squad cars outside with numerous others nearby.

Six local organizations, Concerned Citizens of Lincoln Park, the Northside Co-operative Ministry, EDUC7, Neighbourhood Commons, the Lincoln Park Survival Front, and the Community Review Board, supported the Young Lords and called for descent upon the police station. More than 300 people showed up for the meeting, yet apparently police intelligence failed to find out in advance what was going to happen.

At 8 p.m. the minutes were read and Ramon Valdes, chairman of the meeting, tried to introduce a scheduled speaker. A local minister moved that the agenda be changed. Valdes continued to refuse to consider the motion whereas tremendous booing broke out. Valdes stated that a motion could only be made by someone who had attended three meetings. Cries broke out to "read the rules". When finally found, the rules said only two meeting attendance were required. The motion was passed. After consultation between Braasch and Valdes, Braasch announced his faith in democracy and agreed to answer questions. He looked very unhappy but the crowd was ecstatic.

Braasch replied in vague terms about proper police response to a hypothetical robbery. Braasch time after time continued to express ignorance about what is happening in his district. The one straight answer he gave was to admit that there was a police intelligence division and thinks it likely they are obser-

(cont. pg. 12)

Editorial

Why a YLO Newspaper?

—A Latin American Movement is developing in Chicago for the purpose of putting an end to the injustices, suffering and exploitation which is forced upon our people.

Y.L.O. considers itself as part of that Movement = a movement that wants a new society in which all people are treated as equal; a society whose wealth is controlled and shared by all its members, and not by a few; a society in which men and women view other members as brothers and sisters and not as people to be exploited and hated.

Y.L.O. stands for an end to police brutality and mistreatment; adequate housing for all; descent jobs and living wages for all; community control of the schools, the police, and all other institutions in our community; an end to the colonization of Puerto Rico and all other Third World countries which are politically, economically, or militarily controlled by the U.S. and the U.S.S.R.

The Latin American Movement has not yet decided on the path it needs to follow. That is, some want reform in the system like more Latin American cops (pigs), teachers, politicians, caseworkers, social workers, etc. and believe that little by little L.A. will

(cont. pg. 9)

Y.L.O. vol. 1, no. 1, March 19, 1969
Young Lords Newspapers Digital Collection
Special Collections and Archives
DePaul University Library, Chicago, Illinois

Young Lords Serve and Protect

Hilda Vasquez Ignatin
Y.L.O. vol. 1, no. 2, May 1969, pp. 6–7
Young Lords Newspapers Digital Collection
Special Collections and Archives
DePaul University Library, Chicago, Illinois

How did a Latin street gang in Chicago develop into a political group that recognizes the need to build a vanguard revolutionary group of Latin Americans?

The Puerto Rican colony of Chicago is on the north side of the city. Division Street, scene of the 1966 rebellion, runs down the center of it. There are some black people with more and more moving in, and a large number of Anglos (mostly Polish homeowners) who live in the area. Throughout the area there are at least fifteen gangs and clubs with many members and sympathizers. Their ages range from 12–27, with each person belonging to only one group.

The Young Lords Organization (YLO) centered in the Lincoln Park area, is the first of these youth groups to move in a positive, conscious political direction. They see the need for unity with other Latin groups and seek to implement it. They are seeking to build an organization that can build mass consciousness and prepare the way for fundamental necessary changes. They understand that to be relevant and effective they must be both politically advanced and prepared to defend the Latin colony and its people.

How did it happen? In the hope that the story will be helpful to people organizing in Latin American communities across the country this article will discuss the development of the YLO up to the present time.

GANG YEARS

The Young Lords were formed in 1959 by seven youths. At that time many Puerto Ricans were getting beaten up by white gangs in the area, so the seven formed their own gang for protection. The main purpose and activity was fighting with Italians, "Billigans" (hillbillies), as well as other Latin gangs for control of hangouts, streets, turf. The club grew large and powerful quickly, and formed branches in surrounding areas and high schools so other Latins could join and have hangouts of their own.

During the gang years the YLO was plagued by social workers who were interested in "helping" them—mostly by getting them to play basketball at a local church even though most of the guys had problems with the police, parole officers, drugs, and all the rest.

In 1964 "Cha Cha" [Jiménez] was elected chairman of the Young Lords. He was one of the three who were still around from the original founders. At that time the group began having social activities at a local YMCA. At one of these gatherings trouble broke out over girls, glue-sniffing, and hassles caused by confusion over membership in the various branches of the organization. In 1965 "Cha Cha" got out, organized the club again, and started a group of Lordettes who had their own chairwomen. More socials than before were part of the revival.

Early in 1966 Orlando Davila, another of the original seven, took over as chairman. His term was short, since some of the Young Lords leaders and many of the members were out of Chicago or in jail and the organization suffered. During this time the YLO now included Puerto Ricans, Blacks, Anglos, and other Latins in the area.

A series of fund-raising socials was held in February. Money was used to hold a community summer picnic, give a "Month of Soul Dances" with the Black Stone Rangers, give Christmas food baskets and toys to needy families, and try to get an office for the organization. But through all this time members of the YLO began to realize that often they were acting like social workers, not getting at the root causes of the community problems.

One of the things that taught YLO members that an attack on the root causes of their problems was first necessary, and second possible, was the development of relations with groups from other communities and parts of the country. Meetings with people who were conducting other kinds of struggle, who had experience in organizing, and also those who were facing similar problems helped YLO to broaden its goals.

For example, in October YLO was invited to take part in a meeting with all Latin organizations and organizers in Chicago. One thing that was discussed was a possible Education and Training Program for the Latin community with emphasis on youth. (Chicago has 100,000 Puerto Ricans, 190,000 Mexicans, and 60,000 Cubans). At the city meeting people from YLO met with other organizers and formed strong links with some of them. As a result a YLO member went to an International Conference in Canada. Through this broadening contact, YLO became informed about what was happening in the rest of the country with other Latin groups who were engaged in struggle.

A NEW MILITANCY

In December of 1968 YLO found that three realty companies in the area (Bissell, Crown, and Romano) were planning to move out all the Puerto Ricans from the community. These companies were figuring to buy up the buildings with Latin bars, grocery and clothing stores, and convert the buildings so that other businesses would occupy them and so the people who the Latin businesses served would move. Puerto Ricans didn't go for that shit, and the windows of the realty companies were busted three different times.

One of the realtors (Fat Larry) started making the rounds of Latin families and storeowners waving a gun in their faces and trying to get them to say that YLO had broken the windows, talking about how he was going to blow some Puerto Rican brains out. Because of his harassment of families YLO decided to mobilize a demonstration and go talk to Fat Larry. On January 11, community people and YLO marched outside the realty office carrying posters while "Cha Cha" went into the office to see Fat Larry.

Larry pulled out a .38 pistol and a machine carbine. He held one in each hand while his sidekick called the pigs. Ten squad cars were on the scene instantly, to "protect" Larry and his guns. The pigs searched "Cha Cha" while Larry, and other pigs dispersed the people outside. Like "Cha Cha" later told a group of community people: "When you have money, the pigs are on your side. You can buy the right to threaten people with guns, especially if the people you threaten are Puerto Rican or poor."

The next day YLO put out a leaflet informing the rest of the community of what had happened, detailing the connection between the real estate company, the political machine of the community, and the local banks. The leaflet asked people to support YLO when future actions were taken. The research, the facts that go out in the leaflet were important in winning the support of the Latin colony and its allies.

In January the all-white Community Conservation Council (CCC) which deals with "urban renewal" met. Latins from the area attended the meeting along with the Young Lords. When the members of CCC saw the Young Lords, they got uptight, decided there was no quorum present and told some of the CCC members to leave. Seeing what was happening the Latins got pissed off. Not only weren't they represented on the CCC, not only were they never told of the meetings which decided which houses in their community would be torn down and which remain, but the CCC was now refusing to meet in their presence. Too much! An argument broke out which resulted in overturned chairs, a broken display, and shattered windows.

It was clear: if the CCC could not or would not serve the community and be under the control of the community, it could not exist. The next month the CCC voted unanimously (after plenty of pressure had been applied) not to meet again until the committee had a majority of Latin and Afro-American representatives.

ENTER THE PIGS—OINK OINK

The day after the community showed the CCC they meant business "Cha Cha" was picked up by the police while rapping to some guys on a street corner. He figured it was for the CCC disturbance, but when they got him to the station he was told, "We just want to talk to you . . . we want to open lines of communication to the community." It was the standard ploy and "Cha Cha" didn't bite—no communication.

So the pig pulled out two old warrants and busted him on them. In 1967 he had been told that the warrants had been cleared in the court, but that didn't make much difference. The bond was $2,500. The money was raised and "Cha Cha" was out in three hours. But he said the pigs had been talking to each other about the realty company and CCC thing, making sure he heard them talking, but they didn't have charges to use against him—yet.

That night there was a community School Planning Committee meeting to elect officers which took place at a local high school. Among the blacks, whites and Latins elected was "Cha Cha," who was elected vice president. During the meeting people became aware that there were at least 14 plainclothes pigs in the crowd, who admitted who they were only after being recognized and pointed out. Then someone came in and said there were twelve squad cars outside the building. People were mad. A local minister who attended the meeting, Bruce Johnson, later went to see the local police commander about it.

"IF THIS KEEPS UP I'LL . . ."

Johnson told Police Commander Braash [*sic*] that such police presence hardly encouraged a peaceful and democratic meeting and was especially unfortunate since men like the Young Lords were actively participating in these types of community activities. The commander said he wasn't going to have a repeat of what happened at the CCC meeting, that he would have police at whatever meeting the YLO attended to make sure trouble was stopped before it began. After all, his job was to protect property, and citizens would have to get used to police at meetings attended by the Young Lords. Until he was convinced that YLO was capable of respecting property and exercising creative, responsible citizenship, police would be where the Young Lords were.

Commander pig was sorry that this disturbed citizens, but after all, he had a job to do. He indicated that if the Young Lords and "Cha Cha" continued to do what they had been doing then he would find a way to put "Cha Cha" or anyone else who acted that way into the pen for good.

And not too long afterwards the commander tried to do just that.

THE BUST

On January 30th "Cha Cha" took a friend to the welfare office. The two of them and other recipients had been there all day with no result. At closing time the women decided they would stay there until they were taken care of, and someone accidently knocked over a coffee pot.

The Assistant Director of the welfare office shoved two women aside in order to rush over and protect sacred Cook County property. "Cha Cha" went up to him, shoved him and said, "Push ME, motherfucker." The pigs were called and the assistant director pressed assault and battery charges.

When taken to the police station there was another warrant for his arrest, sworn out by the director of the CCC. The pigs searched for needle marks on his arms and legs and question him about draft resistance. Then he was jailed on two charges: assault and battery ($5,000 bail); and mob action (also $5,000). A thousand bucks had to be raised to get him out. It was raised the same night and he was bailed out.

The next day representatives of various organizations and churches met to discuss police harassment as part of the political repression of the Young Lords. The group decided to raise money for YLO and to set up an on-going bail fund for the Lincoln Park area. The group talked about sending a delegation to Commander Braash [*sic*]. In the end it was decided that those who wanted should go to the monthly police-community workshop, which would be held in two weeks.

POLICE COMMUNITY WORKSHOP

The meeting was scheduled to start at 8, but people started coming at 7:20. YLO came with signs: WE WILL NOT TOLERATE PIG ABUSE. PIGS NEED SPORTS CENTERS TO KEEP THEM OFF THE STREET AND END VIOLENCE. YLO SERVES AND PROTECTS. HANDS OFF CHA CHA. Guys put the posters up on the wall and the meeting was ready to start.

By 7:30, 300 people were in a room seating only 150. YLO had mobilized Latins while a group called the Concerned Citizens of Lincoln Park had organized Anglos . . . all by word of mouth. Apparently pig "intelligence" hadn't been hip to it in advance, and they were falling all over themselves trying to deal with the scene.

People filled the seats, the aisles, sat on tables and desks, lined up double against the wall so everybody could get inside. For the time being, the people had taken over the police station.

At 8 the minutes were read. Then a Puerto Rican "Tom" tried to introduce the scheduled speaker. Latins yelled at him, "Shut up Uncle Tom!" A minister moved that the agenda be changed because people had questions for the Commander. Chairman "Tom" refused to consider the motion, and loud jeers broke out. People began to yell, "We demand our rights!" Commander pig and "Tom" conferred. An uncomfortable commander then agreed to answer questions, "if he could." Before he started he called for a sergeant to come in, while plainclothesmen were taking pictures like crazy. People demanded they stop, called for a vote. The Commander was reluctant. The vote was unanimous. They stopped taking pictures.

SKINNING THE PIG

Reverend Johnson began the questioning by repeating what commander pig had said to him about putting "Cha Cha" away for good. Braash [*sic*] said he didn't remember saying that and continued to feign ignorance of events in the community. People were yelling, "lying pig," and assorted "mother-fucker" after every answer. The only straight answer he gave was, yes, they were most likely investigating the YLO. He said police probably came to YLO in answer to anonymous phone calls. Someone asked him if police could function without little old ladies calling up to tell them about "crime and violence".

He was asked about the killing by a pig of a 15-year-old black youth a few weeks before. He said, "According to the officer's report, a call came in saying a burglary was in progress. When the officer arrived at the scene it was dark. The officer 'heard' the youth charge at him with a knife and shot him in self-defense." Commander pig was satisfied with the officer's conduct.

Uncle Tom figured his Commander had suffered enough indignity and tried to end the meeting. He ignored a motion passed to continue the meeting. The meeting ended—the first where the Young Lords and community people had done a fine job of exposing the real criminals and murderers in the streets of our communities.

The establishment press picked up on the meeting. Their reports explained regretfully that the confrontation had prevented two officers from receiving awards for shooting burglars.

Political and police harassment hasn't ceased. Since the meeting YLO members, including "Cha Cha" have been picked up often, usually released once at the station. In some cases, money has had to be raised to bail out those who were held for crimes like upside down license plates. If January and February are any indication of what 1969 will be like for Puerto Ricans in Chicago, then the answer of the Young Lords is . . . "Right on Brothers!"

THIRD WORLD UNITY

On the weekend of February 15–16th, YLO and BAD co-sponsored a Third World Unity Conference. B.A.D. stands for Black, Active and Determined and is a group of young black men and women organizing in and around the Cabrini Housing projects, just south of the Lincoln Park area. BAD has been organizing for over a year, in high schools as well as the community. The theme of the conference was "Non-Whites and Latins Unite in the Third World." Several workshops were part of the program, along with speakers from BAD, YLO and the Chicago Black Panther Party. Plans for further talks and discussions were set up between the three groups.

At a later meeting of the groups, the Young Patriots, a southern white group from the Uptown area became part of the coalition. The Young Patriots have been organizing white youths and community people around similar issues as YLO has and are working a few blocks north of Lincoln Park.

These meetings have resulted in a coalition of support between the groups for future actions against the pigs of Chicago.

THE YLO NEWSPAPER

The Young Lords have also begun publishing a monthly newspaper. The paper is in both Spanish and English, and has many articles on local struggles and problems. In addition there are articles like: "Chicago Blacks Mourn Malcolm," "Uptown Confronts Pigs," reprints from the Black Panther paper, well written articles on Nixon maneuvers, millionaire tax dodges, Cuba, Latin history and national liberation struggles.

An editorial called "Why a YLO newspaper?" says, in part, "A Latin American Movement is developing in Chicago for the purposes of putting an end to the injustices, suffering and exploitation which is forced upon on our people. YLO considers itself as part of that movement—a movement that wants a new society in which all people are treated as equal; a society whose wealth is controlled and shared by all its members, and not by a few; a society in which men and women view each other as brothers and sisters and not as people to be exploited and hated." After speaking of police brutality, community control, jobs, housing, and imperialism and the need to overcome tendencies toward reformism in Latin American movement, the editorial hopes that the tool of a newspaper can help aid the development of political consciousness in the community and in YLO, help develop revolutionary goals, people, strategy and contacts.

The editorial ends: "The YLO newspaper exists for the benefit of the Latin American community. We welcome all news items and suggestions as to how to make YLO serve more effectively."

MORE ORGANIZATION

As the Young Lords Organization demonstrated to the Latin Colony that it was truly committed to protecting the interests of Latins in Chicago, its support grew. Many young people and adults wanted to join. But YLO felt that it needed to clarify the path it was taking, to strengthen itself to more effectively tackle the job that had to be done.

YLO realized that its members had to develop greater political consciousness and sophistication if they were to help provide leadership to the Chicago Latin movement. Thus, YLO again reorganized.

During the next few months before the summer, YLO will spend most of its energies in educating itself: learning what needs to be done to change it. Besides setting up study groups for all its members and training in karate, YLO will participate in Latin activities that require protection from the pigs and co-sponsoring events that aim at educating the people as to what is happening and what Latins need to do in order to resolve the present situation. By the middle of the summer, YLO should be prepared to work out a more systematic offensive against the injustices plaguing the Latin colony.

There are 350,000 Latins within the city of Chicago, and 12 million Latins in the US (not counting the 2 and ½ million in Puerto Rico). In light of their objective conditions, it is clear that basic change in this country, and thus throughout the world, will require the mobilization and leadership of brown people—as well as black people. The developing Latin struggles for independence and freedom in the Southwest, in Puerto Rico, and in the northern cities will be a key part of the present revolution.

Y.L.O. Wednesday, March 19, 1969 page 3

LATIN POWER to LATIN PEOPLE

Young Lords Organization

Latin Power to Latin People

Y.L.O. vol. 1, no. 1, March 19, 1969, p. 3
Young Lords Newspapers Digital Collection
Special Collections and Archives
DePaul University Library, Chicago, Illinois

McCormick Takeover

Y.L.O. vol. 1, no. 2, May 5, 1969, p. 4
Young Lords Newspapers Digital Collection
Special Collections and Archives
DePaul University Library, Chicago, Illinois

On Weds., May 14, just a few minutes before midnight, a coalition of poor people occupied the brand new Academic Administration Building at McCormick Theological Seminary.

As a result of the take-over, the following demands were won:

- 601,000 for low income housing;
- funds for a Children Center of 100 children that would expand to a 24-hour per day center;
- priority renting of apartments owned by McCormick to poor and working class people;
- (not won) the fence around McCormick to be torn down;
- a Puerto Rican cultural center to be set up by the Young Lords Organization;
- $25,000 for leadership programs for Y.L.O.;
- McCormick will publicly and actively support the Welfare Coalition;
- $25,000 to set up a legal bureau controlled by the Poor People's Coalition to serve the people of the area.

The groups operating with the Poor People's Coalition include the Young Lords Organization, Young Patriots, Black Active and Determined, the Concerned Citizens Survival Front, the Welfare and Working Mothers of Wicker Park, and the Latin American Defense Organization, and others.

For the past two years, McCormick has been under increasing pressure, from internal and external sources, to deal with the problems of the surrounding community. It is important to understand from the outset that McCormick (located at Fullerton and Halsted) has helped to create these problems. It is not an innocent bystander. The biggest single issue is that of housing. McCormick, in conjunction with other institutions in the community (principally DePaul and Children's Memorial Hosp.)

has instigated and supported an urban renewal program in the community which was and is designed to remove poor people and replace them with middle- and upper-income residents. This has been done primarily through the destruction of 1100 family housing units and the removal of 2 to 4 times as many families by institutional takeover of housing or by the housing being priced upwards out of reach of the former residents. In addition to its aggressive action against the community people in this regard, McCormick has been totally insensitive to other needs of the surrounding community.

On Wednesday, May 7, the PPC met with representatives of the McCormick administration and presented a series of 10 demands. In a meeting on Mon., May 12, McCormick presented a series of formal answers to the demands of all the people involved, including the PPC. Their response to the demand for low-income housing funds was that the seminary restated its concern about housing in the community and would explore with all community groups and institutions the potential use and development of properties in the neighborhood. They would ask that their investment committee give first priority to such neighborhood development, recognizing that substantial amounts of unrestricted funds have already been committed. In response to the demands for daycare facilities, McCormick said no, but they would explore with other organizations the extent of the need for such a center and the possibilities of providing the center on a fee basis. To the demand for rental to poor and working families, the seminary said no. To the demand that the fence be torn down, they said no. To the demand for a Puerto Rican cultural center, the Seminary said no, but it offered to help get the money from other sources. To the demands for funds for, YLO, LADO and a Legal Defense unit, McCormick responded that no grants of any kind could be given for any purpose other than educating persons for the ministry of the church. In addition, McCormick indicated that they didn't have the funds anyway. In the response to the request for a condemnation of political persecution, the Seminary replied that such a statement would not be appropriate.

In a meeting held on Wednesday afternoon, May 14, representatives of the PPC made it clear that they considered this response totally inadequate. They had demanded to meet with the executive committee of the board of directors upon being informed of these responses and had been told that it was "impossible" to hold such a meeting without two weeks' notice. Representatives of the PPC told the McCormick people present at the meeting that they were going to be forced to resort to "community education." They did not define that term. At midnight that night, the Stone building was seized. The 80 or so community people efficiently sealed all entrances to the building and controlled all entrance and exit of persons. Their first act after seizing the building was to rename it the Manuel Ramos Memorial Building in honor of a Young Lord murdered the week before by a Chicago pig. The administration was informed of the seizure and the PPC waited for a response.

The response was not long in coming. The meeting with the Board of Directors Executive Committee which was "impossible to set up without two weeks' notice" was scheduled for Thursday afternoon, May 15. A press conference was called by the PPC for 10 AM on Thurs., and 24-hour security was set up for the building. It is difficult to overstate the significance of this action. It is probably the first time in recent years in the US when community residents, poor and working people, have seized and held a major community institution like McCormick for the purpose of gaining the fulfillment of a list of political and economic demands. In addition, the groups who have seized the building are Latin, black and white. They are by and large politically radical and are questioning the legitimacy of the institution and its power, rather than simply trying to force a few concessions. There is talk of a revolution and "serving the people." Little red books are in evidence and the clenched fist is the accepted greeting. Control and power must be won by the people thru force—the rich will never give up anything peacefully.

TENGO PUERTO RICO EN MI CORAZON

YLO

YLO

25¢

Young Lords Organization

Published Monthly Vol. I No. 2 Ministry of Information 2512 N. Lincoln Avenue Chicago, Illinois 60614

Y.L.O. vol. 1, no. 2, May 5, 1969
Young Lords Newspapers Digital Collection
Special Collections and Archives
DePaul University Library, Chicago, Illinois

The New Economic Invasion

Y.L.O. vol. 1, no. 2, October 10, 1969, p. 15
Young Lords Newspapers Digital Collection
Special Collections and Archives
DePaul University Library, Chicago, Illinois

In the last ten years, the economic invasion of Puerto Rico has been accelerated. Seventy-eight percent of the island's economy is today in the hands of U.S. interests.

As William Appleman Williams has written:

> Puerto Rico is essentially a second-class state within the United States, and no Latin American country would care to pay the price for such help . . . Puerto Rico is not being industrialized in the true sense . . . absentee capitalism controls three of every four factories in Puerto Rico and is handled by non-Puerto Ricans.

In an impassioned plea for its right to survive as a nation, the Movement for Puerto Rican Independence declares:

> The so-called "progress" which is said to reign in our land is not a product of an authentic development of Puerto Rican productive forces. On the contrary, these forces have been reduced to the point where they are daily being swindled out of their role in the economy of the country.

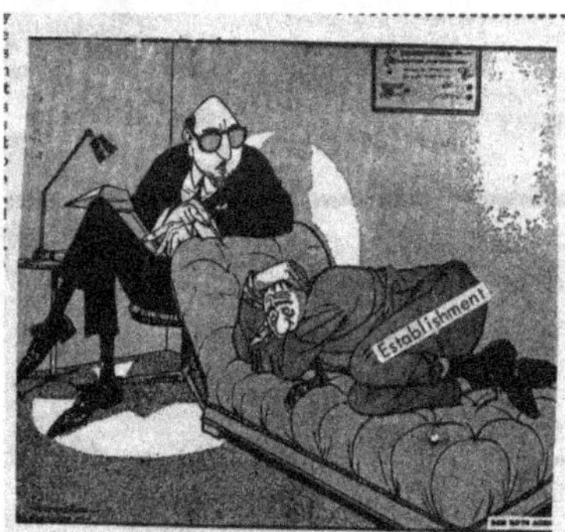

"Apart from being threatened daily by the Young Lords Organization, The Black Panthers, growing militancy among the people, what else is making you nervous?"

You Can't Kill a Revolution

Y.L.O. vol. 1, no. 4, October 10, 1969, p. 3
Young Lords Newspapers Digital Collection
Special Collections and Archives
DePaul University Library, Chicago, Illinois

Two friends of the people, Rev. Bruce Johnson and his wife Eugenia, were assassinated late Sunday night (the 29th) or early Monday (the 30th of September). They were brutally stabbed to death in their home at 2030 N. Seminary.

The YLO mourns this tragic event. Bruce and Eugenia were friends and partners in the struggle to open up the daycare center at the People's Church, where Bruce was pastor. Both Bruce and Eugenia supported and helped the work of the Young Lords. And in a sense, both were in the process of becoming revolutionaries. They had dedicated themselves to the struggles of the poor, especially poor Latins.

Since the Young Lords took over the church in June, the Johnsons' work to bring the people they know to a clearer understanding of the historical and political significance of the church's relationship to the activities of the YLO. The church was renamed the People's Church, a new symbol of the cross bursting the chains of bondage was created and a new creed appeared at the church door. It goes:

> We have a dream. This church, led by the community, confronting the powers which limit our destiny, keeping rulers responsible, assisting man to claim his destiny and celebrating in worship the birth of that power is our dream of a People's Church.
>
> The Good News of Jesus Christ is that each man is of worth as a special creation of God. And Christ's resurrection means that there is no power or establishment which can control a man who claims his own dignity.
>
> This is your faith and your church! Claim them both and join us in this dream.

Bruce and Jean knew they could only serve the people if they entered into the struggle. They knew that no easy reconciliation of the contradictions of our society was possible. They knew that for the church to speak to man's pains, it could not stand as a mere mediator between the forces in conflict. But that the church and its ministers must become part of the forces fighting with the people. They knew this and they died knowing it. As warlord chairman Cha Cha Jimenez eulogized, "Today, too many churchmen are static, like boats tied to the dock, going nowhere, doing nothing. We need to cut ourselves loose and go in search of new ideas, new freedoms, and new ways to get it. We need people who will move across the waters toward the sunlight of freedom, the new land, and the sunlight. If people do that, if they ever arrive at the land of freedom and they look back across the water, they will see the bodies of Bruce and Jeanne Johnson near the land. They will see how close our two friends had come to freedom."

On the morning before the Johnsons were murdered, 10 Young Lords attended the worship service at the church. It was a clear sign of the bond between the Johnsons dream and the work of the Young Lords. Though they are dead, the bond has not been broken. The people demonstrated this at the community meeting Monday night and the memorial celebration on Wednesday night.

On Monday night, the same day the Johnsons were found murdered, 500 community people came to the people's church to plan a memorial service and the future of the daycare center, and people discussed the meaning of the lives and deaths of the Johnsons. It was announced that the memorial service on Wednesday would in fact be a celebration of the Johnsons lives—that people should come to celebrate.

The celebration began with a torchlight March through the community to gather the people to the church. 2,000 people came to hear Bishop Pryor, Jim Reed, Pat Devine and Cha Cha speak words of celebration. Balloons, songs, the kiss of peace—The people all celebrated, saying:

> The bread is rising ** Bread means revolution** God means revolution ** Murder is no revolution ** Revolution is love ** The radical Jesus is winning ** The world is coming to a beginning ** Organize for a new world ** The liberated zone is at hand. Right on!

The members of the Young Lords Organization are deeply saddened by the murder of Rev. Bruce Johnson and his wife Eugenia on September 28 in their home. In the time we have known them, we have come to respect them greatly for their dedication to the oppressed people, to the Puerto Rican community, and to our organization. Reverend Johnson was the pastor of the Armitage Ave. Methodist Church (now Armitage Ave. People's Church) which the YLO used in order to make a reality of the demands of the Puerto Rican community for decent childcare facilities. Instead of attacking us, the way others in his position might have done, Rev. Johnson, his wife, and the board of the church knew our demands were justified and supported us all the way. They helped us greatly in our efforts to open a free daycare center and helped tell others of our needs and the correctness of our action.

In the face of pressure and threats, they stood up for what was right, and continued to defend us from attacks from the police, the alderman and other politicians, and to stop the attempts of building inspectors to close down the childcare center. In the past months, Rev. Johnson often went to court, at least once a week, about legal "violations." The city had threatened to sue him $200/day for the "violations."

This brutal murder of Bruce & Eugenia Johnson is meant as a warning to all people fighting for their just rights, to the Latin American people, to the YLO, and also all other people in their position who show they are willing to learn from and work with the Puerto Rican revolutionary movement. These murders show to what vicious lengths the ruling class will go to prevent the growth of our just struggle.

We will never forget Bruce and Eugenia Johnson. We will not be frightened by their savage murder. We will build them the highest memorial anyone could have, by continuing and stepping up our struggle to win freedom from our people and all oppressed people of the earth, for whom Bruce and Eugenia Johnson gave their lives.

Revolutionaries Serve the People!

Y.L.O. vol. 1, no. 4, October 10, 1969, p. 4
Young Lords Newspapers Digital Collection
Special Collections and Archives
DePaul University Library, Chicago, Illinois

NO ONE CAN DEFEAT ALL THE PEOPLE, FOR EVERY REVOLUTIONARY WHO DIES, A THOUSAND TAKE HIS PLACE.

DAY CARE CENTER

Just before the Puerto Rican Street Festival August 23, the YLO finished most of the work on their Day Care Center in the basement of the People's Church at the corner of Armitage and Dayton. Their hope was to open the center soon after the festival. But the city had other ideas. One day, without being asked, a building inspector from the city came to the church. He told the YLO and the church's minister, Bruce Johnson, that if they tried to open the center there would be trouble because the basement did not meet all the city requirements for day care facilities.

The YLO and Johnson were set on serving the people of Lincoln Park. They finished work on the day care center. Then trouble began. The warning by the building inspector turned to harassment. The city said that the center was in violation of the city building code.

3 broken floor tiles were a violation. The ceiling was a violation because it was too high. The rooms were violations because they were partially below street level. Paint which had been thrown at the murals on the outside of the building was considered a violation. In short, everything was a violation. The city forced Bruce Johnson into court because of these violations.

As one YLO member said, "We were violations to the system the day we were born. The idea of poor people running and benefiting by their own day care center is a violation of city purpose and policy." The point is that although the center doesn't meet all the city requirements, it does meet the requirements of the people in the neighborhood who need it and will use it.

And many mothers will use it. One of the purposes of the center is to free women from being household slaves and to make the caring of children everybody's business. This is especially important for people to understand. Women in Lincoln Park can no longer be mere servants. They must become fully participating members of society, of the new society we are building.

The Day Care Center is beautiful. The YLO built into the basement a dining room, playrooms, napping rooms and equipment rooms. On the walls of each room there are brightly colored paintings which children will love. YLO is opening the center regardless of what the city says, because there is a great need for such facilities.

A working committee of five people has been busy recruiting people, collecting baby toys, contacting doctors and nurses for a medical committee. But more help is needed. This committee needs people to work with people. Offer yourself to the daycare center!

PEOPLE'S PARK IN CHICAGO

(LNS)— People's Park in Chicago began to happen on August 4. After various hip groups had tried and failed to get the project off the ground for a month a coalition of poor people's groups decided to move—and it happened.

The site is a large lot on the busy corner of Armitage and Halsted—Young Lords and Young Comancheros turf. The Lords and the Comancheros are politically minded groups which developed out of Chicago's youth gangs.

People's Park is not being built just for the sake of greenery— it is a holding action for the land.

An estimated 1500 poor people were relocated in 1965, so that the vacant lot could exist. After a few years of uselessness, the city decided the best thing for the land was a Tennis Club, and it began taking bids this spring. As soon as people got wind of it, they started talking about how to take the land back.

Schemes flew back and forth for months: parks, a geodesic-dome medical center, housing of some sort, even a people's shopping center.

It took the YLO and YCO to get it together. After poor people had broken up a public meeting of the Lincoln Park Community Conservation

Council, a rubber stamp for Mayor Daley's urban renewal plans, a Comanchero announced that work on the park would begin August 4—and it did.

Local newspapers have given the park extensive and mostly favorable coverage. The mayor's office has declined comment. Pigs are nowhere to be seen. This ain't Berkeley, and if shit happens, Eldridge's advice—"no more riots—two's and three's"— will more than likely be followed.

The rich white people's stone up-front rip-off of poor people's land is so amazing in Chicago that many people are mesmerized into thinking that there is some kind of legality to it. But booting out 1,500 poor people to make room for a Tennis Club is a bit much, and no one expects to see much public defense of it. This isn't a case of hip people fighting for some greenery; it's poor people fighting for survival in a city that is trying to wipe them out.

El Barrio Está Despierto

Y.L.O. vol. 1, no. 4, October 10, 1969, p. 5
Young Lords Newspapers Digital Collection
Special Collections and Archives
DePaul University Library, Chicago, Illinois

There is much for us all to learn and know about the struggles of the people in Chicago as we come here to join with them and unite to demand that the U.S. GET OUT OF VIETNAM NOW.

This is the story of one part of one struggle, an example of the fight carried on every single day against the pigs by the most oppressed people of this city. Many of these people's organizations have asked us to participate in their fight. We must make every effort to learn from them, as we unite our struggles with the struggles of the Vietnamese in Chicago October 8–11.

The Latin Kings are the biggest Latin youth organization in Chicago, claiming upward of 4,500 members. They have never had a friendly relationship with the Chicago cops. But in the last few years, the cops have come to understand the enormous potential revolutionary power of the youth organization, and since the 1966 Division Street uprising have cracked down heavily on the Kings. This summer between 150 and 300 Latin Kings were in jail at any one time. The Kings defended members of the community against cop harassment on many occasions.

They have been subjected to mass shakedowns and phony raps. They have been shot at by prowl cars in King neighborhoods. There is a rumor in the neighborhoods that the pigs keep a list of the Kings and give each other "points" for busting one. One night in July a King brother was beaten brutally by two pigs at Leavitt and Schiller. Later that night, a patrol car in the neighborhood was fire-bombed. Still later that night, nearly 100 Latin Kings were arrested on suspicion of the bombing.

The cops keep detailed records of information about the Latin gangs and their families and try to bribe brothers and girlfriends to become informers. The cops come around the neighborhood and act real friendly to everyone in the broad daylight, but at night they come around and shoot at us, yell racist insults at black and Puerto Rican kids, and they're too chicken to get out of their cars after dark.

The people have been angry for years. They got even angrier when Manuel Ramos, a member of the Young Lords, and a Puerto Rican revolutionary, was shot to death by an off-duty cop in May 1969. Many parents and young people from the Division Street area came up to the wake and the March we had for Brother Manuel Ramos. The people in the community saw that the cops are the enemy of all the people, black, white and Latin. They had seen many Latin youths ripped apart by police bullets before—but never had the people united and made such a show of strength and rage as we did around the murder of Manuel.

So last week, when brother Pedro Medina was shot in the guts by a Chicago cop, the people were enraged, and they organized together to fight the pigs in the community. They looked for leadership to the Young Lords, who already had the experience of Ramos's murder behind them. The Latin Kings and many other Latin street organizations united and made the greatest unity yet. Here is how it happened.

At 1:30 PM Friday, September 15th, 1969, a Chicago pig attempted to murder a 17-year-old Puerto Rican high school student, in broad daylight.

The pigs reported that the young man, Pedro Medina, was armed and making a getaway when they shot him. They further stated they were in the Puerto Rican community because a burglary had been reported (but they couldn't or wouldn't say what address they supposedly were checking out).

Thirty-five people, mainly Puerto Ricans, who witnessed the incident and know the family said Pedro was running back to school from lunch because he was late. They saw a patrol car stop suddenly, 2 pigs got out and started running after Pedro. When they were about 20 feet away, they fired what the pig claim was a "warning shot" to stop him. When Pedro heard the shot, he turned his head to look back and tripped and fell on his face.

He didn't even have time to pick himself up. The pigs came up to him and rolled him on his back at which time Pedro raised his hands up in surrender and said, "Please don't kill me." One of the pigs held him down with his knee and shot him in the stomach. People who witnessed the whole thing were furious that they would shoot someone who was already caught. They started yelling "pigs," and asked why they had to shoot him. One pig threatened the bystanders and told them to mind their own business and go home.

The other pig went through the victim's pockets and all he found was a pen and $0.20. Meanwhile Pedro's blood was running rapidly down the sidewalk and into the gutter. More and more people gathered and yelled "murderers," "pigs" in English, and in Spanish. By this time the pigs were in the car calling in. Twenty minutes later a paddy wagon came instead of an ambulance. The people's anger continued to burn hotter.

Pedro was thrown into the paddy wagon and driven away. The two pigs went to work: The bullet out of the sidewalk, while the other one tried to wipe up the blood. Then they left. The parents were contacted a couple of hours later. The report they got from pig headquarters was that the officer had seen a gun sticking out of Pedro's pocket, tried to question him about the gun, he ran, and they had to shoot him.

People arrived at the scene minutes after the pigs left and began to work on investigation and rapping to people still there about taking action. Meetings were set up for the following day. Leaflets were distributed throughout the Puerto Rican community inviting all concerned people and especially gang leaders to meet and discuss the incident and others relating to pig harassment and brutality.

The decision was a protest march to pig Daley's office on Saturday, September 13. Out of that first meeting the United Puerto Rican Coalition was formed, made up of 12 youth clubs gangs, Latin church groups, the Spanish Action Coordinating Committee, the Young Lords, and others.

The following five days were spent distributing leaflets informing the community of the incident, the formation of the coalition, and the march on Saturday. The adults in the church groups and "legitimate agencies" try to control the anger and militancy of the youth. But we argued with them and pushed them hard. The march was significant in that the barriers between the youth clubs were broken and they were all aware that YLO was with them struggling against the conservative adults, discussing ideas, urging them to take leadership. The Latin Kings Militant Unit had led the March for the first time appearing in public in full uniform, marching in formation behind the flag of the Puerto Rican Independence Movement. After the March YLO and all the youth organizations met at a park where the march had started.

YLO members split up and offered to inform different groups what we're all about and answer what questions they might have. A lot of good discussions started about "pigs" and pretty soon elevated to political questions, then questions on strategy for revolution.

We have started by deciding to continue with, and function in the Coalition as an organization. Whether the United Puerto Rican Coalition is the answer is not important. But laying down the basis of another united youth forced against the ruling class is Right On!

YLO in Revolution

Y.L.O. vol. 1, no. 4, October 10, 1969, p. 6
Young Lords Newspapers Digital Collection
Special Collections and Archives
DePaul University Library, Chicago, Illinois

The contradictions in this country are becoming sharper. The American empire is crumbling, having lost two wars in the last ten years—Cuba and Vietnam. As things worsen for the rich abroad, it is more important for them to keep things quiet at home. But they must also keep their profits up, so they do this at the expense of the workers. Result: inflation and a near freeze on wages; taxes go up, but services become worse and worse. As the crisis deepens, the ruling class finds it more and more necessary to rely on brute force, the pigs and the army, to keep the people in line. The people revolt in the communities, in the workplace, in the schools. The people demand their rights and fight for them. They demand a government that serves the people, and not one that functions to keep the capitalists healthy. The people are in the majority, but they are out-organized. The people must develop conscious revolutionary groups to lead the struggle.

A revolutionary Latin American organization has been formed in Chicago. The Young Lords Organization is committed to educating the masses of Latin Americans as to the class nature of American Society and the colonization of Latinos in Puerto Rico and the Southwest. YLO is educating the Latinos and raising the level of struggle. YLO has gained considerable mass support in the few months it has been in existence. In the following paragraphs I shall point out the need for YLO, the history of the organization, and the reasons for its continued success.

Latin Americans in the US are workers. Mexicans, Puerto Ricans, and other Latin Americans have produced the vast wealth that came from the West—in mining, farming and industry—pick most of the crops of the Midwest and East, and work in every major industrial center in the country. There are 15,000,000 Latin Americans in this country. The Mexicans were colonized in the Southwest and robbed of their land and riches. The other Latin Americans were forced to come to the US by the super exploitation of American companies in their homeland. So the millions of Latin Americans here also represent their brothers and sisters in the Caribbean, Central and South America that are maintained at mere subsistence for the benefit of Wall Street.

350,000 Latin Americans live in Chicago. They were forced to come north to be exploited by the rich factory owners. The Mexican population (about 160,000) has been in the city for 40–50 years; the Puerto Rican colony (about 100,000) about 20 years.

While in Chicago, we have been involved in a constant struggle against the exploitation at the factory, the robbery by the landlords and the credit sharks, the brainwashing of the schools and the social welfare institutions, and the repression by the pigs and the flunky courts. We have a long history of work strikes, rent strikes, marches, school struggles, pig shootouts, etc.

Considering the fact that Latin Americans alone in this city outnumber all the pigs and flunkies of the pig power structure, we must ask ourselves why we are under their control. The answer, of course, is that the pig power structure has us out-organized. When the people are organized and have a correct understanding of the nature of this racist, capitalist system, they can't lose.

First of all, YLO is a propaganda machine that is committed to educating the masses of people. Our primary task is informing and showing the people why they're being exploited and oppressed, who is responsible, and how they can eventually eradicate the many injustices committed against them.

We are also an armed group prepared to protect our communities from the brutal assaults by the power structure that are committed every day. As the people become more aware of what has been happening, they will turn their guns away from each other and aim them at the pig power structure that has been messing with us for so long.

MURDER OF MANUEL RAMOS

As YLO gained mass support by successfully demonstrating to the people the correct manner of handling unjust, racist institutions, the pig power structure handed down orders to their flunkies on the beat (the pigs) to put us out of commission. But the pigs were unable to move on us in our communities because of the mass support for YLO. But when one of our brothers, Manuel Ramos, was on the South Side at a friend's house, an off-duty pig murdered him. The people put pressure on the government through marches petitions, etc. to bring pig Lamb, the murderer to trial. The Latin people know that the courts are not there to serve them, but we were willing to give it one more try, with the Latin colony of Chicago keeping a close eye on the proceedings. But the pig power structure refused to bring pig Lamb to trial. Instead, six senile flunkies at the coroner's inquest judge the murder of Manuel Ramos "justifiable."

Having exhausted all "legal" means, YLO demonstrated once more that the government and those who control it do not serve all the people, only a few. Since there are no channels open to the people, then the people have the constitutional right and duty to set up whatever structures are necessary, by any means necessary, to have their needs met.

In less than a year, YLO has moved from a social club to a revolutionary organization set on serving and protecting the people. YLO will continue to grow. At present, YLO is involved in establishing a child center on the North Side and stopping urban renewal projects until they are able to meet the needs of the people and not of the greedy speculators and politicians; developing a Puerto Rican Cultural Center; we have opened up a law firm to serve organized revolutionary groups in Chicago; we have forced racist institutions like McCormick Seminary and DePaul University to stop their attack on poor working class people and make retribution for past actions against the people.

YLO has members in most of the Latin American gangs in Chicago, in numerous factories and in all Latin American communities. We are organizing and mobilizing the people. We will continue to grow because we are committed to meeting the needs of the people and we understand the necessity to ally with all other progressive segments of the working class in this country and abroad, and with other progressive elements.

The road that must be taken by Latin Americans in order to achieve freedom is being set by the YLO in Chicago and New York. But it is not clear yet how whites will fight in this just struggle. White students and white workers are rebelling, but these struggles only amount to maintaining their white supremacy in the colleges and in the factories.

The road for white revolutionaries is not clear to some yet, but it must surely include the organizing of white workers at the point of production, in the schools, and in the communities, to a position of solidarity with the black and brown workers of this country and of the third world. The Young Lords Organization extends its hand of revolutionary friendship to white people of Chicago and urges them to join in the present struggle that seeks to benefit all people.

Cosmoe Speaks

Y.L.O. vol 1, no. 4, October 10, 1969, p. 11
Young Lords Newspapers Digital Collection
Special Collections and Archives
DePaul University Library, Chicago, Illinois

If you are a slave and you wish to have freedom, it is useless to talk about becoming free unless you talk about engaging in armed struggle against racism, capitalism, and imperialism in America. That is why we talk about political power coming from the barrel of a gun. We are not striving for civil rights, we are striving for human rights.

Because Manuel Ramos preached the historical necessity of armed guerrilla resistance to capitalism in the US, he was assassinated by the Pig. That is the American story. Every time somebody demands human rights for poor people, he is destroyed by the racist power structure of the U.S. government. We have learned that this is the American story and that is why we began to oppose racist imperialist violence with revolutionary violence.

The YLO was organized to achieve—to accomplish—revolutionary Latin power for the Latin people of this country. When we say "to achieve revolutionary power for Latin Americans or Latin people in this country," we mean power for all persons of African, Asian or Latin American descent in the U.S., as well as progressive whites. We are all being suppressed by the same enemy.

Now most Latin revolutionaries do not get involved in Brown racism. However, when one has been exploited, oppressed, murdered and stomped on for hundreds of years, one naturally develops an unbounded hatred for his enemy and draws a clear line of demarcation between himself and his enemy. We are totally in opposition to all imperialists, and we will move in ALL revolutionary directions to destroy our enemy, regardless of the personal hang-ups of some people.

We don't want to create a brown Rockefeller rather than a white Rockefeller. That is not the goal of the YLO, nor of any revolutionary group. If Rockefeller was brown, he would be our enemy just as much as he is when he is white. If Johnson was brown, he'd be the enemy of the peoples of the world just as he is the enemy of the peoples of the world now. We do not want brown capitalists or brown racists, nor do we want white capitalists.

If we want to be free, we must first understand that we are slaves to neocolonialism because we are powerless and if we wish to become free, we have to understand one historical fact: POLITICAL POWER WOULD MAKE US FREE.

TENGO PUERTO RICO EN MI CORAZON

YLO

Y.L.O.

834 West Armitage Chicago, Illinois 60614

Published Monthly **Young Lords Organization** Vol. I – No. 4

25¢

CHICAGO POLICE DEPT.

REV. BRUCE JOHNSON JR.
1938-69

El Barrio Esta Despierto

Y.L.O. vol. 1, no. 4, October 1969, p. 6
Young Lords Newspapers Digital Collection
Special Collections and Archives
DePaul University Library, Chicago, Illinois

Pa' Vietnam Yo No Voy

Cáno
Y.L.O. vol. 1, no. 5, January 1970, p. 6
Young Lords Newspapers Digital Collection
Special Collections and Archives
DePaul University Library, Chicago, Illinois

FREE PUERTO RICO NOW
OUR SOLIDARITY WITH DRAFT RESISTORS
LONG LIVE THE SPIRIT OF RESISTANCE AGAINST U.S. IMPERIALISM
Puertorriqueños en Todas Partes Repudian el S.M.O

The Young Lords Organization understands the struggle of our Puerto Rican brothers who are resisting the draft here in Puerto Rico. Several of the Young Lords continue to follow these heroes' example.

The exploitation of our Puerto Rican nation by U.S. imperialism is precisely the factor that unites our forces more and more every day. Draft resisting is just one more part of the struggle that our PUERTO RICAN nation has been waging against imperialism since Columbus landed on the beautiful shores of Borinquen in 1493 and thus began the rape and brutalization of our mother country in the Caribbean (we use the term mother country because Borinquen is the only mother country we recognize).

Puerto Ricans began to be illegally drafted by the imperialist government of the United States in 1917 by the grace of a benevolent "act" ratified by the Congress of Babylon (USA). As part of a plan to systematically kill our Puerto Rican people and destroy our nation. This stroke of a pen has gone down in history as one of the bloodiest chapters on genocide and mass murder that continues up to the present time. Several years later, Adolf Hitler would add his own chapter by attempting to exterminate the Jewish race.

Today, less than five and a half million Puerto Ricans remain in the Planet Earth. What makes our particular situation so critical is the fact that our Puerto Rican brothers are being killed in Vietnam at a 20% higher rate, in proportion to our numbers, than both our Chicano and Black brothers.

Throughout the modern history of Puerto Rico, the US imperialists cannot be held totally responsible for being the architects of this planned genocide of our people. They have received ample cooperation from such famous traitors as Luis Munoz Rivera, his prodigal son Luis Munoz Marin, Roberto Sanchez Vilella, and lately the worst of all, Luis A. Ferre, the new progressive statehood party's answer to George Wallace. This traitor serves as "Emperor" Nixon's vassal in Puerto Rico and condones the mass murders being committed against our people. He also directs the political persecution of our patriotic Independentista brothers who are struggling to liberate Borinquen from the grip of US imperialism.

The Young Lords Organization realizes that only through the education of our masses will they be able to "equip" themselves for the long struggle."

This is why we will repeat today what our glorious leaders have said for years and years: The struggles of our people for national liberation, draft resisting and the right for self-determination will only be won when the people rise up against their oppressors.

Ours is a revolutionary history, filled with heroic deeds like our early black and Indian revolts, El Grito de Lares, the Ponce Massacre, our 1950 Revolution, the attack on Blair House, the attack on the U.S. Congress, our armed commandoes for liberation. These are just a few of the dozens of patriotic deeds that have historically characterized the plight of the Puerto Rican nation and its constant and untiring struggle against all forms of imperialism.

Our Draft Resistance Movement adds one more valiant chapter in the revolutionary history of the Puerto Rican nation.

"Cáno" December 1969
Free Puerto Rico Now

"I came down from the mountain to the valley . . . I am a Revolutionary"

Y.L.O. vol. 1, no. 5, January 1970, p. 14
Young Lords Newspapers Digital Collection
Special Collections and Archives
DePaul University Library, Chicago, Illinois

Our brother, Fred Hampton, Deputy Chairman of the Black Panther Party, Chicago, Illinois was murdered by the Chicago pigs Thursday morning December 4.

On this same night an attempt was made to burn the National Headquarters of the Young Lords Organization at 834 W. Armitage, Chicago, Illinois.

The Young Lords Organization would like to inform the community of the seriousness of the gestapo tactics being used by the Nixon Administration and the city against the brother and sisters of all organizations that serve the people.

The political murders of brothers Fred Hampton and Mark Clark plus the wounding of several brothers on the 2300 block of Monroe St., the murder of Manuel Ramos on May 4, 1969, the arrests, imprisonment and murder of our people clearly marked the beginning of Nazi-like extermination being planned and carried out by Richard Nixon and his pigs against our brothers here and in our motherland, Puerto Rico.

This is the reason why the Young Lords Organization has been informing the community and stressing the importance of the struggle that is being waged by the Black, Brown and poor whites for self-determination and the need to bring all struggle of poor people to one united front.

The Young Lords Organization is calling for unity NOW! Or be wiped out by the pigs that continue to vamp on us like Nazi storm troopers.

Let's unite and struggle together under the examples of great men who have died and will continue to die for our people in Puerto Rico and the Americas.

¡FRED VIVE!

"Baje de la montaña al valle . . . "

Nuestro Hermano Fred Hampton lider de los Panteras Negras de Illinois, fue brutalmente asesinado por los "puercos" policia de Chicago en la madrugada de Jueves 4 de Diciembre. Casi a esa misma hora los cuarteles nacionales de la Organizacion Young Lords en Chicago fueron victimas de un ataque para incendiar dichas oficinas con un mecanismo explosivo.

La Organización Young Lords, que defiende los derechos de los Puertorriqueños en Chicago, Nueva York y en todo el país, toma esta oportunidad para poner en alerta y sobre aviso a todas la comunidades acerca de la gravedad y el peligro que conlleva estos ataques en contra de estas organizaciones YLO y Panteras.

Las tácticas de la administración de Richard Nixon, y sus representantes estatales aquí y en Puerto Rico, son las mismas tacticas usadas en contra de el pueblo Vietnamíta y fueron las mismas tacticas utilizadas por Adolfo Hitler y su Partido Nazi Aleman para exterminar la raza Judía.

El asesinato politico de Manuel Rámos, joven puertorriqueño y ademas miembro militante de YLO en Chicago, marcó el comienzo de la ola de represión mas sangrienta y fasista en la historia de America.

Hoy lloramos las muertes de Fred Hampton y Mark Clark. Lloramos también los arrestos que dirige la administracion del titere Luis. A. Ferre en nuestra madre patria Borinquen. Tomando en cuenta la gravedad de estos sucesos llegamos a la conclusion de que el gobierno de los Estados Unidos de America se dispone, en forma abierta, a la sangrienta tarea de exterminar la raza Negra, Puertorriqueña y, o cualquier persona o grupos de personas que traten de una forma o de otra de romper las cadenas del imperialismo Yankee.

La Organización Young Lords ve como un deber patriotico el que se desarrolle una campaña intensa de orientación y de educación en todas nuestras comunidades de habla Hispana. YLO ya comenzó esta campaña y se está ocupando de alertar a nuestra gente sobre la necesidad que hay de unificar todas las razas oprimidas en un solo bloque de lucha colectiva.

La Organización Young Lords hace un llamado a todos los pobres y explotados en America a rededicar sus vidas a la ardua tarea con que nos ha confrontado el imperialismo en el mundo entero. Luchemos juntos bajo los ejemplos sentados por los que han caído en las batallas por la liberación de Puerto Rico, las Americas y todas las géstas gloriosas que han caracterizado las luchas de pueblo y de clases a traves de la historia del universo. Detengamos en esta forma el genocidio de nuestra gloriosa raza.

Todo el poder al Pueblo!
Viva Puerto Rico Libre!
Venceremos!

TENGO PUERTO RICO EN MI CORAZON
YLO

YLO

MACHETE REDENTOR

Young Lords Organization

Published Monthly 834 W. Armitage, Chicago Vol. 1, No. 5 25¢

VIVA PUERTO RICO LIBRE

ALBIZU CAMPOS

¡DESPIERTA BORICUA!

¡En Puerto Rico cada día el rico es más rico, y el pobre más pobre que nunca!

Children playing in the garbage at the Puerta de Tierra Public Housing Project. (Photo by Luis Merino, Jr.)

This, Too, Is Puerto Rico

FREE PUERTO RICO NOW!

Y.L.O. vol. 1, no. 5, January 1, 1970
Young Lords Newspapers Digital Collection
Special Collections and Archives
DePaul University Library, Chicago, Illinois

PAGE 4 Y. L. O. JANUARY 1970

CHICAGO 1969

Y.L.O. vol. 1, no. 5, January 1, 1970, p. 4
Young Lords Newspapers Digital Collection
Special Collections and Archives
DePaul University Library, Chicago, Illinois

PAGE 5 Y. L. O. JANUARY 1970

Esa cuerda está en mi mano,
y la pulso y la conservo;
y estará en mi ronca lira
hasta la muerte,
como el bien más soberano,
que pudiera la fortuna
dar al siervo...
¡Una cuerda larga y fuerte!
¡¡Una cuerda larga y fuerte para el cuello del tirano!!
José de Diego

FREE PUERTO RICO NOW

EL DERECHO DE LA PATRIA A LA INDEPENDENCIA NO SE DISCUTE.

Y SI SE DISCUTE SERÁ A TIROS

Habla el *Maestro*: Don PEDRO ALBIZU CAMPOS

PARA PELEAR DOS PALMOS DE TIERRA BASTAN

En cierta ocasión, una escritora extranjera le preguntó a Don Pedro si él no creía [illegible] Puerto Rico había poca tierra para pelear. Don Pedro le contestó: "Señora, usted se equivoca; es para huir que se necesita mucha tierra; para pelear por la libertad de la patria, solo dos palmos de tierra [illegible]".

Otro periodista extranjero le preguntó si él (Albizu) [illegible] que con un ejército de locos se podía pelear por la libertad de un [illegible]. Don [illegible] respondió: "Cuando los locos están dispuestos a [illegible] por la Patria, es porque han recobrado la razón".

Y.L.O. vol. 1, no. 5, January 1, 1970, p. 5
Young Lords Newspapers Digital Collection
Special Collections and Archives
DePaul University Library, Chicago, Illinois

CARTA DE AZTLAN

¡FREE LOS SIETE!

In the last weeks of April 1969, a big stink was raised by a few merchants on Mission Street in San Francisco. They accused the young men who hang around the area of creating disturbances that were driving their business away. The papers played it up very big and never did report that soon afterwards this was retracted by the Mission Merchants Association. The real reason for loss of business was the new rapid transit system which has torn up many blocks of Mission Street. But the chotas used this as an excuse to vamp down on our young brothers, hauling them into jail and holding them for weeks on things like "obstructing traffic." Hermano Nelson Rodriguez was singled out for special attacks and later was personally apologized to at a press conference. Why were these young men called "hoodlums" and so viciously attacked? We later learned that this was just to set the stage for further repression.

May 1, 1969, 10 a.m. in San Francisco's Mission District Barrio, several brothers were accosted by two unidentified men claiming to be policemen. The brothers were innocently transferring a tv in front of the Rios home at 438 Alverado Street. The two unidentified men, not in uniform, began to harrass and antagonize the brothers. Out of this resulted one man dead and one wounded. Both were later identified as la jura.

Immediately 150-200 chotas were sent to the scene of the incident. The entire area was surrounded by police with guns, rifles and dogs. The fire department was also brought in to hunt out the so-called "criminals." Rounds of ammunition and tear gas were shot into the Rios home without regard to residents of the area. The 14 year old Rios girl was inside the house at the time this was taking place. She was skinned by a bullet and also gassed. The jura were shooting carelessly, even at one another. The furniture in the Rios home was completely destroyed. Persons thought to resemble nuestros carnales were pulled over and questioned. The hunt for these brothers was considered the largest in the history of northern California.

The search went on for 5 days; these were the young men they picked up. Today, Mario Martinez, Rudolfo Martinez, Jose Rios, Nelson Rodriguez, Jose Melendez and Gary Lescallet find themselves in County Prison facing charges of murder and the gas chamber. Another brother, Gio Lopez, is being sought for these same charges. All these brothers worked to help their Raza, en las escuelas, en las calles. Tres carnales as Brown Berets patrolled the streets of San Francisco. They participated in the College readiness program at the College of San Mateo, bringing hermanos y hermanas off the streets into college. They fought this oppressive system in the Third World Liberation Front.

As usual, nuestra gente were harrassed. Constitutional as well as human rights were violated. Persons known as amigos de Los Siete have been stopped by la jura and FBI agents and questioned at gunpoint. Homes have been entered without warrants and ransacked. They have tried to buy off the amigos of the brothers. The Mission District has been patrolled nightly by a troop of super jura. Roadblocks have been set up--people stopped at random.

En la pinta: The brothers have been treated as inhumanly as possible. Were it not for the publicity their case has received and the many visitors they get, there would be no hope for them. The chotas have planted their own men in their cell, lied to them, spit in their food, put them in isolation, but the brothers' morale remains high. Brother Jose Rios has developed hepititis while en la pinta, and it took a court order to get him medical care. Their lawyer, Charles Garry, is the best political lawyer around. We could not find a man more dedicated to la causa, to the rights of human beings to be free. Every time he goes before the court, he provides an education for the entire community.

The parents of Los Siete have organized themselves into a defense group united with the Comite Para Defender Los Siete de La Raza. In the works are a dance featuring a new Cuban movie for the revolutionary Cuban holiday of July 26, and a big rally. Our newspaper, BASTA YA! is working on exposing the actions of the chotas in the Mission. We will not let the jailing of our brothers defeat the movement they are a part of.

Examining this incident and the aftermath it provoked, you can see the political nature of the case. It affects each and every brown person walking the streets of the Mission, or any street in Aztlan. It involves our right to defend ourselves, our people, against this racist oppressive system. One of the first things said against the brothers was "foreign types," "Latin hippies." This is the next step in taking away nuestra tierra, disinheriting us from our birthright.

Why are these things happening more and more? Because La Raza is on the move more and more. Raza is beginning to realize the extent of our brainwashing, that we are not---can never be---gringos. That as brown people we have a proud tradition and a future to determine for ourselves. The rights of brown people in this society have been denied long enough. We are not the passive, manana people the gringos like to think. It is not a question of militancy, but of survival. Any move by La Raza is called violence, while the actions of the chotas are called justice. Our people die of malnutrition in the richest country in the world. It is when La Raza stops fighting among itself and recognizes the true enemy of our people and of all oppressed peoples that the man comes down on us. Today Los Siete, manana usted?

We call on every carnale to help us defend our brothers to keep them from the fas chamber. If one of them is touched, we all die. For more information, write to:

Comite Para Defender Los Siete de La Raza
PO Box 12217
San Francisco, California Aztlan

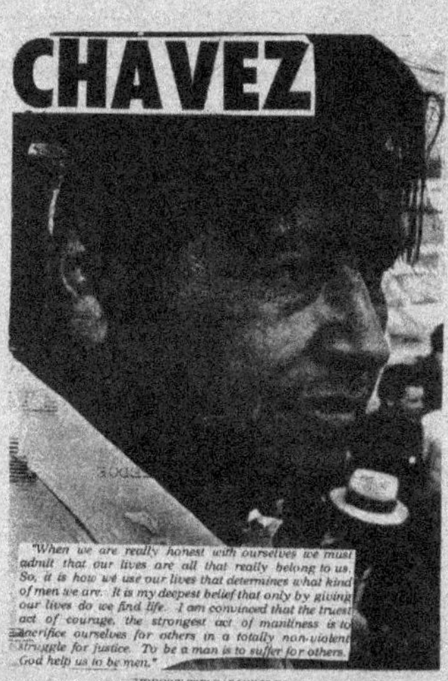

"When we are really honest with ourselves we must admit that our lives are all that really belong to us. So, it is how we use our lives that determines what kind of men we are. It is my deepest belief that only by giving our lives do we find life. I am convinced that the truest act of courage, the strongest act of manliness is to sacrifice ourselves for others in a totally non-violent struggle for justice. To be a man is to suffer for others. God help us to be men."

SUPPORT THE FARMWORKERS

Don't Buy Grapes!

BASTA YA!

The "Sleeping Giant" in the Southwest area of the United States is asleep no longer. Chicanos primarily from the five southwestern states (Texas, Colorado, Arizona, New Mexico, and California) are preparing for a massive Unity Demonstration to be held in Austin, Texas at the foot of the state capitol building.

The Unity Demonstration will focus on the present struggle by Austin Chicano Strikers at the Economy Furniture Factory in Austin, Texas. These determined Chicanos have been on strike since November 27th, 1968. Their battle has been not only with a factory owner that refuses to recognize what is legally their right---that is, to organize and have a voice in their working situation---but it has been and continues to be a bitter struggle with the Sheriff's Department, the District Attorney's staff, the local Police Department, and scab Mexican-Americans. The Chicano strikers are constantly under the watchful eye of people hired by the factory owner with the usage of motion picture cameras and high-powered binoculars---a favorite technique presently being used by the local Sheriff's Department and Highway Patrolmen. There have been dozens of cases clearly indicating that many of the law-enforcing officials are supporting the factory owner who has been ordered by two courts to meet the demands of the Chicano strikers.

Y.L.O. vol. 1, no. 5, January 1, 1970, p. 16
Young Lords Newspapers Digital Collection
Special Collections and Archives
DePaul University Library, Chicago, Illinois

PAGE 17 Y.L.O. JANUARY 1970

Give Alcatraz Back to the INDIANS

YOUNG LORDS SPEND THANKSGIVING WITH INDIAN BROTHERS AND SISTERS ON ALCATRAZ

(YLO/LNS–Karen Wald–San Francisco)

In a proclamation issued November 20, 1969 to "The Great White Father (presumably Secretary of the Interior Walter Hickel) and All His People," the Indians declared the former prison island of Alcatraz theirs by right of discovery prior to Columbus.

Expressing a desire to "be fair and honorable in our dealings with the Caucasion inhabitants of this land,"the Indians offered the following treaty:

"We will purchase said Alcatraz Island for twenty-four dollars in glass beads and red cloth, a precedent set by the white man's purchase of a similar island about 300 years ago." Noting that they were paying comparatively more for their small island than the Dutch had paid for Manhattan, the Indians generously added, "But we know that land values have risen over the years. Our offer of $1.24 per acre," they noted, "is greater than the 47 cents per acre the white men are now paying the California Indians for their land.

Regarding the future of the island, the Indians said reassuringly: "We will give to the inhabitants of this island a portion of that land for their own, to be held in trust by the American Indian Affairs and by the Bureau of Caucasian Affairs to hold in perpetuity---for as long as the sun shall rise and the rivers go down to the sea. We will further offer them our religion, our education, our lifeways, in order to help them achieve our level of civilization and thus raise them and all their white brothers up from their savage and unhappy state. We offer this treaty in good faith and wish to be fair and honorable with all white men."

With this proclamation, 80 young Indians, stoutly supported by their tribal elders, landed on and occupied Alcatraz Island. A week later, with their numbers reaching 300 and still growing, the Indians celebrated Thanksgiving.

The festival was somewhat reversed. Instead of the friendly Indians showing the newly arrived pilgrims their hospitality, white allies of the Indians brought boat-loads of turkeys, blankets, sleeping bags, firewood, fresh water and milk, and other supplies in assorted motor boats, yachts and junks. The on-again-off-again Coast Guard blockade wasn't operating, and boats were free to land on the island, screened only by the Bureau of Caucasian Affairs representatives, who checked out all non-Indians who sought to enter.

Press were welcome--provided that they remain escorted by personnel from the Indian Press Service. So were two Puerto Rican brothers, "Cha Cha" Jimenez, National Chairman of the Young Lords Organization, from Chicago, and "Cano" Miller of San Juan, who came to bring revolutionary greetings of solidarity from their Puerto Rican brothers and sisters.

Our landing party was greeted by a young brave named Dennis Turner, a Mission-Shoshone, who warmly welcomed us and arranged for an Indian sister named Julie the head of the press service, to take us on a tour of the island.

Richard Oakes, a Mohawk, is informally recognized as the leader of the Indians here. It was Oakes who, with 13 other braves, landed on the island for a trial expedition several weeks ago, then went out to gather more Indians from all over California, many of them college students, to reclaim their land for real.

Julie explained that a great deal of organizing was needed once the Indians landed on the island. Now they have committees working on providing food, arranging shelter, clean-up details, guard duty, press clearance, caring for the children and taking care of transportation. Asked by "Cano" whether there was a spirit of resistance against any possible intervention on the island, Julie responded, "We'd use our heads." She gave the example of the blockade that had been set up by the Coast Guard. "Of course we had to do something; we have children to feed. So we ran the blockades all night. Ww weren't hurting anyone, or really resisting, we were just getting supplies in. But is was like guerrilla warfare.

It's a 15-minute climb to the prison buildings. Alcatraz was a maximum-security Federal prison until 1963. Since then it has been abandoned. Some electric power and some running water remain in a few buildings, but everything is in a state of decay.

Recently the federal government decided to pass the land on to the city of San Francisco, which in turn had decided to sell it to H. L. Hunt (right-wing Texas oil millionaire). He was going to make it into a kind of Space Age Disneyland. Some of San Francisco's enlightened citizens objected, and a dressmaker named Duskin put a full-page ad in the San Francisco Chronicle which brought in thousands of letters of protest to Interior Secretary Hickel. A flood of suggestions began pouring in as to what to do with the island.

The Indians at this point conveniently settled the question by occupying and reclaiming their land. Their plans for the island include:

1. A center for Native American studies, teaching native arts and skills, supplemented by travelling universities which would learn from the various Indian Reservations around the country.
2. An American Indian Spiritual Center.
3. An Indian center of ecology to train their people in "scientific research and practice to restore our lands and waters to their true and natural state."
4. An Indian Training School to teach Indians the trades they need to make a living in the world, as well as a center for arts and crafts, including Indian cooking, all of which would be offered to the public.
5. An American Indian Museum which would contain one portion depicting what the white man gave to the Indians in return for the land and life he took: disease, alcohol, poverty and cultural decimation (as symbolized by old tin cans, barbed wire, rubber tires, plastic containers, etc.) as wel' as broken treaties and a history of massacres.

As we wandered around the island, we saw many signs painted on walls or hung over doorways. Even as we first approached the island, the huge government block letters proclaimed "WARNING KEEP OFF. Only government boats permitted within 200 yards. Persons entering without authority do so at their peril." Hand painted letters on the adjacent wall proclaimed otherwise: "INDIAN LAND'" A huge smokestack was lettered "FREEDOM, PEACE ON EARTH'" The word "States" was painted out on another government sign, so that it now read "United INDIAN Property.". At the entrance to the main prison building, a huge sign with an elaborately painted eagle declared "THIS LAND IS OUR LAND!'" Another frequent slogan asserted, "CUSTER HAD IT COMING!'"

All of the Indians, young and old, are enthusiastic. A 47-year-old man who has been involved in the fishing rights struggle in the State of Washington said he came down to "see what we can do to help." "We see the young people as moving not only in the right direction," he commented, "but faster. I think this is real beautiful." Asked about whether there was a generation gap among the Indians, he explained that this didn't occur because of the mutual respect between the young and the old.

A white-haired companion from Southern Californis added, "I support these young people here, because us older people haven't done much for over 200 years, and it's about time we let the young ones do it. At least we're supposed to support them. And I don't think there's much of a generation gap, because they want old people here, and they love us, and that's why I'm here.

Later we spoke with some of the young men who were most responsible for the Alcatraz landgrab, Richard Oakes and Dennis Turner. When asked how this had all begun, Dennis said, "Well, it really began about 470 years ago, when we discovered Columbus, and he was lost...," He then turned more serious, discussing the genocide in Vietnam. "We're now making our stand, and it's a definite stand, and we're gonna stay here."

ALCATRAZ PARA LOS INDIOS

PUERTO RICO PARA LOS PUERTORRIQUENOS

YOUNG LORDS VISITAN ISLA DE ALCATRAZ Y AFIRMAN LAZOS DE SOLIDARIDAD CON HERMANOS Y HERMANAS DE LA RAZA INDIA.

El dia de Accion de Gracias 1969 marco un evento de gran significado historico en terminos de solidaridad entre El Pueblo de Puerto Rico y La Raza India en los EEUU.

Fue en este día que dos líderes de la Organización de Los Young Lords llevaron personalmente, un mensaje de apoyo a los bravos Indios, y a su lider maximo, Richard Oakes, quien dirigiera el "Asalto" a Alcatraz en días anteriores.

Los hermanos "Cha Cha" Jimenez, Primer dirigente de YLO, y "Cano" Miller de San Juan Puerto Rico fueron recibidos con abrazos su llegada a dicho ter fueron recibidos con abrazos a su llegada a dicho territorio Libre.

Los hermanos fueron conducidos a traves de la isla por una escolta de honor. Afirmo Oakes, "Recibo a estos hermanos revolucionarios Puertorriqueños que de tan lejos han venido a apoyarnos con su presencia aquí. Las Razas Indias de los EEUU y todo las Americas reconocen plenamente y agradecen profundamente el apoyo dada a nuestra causa por LA ORGANIZACION DE LOS YOUNG LORDS Y EL PUEBLO DE BORINQUEN."

FREE AMERICA NOW

Y.L.O. vol. 1, no. 5, January 1, 1970, p. 17
Young Lords Newspapers Digital Collection
Special Collections and Archives
DePaul University Library, Chicago, Illinois

Housing Denied to Poor People

Omar López, Minister of Information, YLO
Y.L.O. vol. 2, no. 6, February–March 1970, p. 5
Young Lords Newspapers Digital Collection
Special Collections and Archives
DePaul University Library, Chicago, Illinois

The Poor People's Coalition in Lincoln Park has struggled to develop a housing plan for the poor and working-class people in this area. The first scrimmages the Young Lords had with the Department of Urban Renewal date back to the beginning of the Young Lords Organization as a political group in December of 1968. In January of 1969 the Young Lords Organization was forced to take over meetings of the local community conservation council where a few middle-class whites were making decisions for the whole community. We were told that we should follow the "legal procedures." We did and presented a plan to CCC which after many legal fights was accepted and recommended to be passed by Daley's Department of Urban Renewal. It seemed as if the city had finally become sensitive to the needs of the people in Lincoln Park. On Wednesday, February 11th, 300 angry Lincoln Park residents showed up at the urban renewal meeting when the word was out that Daley had instructed his head puppet Lou Hill to ignore the Poor People's Plan and approve the Hartford bid.

Daley's puppet Lou Hill pretended to go through the motions of voting for the bid and asked that those opposed to the Hartford bid stand up. The City Council chambers were packed with people favoring the Poor People's bid and all stood up. At this point Hill approved the Hartford bid ignoring not only the petitions of the people to speak but the decisions of the people to oppose the Hartford plan.

The people of Lincoln Park have made the final stand with the People's Park. The D.U.R. can no longer make decisions without expecting a strong retaliation from the people. Hartford construction company should be aware of its role in our community and make its decision based on the fact that they are contributing to the perpetuation of the powerlessness of a community.

The city's action is a crime against the people. The people of the neighborhood struggled long to develop a plan and had the support of our plan.

The land belongs to the people! We will take action!

Y.L.O. vol. 2, no. 6, February–March, 1970
Young Lords Newspapers Digital Collection
Special Collections and Archives
DePaul University Library, Chicago, Illinois

PAGE 11 Y.L.O. February, March

¡EL BORICUA ESTA DESPIERTO!!!

El alcaguete Ferre a logrado finalmente la polarizacion en Puerto Rico, y muy facilmente puede ganar el premio de organizador numero uno en contra del imperialismo norteamericano. Las acciones de sus titeres en los recintos de Rio Piedras y otras universidades ha logrado lo que el movimiento estudiantil habia tratado de hacer por mucho tiempo: el de concientizar al estudiantado y al resto de Puerto Rico.

La ocupacion del Recinto de Rio Piedras que es un paralelo a la ocupacion de la universidad de Mexico en 1968, y la ocupacion de la Universidad de Buenos Aires quita el velo a la pretencion de que el Puertorriqueno esta contento con sus condiciones.

EL BORICUA ESTA DESPIERTO!
CUIDA'O!

EN el Recinto de Rio Piedras

SUPPRESSION, REPRESSION, AGGRESSION!

JURY TRIAL + for aggravated assault
LADO WELFARE UNION
1. Josefina Rodrigues
2. Esperanza Gonsalez
3. Maria Perez
4. Vicky Perez

JURY TRIAL

JURY TRIAL - for Mob action, aggravated assault and batery against 2 police officers
LADO- Latin American Defense Organisation.
1. Obed Lopez

YOUNG LORDS CASES
1. Luis Chavez
2. Jose Cosmo Torres
3. Jose "Cha Cha" Jimenez
4. Carlos Juan Morales "Mousee"
5. Sal del Rivero
6. Orlando Davila
7. Pancho
8. Division Pete
9. Adrian Luna "Lucky"
10. Rafael Viera

"Hands Off Loui"

Little Loui Chavez es uno de los muchos Young Lords que estan sintiendo la represion de las cortes en Chicago. Luis ira a Corte este mes por el "delito" de informar a la comunidad de los programas de la Organizacion por medio de hojas sueltas. Los abogados nos dicen que el juez le dara al menos una multa de $500.00dlls. por el "crimen" cometido. Nosotros nos decimos: Que habra pasado con el famoso derecho del que tanto se habla en este pais? ese de "Libertad de Expresion". O sera que Loui no debe de hacer uso de ese derecho por ser un Young Lord?.

La represion no solo se siente en las calles de Chicago y New York, pero tambien en las cortes. Las cortes solo son instrumento para esconder las inconsistencias de este sistema llamando "criminales" a aquellos que se rebelan y tratan de hacer cambios en esta sociedad.

Luis Chavez es inocente de todo delito Los culpables son las cortes, e instituciones del govierno que no implementan los programas que la comunidad necesita y forza a los Young Lords a hacerlo.

¡Justicia para Rafael!

¡Los "4" Lords son inocentes!

¡Hands Off Chairman "Cha Cha"!

DAVID RIVERA

Nuestro hermano David Rivera, que fuera nuestro Mariscal de campo durante el tiempo mas duro en el desarrollo de la Organizacion de los Young Lords, ha sido objeto de varios atentados contra la vida de el y de su familia.

David ha sido baleado dos veces por gente desconosida y en otra ocasion fue casi arrollado por un carro. Su casa ha sido atacada con bombas incendiarias pero sin ningun resultado.

Estos ataques vinieron despues de que David descubrio publicamente los verdaderos motivos de el Departamento de Renovacion Urbana en nuestro barrio al botar a familias Puertorriquenas, y los motivos de el Departamento de la Policia al intimidar a los jovenes del barrio para que terminaran sus actividades en el area.

La vida de David es muy valiosa: esta dedicada a la liberacion del Pueblo Puertorriqueno, por lo tanto lo que le suceda a David sera un ataque a todo Latinoamericano, y los culpables contra-revolucionarios rebenta'os seran traidos a justicia por el Pueblo.

Ministry of Information
Young Lords Organization
National Headquarters

Y.L.O. vol. 2, no. 6, February–March 1970, p. 11
Young Lords Newspapers Digital Collection
Special Collections and Archives
DePaul University Library, Chicago, Illinois

Revolutionary Constitution

Pitirre vol. 2, no. 7, Summer 1970, p. 11
Young Lords Newspapers Digital Collection
Special Collections and Archives
DePaul University Library, Chicago, Illinois

Why a revolutionary constitutional convention? Why a new constitution? It is clear to all oppressed people, and allow me to make reference to the Brown people as a segment of the oppressed people, to say that we understand that the present constitution, with the exception of the Bill of Rights, which was "crumbs" to keep the people down, is an accumulation of laws that deprive poor people of its basic human rights. It is a document designed to put a certain type of people in power and keep them in power.

What brown people are saying is that up to now, under this constitution we've been lynched in Texas and California; murdered in cold blood in the cells of the jails of Chicago and New York (and then they say we hung ourselves); that under this constitution Puerto Rico was made a colony of the United States; that under this constitution the five southwestern states of the US were stolen from Mexico; under this constitution Latin America has been exploited to the bone and under this constitution the needs of poor people are used to make a profit.

Poor people need a constitution that will guarantee us the life liberty and the pursuit of happiness. We need a constitution that will punish criminals that destroy people physically and mentally—to punish the Nixons and Rockefellers; the Ferres and Muñoz Marins; the Echeverrias and Diaz Ordacess. A constitution that will guarantee our brothers and sisters food to eat and a place to live.

The need for a document designed by the people to be a guideline for the actions of all revolutionary organizations is unquestionable. The need is great, and the time is now.

Recordando a Borinquen Festival

Yolanda Lucas
Pitirre vol. 2, no. 7, Summer 1970, p. 17
Young Lords Newspaper Digital Collection
Special Collections and Archives
DePaul University Library, Chicago, Illinois

Once a year the Young Lords Organization celebrates a Festival Recordando a Borinquen (Remembering Puerto Rico). It is a cultural and social gathering of the community people.

Why are we Recondando a Borinquen? Because Puerto Rico (Borinquen) is our motherland, and we are proud of being Puerto Ricans . . . of being Latins . . . of being brown.

There are two reasons for celebrating the Festival on the 26th of July: one to declare our solidarity with the people of Cuba since the date is the 17th anniversary of the Cuban Revolution and as Latins we feel proud that Cuba fought and won her total liberation from Yanqui imperialism and their puppet government in Cuba led by dictator Fulgencio Batista; and second, because of the similarities between Cuba and Puerto Rico.

It was on the 26th of July of 1953 that Fidel Castro, at the head of a small group of brave Cubans, attacked the Moncada headquarters of the puppet government of Batista, setting the base for the Liberation that was to come in 1959, when Castro's guerillas overthrew Batista's regime.

Similarities between Cuba and Puerto Rico go way back into the days of the colonization by the Spaniards. Both islands were victims of the oppression and exploitation by the Spaniards. Both countries began to fight the oppressor simultaneously, progressively fighting towards the same goal: their independence.

Both leaders of the revolutions of Yara in Cuba and Lares in Puerto Rico, respectively, were moved by the same motivations. In the case of Cuba, the fact that the United States supported the revolution against Spain and declared war on Spain in 1898 was because of the U.S. economic interest in Cuba, whereby Puerto Rico was ceded to the United States as spoils of war.

During the Spanish-American war, Cubans and Puerto Ricans fought under the guidelines of men like Betances and Jose Marti who had established the revolutionary Board in New York in order to plan for the independence of the two islands. That explains the fact that the Cuban and the Puerto Rican flags are so alike.

Now Cuba is liberated from capitalist oppression while Puerto Rico is still struggling for independence. On July 26, we declared our solidarity with the courageous people of Cuba and declared our solidarity with the brothers and sisters in Puerto Rico in an effort to unite our ideals of Independence.

Brother Tony Baez of the Young Lords spoke on the development of politics in Puerto Rico in Spanish, sister Jenny spoke on the similarities between Cuba and Puerto Rico in English. Brother Alberto rapped about the summons on the Ramon Emeterio Betances Free Health Center. Towards the middle of the entertainment, a brother of the community sang Puerto Rico's anthem "La Borinqueña." At this point many cries of "Free Puerto Rico Now" and "Power to the People" were released. Fists were raised as a sign of protest, salute and honor, Latin Bands participated free of charge and community people helped serve and clean.

The Young Lords Organization thanks deeply the following people who gave services for the benefit of the "barrio" and the support of our festival. The Soul Mystics, the conquistadores and the Soul Medallions, who proved in more ways than one that we as Latins have talent; thanks to the community who served and Mr. and Mrs. Lorenzi who cooked, like last year, our Latin foods; thanks to the Venceremos Brigade who spent more than a month cleaning the People's Park. Thanks to the donors of foods and materials. Again, we give our Thanks to all who participated. With our revolutionary fervor—All Power to the People . . . Free Puerto Rico Now.

The Government and Repression

El Young Lord: Latin Liberation News Service vol. 1, no. 1, April 1, 1971, p. 9
Young Lords Newspapers Digital Collection
Special Collections and Archives
DePaul University Library, Chicago, Illinois

The government is a wall designed to act as a barrier between the oppressor and the oppressed. In order to understand this statement, we must first look at history and understand that everything is in a constant state of change and that everything is interconnected.

The human race began to divide as the population of pre-civilized tribes grew larger. As they grew larger, people began to split off and form other tribes. This process of development became so widespread that soon even the natural boundaries (rivers, mountains, etc.) separated people who once belonged to a common tribe.

The first government was formed as a result of the tools of production (plows, cattle to pull the plows with, etc.) becoming the property of a few individuals.

The private owners of these tools, at first thinking only in terms of survival, began to use their ownership as a way of exploiting the rest of the population.

Because the ruling class (owners of tools) later saw the necessity for creating a force to stand between them and the people, the government was invented. And along with it the standing army and the political apparatus.

Today we know the standing army in the form of the National Guard, the Federal Bureau of Investigation (FBI) and the Gestapo police who patrol our communities.

The political apparatus is made-up of the corrupt news media (newspapers, TV, radio, etc.) and the pig politicians who claim to serve our communities.

Historically pig repression of the type which we are now experiencing has been strong indication of the presence of fascism.

One can accurately describe fascism as being a condition where: repression of attempts at becoming free have become so intense, that the government has resorted to the use of its standing army as a means of destroying the people. In short, fascism means that we are living under police state conditions.

The fascist murdering and harassment of the people in general and the movement in particular is very evident. When we look at incidents such as the national Chicano moratorium in LA, where three people were murdered on Aug. 29th and again at the recent police riots in Puerto Rico where one student was murdered, we can only come to one conclusion, THAT IT IS NO LONGER POSSIBLE TO DEAL WITH THIS GOVERNMENT ON PEACEFUL TERMS.

We must now understand that in order to combat this government's repression, we must take a look at our liberation struggle in general and understand that the small amount of work that we have done is not enough. We must fight the standing army with a standing people's army.

When we find that we're in a situation where the government's repression has grown so strong that we find ourselves acting spontaneously or reacting on the spur of the moment, then we must retreat. When we find that we're trying to avenge the deaths of a few rather than avenging the deaths and persecutions of all the people, then we must retreat. When we think that it is more important to organize a demonstration rather than to organize a revolution, then we have found that we must retreat and reorganize ourselves internally.

In short, the only way that we can deal with our situation is to: 1) understand that everything that we become involved with must be strategical and of a qualitative nature, 2) that all our activities must be geared toward educating, organizing, and arming the people at all times, 3) that while becoming involved in the other two points that we be prepared to protect and defend ourselves and the community from further pig attacks. Then and only then will we be in a position to deal with the government and repression.

HASTA LA VICTORIA SIEMPRE!
VENCEREMOS!

Young Lords Health Program

El Young Lord: Latin Liberation News Service vol. 1, no. 1, April 4, 1971, p. 11
Young Lords Newspapers Digital Collection
Special Collections and Archives
DePaul University Library, Chicago, Illinois

In February 1971, the Dr. Ramon Emeterio Betances Health Program celebrated its first anniversary having provided free health services in the community for one full year, despite mayor Daley's determined effort to close us down by dragging us to court for nine months. The Betances Health Program keeps serving the people and keeps showing who in Chicago is really interested in decent health care. This past year, with little money, the program has offered preventive care, general medical care for adults and children, prenatal care and eye care. The Chicago Board of Health, with $18 million for one year, offers only prenatal care and well-baby care at its dilapidated and poorly equipped clinics. Yet, instead of improving its own services, the Board of Health has dedicated itself to shutting down the free clinics operated by the Young Lords, the Young Patriots, and the Black Panther Party.

To begin the new year of the Program, the health workers on the staff pledged their support for three community women who are working for the Betances Health Program to increase community participation and community control. The three community workers are involved in the new eye program—a program of vision screening, eyeglasses, and eye care—and in the outreach program—a program where the health workers "reach out" to families in their homes to begin preventive family care (TB tests, baby shots, urine tests, family medical questionnaire).

A patient advocacy program was also begun because the Young Lords saw that the community people were being harassed and cheated at Grant Hospital—the hospital that says it serves the community. All patients from the neighborhood are accompanied by an advocate to prevent mistreatment and fees of any kind. But what the advocate found out is that hospital workers were not mistreating patients—the workers themselves were confused because their bosses, the hospital administrators, had not communicated our arrangements to them. The hospital workers were simply ignored when the administrators negotiated with us. The Young Lords and the health staff of the Betances Health Program know that our struggle is not against the hospital workers, but it is with the workers against their bosses!!!

In February 1970, the Young Lords Organization opened a free health center to meet a basic need in the community. Most poor Chicano and Puerto Rican people live their lives without any health care until they are so sick it is very critical. And why? Because it costs too much money to try and get well! But another more important reason exists for the health center, it is a model for the kind of healthcare and community program we believe in. At the Betances Health Program, a patient is not regarded simply as a disease. He or she is regarded as a person deeply involved in the family, in our culture, and in this community which is struggling to survive.

So while the Betances Health Program is a "survival program" on one hand, on the other hand it is a political lesson. When we say "free healthcare," we do not mean you don't have to pay. We mean that by being kept poor by the capitalist, by being a worker in a factory, in a hospital, or in a household, you have earned the right to good healthcare and good health.

FREE HEALTH CARE IS A HUMAN RIGHT!!
POWER AND HEALTH TO THE PEOPLE!!!!

Free Culebra

El Young Lord: Latin Liberation News Service vol. 1, no. 2, April 15, 1971, p. 9
Young Lords Organization
Freedom Archives, digital reproduction

Culebra, a ten square mile island, 20 miles east of Puerto Rico, was invaded by the United States Navy in 1902. Today, 36% of the land is being used for military purposes. From here, an immense naval base operates in the Caribbean.

Because of its strategic location Culebra is used as a base for protection of the Panama Canal Zone. and serves as a base of operations for the Central Intelligence Agency (C.I.A.). The Navy's target practicing provides a useful cover.

At the beginning of the century there were about 4,000 inhabitants in the island. Today, approximately 750 are left. The families at the northwest section of the island were moved out so that the Navy could set up its target practice there. More than 20 nations from all around the world use Culebra as a target for their naval practicing. And the US gets all the profit from it. People in the island called the naval practice section "Vietnam."

Damage has been done to livelihood sources, like fishing, on which many islanders depend for food. Bombing errors constantly endanger the lives of civilians (people have been reported dead and many injured) as well as Navy men (9 sailors were killed when an aircraft accidentally bombed an observation post).

Since the Navy started to use the northwest of the island as practicing grounds people have been increasingly harassed and threatened, not only by the immediate danger of a bombing mistake but by the confusion created in their own lives as the noise and pressure from the Navy has mounted. People of the only city on the island called "Dewey" after the invader that stole their land—started to question the whole game that was being played. Legal research was done and, although Culebra was taken over—as part of the Puerto Rican Nation—by the United States in the Paris Treaty of 1898, legal questions have been raised as to whether Culebra was actually included in the treaty.

At this moment Culebrans started to move and organized around the idea of asking the Navy to leave. The United States responded with a bill introduced in Congress by some pig senators aimed towards moving out all Puerto Ricans off the island so that the Navy could use the entire island as a military base. The bill wasn't passed but on January 11th a treaty was signed by the Navy, the millionaire governor of the island—Luis Ferre—the president of the Puerto Rican Senate—Rafael Hernandez Colon—and the mayor of Culebra—Ramon Feliciano. It didn't take long for the people to understand that with this treaty they were agreeing to stop protesting against the Navy.

A major practicing operation—"Operation Springboard"—which takes place every year, was scheduled by the Navy for mid-January. Some people from the Puerto Rican Independence Party (PIP), the "Save Culebra Committee," and a Quaker Action Group from the United States, got together and decided to invade the practicing grounds. They did, and when they arrived, they were met by the US Marines. The latter tried to stop them and engage in hand-to-hand combat with the unarmed courageous people. The Marine commander had to call for a retreat and the demonstrators managed to enter the area where they built a chapel. Several days later six of the demonstrators got arrested. Four of them members of PIP, including their president, Ruben Berrios. All six were sentenced to serve three months in jail. Later, eight more people were arrested.

All these brothers and sisters are political prisoners of this country. It's the United States whose keeping them in jail because they were a threat to its interest in Culebra.

On February the 8th, 1971, 100 marines were ordered to tear down the Chapel. They waited til nightfall. Culebrans that had been waiting went for reinforcement in town and when they returned, they were received with tear gas. One demonstrator was arrested. The rest had to retreat. Even the mayor Raymond Feliciano, was tear gassed.

More people have been arrested and must still go to court.

The Young Lords Organization understands that all these brothers and sisters are political prisoners . . . That such cases are generated by U.S. imperialist policies against people all around the world and in this particular case Puerto Ricans.

The army of the ruling class of this country will not leave Culebra until they are thrown out. Like the people in the island say: "If the Yankees don't leave . . . We'll make them leave."

ALBIZU CAMPOS

EL YOUNG LORD
LATIN LIBERATION NEWS SERVICE

EMILIANO ZAPATA

OFFICIAL ORGAN OF THE YOUNG LORDS

PUBLISHED WEEKLY
VOLUME 1 NUMBER 2
25 CENTS

MINISTRY OF INFORMATION
BOX 5024
MILWAUKEE WISCONSIN 53204

El Young Lord: Latin Liberation News Service vol. 1, no. 2, April 15, 1971
Freedom Archives, digital reproduction

Page 4 EL YOUNG LORD April 15, 1971 NACIONALES

LOLITA LEBRON
PRISIONERA POLITICA

Mientras la Organización de Estados Americanos (OEA) debatía sobre la situación reinante en la América Latina de principios de la década, marzo 1 del 1954, un grupo de cuatro valerosos boricuas residentes de Nueva York, tiroteaban la Cámara de Representantes de los Estados Unidos de Amerikka hiriendo a cinco congresistas.

Los boricuas, bajo el liderato de Lolita Lebrón, habían planeado el golpe desde el 22 de Febrero--día del natalicio de Washington--en la ciudad de Nueva York y se proponían llamar la atención de la OEA en Caracas y del mundo entero expresando así, como hicieran los heroes de Lares en el 1868, como hicieran los nacionalistas en Jayuya (1950) y como hicieran Oscar Collazo y Griselio Torresola en su atentado contra el Presidente Truman, sus ansias de libertad a su madre patria, Puerto Rico.

La noticia conmovió al mundo entero ya que era la primera vez en la Historia que sucedía cosa igual en la capital de Amerikkka. Se hacía muy extraño para la Amerikkka racista reconocer que cuatro boricuas habían tiroteado a más de 200 congresistas en la Cámara y que luego desplegaran la bandera de Puerto Rico con un grito de VIVA PUERTO RICO LIBRE.

Los asaltantes: Lolita Lebrón, 34 anos de edad; Andres Figueroa Cordero, de 29 anos; Rafael Cancel Miranda, 25 anos; Erving Flores de 23 anos; parapetados en las galerias de espectadores, habrieron fuego sobre los congresistas cuando culminaba una votación sobre una ley referente a los trabajadores agrícolas mexicanos...víctimas también de la más cruel explotación y descriminación por los Estados Unidos que robó sus tierras e intenta destruir su identidad como nación.

El intento de los nacionalistas de expresar al mundo su repudio por la política de intervención norteamericana en Puerto Rico y en el mundo entero, especialmente en el momento en que se llevaba a cabo una votación sobre el obrero mexicano y una Conferencia Inter-Americana en Caracas, llevó a que los cuatro fueran reconocidos como: "Los Caballeros de la Raza".

Por el otro lado, los Estados Unidos hicieron uso de este intento para atacar y arrestar a otros puertorriqueños, 11 en total, residentes tanto de Nueva York como Chicago. Muchos de estos recibieron de 16 a 50 años de prisión; los otros tres hermanos recibieron sentencias que iban de 25 a 65 anos de prision. Ninguna comparable a la sentencia de reclusión perpetua que dictaron a Oscar Collazo, sobreviviente al tiroteo contra la casa Blair donde se encontraba Truman.

Mientras tanto, el gobernador títere de la Isla, Luis Muñoz Marín, llegaba a los Estados Unidos en "vista de desagravio" al presidente Eisenhower, su amo Como buen siervo le hizo claro al presidente su promesa macabra de acabar con el " grupo de fanáticos nacionalistas" residentes de la Isla. Sin investigar si había o no relación entre los miembros del partido Nacionalista en la Isla y los hechos acaecidos en Washington el títere de Muñoz Marín se adelantaba a proponer al amo sus intentos de acabar con la membrecía del Partido en Puerto Rico, por el sólo hecho de ser miembros de la misma agrupación política luchando por la Independencia de Puerto Rico.

Fue así como, a su llegada a la Isla, a pesar de las declaraciones de Lolita y demás que señalaban que todo fue planeado por ellos en Nueva York, y se responsabilizaba Lolita de todo, Muñoz Marín ordenó el saqueo de más de cincuenta residencias de familias en la Isla arrancando violentamente de sus camas hombres y mujeres que nada tenían que ver con lo sucedido y cuyo único delito era el de amar la independencia de su patria.

A la par, ordenó el asalto a la casa del líder nacionalista Don Pedro Albizu Campos. Allí, por espacio de dos horas, los valerosos nacionalistas guiados por Don Pedro, se batieron con la policía. Al ser capturado el gran líder, tras caer bajo los efectos del gas lacrimógeno, dejó su mensaje al pueblo: "Hemos cumplido con nuestro deber"

Don Pedro, quien había recibido clemencia tras cumplir varios años de una sentencia de reclusión perpetua a causa de los sucesos del 1950 en Jayuya, fue encarcelado de nuevo hasta que murió asesinado por las torturas que le aplicaron mientras estaba en la Carcel, en el 1965.

Aún Lolita sirve prisión en Virginia y, los otros tres hermanos que participaron se encuentran retenidos en Leavenworth, Kansas. Oscar Collazo aun se encuentra sirviendo reclusión perpetua. El único crimen cometido por los cuatro hermanos y la hermana Lolita, fue el de luchar por la Independencia de su patria.

El ejemplo que nos legaron nos prueba que la teoría de la clase dominante en relación a la docilidad del puertorriqueño es errónea así como es errónea la idea de que el puertorriqueño está conforme con la opresión que practica los Estados Unidos de Amerikkka contra ellos, tanto en la Isla como en este país, a donde son forzados a venir por la condición de colonia en que se encuentra Puerto Rico.

Es nuestra tarea como Young Lords, seamos puertorriqueños o Chicanos exaltar nuestra solidaridad con los presos políticos puertorriqueños ya que estos son un reflejo del racismo y opresión que sufren todas las Comunidades y Naciones Latinas.

LIBERTAD PARA TODOS LOS PRESOS POLITICOS!

VIVA PUERTO RICO LIBRE!

DOS DE LA RAZA EVADEN PRISION

Soy Daniel Meléndez, uno de Los Siete de la Raza. Los siete de la Raza están forzados a tomar una rutas separadas, pero, para unirnos a ustedes otra vez, luchar en el revolución de la gente.

En primer lugar quiero aclarar que somos considerados "armados y peligrosos." Somos considerados fugitivos de la ley, mas; no somos criminales! Somos revolucionarios que luchamos por la liberación de nuestra gente. Lucharemos hasta la muerte si es necesario. Les digo a ustedes, gente de la república Revolucionaria, recojan su fúsil como nosotros lo hemos hecho. Pues luchar quiere decir ganar y ganar quiere decir una vida nueva para todos los hermanas y hermanos:negros, trigueños, rojos o cual quiera que sea el color.

Es muy triste en el presente que no pueda caminar libremente entre ustedes, pero como dije antes los caminos por donde pasara la artillería de guerra nos unirán otra vez. Lucharemos al lado de ustedes en la revolución de la gente.

Quiero decir, antes de que me vaya lejos al tercer mundo que si algún agente y puerco trata de obstaculizar mi libertad, yo dispararé a matar. Ya que la ley me considera armado y peligroso.

Yo estoy armado. Sólo soy un peligro y una amenaza a esos que son un obstáculo a mi libertad.

Nosotros Los Siete, debemos huir de la "justicia" de esta sociedad racista y capitalística. Por 18 meses, no hubo 'justicia' para nosotros. Por 18 meses sufrimos por un crimen que no cometimos. Sufrimos a causa de un puerco. Que mató a otro puerco. Debo establecer que deseo la muerte de todos los puercos. Me gustaría añadir que sobrevivimos a los 18 meses que pasamos en la cárcel de San Francisco, gracias al espíritu de solidaridad de la gente. Hay más gente que puercos, yo digo "Fuera los puercos!", estoy dispuesto a morir. Y estoy dispuesto a morir por una causa valiosa. Si yo muero o, mejor dicho, caigo asesinado, será por mi gente. Muero luchando por mi gente, por mis hermanas y hermanos y por toda la gente oprimida aquí en Amerikkka. Digo, a demás, que debemos librar al prisionero político número 1 en los Estados Unidos, Reies Lopez Tijerina! Ustedes deben librar a todos los prisioneros políticos. Y digo a todos que luchen por la Libertad de "Los Siete!" Porque, sin su apoyo, yo no hubiese hacer esta grabación.

En mayo primero de 1969 fue el punto culminante en las vidas de "Los Siete de la Raza." Tony Martinez, Mario Martinez, José Rios, Gary Lascallet, Nelson Rodriguez y yo, Daniel Meléndez. Nosotros ya no podemos vivir una vida normal. Nuestras vidas estan en peligro constantemente, como es el caso siempre que la gente no gobierna. Y todos nosotros estaremos en peligro hasta que el verdadero poder sea regresado a la gente. Ché dijo, "aprendemos, de la gran fuente de sabiduría que es el pueblo." Yo he aprendido mucho de mi querida raza. Digo otra vez, estoy dispuesto y listo para morir por mi gente. Luchemos por la libertad de Los Siete para que un día regresemos a vivir y a luchar hombro con hombro junto a todos en la Revolución de la Gente. Todo el poder a la gente. Que viva mi querida Raza!!!

Esta fue carta enviada a la Revista La Raza por Daniel Melendez y Gary Lascallet

Lolita Lebron Prisionera Politica

El Young Lord: Latin Liberation News Service vol. 1, no 2, April 15, 1971, p. 4

Freedom Archives, digital reproduction

LOCALES April 15, 1971 EL YOUNG LORD Page 7

YOUNG LORD MURDERED

--BROTHER FROM CHICAGO MURDERED--

On Sunday April 11, 1971 at 5:00 A.M. Jose Luis Lind also known as "Pancho" to many of the sisters and brothers on the block, was pronounced dead at St. Mary of Nazareth Hospital of a severe skull fracture, inflicted by baseball bats.

Friday, April 9, around midnight "Pancho," his brother José Ramon, and his brothers' wife Virginia, were walking in the vicinity of Chicago and Damen Avenues- on the near north side of Chicago,- after visiting relatives, from that community, were approached by a group of about 12 white men who attacked them, swinging baseball bats with no warning or cause , except that they were Black Puerto Ricans in a racially tense community.

By the time the police arrived, "Pancho" laid unconscience on the sidewalk, his brother had a broken wrist, and his wife's body was badly bruised by the beating they received. As the police arrived on the scene, the group of white men fled, with no attempt by the police to apprehend them. Not even one of them was arrested.

"Pancho's" history as a member of the Young Lord's Organization can be traced to it's earliest days even before the group turned political. Even though the brother did not hold any position in the organization, he actively supported it.

He was in the McCormick Seminary take-over (which resulted in a pledge of $600,000 to be used for low income housing in the community) and the People's Church takeover, where now the Ramon Emeterio Betances Health Program is located and, also, the National Headquarters of the Young Lords Organization.

Pancho had been arrested and charged with aggravated battery against the police, when harassed by the pigs prior to a welfare demonstration. He was also arrested on trumped up charges for being one of the four Young Lords, who witnessed the murder of brother Manuel Ramos, by an off duty policeman.

Because of the pressure of the charges and responsibility to his wife and his four children, he was forced into a less active role.

We, the Young Lords Organization, out of the understanding that racism prevails in this country as a result of conditioning by the ruling class and understanding that the struggle in this country is of a class nature, must declare that Jose Luis Lind was a victim of that racism generated and perpetuated by the real enemy of all the masses--the U.S. bourgeosie.

To those brothers and sisters on the block who think we're "punks" for not going to the neighborhood and "shooting it up" like we used to do before when we were a street gang. Let us just say, we don't want to deal with other victims of this racist system, but instead with the real enemy the rich ruling class.

We are not saying Pancho's murder should not be avenged, but instead, all those sisters and brothers who were planning to go out gang bangin should organize themselves and so we can gang bang together with the Y.L.O., so we can "gang bang" against the system.

ANGELA DAVIS POLITICAL PRISONER OF AZTLAN

Sister Angela Davis is one of the many freedom fighters of Aztlan who is now a political prisoner. California's Governor Ronald Reagan and the racist judicial system of this country is accusing the sister of having master minded the August 7 liberation raid on the Main County Courthouse. In the raid brother Jonathan Jackson attempted to liberate three brothers who had been accused of offing a known racist pig, from the "claws of injustice."

The sister was not present at the time of the raid yet she is charged with kidnapp, murder and conspiracy to commit both. California injustice states that "All accomplices to a felony are guilty of said felony, whether or not they actively participated."

Laws are made to the advantage of the oppressor. The pigs of this society not only want to hang sister Angela on trumped-up charges, but they are also trying to bribe Ruchell Magee, a black brother and co-defendant into making false statements in exchange for saving his own neck and getting off "free."

Nixon tried to play a game on the people by inviting Russian Scientists to be present at sister Angela's court proceedings when thegrand jury handed down indictments against her. The fool tried to make people believe that there is fairness and social justice in this land. But what this puppet of the ruling class, with his "let me make it very clear" attitude, fails to say in his "message to the people," is that if there was any kind of social justice in the first place; sister Angela would not be on trial.

When asked to enter a plea relating to the charges, sister Angela replied, "I am innocent. As a preface to these brief remarks I now declare before this court and before the people of this country that I am innocent of all charges leveled against me by the State of California. I am innocent, therefore I maintain that my presence in this courtroom today is unrelated to any criminal act. I stand before this court as the target of a political frame-up."

The Main County Courthouse which seats ninety to ninety-five people. Has sixty of it's seats taken up by the capitalist press. The rest are occupied by strange looking people in suits and ties who are believed to be members of "J. Edgar Hoover's pig force" the F.B.I..

The fools think they are hiding the cruelties of injustice from the peoples eyes . But they fail in this too, because all we have to do is look around us and walk down the streets of our barrios to see and know all of what they are doing to our sister and us.

As members of the Latin Communities we must point out the true nature of this society, we must expose the contradictions. We must oppose everything the power structure tells us to support. We must take a stand and devote our lives to the struggle for justice, equality, and freedom! We must take a stand for Angela, for all political prisoners, for Aztlan, for all oppressed people!

FREE ANGELA DAVIS!

FREE ALL POLITICAL PRISONERS!

Young Lord Murdered / Angela Davis Political Prisoner of Aztlan
El Young Lord: Latin Liberation News Service vol. 1, no. 2, April 15, 1971, p. 7
Freedom Archives, digital reproduction

El Young Lord: Latin Liberation News Service vol. 1, no. 3, May 3, 1971
Personal collection

La Mujer Como Revolu

Hay muchas preguntas y raras las respuestas dentro de la lucha para tomar control de nuestro destino, una de esas preguntas esta relacionada en el papel de la mujer en la revolución socialista.

Opuesto a la creencia popular, acontecimientos historicos indican que en un punto en la prehistoria del hombre y la mujer, la mujer era la principal procedora de la familia. En ese tiempo esto significa que ella estaba en control directo de las heramientas de producción. Ella realizaba las funciones esenciales mientras el hombre vagaba la foresta en busca de caza.

Mas tarde con la evolución de la especie humana, la posición predominante cambia de operario (de mujer a hombre). Esto ocurrió por la clase de producción que empezó a efectuarse, la ganadería en donde los principales instrumentos de producción eran lanamiento, lanza y arco. La primera gran división de trabajo empezó con este cambio por el desarrollo o las areas de producción.

La explotación de la mujer empezó como maquinaria se hizo más y más común. Entre más maquinaria se usaba más productos excesibos eran producedos. El manejamiento de estas maquinas no requería la fuerza del hombre, por ello una fuente nueva de trabajo fue hayada, la mujer. Ya que la mujer en el pasado trabajaba principalmente dentro de los limites de la familia (la agricultura era la anterior fuente de supervivencia) ella era automaticamente considerada inferior y su trabajo era pagado menos.

Esta no es la única area donde las hermanas son explotadas. La supremacia masculina primeramente principio su senda en historia cuando la propiedad privada y la ganancia se convirtieron en un medio de vida. El hombre, para poder protejer su fortuna tenia a su esposa sobre candados y llaves. Esto era un aseguramiento para que el hijo que heredara su dinero fuera de el. El hijo pertenecia al sexo masculino a quien en cambio dejaba su fortuna. Evaluando las presentes condiciones económicas en general de la gente oprimida y especialmente la gente Latina uno puede ver como el "machismo" y la supremacia masculina, no son ni siquiera validos. Hoy día, por el hecho de que la mujer en muchos casos es la ganadora del pan en la familia ningunas bases de supremacia del hombre existe dentro de las familias de gente oprimida.

La supremacia del hombre, la antigua tradición de los ricos es vista por gente oprimida como si fuera una condición normal, sin reconocer que no es una parte verdadera de nuestra cultura pero de la burguesía (clase de gente rica y dominante).

La mujer es una de las gentes más oprimidas en la tierra. Si ella, es parte del mundo tercero, es automaticamente oprimida en tres areas generales: 1) ella es oprimida como gente de color, descriminación, 2) ella es oprimida por el simple hecho que está viviendo en un país capitalista donde toda la gente, que no es de la clase dominante es explotada, 3) está oprimida como mujer que es.

Hoy día la posición de la mujer en la sociedad es claramente como de esclava. Mujeres son explotados en cualquier manera posible. Solamente el socialismo puede relevar a la mujer de su presente posición. Solo entonces las mujeres seran libres y emancepadas.

Se ha comprobado el hecho de que el éxito de la revolución depende de la extensión en la que la mujer toma parte.

Las mujeres son las reservas más grandiosas de la clase oprimidas. Estas reservas constituyen más de la mitad de la población del mundo. El destino del movimiento socialista, la victoria, o el derrotamiento de la revolución depende de la reserva de mujeres sea o no en favor o en contra de la gente oprimida.

Sin embargo la mujer no es solamente una reserva. Ellas pueden y tienen que ser un ejercito realmente de los oprimidos, luchando contra los burgueses.

Tocante a la igualidad de las mujeres, uno tiene que estar seguro que la igualidad no se cumbierte solamente en otra ley formal, pero un tipo de ley que este escrito en las acciones del pueblo. Igualidad verdadera. La mujer tiene y debe ser parte del liderato en la lucha revolucionaria. En la misma manera que la gente oprimida se libere, librara a otra gente oprimida, así es como tenemos que ver la pregunta de la mujer; la mujer tiene que estar en la vanguardia de la emancipación de ella. En cada revolución dentro de la historia, mujeres en la lucha han comprobado ser unas de las más valerosas, tienen una participación sacrificadora. La lucha aquí en norte américa no sera diferente. La mujer en general y particularmente la Latina debe de estar preparada para alzar la pistola en defenza de su sobrevivencia, para la supervivencia de su familia y para toda supervivencia de la perdurable existencia de la raza humana.

La mujer, tiene que comprender, no solamente su participación en la lucha armada pero, también tiene que entender la importancia de los aspectos teoreticos de la lucha. Ella tiene que estar preparada tanto idiologicamente como fisicamente. Ella y el hombre tienen que aprender todos los niveles.

Las demandas y luchas de la mujer deben ser unidas con el objeto de ligar un poder, estableciendo un mundo gobernado por las masas de la gente oprimida. Sus batallas deben de estar de acuerdo con el nivel de lucha que compruebe ser la vanguardia: Resistencia, Armada y Politicalización en masas.

Entendiendo que la explotación de la mujer es nada menos el antiguo juego capitalista, dividir y conquistar es el primer paso de rehabilitación para el hombre. La mujer encontrara que ella probablemente se encuentre en un a posición en donde va a hacer esencial que ella eduque a el hombre en este motivo. Los dos entenderan claramente que no podemos ir adelante sin la participacion de la lucha revolucionaria.

adelante sisters

La Mujer Como Revolucionaria

El Young Lord: Latin Liberation News Service vol. 1, no. 3, May 3, 1971, p. 8

Young Lords Newspapers Digital Collection, personal collection

Ya la mujer despierta
y empieza a luchar;
Sus temores ya no existen
y su corazon persiste
palpitando con ansiedad.
Sus dolores son muy fuertes
y pendientes por la LIBERTAD!

cionaria

There are many questions within the struggle to take control of our destiny which are seldom answered. One such question is in regard to the role of the Women in the Socialist Revolution.

Contrary to popular belief, historical circumstances indicate that at one point in the unwritten history of Man and Woman, that the Woman was the primary provider for the family. At that time this meant that she was in direct control of the tools of production. She performed the main functions, while the men roamed the forest hunting game.

Later as the human species developed, the predominant position changed hands. (Female to Male). This happened because of the kind of production that began to take place, Stockbreeding, in which the principal instruments of production were the lasso and the bow and arrow. The first great division of labor also began with this change, because of the increase or area's of production.

The exploitation of women began as machinery became more and more common. The more machinery was used, the more surplus products were produced. The running of these machines did not require the strength of a man so therefore a new source of labor was sought, the woman. Because the women in the past worked mainly within the limits of the household (Agriculture had been the previous source for survival) she was automatically deemed inferior and paid less money.

This is not the only area in which sisters are exploited. Male supremacy first found its way into history when private property and profit became a way of life. The male, in order to protect his fortune, kept the wife under lock and key. This was his insurance that the child whom inherited his money was his own. The child was of the male sex, whom in turn would leave his fortune to his son. In evaluating the present economical conditions of oppressed people in general and Latin people in particular one can see how "machismo" and male supremacy are not even valid. Today, because of the fact that the woman is in many cases the breadwinner of the family, no basis for any kind of male supremacy exists in the oppressed peoples household.

Male supremacy, the age old tradition of the rich, is looked upon by oppressed people as being normal condition, not realizing that it is not really a part of our culture but that of the bourgeoisie(rich ruling class).

The woman is one of the most oppressed persons on earth. If she happens to be of the third world she is automatically oppressed in three general areas; 1)she is oppressed as a person of color, discrimination, 2)she is oppressed by the mere fact that she is living in a capitalist country whereby all the people not of the ruling class are exploited, 3)she is oppressed as a woman.

Today, the position of women in society is clearly that of a slave. Women are exploited in every way possible. Only socialism can relieve the women from her present position. Only then will women be free and emancipated.

It has been proven a fact that the success of a revolution depends on the extent to which women take part in it.

Women are the greatest reserve of the oppressed class. This reserve makes up more than half the population of the world. The fate of the socialist movement, the victory or defeat of the socialist revolution, depends whether or not the reserve of women will be for or against the oppressed peoples.

The women, however, are not only a reserve. They can and must become a real army of the oppressed, fighting against the bourgeoisie.

In regard to the equality of women, one must be sure that equality does not become just another formal law, but the type of law which is written in the actions of the people... real equality.

The women can and must become a part of the leadership within the revolutionary struggle. In the same way that it will take oppressed people to free oppressed people, this is how we must view the women question; the women must be in the vanguard of her emancipation.

In every revolution thru-out history, women in the struggle have proved themselves to be some of the most courageous, self-sacrificing participants. The struggle here in north-amerikkka will not be any different. The women in general and the Latin women in particular must also be prepared to pick up the gun in defense of her survival, for the survival of her family and for the very survival of the continued existence of the human race.

The women must realize, not only the importance of her participation in the armed struggle, but, she must also understand the importance of the theoretical aspects of struggle. She must be prepared ideologically as well as physically. She, and also the man, must learn to struggle at all levels.

The demands and struggles of the women must be bound up with the object of seizing power, of establishing a world governed by the masses of oppressed people. Her struggles must correspond with the level of struggle which proves itself to be in the vanguard. Armed Resistence and Mass Politicalization.

Understanding that the exploitation of women is nothing more than capitalism's age old game of divide and conquer, is the first step to rehabilitation for the man. The women will find that she will probably be in a position where it will be necessary for her to educate the man to this fact. They will both have to clearly understand that we cannot go forward without the participation of women in the revolutionary struggle.

in the struggle !

YLO newspapers ready for distribution in front of headquarters on Wilton and Grace Streets, ca. 1972. Photograph by Carlos Flores.

3.

YLO SPEAKS

I.
Seeds of Rebellion: From Gang to Political Consciousness

History from Gang to Club to Organization

(1968) Cha Cha Jiménez and Raphael Rivera
Lincoln Park Press, November 1968, p. 5
Lincoln Park Conservation Association Collection, Box 131
Special Collections and Archives
DePaul University Library, Chicago, Illinois

The Young Lords, for many years a large and powerful Puerto Rican youth group in the Lincoln Park neighborhood, has recently decided that the purpose of our organization should be the improvement of the conditions and standards of the community. This is a change from earlier days when the purpose of our group was to fight competing gangs and to provide dances and other entertainment for our members.

Gang Years

The Young Lords formed in 1959 under the leadership of Joe Vicente, the first president. Along with Vicente, some of the other founders, all Arnold and Waller students, included Orlando Davila, Raphael Rivera (Al Shades), Jose Jimenez (Cha Cha), Bennie Perez, Saul Del Rivero (King Cade), and Santo Guzman (Al Capone).

At the time we started the Young Lords, many Puerto Ricans were being beaten up by white gangs in the neighborhood. We felt that it was time Puerto Ricans joined together in their own gang for self-protection, to fight the whites and to rule the neighborhood.

So during the first two years of Vicente's reign, our main purpose was to fight and to take control. We fought an Italian gang at Roma's restaurant, Hillbillies (or as we call them "Billigans") at the Oasis, the Gaylords, the Galahads and gangs from 18th St. and Addison. Our turf was Bauler Playlot and Adams Playlot.

The Young Lords grew fast and by the end of the first two years our gang included, not only Puerto Ricans, but also a few Blacks and a few Billigans. During this time and for a number of years to come, Lou Nagy, a volunteer from Wright Junior College, was our sponsor and a friend of everyone in the gang.

In 1961, Nick Garcia became president of the gang. Nick taught us Puerto Rican consciousness and formed the first branch of the Young Lordettes. During Garcia's reign, we continued to fight but also started other activities. With the help of Josephine Aragon, whose son Freddie was a member of the Young Lords, we threw a banquet for our parents and held dances to raise money for Young Lords sweaters.

During 1962 and 1963, Estill Miller, a Billigan, was president of the Young Lords. Miller continued the fighting, but also involved us in sports, got our sweaters, and expanded our social activities with many parties. This was the beginning of our years as a club.

Club Years

By 1964, the fighting power of the Young Lords and our social activities had attracted so many Puerto Ricans to the gang that we no longer could keep track of all our members. Branches of the Young Lords formed on Wrightwood, on Chicago Ave., on Howard and in Sullivan High School. Other branches formed among Mexicans and Cubans. It seemed that everyone was wearing a Young Lords sweater.

To keep the group of Young Lords who lived in the neighborhood together, we decided that we needed to have our own hangout, so we went to Old Town and got a place at the corner of Wieland and North Avenue. The other hangout in the neighborhood was Halsted and Dickens.

During 1964 Cha Cha Jimenez was president and began throwing socials at the Isham YMCA. It was at the socials that a lot of trouble started. There was glue sniffing, fights over girls, and fights between branches of the Young Lords about who was a member of the club. Many club members were arrested and finally Cha Cha ended up in jail.

While Cha Cha was in jail, the club was without a strong leader and separated into two groups, the Latin Lords and the Young Lords with Jose Coss (Wito) as president of the Latin Lords and Fermin as president of the Young Lords.

When Cha Cha was released from jail in 1965, he returned to the club and started a new group of Young Lordettes, with Margaret Trinidad as president. The new Young Lordettes were very helpful in getting the club in swing again with many socials.

In 1966, Orlando Davila took over as president, but his term was short as the membership and many of the leaders moved or served time in jail. The only remnant of the club in 1967 was a summer coffee house on North Avenue called Uptight II.

New Organization

In January of 1968, Cha Cha Jimenez returned to Chicago and reorganized the Young Lords. The new Young Lord Organization is just that, an organization, no longer a gang or a club. The purpose of the new organization is to unite people in the community for the improvement of the neighborhood. As an example to the rest of the community, the membership of the new Young Lords includes fellows and girls as well as Blacks, Whites and Puerto Ricans. Activities of the organization are for the benefit of the rest of the neighborhood.

This summer the Young Lords held a dance, raised money, and, with the money raised, held a splash party and picnic for other people in the neighborhood. Some of the Young Lord members are now setting up a drug addiction program to educate other young people in the effects of drugs. We hope that this Christmas we can have a food and clothing gift basket project for other poor families in the neighborhood.

Our immediate project is the Young Lords' Month of Soul. Each Saturday evening during November we will sponsor a dance at Saint Michael's gym for all young people in the area. Black and Puerto Rican bands will play soul music. With the money we make on the dances, we hope to open an office, have money for the Christmas project and begin a business.

Collection on the Young Lords, Box 5, Folder 9
Special Collections and Archives
DePaul University Library, Chicago, Illinois

From Rebellion to Revolution: The Division Street Uprising, LADO, and the Rise of Puerto Rican Activism in Chicago

(2024)
Omar López Zacarias, Minister of Information, YLO
Exerpt from unpublished memoir
Personal collection

> *. . . Todo parecía en silencio, aquel domingo callado,*
> *cuando un error policiaco a todo esto dio comienzo . . .* *
> **Décima "Los Motines de Chicago"**

In the late afternoon of Sunday, June 12, 1966, a police officer shot Arcelis Cruz, a member of the Young Sinners street gang, by the alley at Damen Avenue and Crystal Street, sparking a three-day and three-night rebellion in the Puerto Rican community of West Town/Humboldt Park. This unexpected uprising, fueled primarily by young people, changed the way city authorities perceived the growing Puerto Rican community and triggered a series of changes that dominated the community's political development for decades. At that moment, it never even crossed my mind that I was stepping into a paradigm change that would shape my life—and our community—for years to come.

In 1966, the established Puerto Rican leadership demonstrated significant progress in their efforts to gain recognition and institutional support from the city of Chicago. One sign of this was the acknowledgment from Mayor Richard J. Daley, celebrated in the usual ethnic Chicago way with the first Puerto Rican Parade on State Street and a festival in Humboldt Park. Before 1966, the Puerto Rican community's annual celebration of San Juan Bautista Day was organized by the Caballeros

* ". . . Everything seemed silent, that quiet Sunday when police misconduct started all of this . . ."

de San Juan. That year, the leadership united to form the Puerto Rican Parade Committee by merging the Caballeros de San Juan's activity with the broader community efforts. The committee organized a series of activities leading up to the parade date, but perhaps the most significant, aside from the festival and parade itself, was the election of the first Puerto Rican Parade Queen: a young woman named Myrna Salazar.

The adult leadership established organizations that provided cohesiveness to the Puerto Rican community, which by then had several enclaves in Chicago, including Lincoln Park, areas along Clark Street between Division and North Avenues, a community in South Chicago, as well as on Harrison Street and Western Avenue where Mexican and Puerto Rican communities thrived. Principal organizations that gave the community structure included the army veterans' Posta Boricua, the Catholic Church's Caballeros de San Juan, the Puerto Rican Congress of Mutual Aid, and hometown associations like Los Hijos de Cidra and Los Hijos de Orocovis. The presence of Puerto Ricans in Chicago was so significant that the island's government also opened an office on LaSalle Street, the Office of the Commonwealth of Puerto Rico, to tend to business between the island and the mainland.

The growth of the community prompted local churches to offer services in Spanish. St. Mark's Church, located on Campbell and Thomas Streets, was one of the first Catholic churches to open its basement to Puerto Rican families to celebrate mass. As the community grew, St. Aloysius Church also opened its basement for worship in response to the increasing number of Puerto Rican families moving into the area. Initially, most of these arrivals were of the Catholic faith, but this profile gradually changed as the charismatic movement within the Catholic Church spread into Pentecostal denominations. The Archdiocese of Chicago also established the Cardinal's Committee for the Spanish-speaking, which became involved in the community at various levels.

Like many immigrant groups before them, the youth socialized through various activities, attending dances at the Crystal Ballroom on North Avenue and Washtenaw, joining baseball leagues, and boxing through the CYO (Catholic Youth Organization). The Division Street YMCA produced top bodybuilders like my friend, Angelo Castro, the first Puerto Rican to win the Mr. Division YMCA title. The Puerto Rican

Congress nurtured young musicians, forming Salsa bands, one of which eventually performed at Madison Square Garden in the early '70s. Sports played a crucial role, with baseball teams forming in the Clark Street area and later playing in Lincoln Park, which became a hub for Puerto Rican baseball. Some players carried their talents to high school, strengthening their teams and pushing them into city and state title contention.

The community also enjoyed robust radio programming throughout the day, with DJs like Turin Acevedo, Tony Quintana, Raul Cardona, Juan Carlos Arroyo, Orlando Miranda "Pelencho," and the popular "Boricua Argentino," Carlitos Agrelo, broadcasting on stations like WOPA-AM. These personalities gathered a loyal audience, and Puerto Rican broadcasters rivaled Mexican broadcasters in number. One program heard by many was Jose E. Chapa's morning show, *Serenata Matutina*. Division Street also had its movie theater, the Biltmore (later renamed San Juan Theater), which played an entertainment role and, in 1966, served as an organizing site during the Division Street Rebellion.

Neighborhood schools like Von Humboldt, Lafayette, Anderson, and Sabin absorbed large numbers of Puerto Rican students, especially those moving from Lincoln Park to Humboldt Park. When my family arrived in Humboldt Park from Mexico in 1958, I enrolled in Yates Elementary School. As one of only three Latino students—and the only one who didn't speak English—I soon began to look for places where other Spanish-speaking youth gathered. Teenagers carved out hangouts in the community: the Latin Kings did so on Leavitt and Schiller, the Young Sinners on Damen and Division, the Latin Angels on Maplewood and Division, and the Trojans at California and Division. Lincoln Park had its youth groups, like the Paragons, Continentals, and Young Lords, while the West Side had the Harrison Gents.

Throughout the 1960s, Dave's Hot Dog Stand at Maplewood and Division became a key gathering spot west of Western Avenue, claimed by neighborhood youth after confrontations with Polish and Italian gangs who had previously dominated the area. I worked there with my friends Marcos Delgado and Angelo Castro while we attended Tuley High School. From that corner, Kenny Smith and I, in my four-door 1952 Mercury, went looking to pick a fight with Chi-West gang members near Chopin School. Outnumbered, we had to make a quick escape.

Kenny suggested we find his friends, the Young Lords, at a playground on Armitage and Burling. Although none of the Young Lords were there that day, it was the first time I heard of them.

As the neighborhood grew due to displacement from the Carl Sandburg Village project, this corner became a launch pad for incursions into Polish and Italian territories. Joe Delgado, a youth leader and CYO boxer, and his crew often returned to the hot dog stand to celebrate victories or recover from defeats. Despite offers for retaliation from a young Afro–Puerto Rican with blond hair and green eyes, Joe, valuing his boxing discipline, refused, saying, "They fought fair." Another hangout was the corner of Division and Damen, where the nascent Latin Kings, led by Phil Juarve, his brother Carlitos, Hush Puppy, Little Tarzan, Big Tarzan, Watusi, and Papo, gathered. Their main base was at Leavitt and Schiller, across from Sabin School, recognized as the birthplace of the original Latin Kings.

These groups quickly drew the attention of the Chicago Police Department, which began targeting young Puerto Ricans, stopping, frisking, and roughing them up. This harassment was indiscriminate, affecting even those unaffiliated with gangs, including church-going students active in the community. The youth grew resentful, feeling unsafe rather than protected. Now we had to be wary of both rival gang members and the police. While we could retaliate against gangs, we felt powerless when stopped by the police, especially when walking our girlfriends home or heading to a dance.

During autumn and winter, the hot dog stand became the meeting point for Friday night dances at Crystal Hall on North Avenue and Washtenaw Street. Girls wore fashionable 'A' skirts with beehive hairstyles, while boys sported shoes with "Cuban heels," quarter-length black leather jackets, and their hair slicked back with a casual curl, or "moña," in front. The Crystal Hall became an easy target for police because the dances ended early, and most girls had to be home by 9 P.M. On their way home, couples were often stopped by police, and the young men would push back to save face, which usually ended with both of them being taken to the Wood Street police station. The youth now had another enemy: rival gangs, the police, and disapproving parents who warned daughters to avoid these boys.

Resentment grew when it was discovered that some harassing policemen were former gang members, including fathers of Gaylords and

C-Notes members who had become policemen and knew the territory well. In the Division Street neighborhood, it was common for police to pick up Puerto Rican youth and drop them off in enemy gang territories, making the Chicago Police Department the youth's primary enemy.

This tension set the stage for what came next. The Division Street Rebellion of 1966 erupted after Arcelis Cruz, a member of the Young Sinners, was shot by a police officer in an alley near Damen and Crystal. Although his wound wasn't life-threatening, it enraged his friends and the community, who were out celebrating the last day of the Puerto Rican festival. The crowd protesting Arcelis's shooting kept growing, and the patrolmen began to feel increasingly unsafe. Cruz's friends refused to wait for an ambulance and carried him to a car, and the sight of a wounded young man being taken away like a casualty of war only intensified the crowd's anger. Feeling they were losing control, the patrolmen called for backup, and a K-9 unit arrived.

The use of dogs only intensified the crowd's anger, which many saw as a dehumanizing tactic. The move backfired. Word spread quickly to the Latin Kings, who began arriving after hearing that the police were under siege on Division Street. Young and old alike confronted the officers, blocking them from reaching their vehicles. In those years, there was no animosity between Latino gangs, and crossing into each other's territories was common. Eventually, the police were forced to retreat, leaving behind a patrol car that the youth set on fire.

As the evening wore on, some youth took to the rooftops along Division just west of Damen, throwing whatever they could find at police cars below. Toward the evening, I chose to stay on familiar ground at the corner of Maplewood and Division. Those of us there knew the gangways, basement entrances, and porches that were good for hiding after throwing rocks and bottles at squad cars. Some of the guys over by Rockwell, however, did end up getting arrested.

The community's response was overwhelming, and its intensity not initially understood. Radio personality El Boricua Argentino broadcasted his Sunday evening show from an office in the San Juan Theater complex on Division and Hoyne, which provided him with a direct view of the disturbance. Carlitos Agrelo's on-the-air descriptions drew hundreds to the streets. As news spread, several newspaper photographers arrived but were confronted by the youth, who refused to be documented. Around

9 P.M., Nermín Ortega, another one of my high school friends and a neighborhood bodybuilder, intervened when a photographer was threatened by a growing crowd, convincing them to let him go, though without his camera. By the second night, national media coverage had alerted the Puerto Rican community in New York, sparking rumors that a caravan from New York's Golden Dragons gang was heading to Chicago. We were excited, imagining the Dragons joining us to fight the police.

However, we had our own gangs and leaders who showed sophistication and discipline. I remember Ricky's Diner on California and Division, where young Latin King founder Phil Juarve received updates from Kings running up to him, then dispatched orders to members stationed at different corners, keeping the rebellion alive.

Meanwhile, Graciano Lopez, first president of the Puerto Rican Parade Committee and member of the Posta Boricua, convened leaders from various organizations, including Father Headley from the Cardinal's Committee and Jesus Rodriguez of the Caballeros de San Juan, to devise a strategy to end the rebellion. Graciano held several meetings, gradually crafting a response and list of demands for City Hall. A pivotal meeting took place at Association House, 2150 North Avenue, where adult and youth leaders gathered to plan an end to the rebellion. Another leader, Juan Diaz, organized a meeting at the San Juan Theater, where New York Puerto Rican housing leader Ramon Velez urged unity. These meetings began to stabilize the situation. By Wednesday evening, police regained control of the streets after arresting and jailing hundreds of youngsters. Now the pressing question was what would come of this new awareness that all was not well in Chicago's Puerto Rican community.

Two distinct organizations emerged from the rebellion: the Spanish Action Committee of Chicago (SACC) and the Latin American Defense Organization (LADO). SACC was established immediately after the June rebellion, while LADO formed in September. Both groups arose from the same event but had different objectives: SACC focused on political solutions, while LADO addressed the social issues that became evident after the rebellion. One of LADO's first initiatives was raising funds to post bail for young people arrested during the three days and nights of unrest. Juan Diaz served as president of SACC, and my brother Obed Lopez Zacarias organized and founded LADO. With financial support from Spanish-language theater owner John Rosen, LADO bought hundreds of 78 RPM records of a décima by Simón Gómez titled *Los Motines de Chicago*, which depicted the rebellion, intending to sell them to raise bail money.

When the uprisings began, Obed had limited knowledge of the Puerto Rican community's dynamics. For the previous eight years, he had been involved in the Cuban Revolution, supporting Chicago's Movimiento 26 de Julio chapter and later cochairing the Fair Play for Cuba Committee. He also organized events marking cultural and historic Mexican dates. Between 1957 and 1959, the exiled Cuban community in Chicago actively raised funds for Fidel Castro's rebels in Sierra Maestra. Though their numbers were small, they raised awareness of Batista's atrocities through activities within the Mexican community. Every Sunday, young Movimiento 26 de Julio members distributed leaflets along Halsted Street between Roosevelt Road and Taylor Street, where the Mexican community gathered to buy goods, newspapers, music records, and fresh tortillas from the first El Milagro tortillería.

Obed's political organizing began as a freshman at San Luis Potosí's State Teachers College, la Normal School, where he and our older brother, Efraim, led a successful campaign to win control of the Student Association. Traditionally dominated by seniors, this election was different, as freshmen broke the seniors' streak through sharp, effective organizing. Influenced by the Mexican Popular Socialist Party and the PRI (Institutional Revolutionary Party), Obed developed a keen awareness of major political events. On June 12, 1966, Obed and I were just a block away from where police shot Arcelis Cruz. The event laid bare the deep conflict between youth and police. It sparked Obed's drive to organize, pushed him to make sense of the situation, and ultimately compelled him to get involved.

The political and social landscape of 1960s Chicago created fertile ground for Puerto Rican activism, especially after the Division Street Uprising of 1966, which erupted in response to police brutality and broader disenfranchisement. To calm the unrest in Humboldt Park, Mayor Richard J. Daley quickly met several community demands and inadvertently opened Chicago's political system to Puerto Ricans. The 26th and 31st Wards began to recruit precinct captains from street organizations, until finally in 1981 Joseph A. Martinez became the first Puerto Rican alderman in the 31st Ward, a development that signaled a major shift in the integration of Puerto Ricans into the political machine.

In this shifting environment, LADO became a critical force in organizing the Puerto Rican community. LADO addressed systemic injustices affecting Latinos, including housing, employment, and police brutality. Under Lopez's leadership, LADO built coalitions with other marginalized groups, including the Reverend Martin Luther King Jr.'s "End the Slums" movement, and operated with four core action principles:

- Unity among Latin American people
- Unity with other sectors who face the same injustices
- The necessity of creating our own institutions
- Direct action when there are no other means to claim our rights

These principles were the backbone of LADO's organizing. Despite police attempts to discredit Obed and other LADO leaders as communists, their work continued, driven by a commitment to justice.

One of LADO's key initiatives targeted employment disparities at the National Food and Tea Company, encouraging the community to support Puerto Rican–owned stores. LADO also supported new Puerto Rican families, especially young mothers navigating the welfare system, with help from sympathetic welfare workers like Olga Pedroza and Kathy Logan. Women such as Pedroza, Carol Lee Tatman, and Dolores Varela were vital in the organization's outreach.

LADO's dedication to community needs led to broader political engagement. In September 1966, LADO endorsed David Cerda, the first Mexican American candidate for judge in Chicago, marking a milestone in Latino representation. The relationships built through LADO would later support the Young Lords as they evolved from a street gang to a political organization.

The Division Street Uprising and LADO's efforts helped shape the rise of the Young Lords Organization. The rebellion pushed the city to address Puerto Rican demands, while LADO's focus on unity, institution building, and direct action laid a foundation for future activism. By championing these values and building coalitions, LADO empowered Chicago's Latino community and left a lasting legacy in the fight against systemic inequality.

Top: Omar López Zacarias and Welfare Union march, photographer unknown. Right: Cha Cha Jiménez and Omar López at rally, Carlos Flores Photo Collection. Bottom: LADO rally at Daley Plaza, 1968. Collection on the Young Lords, Box 2, Special Collections Department, DePaul University

II. Personal Journeys and the Formation of Political Identity

Becoming a Young Lord

(1974)
David Rivera, Field Marshal, Young Lords Organization
Unpublished memoir written in USP Terre Haute, Indiana
Personal collection

I was born in a section of Coamo, Puerto Rico, called Sta. Catalina. Our house was a three-room shack made of wood with a zinc roof. It was located on the side of a hill about fifty yards from the dirt country road.

After I left there with my grandparents, I didn't see that house again until I was twenty-four years old. My parents had come to the United States around 1950. They came to get jobs and later sent for the children who had stayed in Puerto Rico with my maternal grandparents.

They ended up in Chicago, where they rented a one-room apartment in a small hotel called the Golden Ox. While my father worked in a furniture factory with my uncles and other relatives, my mother stayed home, cooking for ten or fifteen men who paid her on payday.

After a couple of years, my parents moved to a five-room apartment on the second floor of a three-story building on Dayton Street on the North

Side of Chicago. The only entrance was through the back door from the alley. In front of the building, the landlord had corn and tomatoes planted.

After furnishing the apartment, they had some money left, so they sent for the family. Five children and two grandparents, four boys and one girl. She was the oldest. I was the fourth one. I was about five years old; the youngest was four.

I don't remember much about my trip on the airplane. I do remember seeing them at the airport. I remember the long ride on a highway in a car with a white interior. I remember my parents' happiness and how they talked with my grandma and grandpa, asking if we had a good trip.

It was August, a hot day. When we pulled up to the house, there were all kinds of people on the street. The neighborhood consisted of Puerto Ricans, Blacks, and a few whites. Kids with no shoes on and wearing shorts and dirty T-shirts were running and playing on the streets and sidewalks. I didn't realize back then that this neighborhood would be my home until I got married fourteen years later.

Well, we lived in this house for about two years. Then we moved to a house my parents bought further down and across the alley. The only difference was that this house was a two-story building and it had a front door to the first and second-floor apartments. By the time I moved from this house, I was seventeen years old and had responsibilities.

Every week was the same. Come Friday, which was payday, my father would give my mother the money she needed for the family and house. He would give all the boys a quarter, and my sister, being the oldest and the only girl, got a half dollar. After he had done all that, he would bathe, dress, eat dinner, say goodbye, and walk out the door. Headed to the bar at the corner of Willow and Dayton Street, two blocks away.

The funny thing is, here I am in this prison cell, and I can remember those terrible Friday nights like they just happened. My father would come home around two in the morning, falling down drunk and calling for my mother to get up and make him some coffee. He would yell obscenities at her while my mother quietly made his coffee. After a while, seeing that she wasn't going to argue, he'd jump up from the chair, grab her by the hair, and start beating her, like she was his worst enemy.

Us kids would see this with our own eyes. We would jump up and down, screaming to my father to please stop beating mommy. The fight would go on until my grandmother—my mother's mother—came into the room. Then, and only then, would he stop, lay down on the couch, and sleep until mid-afternoon the next day.

You see, our family had the biggest respect for my grandmother. Even my grandpa didn't argue with her. "She was boss."

My mother is a short woman, about five feet tall. She is light-complected and a little on the heavy side. Hazel eyes and light brown hair. So, in the morning, you could see the black and blue marks my father's beating had left on her face and body.

This happened often. Many, many times, my mother had to call the police to calm him down. It was strange because he never hit us kids, especially my brother Anibal, who was his favorite. Now, Monday to Friday, he was the perfect daddy.

The years passed by. I started school. I was nine years old when I got crippled by some bone disease in my right hip. I was running home from the playground under the tracks behind the building on Bissell Street when I fell. When I got up, I could hardly walk. My mother asked, "What's the matter with you?" I was scared, so I told her that the cardboard I used in my sneakers had slipped. We put cardboard in our tennis shoes when the holes got too big, just to protect our feet from the heat and glass.

It was funny because in school I tried never to let any of the other kids see the bottom of my sneakers. I didn't want them to know I had cardboard for a sole. We were a poor family and that was all I could do until my mother could afford to buy me some new ones at the five and ten-cent store for a dollar ninety-nine.

After a few weeks, my leg started to hurt more, and I walked with a limp. My mother thought I was just trying to get away from going to school, so she told my grandmother. Boy, oh boy, I wish she had never done that. My grandmother got her leather belt, took me to the living room, and made me walk back and forth. Every time I limped, she'd hit me hard across the legs and butt. That went on for about an hour.

Eventually, they took me to the hospital, where they discovered the problem, and I stayed for some time. In the hospital, volunteers and visitors came to see me. They brought me some money. Dimes, quarters, and sometimes a dollar bill. By the time I got out, I had about seventeen dollars, more money than I'd ever seen in my life. I felt like a rich man.

But not for long. The same day I left the hospital I was broke again. Yes, I was broke again but I was happy. I was very happy because days before I left the hospital my mother had told me that my sister didn't have clothes for school and that my brothers needed tennis shoes, and she didn't have money to buy them.

When I got home, the first thing I did was give my sister five dollars so she could buy a couple of cheap skirts, and I gave my brother money for tennis shoes. By the time I finished, I didn't have enough to buy the rubber tips for my crutches.

But I remember that day mostly because my grandma had called for me. At that time, she was living in the rear apartment on the first floor. It was only a one-and-a-half-room with a small kitchen and bathroom. The main room was the bedroom as well as the living room.

When I walked in on my crutches, she told me to sit down on the floor by her rocker. She gave me her blessings and asked why I'd given all my money away. I didn't want to say, but finally, I just buried my face in her lap and broke down, telling her I couldn't stand to see my family suffer.

She stroked my hair and said with a very gentle voice that God was going to bless me because I had a good heart. As I sat with my face in my grandma's lap, I wished that someday I would be rich. Then I just fell asleep.

When September came around, they enrolled me in a school for crippled children. But I didn't mind. Every time we had a lot of snow I didn't have to go to school. Plus, I liked the school. We had a swimming pool, and we had a rest period, and I learned one of the most important things of my life: never look down on a person and that life, no matter how many adversities you have is always worth living. I also learned to help myself as well as others.

But being crippled wasn't easy, especially around the neighborhood kids. They didn't let me play in their games and laughed at me because I couldn't walk. So, every chance I got, I'd hit one of them with my crutches and scream at them that I could play by myself. If they were going to make fun of me, I was going to defend myself. I would walk away and hide behind the house, pressing my back against the wall and cry until my mother called for me to go inside.

By the time I got to seventh grade, I wasn't using crutches anymore, but that didn't mean I was ready for what came next. My first day in public school was terrifying. I wasn't used to all the noise, the running around. Plus, I was scared of the gangs in the school and in the neighborhood. Seeing white gangs with sweaters and jackets with their name on it. Puerto Rican gangs also with black t-shirts with their club's name and emblem printed on the back of them. I was scared!

I was never a very big fellow. As it is now, I am only five feet seven inches tall and weigh one hundred and sixty-five pounds. At that time, I was a puny kid. But the experiences I had taught me to look out for myself. That's one thing I had to be thankful for. But I only knew how to fight by hitting my enemy with my crutches. And I didn't have my crutches anymore.

When I reached my first-period class I was a little late, so I rushed in. That was a big mistake. In my hurry, I bumped into another boy and knocked his books down. Without looking, I picked up his books and handed them to him and said I was very sorry, that I didn't mean it. But when I looked carefully, I saw that the boy was wearing a club jacket, and it had the name of Mohawks on its back. He was a slim boy about fourteen years of age, and he was about three inches taller than me.

I turned to walk away but he grabbed my arm, pulled me back, and called me a spic. I didn't know what to say. By this time there were a bunch of boys and girls all around us. Most of them wearing the same kind of jackets. Out of nowhere, I hear another voice that said, "Hey white boy, you want to fight with him, why don't you meet him in the open lot after school?" It was a Puerto Rican boy wearing a black t-shirt with Young Lords printed on it.

The boy with the Mohawk jacket said, "Alright!" With that, the crowd dispersed, and I sat down to class.

All that day the only thing I had on my mind was the coming fight. How the hell did I ever get into such a mess? And every time I think of what I would do to the guy, I build up my confidence. But when I thought of what he could do to me, my heart started to beat so fast I thought it was jumping out of my chest. What scared me the most was what my mother going to say or do if I got home with a black eye or torn clothes. But I decided that I would rather get it from my mother than get bullied by everybody in school.

When the final bell rang, I gathered my books and walked down the hall to meet Orlando, the boy who had stood up for me. "Are you ready?"

he asked. I smiled and said, "As ready as I'll ever be!" We headed to the open lot, where about forty kids were waiting: White, Puerto Rican, and Black. The Mohawk kid was there, smirking at me. "You want to give up, spic?" he sneered. I was about to back down when one of the Young Lords yelled, "Man, he ain't shit if he gives up!"

Before I could react, the Mohawk kid tackled me to the ground, pinning me with his weight. I looked up at the Mohawk kid sitting on my chest, and I shouted, "Hell no!" But no sooner had I said it than I saw stars. And before I could clear my head, I saw them again. I was really getting it, but before he could hit me again, I threw up my legs and caught his head between them.

Now it was him on the ground. I went wild, swinging at him with everything I had, hitting his back, his face. I didn't care where I hit him. Then I heard his cries, "Okay! Okay! I give, you win!" But I kept on hitting him until some of the Lords pulled me off him. They were all laughing and patting me on the back. I'd won my first fight against a gang member.

All through my seventh and eighth grade, I went to all the gang fights, socials, parties, and did everything the gang would do. By then I had lost my fright. I had hardly any respect for my parents or the teachers in school. I was always getting called to the office for some reason or another. A few times my mother had to go to school about me. But I didn't care, no one was going to push me around. I was a Young Lord, and I was tough (even though the biggest thing we did then was smoke marijuana and drink wine, steal hub caps from cars, and fight the white gangs in the neighborhood).

You see in the gang I felt needed, wanted, secure—everything I never felt before. I didn't care about anything except the gang. I didn't even care about my family slowly falling apart. Nothing mattered but the club.

Finally, the big day came. We were going to graduate from eighth grade and start our summer vacation. That was the summer of 1963. It was a big day for everybody. Even me. I was fourteen years old going on fifteen. I was proud of myself for making it despite all the trouble I gave the teachers. I almost felt like they were giving me my diploma just to get rid of me.

It didn't matter. What mattered was that come September, I was going to be in high school. Waller High School. What I didn't see then was that this was going to be the beginning of my manhood. Looking back, I wonder if I was truly ready for it. But back then, I didn't have time to think about it. I just knew that whatever lay ahead, I had my brothers in the Young Lords and a place where I finally belonged.

David Rivera, YLO Field Marshal (far right). Courtesy of José "Cha Cha" Jiménez personal collection.

David Rivera speaking before a crowd, *Y.L.O.*, vol. 2, no. 6, February–March 1970, p. 11. Courtesy of DePaul University Special Collections and Archives, Richardson Library Digital Collection.

Angie Speaks

(2003–2004)
Angela Lind, Communications Secretary, YLO
Excerpts from oral history interviews conducted by Jacqueline Lazú
Personal collection

I was born on February 23, 1951, in Lincoln Park, Chicago. I went to Saint Vincent de Paul grammar school, but I didn't go to DePaul High School because, at the time, it was just for boys. So I ended up going to Holy Name Cathedral for high school. I lived in Lincoln Park for twenty-one years, eighteen of those years on Armitage, and then the other three just around the corner. We were all working class, and that's how we started hanging out together, just a bunch of young people from the same area.

My father and mother were both born here, but my dad's parents took him back to Sicily when he was just a year old. At home, all we spoke was Italian—Sicilian, really. My mom could speak English, but my dad didn't, not really. He worked as a laborer for the railroad, and my mom worked in a factory. My mother didn't really have a lot of political views, but she was able to read and write. She had graduated from eighth grade, which was a big deal back then, so she ran the house, handled the bills, and took care of everything. My dad cooked. We didn't talk about things like equality between men and women, but in my house, that's just how it was. My mom ran things, and my dad respected her.

I came from a real strong family environment, and I have to thank them for that. I grew up with these morals, things I've carried with me my whole life. We were Catholic, really Catholic. Church was a huge part of our lives, Mass every Sunday, confession, and all the holy days. My parents always told me, "Everyone is equal in God's eyes," and that stuck with me. When my grandfather first came over from Sicily, he worked cutting sugarcane in New Orleans. I imagine he probably felt a lot of prejudice doing that kind of work. I keep reflecting on him because, in a way, I think he helped shape who my dad was, and that really helped to shape me too.

My dad wasn't what you'd call political, but he had strong opinions, especially about fairness. He used to say, "This United States, they treat people different because of their color. It's not right." He noticed how Black people were treated unfairly, and it bothered him. "You treat people the same, no matter what," he'd tell me. He wouldn't stand for the national anthem, not because he hated the country, but because he felt it didn't represent everyone. He had a lot of Black friends, and fairness was everything to him. He didn't belong to any political organizations, only Catholic ones, like Italian Catholic groups. A lot of people didn't agree with him, but he didn't care. He never made politics the center of his life. I guess because he was illiterate, he didn't get into intellectual discussions with people, but he knew what to avoid and who to avoid talking to.

I grew up on Armitage, between Bissell and Fremont one block away from what was eventually the People's Church. When I was growing up, the neighborhood was diverse. You had pockets, maybe one block had more Italians, another had more Germans, and another might have more Irish. It wasn't like the area belonged to any one group or ethnicity. Not really. But over time, it started becoming more Hispanic. That's when the developers started showing up. People came to my parents, saying, "Well you know you really ought to think about moving out of here because the Puerto Ricans are moving in here and the neighborhood is getting bad." They did not sell right away. My father had some sisters come in from Italy who moved to New Jersey. Only then he said, "Well, maybe it is time to sell."

My mom and dad had a three flat brick building, and they ended up selling to developers and going to New Jersey. It was all part of the master plan, and I think they were able to grab the property for real cheap, less than reasonable. Dirt cheap is more like it. They knew the area was geographically perfect. It was a prime spot. The transportation was there, you could get to school from there. It might've been a little farther out for some, but it was still a prime area. Everything was right there; you were basically close to the Loop. Looking back, it didn't matter if you were Italian, Puerto Rican, or whatever, if you were working class, they wanted you out.

I first met José "Cha Cha" Jiménez when he was about nine. He lived around the corner from me on Armitage, renting from an Italian family we knew. Back then, there wasn't a Young Lords Organization; it wasn't political. We were just neighborhood kids, playing basketball and hanging out at the candy store on Fremont and Armitage. We called ourselves a gang, but not like gangs today. You had your turf, it was kind of like, "Stay off my area." Most of the time, it was just things like swim parties at the YMCA as we got older or Wednesday night socials at the Isham YMCA on North Avenue and Ogden. We'd go to dances at Immaculate Conception or parties in basements. The guys would wear their sweaters. If you had one of the guys' sweaters, it was like, whoa! I remember my husband had one.

Around that time, we started hanging around North Avenue and Wieland a lot. We had kind of left Armitage for a bit. That was Old Town, North Avenue and Wieland, right off Wells. If you stop and think about it, I think it was because a lot of our social activities were up in that area. It must have been 1964 or 1965. Some of us were living around North Avenue, but I still lived on Armitage. Cha Cha lived on Armitage, too, and so did Sal [del Rivero]. Eventually, we ended up coming back to the neighborhood.

Girls sometimes got into fights too. We were called the Lordettes. I remember going down to Orchard Street and beating up the gypsies. Don't ask me why, we just did it. It was one of those things where somebody didn't like somebody else, so it was like, "Let's go kick their asses." That's just how it was sometimes. Like I said, it was a turf thing, and sometimes it was racial. You had the Mohawk Boys—they were all white, and if they didn't like someone, they'd jump them, and then you'd have to go back and avenge whoever got jumped. They didn't like us, and we didn't like them. But it wasn't what you see today with gangs, no guns or anything like that. They used a car antenna or, sometimes, a knife, but it wasn't as violent as things got later on.

The people we hung out with weren't all Puerto Rican. I'm Italian American. There were some Irish and white kids who hung out with us too. For example, my sister-in-law was Irish, and she and her sister used to hang around with us. I don't know if it's really fair to say we were a Puerto Rican gang. The neighborhood wasn't just about race, it was about class. But Puerto Rican culture was so present in Lincoln Park, and we related even though we knew there were differences. We were working-class kids, and the people moving in weren't. You started to notice how the ground was shifting, how people with money were starting to take over.

I think I was about fifteen when I started to get political. It wasn't something I planned or even thought much about at first. Back then, I didn't even know what "political" really meant. It wasn't like we sat around reading books about revolution or anything, at least not in the beginning. I remember one day running into Cha Cha at the candy store. At the time, he was living on Dayton, but I remember him being really upset because his family had to move again. The landlord had raised their rent, and they couldn't afford to stay. It wasn't the first time something like that had happened to them. They'd already been pushed out of Clark Street before coming to Armitage, and now it was happening again. You could see the frustration in him, and it wasn't just him, it was a lot of people, especially Puerto Rican families. They were being forced out, one by one. That's when it started to click for me: this wasn't random. It was part of something bigger.

Around that time, the developers started showing up in the neighborhood. You'd hear about people getting offers to sell their buildings for practically nothing. Whether you were Puerto Rican, Italian, or Irish, if you were working-class, you were getting pushed out. But the Puerto Rican families had it the worst. You'd hear stories about landlords refusing to rent to them or charging outrageous prices. People were being shuffled from one place to another, barely able to keep up. I didn't know the word for it back then, but now I'd call it displacement.

I mean, we weren't all on the same level. Jesus Christ, we were seventeen or eighteen years old. We weren't sitting around thinking too deeply about it. We were talking about unity, not about kicking people's ass anymore. The only ass-kicking we still talked about was self-defense. It was political at that point, things like dealing with the cops and the Red Squad. Overthrowing the government? Yeah, that came up, but it wasn't something we obsessed over. That might sound sour to some people now, but my attitude was always, if you love America, you try to change it. I'm not saying it was the best way to go about it, and I'm not going to overthink the idea of an actual revolution. But if you love something, you try to change what's wrong about it. You don't just sit back and do nothing.

Cha Cha was the one who really started putting it all together. He saw what was happening before most of us did and he was good at organizing people around things. He'd talk about how landlords and developers were buying up the neighborhood, how people with money were moving in and pushing everyone else out. It wasn't just about housing, though, it was the schools, the jobs, even the parks. Everything was changing, and none of it was working in our favor. Little by little, the rest of us started seeing it too. And it wasn't just the neighborhood. By the mid-1960s, there was so much else going on. The Vietnam War was tearing families apart. We all had friends or family getting drafted, some of them not coming back. The Civil Rights Movement was in full swing, and we couldn't ignore what was happening to Black people in the South or even right here in Chicago. On top of that, you had police harassment. If you were a young Puerto Rican guy walking around Lincoln Park, the cops were on you. They'd stop you for no reason, search you, hassle you.

I got married in 1966, but I'd been going out with my husband, Pancho Lind, since the summer I graduated from grammar school and started high school. He was part of the Young Lords too. He wasn't originally from our neighborhood, though; he was from North Avenue. I met him when he switched neighborhoods for a while. In the organization, he didn't hold a titled position, but we were always together for the takeovers, the marches, and everything else. He was a cadre, and he was one of the Cuatro Lords who got arrested when Manuel Ramos was killed. That happened on the South Side in 1969.

It was a house party hosted by Edie and her brother Manuel, both Young Lords. Manuel and Ralph, also a Young Lord and my daughter's godfather, were standing in the doorway while, across the street, an off-duty cop, James Lamb, was painting an apartment. Things got loud, and Lamb came out to complain, but he didn't say he was a cop; he just started arguing from across the street. During the argument, Lamb claimed Manuel pulled a gun, but Manuel never carried a gun. Sure, some people did, that was the reality, but not Manuel. It turned out to be a silver comb, one of those shiny steel or aluminum ones. Lamb shot Manuel, killing him, and Ralph was shot in the neck. The guys at the party, including my husband, jumped Lamb, not knowing he was a cop, just knowing he shot Manuel. They all got arrested, and that's how they became known as Los Cuatro Lords. Lamb stayed on the police force. They didn't fire him; they just moved him to a different area like nothing ever happened.

When the political work got started, it felt like we were going twenty-four hours a day. I had my first child when I was sixteen and three more after that, one right after the other. It was a lot, raising babies, so I couldn't be as involved in the Young Lords at first. But as my kids got a little older, I started taking on more. I was part of the negotiations with McCormick Theological Seminary about the day-care center. I was involved in all the takeovers. When we took over McCormick, people stayed there for a long time. I was there for two days with my kids; they came in with me. Nobody took anything or touched anything they weren't supposed to. Nobody went into people's offices. It was all very disciplined. When we were political, there were certain rules you had to follow. I never put myself in a position where I'd be in real jeopardy because I had kids to think about. As they got older, I got more involved. I became the communications secretary and later an area coordinator when Cha Cha ran for alderman.

The Young Lords were doing so much during that time. We took over the Armitage Avenue Church and called it the People's Church. We were fighting for affordable housing and community programs. We wanted to turn the church basement into a daycare, but the city wouldn't approve it. They said the ceiling was too high or the floor was too low, just excuses to block us. Cha Cha even got in trouble for stealing $23 worth of lumber to fix it. He wasn't hiding it; he did it because it needed to be done. That's just how it was. We also ran a health clinic and worked with the Black Panthers on their free breakfast program for kids. The church was more than a place to meet; it became our headquarters. People lived there, organized there. It was where we made things happen.

The women in the group were a big part of that work. There was Hilda Ignatin, who was always involved, and Judy Pacheco, though she moved away later. Pat Devine stands out too. She was a communist and an organizer. She used to talk with Cha Cha a lot in the early days and helped push him more into the political side of things. Women weren't always in the spotlight, but we were there, holding things together and making sure the work got done. The health clinic was something we were really proud of. Doctors came and volunteered their time, and we ran a very good clinic in the basement of the church. We also tried to get a daycare center off the ground. We started by taking care of our own kids during activities and actions, the kids of the members. The goal was to expand it into a larger daycare for the whole community, but unfortunately, it never happened.

At that time, there was also a growing conversation about "the woman's question." It was an issue for all women, but if you were politically progressive, you had to engage with it. Some women in the group understood and connected with it more deeply, especially those who were involved 24/7. I think a lot of women expected the men to just wake up one morning and say, "I'm no longer a male chauvinist." But things aren't that simple. The organization did try to take a very disciplined stand on these issues, but it was still hard to deal with. Even though it was structured, there was still a lot of fooling around going on. We were part of the hippie movement at the time, and there was this attitude of, "It's your right to love and sleep with whoever you want, and as a woman, I'm going to exercise that right." I was more sheltered from it because I was still with my husband. At the same time, nobody forced you to think or feel a certain way. It wasn't like someone told you, "You have to believe this." You did what you felt you could do when you were ready to do it.

In the beginning, we focused on local issues like housing and police, but we quickly started learning and becoming more international. There was the question of Puerto Rican independence and the Rainbow Coalition with the Black Panther Party and the Young Patriots. The Young Lords from New York came to Chicago to ask permission to form a chapter, and chapters also started up in Connecticut and Philadelphia, while Steve worked in Los Angeles. We built national coalitions with groups like the Brown Berets and with Corky Gonzales. The newspaper reflected this growth, covering both national and international issues, and we linked up with progressive groups everywhere. We even sent people to Cuba with the Venceremos Brigade. Study groups started in people's homes before becoming regular at the church. Once I got involved, I began reading a lot. Early on, it was mostly Lenin and Mao, but as time went on, we read more philosophical works. When we were underground, we studied materials on dialectical and historical materialism, Cornforth and writers like that.

As the Young Lords grew and started connecting with other organizations, we began taking real positions on broader issues. That's when the city started feeling threatened, and things got more aggressive. They considered us subversives. If you were standing on the corner wearing purple, they'd stop you. If you were headed to a meeting, the Red Squad would be following right behind. We were seen as a threat locally to Mayor Daley and Ed Hanrahan, and nationally to people like J. Edgar Hoover. Fred Hampton was murdered. Reverend Johnson and his wife Eugenia were murdered. My husband was murdered.

One of the hardest things I've ever been through was losing my husband, Pancho. He was killed in a racially motivated attack while I was away at a women's conference. He was walking with his brother and some cousins when a group of Italian men started calling them names. A fight broke out, and they beat him with baseball bats and pool cues. It happened on Good Friday, and he passed away on Easter. Like I said, I wasn't even there. By the time I got back, it was too late. There were about eleven guys involved in the attack, but they even turned on one of their own and killed him later. I couldn't blame just one person for what happened. It's the system that keeps people divided by race and poverty. That's what I've always believed.

As things got more intense, some of us had to go underground. I moved to a farm in Wisconsin with my kids. We set up a training school there where we studied politics and did a lot of reading. The kids didn't do what we were doing; they played and had fun while we worked. We all took turns watching them. I'd drive back to Chicago when I needed to, but mostly, we stayed on the farm. After about a year, I decided to come back for good. My kids were getting older, and I didn't want to keep living like that. There was no animosity about it; everyone understood. It was just time.

While we were underground, we had to take a step back and reevaluate. It was a time to redevelop, to rethink how we could organize without giving up our ideals. We started building a base again, and that's when we thought electoral politics might be the way forward, not to put all our hopes and prayers into it, but as a tactic. You have to adapt to changes, educate people, and organize them. Philosophy teaches you not to remain stagnant but to always be aware of your surroundings and reevaluate. That's what we did. We weren't giving up our beliefs; we were just approaching things differently. Part of Mao's theory was encirclement and suppression, organizing the people to surround the enemy. But if you don't have enough people, you're out there on your own, and while you might win a battle, you won't win the war. So we leaned more toward organizing through electoral politics while staying true to our principles. Some might argue about it, but we felt it was a practical way to apply dialectics.

Cha Cha ran for alderman around 1974, and he was the first Hispanic to do it in Chicago. The Young Lords still had an office on Wilton and Grace, which eventually became the 46th Ward Service Center for the aldermanic campaign. That campaign taught us a lot about how the Democratic Party worked, especially their precinct organizations. Like it or not, those precinct systems were effective. The problem was Daley's regime; it wasn't open to everyone. It was very selective. There's something to be said for the ward committee setup, not just for patronage jobs, but for helping the ward. That's what it's supposed to do. But under Daley, it was locked up tight. We'd go to City Council meetings, and if Daley didn't like what you were saying, he'd just shut off the microphone. Come on, that's not democracy. You can't preach democracy while running things like that. If we were going to get involved in aldermanic elections, it was our version of encirclement and suppression, our way of building our own ward structure.

We worked a lot with Slim Coleman during that time. I remember going to City Hall with Slim. Mayor Daley's people kept shutting off our microphones. Slim jumped up, grabbed a mic, and they carried him out by his arms and legs. Those little moments of defiance stick with me. Slim supported the Black Panther Party, and a lot of the folks in the Intercommunal Survival Committee in the 46th Ward supported them too. It was mostly white people, and they really believed the Panthers were the vanguard. We joined forces with them and worked together to organize a ward structure. Cha Cha didn't win, but he did a hell of a job, especially for being the first Hispanic candidate. And it wasn't easy; this was the 46th Ward, around Wrigley Field.

After the campaign, we stayed busy. We built a coalition with the farm workers and joined their marches. There was even a big rally we held at a theater on Irving Park and Sheridan. By then, we'd moved our base from Lincoln Park to the 46th Ward, shifting our focus back to local issues. We weren't as active with international causes anymore, except for the independence of Puerto Rico—that was something we always supported and stayed committed to. But locally, we had to deal with what was right in front of us. People were still being displaced, first in Lincoln Park, and now it was happening around Wrigleyville. The community we had in Lincoln Park was gone, and you could see people being pushed further west to Division Street and beyond. It isn't as blatant as what had happened in Lincoln Park, but it's still happening.

We stayed involved in everything we could, though we weren't as radical anymore, more low key. We just kept pushing, doing what we could to help the community. When I look back, the Young Lords are and will always be about justice. We marched, protested, and ran programs that made a difference. We worked with the Black Panthers and others, forming coalitions to make our voices louder. Together, we were strong. I wish we could've done more with housing in Lincoln Park. Seeing my community pushed out still hurts. But I'm proud of what we did. We showed people that change is possible, even if it starts small. Those were hard times, but they gave us a purpose. We believed in what we were doing, and that belief has kept us going.

Angela Lind (née Rizzo), ca. 1968. Courtesy of Angela Lind family collection.

Angie and Pancho Lind, ca. 1969. Courtesy of Angela Lind family collection.

Angie speaks at YLO National Office/46th Ward Service Center on Wilton and Grace, ca. 1974. Photograph by Carlos Flores.

Below: Mothers and Others lead a march at the People's Church Heritage Festival, *Second City*, August 1969. SpC. 071.05 S445g, Special Collections Department, DePaul University.

III. Radicalization, Repression, and Revolution

Cover of the first printing of José "Cha Cha" Jiménez's *Que Viva el Pueblo* (1972), written while he was serving a one-year sentence for allegedly stealing scrap wood. At the time, after briefly stepping down as chairman, this communique identified him as the YLO's General Secretary. Author's personal collection; a digitized version is available via the Marxists Internet Archive.

Que Viva el Pueblo

(1972)
José "Cha Cha" Jiménez, General Secretary, YLO
Pamphlet, personal collection

Cha Cha's story shows the lengths to which the rich who run this country will go to keep poor people and Latinos down. Born in Puerto Rico and raised in a US slum is only a little different from other Puerto Ricans; that is, he has already spent ten years of his life in court and in jail for rebelling against the system. Those near him in his teenage years would ask if he had been anything more than a drug addict and a gang member. But what is a gang but a group of young people—products of the ghetto in rebellion—directing their hostilities toward other poor victims instead of their oppressors. Drug addiction is only an extension of the gang.

Although confused for many years as to who the oppressor was Cha Cha used his time in jail to think. He left jail with a vague conception of an oppressor, a conception he sharpened as he experienced continued abuse. He saw that his problems were not unique but common among the poor, especially among Latinos. He reorganized the dissolving gang—then on the verge of falling into drugs—and turned it into a political organization fighting for the self-determination of Latinos and other poor and oppressed peoples.

The Young Lords Organization was concerned with the issues of welfare, health, daycare, and police brutality. It also dealt with questions of Puerto Rican independence and urban renewal. These were the issues which brought repression from the oppressor. Mayor Daley and his "Máquina Democratica" who had dominated the Latino vote ever since we can remember could not tolerate a Latino organization opposed to their scheme for driving the poor out of their neighborhoods so that suburbanites could return to the inner city. Daley drove the Latinos from the areas now occupied by the Carl Sandburg Village and the University of Illinois. When he promised them relocation and decent housing he swindled them. He did the same thing to the Lincoln Park community. But Cha Cha, the Latinos, and the poor people of Lincoln Park who had been driven out of their homes too many times saw through Daley's demagoguery and protested. This Daley could not tolerate. A deluge of indictments poured out of state attorney Hanrahan's office to Lincoln Park residents and Young Lords. The Young Lords' leaders got four and five cases each—they were charged with everything from leafletting too close to a school to mob action. Cha Cha alone got 18 cases dumped on him. He was given a year for taking $23 worth of lumber. He has now won 13 cases. He still has four cases pending.

What were the crimes committed by the poor and Latinos of Lincoln Park in 1969 and 1970? Demanding self-determination in a democratic society? What was so diabolical about a former street gang and its leader trying to serve the people? Why was the news media used to slander them? As long as street gangs kill and brutalize their own people they are ignored and sometimes even aided by the oppressor, but when they attack the root of the problem, the creators of the ghettos, the actual criminals of this society—the oppressors—will utilize every means in their power—the courts, the police, the state's attorney's office, etc. to suppress them.

The only crime that Cha Cha committed has been to wage a struggle for self-determination and to refuse to humble himself before the oppressor. For this he is now in jail. As Cha Cha himself said after the Young Lord Manuel Ramos was murdered in cold blood by an off-duty policeman:

> They can jail us;
> They can brutalize us;
> They can even kill us—
> But they can't stop us!

CHA CHA JIMENEZ

Jose (Cha Cha) Jimenez was born on August 8th, 1948 in an apartment in "El Millón," a slum of Caguas, Puerto Rico. His parents came from a rural area. The youngest of 15 children, his mother Eugenia had been raised in a convent because her father was blind and there was no one to take care of her. At the age of 16, she left the convent to marry Cha Cha's father Antonio. In her pregnancy, she went to Caguas to be near a doctor. Antonio had already left to find a job in the United States; He was in a migrant camp near Boston when Cha Cha was born. Cha Cha's older sister died of pneumonia shortly after his birth leaving him the only male and eventually the oldest of four children.

When Cha Cha was two years old, Antonio had earned enough money to send for him and his mother. They lived near Boston for a year, then moved to Chicago with a newborn sister. There they became tenants in a hotel which had been converted into rat- and roach-infested apartments known as the Water Hotel. It was on the corner of Superior and LaSalle streets on the Near North Side in the old Clark Street area. There, the family lived near relatives and friends who had left Puerto Rico for similar reasons.

In the late '40s and early '50s, migration of Puerto Ricans to US cities skyrocketed from an average of 10,000 people a year to 50,000. They came looking for jobs to establish some savings with the hope of eventually returning to their homeland. In Chicago, two centers of the Puerto Rican community grew—an area around Madison Avenue from Ashland to Kedzie and the neighborhood where Cha Cha lived from Ohio to North Avenue with Clark Street as its nucleus. Among Puerto Ricans, these "barrios" were commonly called "La Madison" and "La Clark." "La Madison" had been an established residential area with two- and three-story apartment houses. It had a sense of community with Latino businesses, theaters, and agencies. "La Clark" was different. Long before the Puerto Ricans moved there, it had been an area under syndicate control. "Los Chinos" from "La Clark" had a firm grip on "la bolita" (the numbers game); There was a lot of gambling, drugs, prostitution, etc. La Clark had mixed housing if you could call it that. Although many Puerto Ricans lived in the Cabrini projects, most of "La Clark" was made-up of dilapidated hotels bandaged and divided into apartments and single rooms. In renting these buildings, it seemed as if the landlords were trying to con the last bit of profit from their Puerto Rican tenants.

Cha Cha's family lived in the Water Hotel for a couple of years until it was finally condemned and torn down. Drifting northward two or three blocks at a time, by 1956 the family had reached the boundary of "La Clark." In a total of six years, they had been forced to move nine times all because of urban renewal. It never dawned on them that the city deliberately intended to push the Puerto Ricans out of their homes. The Puerto Ricans thought the buildings would either be renovated or leveled and then reconstructed so that they would be able to return to live in them. The men who ran the city had a different plan. Today the expensive areas of the Carl Sandburg Village and "Old Town" have replaced most of "La Clark" and Puerto Ricans are a rarity. To make way for the rich, the Puerto Ricans from "La Clark" were pushed into the adjacent community of Lincoln Park or into the new barrio of "La División." People from "La Madison" poured in there too. The other pockets of the Puerto Rican community in Chicago "La Blue Island," "La 63," "La Sheridan," etc.—grew up later.

Cha Cha had already attended Holy Name Cathedral, Saint Joseph's and Franklin schools when he entered Newberry Elementary School in Lincoln Park in the third grade. At first he had a difficult time adapting. Lincoln Park was a community of poor white Americans—Irish, Italians, people from Appalachia, etc. Cha Cha's family was one of the first Puerto Rican families in the neighborhood. Kids at school would call the few Puerto Rican children spics and beat them up on their way home. Cha Cha came home injured many times. He told his parents he had tripped and fallen, but they understood otherwise because they had seen a fight in the alley next to their home. The scuffle began among gypsy youth, whose families shared the building with Puerto Ricans. All the residents of the apartment house got a panoramic view from their windows as if they were watching from separate booths in an outdoor stadium. The youths were belting a young gypsy who was Cha Cha's friend. When Cha Cha ran outside to help him, the gypsy youths converged on him. When Puerto Rican youths poured out of the building, the fight shifted to a battle between gypsies and Puerto Ricans. Even Cha Cha's friend sided with his kinfolk. The spectators began casting their ballots arguing with each other, screaming and cheering victory for their side. After letting the fight go on for some time, the adults intervened and brought it to a halt.

As more Puerto Ricans from la Clark moved into Lincoln Park, Cha Cha's family followed the currents of block upward as Irish, Italians, and Appalachian whites moved further north. Cha Cha's father began guzzling liquor (two of his uncles had already died from liver infections caused by alcohol). To get her husband to stop drinking, Doña Eugenia made a "promesa" to dress in black for a year. She persuaded her husband to join the Knights of Saint John, a Latino organization formed by the Catholic Archdiocese of Chicago. Through the aid of a priest assigned to

Latinos, she organized Spanish catechism classes in her home for Puerto Rican children in the area.

Meanwhile, Cha-Cha was getting into trouble—according to the neighbors who tried to keep their sons away from him. Cha Cha couldn't understand the difference between his actions and those of the neighbor kids nor did he know why people were talking. In fact, a recording at the time with the title "Everybody Else's Son's a Troublemaker But Mine," would have been appropriate.

At his mother's request, the priest talked with Cha Cha and met with him all summer. Soon he became an altar boy at the Spanish mass in Saint Michael's church. His mother arranged with the priests to enroll him in Catholic school—Saint Teresa's. Though a poor family, they did not have to worry about tuition which the priests had taken care of. Most of the classrooms in St. Teresa's were filled with Germans, Polish people and Italians. There were only a few blacks and Latinos in the school. In Cha Cha's 6th grade class, there were none.

When he entered St Teresa's, he had been completely transformed from mischievous to piety. His teacher—a nun—took special interest in him and became his friend. He put his mind to his studies and no longer spent much time with his neighborhood friends, who people thought had been the cause of his mischief. Before and after class and on weekends, he helped around the church and school shoveling snow, sweeping, mopping and waxing the floors, and dusting the pews in the chapel. In the three years he attended St Teresa's, he was always first or second in the number of candy sales made to raise funds to build a new church. Continuing as an altar boy as St. Teresa's he also sang in the choir.

Near completion of her "promesa," Doña Eugenia had set up an altar in their home. Latino neighbors often asked her to lead in the recitation of a rosary; It became part of the daily schedule at home. It was not surprising then that at age 11, Cha Cha had made up his mind about his future. After graduating from 8th grade, he wanted to enter a seminary to prepare for the priesthood.

Meanwhile, although there were still only a few Puerto Rican businesses in Lincoln Park, the influx of Puerto Ricans continued. It was the early 1960s and street gangs were spreading over the city. There were a few gangs in Lincoln Park among the European minorities, but none as yet among the Puerto Ricans. When Puerto Rican newcomers were detected in non-Puerto Rican sections of Lincoln Park, they were beaten mercilessly like someone was beating dust out of a carpet. From time to time, the Puerto Rican Grapevine reported incidents like this. Saint Teresa had no gangs although there were a couple of gang members in the school, which was located in the territory of a European gang.

In hopes of preparing for the priesthood, Cha Cha stuck to his studies. In the spring when the gangs surfaced, he became inadvertently involved in an incident. A group of Puerto Ricans who later the same year would form the Black Eagles, the Paragons or the Young Lords, retaliated against some of the European gang members. Because some of their own had been hurt, the European gang was out for revenge. Although Cha Cha had not been involved in the incident, some of the gang members remembered him from Newberry. One day as he was walking home from school, they caught sight of him across the street and yelled his name. He kept walking and pretended not to hear. They yelled again. This time he looked at them, turned the corner, and ran down the block. The gang dashed after him chasing him until he got into the Puerto Rican section. To avoid further beatings, Cha Cha found a new route home from school.

More fights occurred between Puerto Ricans and European gangs. The Puerto Ricans who by now had grown a number began to organize themselves in self-defense. Orlando Davila, founder of the Young Lords, asked Cha Cha to a meeting. He had met Cha Cha at his mother's catechism class. Cha Cha decided to attend the meeting along with nine other youths. At this meeting, the Young Lords were formed. The Young Lords remained a nominal organization for Cha Cha: he was not an active participant. Most of the battles were fought at the public school while he was at the Catholic school. Further, at this time, gang organization and Lincoln Park was just beginning.

During the summer vacation, Cha Cha was in a few scattered fights at the beach, but when classes resumed, he split from the gang to readapt himself to a different environment. He returned to his studies. Now he was in the eighth year—the year of decision. He sent his application to a Redemptorist seminary in Wisconsin for which he needed letters of recommendation from the principal and pastor of St. Teresa's. Although Cha Cha had behaved himself all semester, toward the end of the term he and another classmate were caught throwing eggs at a bus in which—they found out later—the pastor was riding. They were suspended from school for a few days. Instead of a letter of recommendation, the pastor asked the seminary to deny entry to Cha Cha. The seminary wrote him to try again the following year. This would be difficult. Because Cha Cha could not afford tuition to a Catholic High School, he would be going to Waller, the public school, which would make it less easy for him to be accepted at the seminary the following year. Further, Waller was a school which the Young Lords and other neighborhood gangs would attend.

Like his other classmates, Cha Cha tried to find people from Saint Teresa's who would be going to his new school. Although Waller was the nearest high school, only one other classmate planned to go so Cha Cha didn't find many associates. Soon after graduation, some of his classmate's families organized a graduation party to which neither Cha Cha nor his family were invited—an example of anti-Puerto Rican feeling which he had experienced consistently at St. Teresa's. He found out about the party while walking down the street with two other Young Lords dressed in their purple and black sweaters. Two of his fellow classmates stepped out of the storefront where the party was being held. When they saw Cha Cha they asked him why he wasn't at the party. "I just didn't feel like going," he replied. The Young Lords were anxious to move into the dance, but Cha Cha persuaded them not to.

By now, Lincoln Park was flooded with Puerto Ricans and other Latinos. By summer, gang fights were routine. When either side in the conflict had its members roughed up, both sides would come together quickly like soldiers in a fort after the sounding of reveille—with their weapons and ready for battle. However, gang fighting was not the only wave of action the gangs created in Lincoln Park. The Puerto Ricans hung out on the playgrounds in their idle time. Cliques of twos and threes would disappear for hours at a time to get drugs, sniff glue, smoke marijuana, shoot heroin, burglarize homes, strip cars, snatch purses, and stick up people. After a while, the Young Lords—the youngest of four or five Latino groups on the playground—got into this. Cha Cha's Catholic education and previous environment did not help him here. If he wanted to be accepted by the crowd—or as it was called then, if he wanted to be considered "a regular"—he had to change his ways. He did so and after a while he found himself in jail. In fact, by the time classes began at Waller, he had been arrested many times, had spent nearly two of his summer months in a juvenile home, and had been placed on a year's probation.

By the time Cha Cha was 17, he had developed from a "regular" to the president of the Young Lords not for being tough but for being "trusted" after so many trips to jail. It was 1964 and gang fighting had stopped some. Cha Cha and most of the other members concentrated more on social activities and their girlfriends, but the police wouldn't leave him alone. They caused trouble for him and his girlfriend. Because they eloped and because Cha Cha had a long police record, his girlfriend's probation officer tried to keep the couple apart by forcing her family to leave the community. It was difficult for Cha Cha to accept this. He had been discharged on parole after two more months in the juvenile home and now her probation officer and his probation officer had taken it upon themselves to keep the couple apart. Cha Cha and his girlfriend managed to meet secretly for some months, but after a while the girl found another romance in her new school. The authorities' scheme worked.

When Cha Cha's friends told him, he let it ride at first, but one day they raised the subject again while drinking wine. Cha Cha and three other Young Lords took the L to the neighborhood of the girl's school where they found her with her boyfriend in a small restaurant. One of the Lords had given his knife to Cha Cha because they thought Cha Cha too tipsy to fight and they didn't want to stab the youth. When the Lord threw the first punch, the boy started to run. He ran straight into Cha Cha who had been standing near the door. Cha Cha reached into his pocket, pulled out the blade, and stabbed the boy three times. The boy reached the other side of the street when a gathering from the school stormed Cha Cha and the Lords. When Cha Cha lunged at the group with a cleaver, they took off. The girl also pushed her way into the fight. Cha Cha belted her and stabbed the boy two more times, then took off with the Lords leaving the youth stretched out on the street with the five knife wounds. Chasing the Lords, a group from the school cornered them in a drug store until the police came and arrested them. When they went to court, Cha Cha took the blame and got six months in a state penal farm. The other Lords were discharged.

When Cha Cha got out in mid-1966, the street gang had broken up. Most of them were in the service, in jail, or married. A few stayed together on the corner but there were no more meetings and no gang structure. Besides the few Lords on the corner, there were others who came just to loiter and get high. If there were any fights, they were with this combined group rather than with the Young Lords street gang. This situation was pure gold for Cha Cha because he had no desire to be part of a gang.

When he got out of the penal farm, he found a job as a stock boy in a nearby factory making $1.65 an hour. He found a new girlfriend whom he began to take seriously. Problems arose when the girl's family found out about Cha Cha's police record. Without telling him, they left the community. This time, however, Cha Cha managed to keep in touch with his girlfriend.

All was going well until he got into an argument with a neighbor. Because he had spent so much time in prison, Cha Cha didn't know his neighbors. It was a Friday evening and Cha Cha had come home from work with Manuel Ramos. They had stopped to have a few beers before reaching Cha Cha's home. They plan to wait for each other while they change clothes and washed up. They were going to a dance that night. While Cha Cha washed up, Manuel decided to leave because he didn't want Doña Eugenia to see him in a slightly drunken state. He left a message to tell Cha Cha he'd see him later at the dance. When Cha Cha got the message, he walked down the block to catch up with Manuel to tell him his mother wouldn't mind, but he couldn't find him so he turned around and walked back toward home. From a distance next door to his house he saw an older man yelling at a young girl, who took off toward the backyard. A little drunk, Cha Cha mistook the girl for his sister. Not knowing that Cha Cha was his next door neighbor, the man thought Cha Cha was provoking him. He told Cha Cha to "mind his own business and to go to hell." Anytime he wanted to, he said, he would yell at the girl. He felt perfectly in the right since the girl was his own daughter, but Cha Cha took a swing at him and his son, who had come down to help his father.

Doña Eugenia came out to explain that Cha Cha was her son, he was a little drunk, etc., she told Cha Cha that his sister had been in the house all along. Apologizing to the man and his son, Cha Cha shook hands with them and started toward home. At that point, a police car drove up. The officer ordered Cha Cha to get into the car. In broken English, Doña Eugenia tried to tell the policeman that the problem had been settled. "No trouble, no trouble," she repeated. While she was telling Cha Cha to go upstairs, the policeman kept pressing him to get into the car. Cha Cha told his mother not to worry—he would explain to the policeman and everything would be all right.

Cha Cha never got a chance to explain. The policeman—angry because Cha Cha had not come right away—grabbed him by the collar. When Cha Cha reacted by grabbing him by the collar, another policeman came up from the rear and cracked his his club over Cha Cha's head. Cha Cha lay unconscious on the pavement. The policeman knelt down on his arms and began banging his head on the sidewalk. In tears his mother screamed, "My son my son! Por favor, no hit my son!" She and one of her daughters tried to pull the policeman off Cha Cha; Another sister put her hands under his head as the policeman banged it on the concrete the third sister grabbed the policeman's club and hurled it across the street. The neighbors—including the man and his son whom Cha Cha had hit—screamed at the police to stop when Doña Eugenia picked up a bottle and threw it at the officer. Blood streamed from his mouth along with two of his teeth.

When he came to, Cha Cha was in a police wagon with his mother, who was praying over a rosary. Though not arrested, his three sisters had asked to go to the police station with their brother and mother. Cha Cha did not know his mother had been arrested. When he found out he was so shocked and infuriated that he began to fight with the policeman again. This time at least 10 policemen beat him black and blue. He was lucky to be alive the next day when he appeared in court. His face was swollen; His neck showed signs of internal bleeding where they had choked him; He was limping on one leg where they had kicked them. The neighbor who had argued with him brought no charges against him. The only charges brought against him were those of the policeman. Cha Cha was accused of knocking out his teeth—or aggravated battery.

Cha Cha's mother was charged with disorderly conduct, but her case was later dismissed. After the dismissal of her case, Cha Cha eloped with his girlfriend and left the city because he knew that he would lose his case in court. The court would uniformly accept the policeman's word. Because of his previous police record, whatever he said in court would be of no value.

After about a year, he and his underage wife decided to return to Chicago. She was pregnant. They both felt they could clear up their differences with her mother while Cha Cha wanted to clear up his case with the courts before the baby was born. When he went to the police station, the police could find no warrants for his previous arrest so they told him to forget about the case. The girl's mother, however, did not want a "criminal" for a son-in-law so she visited the court and had Cha Cha jailed. She got a court order preventing him from visiting his wife or his newborn child. Cha Cha went to the penal settlement again. This time he returned he was really depressed. He began shooting heroin daily until he was addicted, and later, for what seemed like a Millennium, he kept taking narcotics. He was in and out of jail until in 1968 while in prison he made-up his mind to beat the drug problem.

At the time he was in maximum security because of a rumor that he and 12 other Latinos were trying to escape from the House of Correction. He had not read a book in its entirety since the 8th grade, but in his isolated cell, there was nothing else to do. At first, he started with religious books *Seven-Story Mountain* by Thomas Merton. He began to think about his life. He got into religion. He wanted to go to church service, but he couldn't get out of his cell except to shower once a week. Still, he began mental invocation and regretted the mistakes of the past. He asked to see the priest and, on his knees and his cell, confessed his sins through the bars.

He read every book he could get his hands on. When a cousin who was also in jail told a Muslim trustee that Cha Cha was Puerto Rican, the Muslim began to supply Cha Cha with political books. He could not see Cha Cha as a Puerto Rican at first because of his light complexion. Jokingly he would say, "But he looks like the devil— the beast." They would all break out in laughter.

While Cha Cha was in maximum security reading about Martin Luther King, Jr. and other political leaders, protests were flooding the nation. It was 1968. Martin Luther King Jr. had just been murdered, and rioters were streaming into the jails. He saw them as they passed the maximum-security cells. Along with the rioters he watched Mexican immigrants being brought in—100 and 200 hundred at a time—for having no passport papers. Cha Cha talked with them in Spanish. They told him they had come to this country to get jobs so they could feed and clothe their families. They had never been arrested until now when they were picked up at their workplaces. They would be flown back to

Mexico, but they would return again to look for another job. The prison guards shoved them around because they could not speak English. Cha Cha and the other Puerto Ricans translated for them from their cells and yelled at the guards for harassing them.

When Cha Cha got out of jail, he returned to Lincoln Park. The drug addicts on the corner offered him heroin but he had decided now that he wanted to help his people. He didn't want anything to interfere. He knew this was their way of telling him they were happy to see him out, so he politely told them he didn't want drugs. They weren't surprised: people who got out of jail usually said that at first a couple of weeks later they were back on drugs.

But Cha Cha was serious. He kept on reading and studying—about Malcolm X, the Massacre of Ponce, Don Albizu Campos, etc. He found other people in the community who thought like him. They invited him to urban renewal meetings. The people at the meetings were all white middle-class people. There were no Latinos or other poor. Cha Cha began to see how, with the help of these white middle-class people, urban renewal plotted to force the Latinos and other people out of Lincoln Park. He was angry, but what could he do? If he told his friends, why would they help? They seem to be interested only in drugs and gang fighting. Still, he knew some of them had been forced out of "La Clark" before and he knew that only the people could stop Daley's urban renewal plans, so he began to talk with them in the taverns, on the corners, and any place he found them.

He put together 3 organizations. The first, the Concerned Puerto Rican Youth, was co-opted by the YMCA and the same white middle-class people who were pushing Latinos out of Lincoln Park. Concerned Puerto Rican Youth preferred to play basketball and baseball; They spent their time going to dances to earn money for more sports activities. Cha Cha could not see himself doing this while his people were being forced out of Lincoln Park so after quitting them, he organized the Puerto Rican Progressive Movement, which held classes on Puerto Rican issues. Later the Puerto Rican Progressive Movement disbanded to become part of the Young Lords which Cha Cha reorganized. It wasn't difficult for the Young Lords to understand what Cha Cha was saying about urban renewal, racism, police brutality, etc. After all, they lived it. They developed quickly. At first, Cha Cha turned his apartment into an office and organized classes. Later they shared an office with another organization until eventually they occupied a church, renamed it the People's Church, and turned it into their national headquarters.

The Young Lords held meetings in Lincoln Park on the problems of housing and urban renewal. From early morning until late at night they would distribute leaflets announcing their meetings until all Lincoln Park had been covered. In the cold winter months, poor people would come to People's Church with their children to tell the Young Lords the sheriff had evicted them from their homes and dumped their belongings on the sidewalk. Taking the family's belongings into the church, the Young Lords would ransack Lincoln Park looking for a vacated apartment. Because many landlords were remodeling to raise rents, many apartments were empty then. When the Lords found one, they would move the family in, visit the landlord, and pay him the first month's rent if the family had no money. They would tell the family to call on them if the sheriff returned. The sheriff, who had built no bonds with the people of Lincoln Park, usually took off when community people gathered.

The Young Lords helped to organize the Poor People's Coalition of Lincoln Park, an organization of all races which protested Daley's urban renewal and fought for low-income housing. With 250 poor families, they seized and occupied an empty lot at the corner of Halsted and Armitage to protest the construction of an exclusive Tennis Club (membership fee—$1,000) where Latino homes had once stood. In May of 1969 the Young Lords and other community groups confronted McCormick Theological Seminary, an influential backer of urban renewal. Among other demands, they requested $601,000 for low-income housing. When the administration of the seminary refused the demands, community people—Latino, black, and white—took over the Stone Administration Building and occupied it for four days in one of the first community occupations of its kind in the country.

They renamed the Stone Administration building after Manuel Ramos, the Young Lord who a few days before had been shot down in cold blood by James Lamb, a Chicago policeman. Lamb was not on duty at the time; when 4 Lords turned him into the police, the police pressed charges against them, not Lamb. Recognizing that Manuel's murder was part of a broader movement of repression in the United States, the Lords immediately organized a March of 3000 people from People's Park to Division Street, the heart of the Puerto Rican community. Shouting "Manuel Ramos vive en todos revolucionarios!" and demanding the arrest of Lamb, they were also marching for the independence of Puerto Rico.

The Lords were the first to bring the issue of Puerto Rican independence to Chicago. Over 3,000 people took part in the well-disciplined Albizu Campos March. In addition, the Lords sponsored cultural festivals for the community with entertainment, food, and cold drinks free to all.

They were involved in welfare marches to protest the harassment of Latino and other poor women not receiving their welfare checks. They set up a free breakfast program for children, a clothing program and a free health clinic for families. Chapters of the YLO grew up all over the country—in New York, New Jersey, California.

They were in the process of setting up a free daycare center and a drug abuse program when Daley's systematic repression began. Mayor Daley could buck no interference with his urban renewal scheme. Getting funds from the federal government, he could not afford to be embarrassed or to frighten the federal officers from HUD (Housing and Urban Development), so when the Latinos and other people of Lincoln Park under the leadership of the Young Lords became an obstacle to Daley's plans, he summoned a press conference to announce his "war on gangs." To carry out this war he appointed his close friend Edward Hanrahan, who followed his orders well. From the way it looked, as indictments hit all Lincoln Park residents objecting to urban renewal, Daley thought all Latinos and poor people in the area were gang members.

The repression began a few months before Manuel's murder—in January 1969 when Cha Cha was picked up and charged with two old warrants from 1967. He was standing on a corner explaining urban renewal to a crowd of young people when a car with two policemen from the Gang Intelligence Unit drew up and ordered him to get in. "Am I under arrest?" he asked. "No, we just wanna talk with you," they replied. "Well, I don't want to talk with you," Cha Cha answered. The two policemen jumped out of the car and told Cha Cha he'd better get in. The young people began to taunt the policeman telling them Cha Cha didn't have to get in the car. Cha Cha told them to cool it and got into the car.

The young people then rounded up community people and lawyers and marched to the police station.

At the station, the police kept Cha Cha upstairs for two hours while the officers combed their files for warrants. Cha Cha was into what seemed to be a friendly argument with the police about Daley's urban renewal. The officers upstairs were all police who had arrested Cha Cha in his gang years—like Commander Brasch [*sic*], who is now under indictment for extortion. In the conversation, they brought up Cha Cha's police record and advised him to "quit while the quitting was good." Cha Cha replied that he didn't see anything illegal in what he was doing. He had been in jail before for stealing from his people. If he had to go to jail now for helping them, he didn't mind. The police downstairs finally came up with two old warrants for Cha Cha's arrest from the aggravated battery case in front of his parents' home. Cha Cha told them the police hadn't been able to find these warrants when he turned himself in for them long before, but the police were bored with talking to him and stuck him in the lock-up.

The Puerto Rican young people raised the bond money which got Cha Cha out, but the repression continued. A week or so later, Cha Cha and twelve others were arrested at a welfare demonstration and charged with "mob action." The other twelve were let off: Cha Cha was not. The same day they charged him with another "mob action" in relation to an urban renewal meeting. Again, he was the only one indicted. Three times he was arrested for disorderly conduct—a charge placed on people when nothing else can be found. He was then accused of aggravated kidnapping of his own child. The child was with its mother who had been separated from Cha Cha for some time. It was his mother-in-law who with the generous help of the police department had filed the complaint. The case was so ridiculous the judge got mad and dismissed it the next day.

As the Young Lords left People's Church for another welfare demonstration, Cha Cha and eight or nine others were arrested for aggravated battery against a policeman. (No policemen were taken to any hospital for injuries—no one was bruised or scratched. No one had been touched. In court, however, policemen are considered infallible). Meanwhile, other Young Lords were getting traffic tickets and being checked for identification. The idea was to keep all of them out of the welfare demonstration.

Two policemen told Cha Cha they had two warrants for his failure to appear in court. Cha Cha was sure he had not skipped a court date so he asked if he could phone his attorney to have his lawyer speak with them. They agreed. They couldn't do much else; after all, when Cha Cha asked them to show him the warrants, they had none. While Cha Cha was phoning his lawyer, community people began to gather. This was enough to prompt the policeman to make Cha Cha get off the phone. They shoved him into the car and drove away. The lawyer went to the station to tell them there were no warrants for Cha Cha missing a court date, so when the police could find no warrants, they charged him with resisting arrest.

The arrests and indictments continued through 1969 and early 1970 until they totaled 18. The police tried everything in their power to isolate Cha Cha from the community. Because they had many cases against him, he not only had to appear in court three and four times a week, he had to appear in different courts at the same time. When he arrived late, the court would issue a warrant. When lawyers told the court Cha Cha would appear later, the irritated judges invariably answered they weren't interested in talking to attorneys, they wanted to see Cha Cha. When all calls for arrest were exhausted, they started charging him with possession of marijuana.

It is true that Cha Cha voluntarily pleaded guilty on petty theft charges of taking $23 worth of lumber. However, the State's Attorney's office acknowledged that this was the only case Cha Cha was guilty of. They placed it first on the court case agenda while shunting and procrastinating on the prior cases. Because Cha Cha had already pleaded guilty, he did not think a trial was necessary. However, at the last moment, the State's Attorney, who "wanted to give Cha Cha all his legal rights," added the charge of burglary to the same case which made the trial necessary. If Cha Cha were convicted of burglary, instead of the one-year sentence, he would get five years for a pile of lumber worth $23.

Of those protesting urban renewal in Lincoln Park, Cha Cha was not the only victim of repression. Because of his leadership role, he got the most indictments and is currently in jail. But many community people were harassed for nothing more than entering People's Church. The "Red Squad" and "Gang Intelligence Unit" photographed the people from their cars and later visited them in their homes. They stopped and questioned people wearing buttons distributed by the Young Lords like the one which read "Tengo Puerto Rico en mi corazon." (I have Puerto

Rico in my heart.) They were arrested at demonstrations protesting welfare, urban renewal, and police brutality. Members of the central committee of the Lords got four and five indictments apiece. Along with Cha Cha, other Young Lords and community people were forced into hiding to avoid Hanrahan's and Daley's repression.

Although the indictments were supposedly related to Daley's war on gangs, the Young Lords Organization proved to the poor—especially Latinos—that they were not a street gang as their enemies portrayed them. They were not in any gang fights. Instead of harming the people, they served them. Cha Cha Jimenez was no gang leader. He was the leader of a bona fide Latino political organization struggling for self-determination within the confines of the United States.

CHA CHA'S LUMBER CASE

In August 1970, Cha Cha pleaded guilty to taking $23 worth of lumber from a building contractor in Lincoln Park. As he stood unemotional and silent before Judge Romiti, he was given the maximum sentence one can receive for petty theft—a year. He is now serving the one-year sentence. We have included this section as part of the pamphlet because we feel that it is important for people to know the circumstances of the case.

In the spring of 1969, the Young Lords Organization began planning a new daycare center where welfare mothers could leave their children while looking for work. It was also seen as a means of involving welfare mothers in the community—especially in the issue of urban renewal, as they would be most affected by Daley's innercity removal of the poor.

The community responded well. Many persons dropped into People's Church to offer their services. The Young Lords gathered long lists of children, parents, teachers, and personnel who along with the Young Lords would make up the center. They had visited other centers to see how they were managed. They repainted the church in bright rainbow colors for the children. Community residents painted colorful pictures of clowns, birds, and animals on the walls inside the church. It was to be named after Manuel Ramos, whose portrait was painted on the wall. Community residents also put together a mural of Puerto Rican history.

Preparatory meetings began with people who would be involved in the center. The opening date was set. People's Park was to be used for recreation. Nutritionists were busy making up menus. A few large companies and many small community stores promised to donate food and supplies. There were more than enough nurses available. The Young Lords refused any aid from the federal government or the city. They did not want the program co-opted.

As opening day approached, Mayor Daley began to move. The Board of Health and the Fire Department paid a visit to People's Church. At first, the Young Lords prevented their entry, but the center staff and the congregation—satisfied that the church was in perfect condition—told the Young Lords that no harm could be done. For two or three hours, the officials inspected every corner of the church. When they finished, they ordered fire exit signs be put up in all entrances. They concluded that the church floor (the size of a gym) had to be raised two or three feet. They also decided the ceiling was too high. They insisted that if these things were not done there would be no daycare center. They announced they would come to the church on a weekly basis to check for more violations. Meanwhile, the Young Lords and the daycare center staff who were distributing flyers about the center were harassed by the police and charged with disorderly conduct, leafletting too close to a school, etc. Attention had to be refocused on the people being jailed for whom bond money had to be raised.

The health department took the minister and congregation to court over code violations. The judge imposed a $200 fine for every day the church stayed open. A trial had to take place to determine whether or not the church could remain open. This involved not only the fate of the daycare center but the fate of the church and the Young Lords' office.

Authorities had ordered that room partitions be built along with the enormous floor. The Young Lords and the center staff went around to all the lumberyards in the area asking for donations. They came back with two or three scraps of wood. Cha Cha could not understand why these huge lumber yards could only donate a few scraps of wood when they supplied the same building contractors who were pushing the poor out of Lincoln Park. He went himself to ask for donations. When they brought Cha Cha more scraps, he told them angrily, "You keep that garbage. We didn't come here to beg from you. This donation is something you owe to the community." With that, they left, got into their car, and drove off to the office. That night Cha Cha and a friend were arrested. At the police station, Cha Cha told the Young Lords that he did take the lumber; that he had mistakenly reacted and that he would be willing now to pay the consequences.

In court, the building contractor could not prove the wood belonged to him. Further, Cha Cha had been given a receipt for the wood. There were no witnesses who had seen Cha Cha take the wood. In the laboratory, sand, dust, and wood particles had been found in the defendant's clothing, but in court, the lab technician said that these particles could be picked up almost anywhere. The only reason Cha Cha was found guilty of taking the $23 worth of lumber was because he himself told them he took it. The only reason there was a trial was because at the last moment the State's Attorney placed another fictitious charge on Cha Cha related to the case. If he had been found guilty of the other charge, he would have gotten five years instead of one—all for $23. The other defendant got 30 days in jail for the same case: his sentence was later nullified.

CHA CHA'S BOND JUMPING CASE

At the end of June or in early July of this year, Cha Cha will go to trial for three counts of bond jumping related to the fact that he did not show up in court when he was supposed to start serving his one-year sentence for the lumber case and begin trial for the remaining cases, which at the time totaled nine. The charge of jumping bond is usually dropped, but Cha Cha is not just another case. Before Hanrahan left office, he made sure Cha Cha—although away from the community at the time—got charged with jumping bond, which brought the total cases pending to ten.

Bond jumping is a case which carries a maximum sentence of not less than one year and not more than five years for each charge. When a person fails to appear in court, he has issued a warrant and has 30 days to appear to quash the warrant. It is very easy for the State's Attorney to prove a person guilty of jumping bond. All that is necessary is to place the clerk of the court on the witness stand to declare that the defendant did not appear. The judge then finds the defendant guilty. However, if it is a jury trial—as Cha Cha will have—it is up to a jury to hear the defendant's side of the story to find him guilty or not guilty of intentional bond jumping. The whole matter hinges upon intent. Did the defendant have intentions of jumping bond or was he placed in a position where he had no other choice?

The matter now will be in the hands of the jury. It will be interesting to see what type of jury Cha Cha gets. There are not many Latino jurors. So the case rests on 1) whether there is a jury of Latino peers to listen to the evidence; 2) whether the judge and State's Attorney will permit the choosing of Latinos if there are any Latinos to be chosen; 3) whether the jury will be able to understand Cha Cha's background and culture; and 4) most importantly, whether or not there will be a fair trial.

CALL FOR ACTION

The hypocrisy of the judicial system in this country is clear in the fact that poor and oppressed people can't get a fair trial by a jury of their peers. This in turn reflects the falsity and contradictions of the so-called democratic way of life. The self-determination and spirit of struggle of an oppressed people can never be totally repressed as shown by the heroic struggle of the Vietnamese people and as reflected in the words of Cha Cha Jimenez:

> They can jail us;
> They can brutalize us;
> They can even kill us;
> But they can't stop us!

Cha Cha represents this growing spirit of "lucha" and political consciousness among Latino people in the US. That consciousness comes from the injustice, the repression, and the exploitation which victimize us. We can clearly see how this process comes about when we look at the transformation of the Young Lords from a street gang defending itself against other street gangs—including Latinos—to a true Latino political organization defending Latinos against Daley's gangs including the Police Department and the court system.

We should fight against the injustices of this yanqui government which wants to oppress us and put Cha Cha in jail. We should fight against the injustice of poor housing which forces our people to live in rat-and-roach-infested ghettos, where falling plaster and cheap paint give lead poisoning to our children—our children who don't know what it means to live in one place for more than four or five years because urban renewal pushes our families from one ghetto to another.

We should fight against the injustice of racism which keeps all poor and oppressed peoples divided because of color and keeps Latinos divided among themselves. Hermanos are constantly fighting each other for jobs, government funds for education, and turf, while this racist government makes no color distinction when it decides who it will oppress—economically, educationally, or by means of open aggression including police brutality. We should fight against the injustice of a court system which places high bonds our people can't afford, so they have to stay in jail separated from family and friends until they are called to court, where their "court appointed attorney"—alias PUBLIC DEFENDER—has made a deal for them with the State's Attorney's office to get them less time for a crime they did not commit.

We should fight not only against these injustices but I guess all the injustices of this yanqui government which forces its culture and lifestyle on our country and forces our people out of our country by promising them bigger and better jobs, homes, and lives, that do not exist here in the American ghettos. We should and must fight against all the injustices of this yanqui government that wants to put people who struggle—people like Cha Cha—in jail.

Que viva el pueblo!
Libertad a Cha Cha!

Puerto Rico: Republic or Federal State?

(1971)
Tony Baez, Minister of Education, YLO
The Rican: Una revista de pensamiento contemporáneo Puertorriqueño, Fall 1971, pp. 48–51
DePaul University, Richardson Library Microforms Collection

There are several points to emphasize in regard to the general elections of 1968 in Puerto Rico. One, that the election of the present governor, Luis Ferre—millionaire, supporter of federal statehood, does not imply that the people of Puerto Rico favor statehood. Two, the fact that the Puerto Rican Independence Party obtained less than 5 percent of the votes required in order to remain registered as a political party does not imply a total rejection of the ideal of independence, and much less a farewell to the possibility of obtaining independence for the island.

I will attempt to give a better understanding of political developments in Puerto Rico before and after the elections.

In 1967 the people went to the ballot boxes in order to demonstrate their support in a plebiscite for one of the three forms of government proposed for the island: "Free and Associated State" (Commonwealth), "Federal State," or "Independence."

This plebiscite, planned completely by the Popular Democratic Party (PPD) in power from 1940 to 1968 and the founder of the free and associated state, was destined to play around once again with the Puerto Rican people. The PPD knew that the people repudiated the Republican Party and its top leader, Miguel Angel García Méndez. Moreover, it knew that the people rejected independence out of the fear created in the minds of the majority that independence would mean a total separation from the United States and thus would bring hunger, misery and desolation. On top of this, there was a great deal of propaganda by the system and the Cuban exiles against Fidel Castro and the establishment of a socialist regime in Cuba. Thus, the situation was in their favor, and even more so when the two opposition parties, the old Republican Statehood

Party [PER] and the [Puerto Rican Independence Party] PIP decided not to participate in the plebiscite elections.

Miguel A. García Méndez knew very well the strategy of Luis Muñoz Marín (leader of the PPD and governor of the island from 1948 to 1964), just as it was well known by Gilberto Concepcion de Gracia, president of PIP. Neither of them was willing to be a toy in the little game of Luis Muñoz Marín.

The division in the leadership of the Republican Party and the Independence Party brought as its consequence a division in the ranks of both political parties. In the Republican Party, Luis Ferré decided to form a group which, defending statehood, would participate in the plebiscite. In the Independence Party, Alvarez Silva also decided to form a group to participate in the elections. Muñoz Marín was overjoyed at the split, which would help more than anything to further his aims: to strengthen in the colonized Puerto Rican mentality the idea that we have to continue being a colony (synonym of "Free and Associated State"), because the people would "democratically" decide to do so. Muñoz Marín and his gang triumphed in the plebiscite elections. The Republican Party ended up so divided that there emerged a new party. The New Progressive Party [PNP] that was to be led by Luis Ferré. It emphasized that it wouldn't tell the people that it sought statehood but would instead hide it. Moreover, Alvarez Silva returned to the PIP only to be completely defeated in the internal party elections. He ended up resigning formally from the party in 1969.

But the PPD didn't remain free of problems. Roberto Sánchez Vilella, who served as governor from 1964 to 1968, was the target of defamation following personal conflicts with his party's leadership. During the Popular Democratic Party convention held to select candidates for the 1968 general election, he was defeated. He chose along with other dissatisfied general "Populares," to found the People's Party (PP).

1968—year of the general elections for the Puerto Rican masses, who are ignorant of the political schemes of the puppets of the colony, the political conditions of the island are more confused than ever before. As a result of internal disagreements within the PPD, a series of personal attacks by petty politicians erupted, leading to the public exposure of numerous illegal and abusive actions committed by the PPD during its twenty years in power. The people, fed up with so many unfulfilled promises and with the abuse of power by the leadership of this party, reacted against the party. From then on, the issue has been to remove the PPD from office.

This leads us to underline three details which should never be forgotten when one thinks about the 1968 elections: first, the People's Party would act as a disruptive element within the ranks of PPD. Second, that its participation in the elections (its leadership supporting Estado Libre Asociado) took away a great number of votes from the PPD, which would be the decisive votes for its defeat by the PNP. Thirdly, the young PNP, led by the millionaire Ferré and supported by wealthy classes and Cuban exiles who are always used by the system as propaganda tools, would turn all its electoral propaganda efforts toward defaming the PPD and towards making a number of vain promises which cannot be fulfilled as long as Puerto Rico remains a colony.

In the meantime, the governmental candidate for PPD did not have the necessary political qualities to struggle against the party and against the internal dissension within its ranks.

To repeat: the final result was the defeat of the Popular Democratic Party and the coming to power of Luis A. Ferré. Therefore, it is demonstrated that the victory of Ferré doesn't imply that the people want statehood for Puerto Rico. The votes given to PNP were defeatist votes, not votes conscious of the consequences of the coming to power of the PNP.

Despite the defeat of the PPD, it was to dominate the Puerto Rican Senate, and the House of Representatives was to be dominated by the PNP in Puerto Rico, the legislature is divided into two governmental bodies: the Senate and the House of Representatives. This has led to a continuous power dispute among the dominant parties and groups mentioned which always puts into last place the interests and needs of the people.

The fact that the people still support the so-called "Estado Libre Asociado," Free and Associated State shows us once again the degree of colonial indoctrination the New Progressive Party is subjecting our people to, with great maliciousness. The people are afraid both of independence and of federal statehood.

The game between the two parties in power (a game which North American executives watch with delight, while the Puerto Rican people suffer), is what is called democracy in Puerto Rico. . . . It is what is used to tell the Puerto Rican people that it has the power to decide its own destiny.

Then again, as the second point brought out in the introductory paragraph, the fact that the Independence Party obtained less than 5% of the votes required to be registered as a political party does not imply a total repudiation of the ideal of independence, and much less, of the possibility of not achieving Puerto Rican independence in the future.

Let me clarify this point. The fact that in a colony there are elections does not imply that the people are given what is necessary to be free to decide their destiny.

In order for the people to be able to decide freely they must be educated politically, they must be conscious of what happens in the political environment where they live. In a colony, the political parties in power want to keep themselves in power and thus during their administration help to keep the people in political ignorance. At the same time their propaganda machinery works to condition the mentality of the people and to shape it so that people will not react against the class which holds political power. The people of Puerto Rico cannot decide freely. This is a myth. Therefore, we must fight against the political ignorance and must create consciousness among the people about their condition as a colony and how this fact affects the mentality of everyone, of how this fact sickens us all.

The Puerto Rican Independence Party was conscious of not being able to win the general elections. But its participation was used as a means for educating the people and exposing the existing contradictions in the colonial structure. All of this without taking into consideration the fact that there are several groups, independence advocators that because of ideological tactical difference with PIP do not participate in election: hence reducing what could be considered an approximation of the "boricuas" who are for independence in Puerto Rico.

On the other hand, it should never be thought that the possibility of achieving independence is null. The people of Puerto Rico are progressively reaching political awareness thanks to the work being done by the majority of the liberation movements on the island. These, day after day, expose North American capitalism. This is the economic exploitation of our people, the destruction of our values and genocide against our people (the death of Puerto Ricans in US wars, the assassinations committed by the US army in our country and here in the US, the sterilization of our women, immigration, etc.).

If we analyze the economic and political development of Puerto Rico, it will be understood that there is only one solution for the problems faced by the island today and that is political independence. . . . The total rupture of political and economic relations with the US of America.

The fictitious progress observed in San Juan, the capital of the island, is never comparable to the misery and desolation perpetrated by the colonial administrations in more than half of the island's municipalities, where more than 25% of the families live with less than $500 a year.

...La blanca cruz en ella significa
ansia de patria y de redención,
el rojo la sangre vertida
por los heroes de la rebelión,
y la estrella en la azuel solidad,
libertad, libertad, LIBERTAD . . .

Luis Lloréns Torres

Cover of the first issue of *The Rican*, the first US journal of contemporary Puerto Rican thought, published in fall 1971. Produced by the Midwest Institute of Puerto Rican Studies and Culture at Northeastern Illinois University, it was edited by Abdin Noboa and Dr. Samuel Betances and featured an essay by Tony Baez, YLO Minister of Education. Courtesy of John T. Richardson Library, DePaul University, Microforms Collection.

Political Activism in Puerto Rico, the YLO, and Early Activism in Milwaukee

(2024)
Tony Baez, Minister of Education, YLO
Excerpt from unpublished memoir, *Barrio Borinquen*, personal collection

When I was in the first grade, my parents moved to New York where they worked for a brief period in the garment district before resettling in el Barrio Borinquen. I attended Cipriano Manrique Elementary School, a rural school with two classrooms. Because I learned some English in New York, I stood out. When I graduated from sixth grade, I went to the Escuela Intermedia Luis Ramos Gonzalez in Caguas. My father insisted that I not attend the rural middle school located in San Salvador where José "Cha Cha" Jiménez, later the leader of the Young Lords, was from. On the recommendation of Mrs. Diaz Alfaro, a math teacher, and sister of the famous author Abelardo Diaz Alfaro, I joined a small group of advanced-level students nicknamed *el grupo de estofones* (the bookworms), an experimental initiative by the Puerto Rico Department of Education.

There were only a few of these programs on the Island. We often participated in televised debates. Once, I broke the tie during a televised competition, sending people in my barrio and school into a frenzy. By the end of high school at Escuela Superior Gautier Benítez, we were excelling in advanced science, math, and English, Latin American, US, European, and Russian Literature. Many members of the group became doctors, leaders in health issues, politicians, educators, and other fields. One teacher who left a lasting impact was Mr. Yinat, an English teacher and Vietnam War veteran with strong antigovernment views. He requested to teach us a bilingual course in universal literature, introducing us to poetry, plays, and global classics. Once he asked me to accompany him to a bookstore close to the University of Puerto Rico (UPR) to buy books for students in our course, and it was the first time I traveled to the university. He knew I was a political activist and quietly supported me.

During this time, I joined an anticolonial youth group's after-school reading circle, where I forged lifelong connections. Among them was

José "Che" Solá, who later became the poet laureate of Caguas and the national poet of Puerto Rico. Others included my cousin Benjamin, who founded a progressive school on the island; Pedro, who joined the Sandinistas and became a professor of Caribbean studies; and Victor, a philosopher and social worker who shared my activism in Milwaukee before his tragic death. These friendships shaped my worldview and strengthened my commitment to social justice.

I was still in high school when I was recruited by members of the Puerto Rican Independence Party. I started to attend PIP youth meetings in Caguas and was soon fully involved in the fight against colonialism and the Vietnam War. I led several large youth demonstrations against the war where I made some of my first speeches. During my last year in high school, fighting broke out between youth street organizations in two barrios: the urban, Barriada Morales, in Caguas, and my rural barrio, Borinquen. During one major fight, scores of youths and police were hurt. I was identified as the leader of the Come Plátanos de Borinquen, as we were then known. We established a reputation as a tough barrio. Later we would become one of the most dangerous and violent barrios in Puerto Rico.

At the time I was also leading the fight against the opening of an office of the ROTC at City Hall. Late in the night, I would lead a group of us in plastering the walls of City Hall with *pasquines*, large flyers, against the military and the Vietnam War. City Hall in Caguas became known to folks as the shitty-looking building ruined by radical youth against the ROTC. We forced the city of Caguas to ask the ROTC to leave. This attracted the attention of politicians who claimed I was both a political danger and a so-called gang leader. My first encounter with a politician occurred when, after the fight, the police arrested me at school despite the objections of my teacher, Mrs. Colón, who explained that I was one of her best students. They did not charge me but took me straight to the mayor's office. I still remember him spitting profanities in my face about how he was not going to allow *un jibarito* to fuck up his city. He let me go but I became the talk of the school because of how the police came to arrest me.

In the fall of 1966, after graduating from high school, I attended the University of Puerto Rico on a scholarship. I was very poor and had to commute daily from Barrio Borinquen to Caguas and then to UPR in Rio Piedras—a three-hour round trip by *guaguitas públicas*. To subsidize my meals, I hustled pool in the Student Union, where I often played against wealthier students. I had been a pool champ in my neighborhood. Thanks to my winnings, I ate well during my time at UPR. At the same time, my leadership among the youth in my town connected me to the student leaders at UPR through the Partido Independentista Puertorriqueño. I quickly became involved in massive student demonstrations against the war and colonialism, immersing myself in the political struggles of the time.

At eighteen, I joined El Comité Sixto Alvelo Pro Defensa de la Juventud Puertorriqueña, named after Sixto Alvelo, who was killed by a US bomb while visiting a school in North Vietnam. Led by Bishop Antulio Bonilla and Dr. Piri Fernández de Lewis, this non-partisan movement aimed to stop the forced enlistment of Puerto Rican youth. My leadership in student protests in Caguas drew their attention, and I was appointed regional vice president. We opposed el Servicio Militar Obligatorio, which disproportionately sent Puerto Rican men to Vietnam. I became a "resister," not a "conscientious objector" like many in the United States. My activism caught the attention of the Cuerpo de Investigación Criminal (CIC), the colonial FBI. After a large protest at UPR, I was arrested, beaten at the police headquarters, and later released thanks to the dean of UPR law school. Years later, my father told me the CIC had kept a *carpeta* on me, but I never bothered to retrieve it.

I became close friends with a middle school teacher from the nearby barrio of San Salvador, Miguel Hidalgo, who often stopped by for a beer and to chat about *independentista* politics. My brother Tito and others were popular musicians, and Miguel, a talented *trovador*, often joined them. Using a small typewriter my uncle brought from the Bronx, I helped Miguel type an anticolonial song he had been working on. He performed "Como el filo del machete" at a protest in Ponce, where it became an instant hit. The chorus, "Oye, boricua, yo te canto esta canción: viva la patria, viva la revolución," is still sung across Puerto Rico today:

Betances me está llamando
Me está llamando y ya Ruiz Belvis me hace seña
Manolo prende la leña
Oiga la leña y Brookman la está soplando
Ya Mariana está bordando
Está bordando bandera en mis cafetales

Y ya por todos los lugares
Ay los lugares se escucha un pueblo que grita
¡Coño despierta Boricua!
¡Oye Boricua y ven a buscarme a Lares!

The song was later recorded by the folkloric singer Andrés Jiménez, and many people believe it's his, but it's not. I still remember my brother Tito working with Miguel on the music. Miguel would often say, "It's in the style of llanera, Tito." When we finished typing the song, I asked Miguel how he wanted to sign it. His response was, "Guarionex Hidalgo y Africano." It's incredible to think that such a historic and patriotic song was composed in my father's kiosk, typed on my typewriter, and first sung in my barrio. Later, other famous folkloric artists, like Los Hermanos Morales, sought out my brother Tito Baez to help shape their music.

In Borinquen, I also participated in community-based struggles, such as advocating for *parcelas de vivienda* (housing plots), which were major issues at the time. I spoke on behalf of the *parceleros* before the Caguas city council—it was my first appearance before a governmental body. Together, we challenged the politicians and helped establish a large housing project called "Las Parcelas de Borinquen," which still exists today as a sprawling complex. I also started a community newspaper opposing colonialism and the Vietnam War, called *El pitirre: Cada guaraguao tiene su pitirre*. It was a mimeographed political publication with limited distribution in Borinquen and Caguas. My friend Ramón Gely, now in Milwaukee, did the cover art and helped produce and distribute it. In the summer of 1970, it inspired a Young Lords paper in Chicago by the same name, and later, it briefly became another community-based newspaper in Milwaukee.

In late 1968, at 20, I moved in with my high school sweetheart, and we soon had a child. My activism had deeply influenced my life, and we eventually separated. She was pregnant again and moved to Chicago with her family, while I stayed in Puerto Rico as a substitute teacher in Cidras and Caguas. I encouraged my students to question war and colonialism, which upset school authorities. Concerned for my safety, my parents urged me to leave. They bought me a one-way ticket to Chicago, where I could be closer to my children.

I arrived in Chicago on February 5, 1970, to live with relatives of my children's mother. Many in the family had been involved in the Puerto

Rican independence movement before relocating to the city, and they remembered my activism back on the Island. As soon as I arrived, they told me about the 1966 Puerto Rican riots and the ongoing struggles for Puerto Rican rights. They also informed me about several Latino organizations in the Humboldt Park community fighting for the Puerto Rican cause, such as the Spanish Action Committee of Chicago (SACC), ASPIRA Association, and Los Caballeros de San Juan. It seemed that Puerto Ricans in the diaspora were making their voices heard in this city, and as I would later discover, other Latinos were just as engaged in the activism.

What impressed me most was when they told me about the Young Lords Organization and its leader, José "Cha Cha" Jiménez. They knew Cha Cha well. He was from the same neighborhood they came from, San Salvador, just minutes from my barrio, Borinquen. They told me that he and other Puerto Rican youth were facing trouble at a place called People's Church, which was still often harassed and surrounded by the Chicago Police Department (CPD). What drew me in the most was hearing that a group of young people in Chicago was not only advocating for Puerto Rico's independence but doing so with a strong socialist agenda. It sounded just like what we were doing in the independence movement in Puerto Rico but, as Cuban freedom fighter José Martí would say, "en las entrañas del monstruo"—in the belly of the beast.

It took just a few days of that chilly winter for me to visit the People's Church. After the family explained how to get there, I took the bus—my first time on Chicago's public transit. As I approached the church, I noticed police officers watching me, much like in Puerto Rico. Ignoring them, I knocked on the large door, and it was opened by Omar López Zacarias, someone I would later know well. I remember thinking he did not fit the Mexican stereotype I had seen in movies. Omar was my first real encounter with a Mexican, and I soon learned many YLO activists came from different Latino backgrounds, not just Puerto Rican. Cha Cha and I connected quickly, especially when I mentioned people we both knew from San Salvador and Borinquen. He even said he had heard of me from his uncle, Dimas Rodriguez, an anticolonial activist. He jokingly mentioned he was not too happy with me because of an article I had written about a knife fight at his house, but we eventually made peace.

From the start, I got into the habit of working during the day and spending my evenings at People's Church. With my new job, I was able to dedicate even more time to the organization. I immersed myself in its history, learning from those who had been involved from the beginning and those who fought to acquire the church building. I quickly caught up on the programs for children and the community, as well as the political issues the YLO was engaged in. I often heard about the deaths of Manuel Ramos, Reverend Johnson and his wife, and Fred Hampton. Their loss deeply affected the YLO, and it felt like the organization's actions were a way to honor their memory, ensuring they were never forgotten.

My involvement in the Puerto Rican independence movement gave me credibility within the YLO, making me the go-to expert on anticolonial struggles in Puerto Rico. I was soon trusted to speak on behalf of the YLO on political issues. Cha Cha called me the Minister of Education, a title with which I was never comfortable. The term felt too rigid and hierarchical, conflicting with my belief in grassroots activism and collective leadership. I was often asked to speak to other YLO members, the Black Panthers, and groups like Rising Up Angry. I once spoke at a student rally in southern Illinois with Bernardine Dohrn and Bill Ayers. It was my first time addressing a large US crowd in English. After our speeches, we rushed back to Chicago, and I did not see them together again. I later reconnected with Bill while working on school desegregation and teacher training in Chicago Public Schools.

I also met others involved in the Rainbow Coalition, which had been active during Fred Hampton's time, before I arrived in Chicago. In Puerto Rico, I had never experienced such intense solidarity and awareness of other ethnic groups. The Chicago YLO opened my eyes politically, and though it was a lot to take in, my eagerness to learn impressed many. I soon became part of the YLO family, included in political discussions, protests, and confidential planning. I became a confidant of Cha Cha and was sent to represent the YLO at protests in New York. Later, I represented the YLO in Lares, Puerto Rico, at the independentista event on September 23, 1970, where I briefly spoke to a crowd of over 100,000 in support of the anticolonial struggle.

I remember the day we went to clean up the People's Park at Halsted and Armitage in Lincoln Park. It was a wonderful day, and many of us, led by Cha Cha, were busy with the work. The police kept circling the area, and eventually, one officer approached Cha Cha with a bad attitude, demanding to know what we were doing. A verbal exchange followed, and when the cop tried to seize Cha Cha, we stepped in to protect him. Suddenly, dozens of squad cars appeared, and the police violently grabbed and beat many of us. I saw Cha Cha wrestling with an officer and Omar pinned to the ground. I was thrown down but managed to get away in the chaos. Cha Cha and others were arrested, and some of us regrouped at the church to start organizing bail. I was struck by the leadership at People's Church, the anger, and the intensity. It reminded me of leading protests in Puerto Rico during police attacks.

We got Cha Cha and the others out of jail, and after that, we had many meetings about the increasing police harassment and attacks around the church. It was clear the police wanted to harm us and break up the organization, especially after hearing about Mayor Daley's "shoot to kill arsonists and shoot to maim looters" order. There was a lot of concern, which led to serious discussions about the future of the YLO. Even though we stayed together, things were not the same after that.

While at the YLO, I started learning circles to discuss political ideology. We built on the political consciousness developed by YLO members and community leaders who had previously taught about Puerto Rico's colonial status and our migration to Chicago. We talked about the need for Puerto Ricans to fight back and stand in solidarity with other Latinos and Third World struggles. We also discussed the 1966 Division Street Uprising, which sparked activism in the Puerto Rican community. However, YLO members felt that other local organizations were less militant and more complacent. Cha Cha often distinguished the YLO's fight for Puerto Rican self-determination and community control from what he saw as the more assimilationist approaches of groups like Los Caballeros de San Juan, SACC, and ASPIRA. He did not criticize them harshly but noted their differences from our youthful organization. We frequently discussed leaders like Ruben Cruz, Juan Diaz, Mirna Ramirez, and Obed Lopez.

Latinx organizations regularly emerged to address health, education, social services, youth, jobs, and housing, and they were crucial to the growth and resistance of the Puerto Rican community and others of color. While I was with the YLO, we had little contact with these groups. Cha Cha never spoke negatively about them but often disagreed with their approach. The only group that interested Cha Cha and others in the YLO was the more radical Latin American Defense Organization (LADO), led by Obed López Zacarias, Omar's brother. Cha Cha also had strong connections with leftist members of the Puerto Rican Nationalist Party, like Mecca Sorrentini and Jim Blout.

A few years ago, Omar invited Dr. Samuel Betances as the keynote speaker for the fiftieth commemoration of the 1966 Chicago riots, and I was asked to serve as master of ceremony. Dr. Betances shared his experience from the late sixties when he worked with established Latinx organizations in Chicago to assess the community's needs after the riots. At the event, some attendees from those organizations mentioned they knew little about the YLO back then and saw them as rebellious nationalistic youth. Dr. Betances and Abdin Noboa, who led the creation of Roberto Clemente High School, acknowledged knowing about the YLO but did not view it as central to the broader changes in the Latinx community. At the time, the sprawling Latinx community in Chicago was fragmented, much like today, with organizations spread out, and their efforts often unknown or misunderstood by others, especially without the connectivity we have now with social media or cell phones.

What I gradually learned was that YLO members practiced an oral pedagogy of liberation, much like in Latin America and other colonial contexts where reading was suppressed during slavery and oppression. This approach became clearer to me when Paulo Freire visited the YLO at the People's Church in 1970, and we discussed pedagogy. Freire, not yet widely known among Latinos, discussed his work in Brazil, where he realized that expecting people to learn through reading was not always effective. Instead, he emphasized building education around what people already knew and how they learned best. Inspired by this, I adopted an oral pedagogy at the YLO, using one-on-one political conversations that encouraged critical thinking without requiring formal reading. Unlike my student days in Puerto Rico, where we had structured debates with brilliant speakers like Rubén Berrios and Juan Mari Bras, the YLO's method was rooted in street smarts and lived experiences. There was no formal curriculum, just conversations that fostered understanding and political growth.

The YLO youth embodied the broader consciousness of young people involved in battles against racism and ethnic identity, fueled by the civil rights movement and resistance to wars like Vietnam. While focused on local fights against racism and gentrification, the YLO stood in solidarity with other youth movements fighting colonialism and imperialism, making it one of the most important Latinx organizations in this struggle. Its socialist and ethnic-nationalist stance set it apart from more traditional Latinx groups. Youth organizations of other nationalities, and even white student groups, now had a Latinx organization to align with. Like el Partido de la Raza Unida in Texas, the Brown Berets in Mexican communities, and the Black Panthers, the YLO represented the boldest, most defiant expressions of their communities.

After the Young Lords expanded beyond Chicago and a New York chapter emerged, tensions over leadership and political direction led to a formal split between the original YLO and the newly established Young Lords Party in New York. In the aftermath of the split, Cha Cha fell back into drugs. I understood when someone needed help with controlled substances. I vividly recall one night in my barrio, when I was around ten years old, I found my uncle Toño lying on the floor, clutching his stomach. He was going through heroin withdrawal. That night was the first time I witnessed someone going through heroin withdrawal, and it left an impression on me. Years later, at the People's Church, I saw Cha Cha going through the same thing. I took him home with me and arranged for him to stay in a small empty room in the house I was living in at the time. Cha Cha spent over a week with us as he went through withdrawal—and he did well. That experience created a bond between us that lasted.

Sometime later, Cha Cha went underground. He was not going to go back to prison on trumped-up charges. He was still the leader of the YLO. In his absence, things became difficult for all of us on a day-to-day basis. Disagreements over programs and issues caused divisions, and soon we conflicted with one another. I had just moved to another apartment on Division and Rockwell when I received an unexpected visit from Alberto Chavira, his wife, and a few other YLO members. They accused me of wanting to take over the leadership of the organization and spouted other nonsense. It really broke my heart. That meeting made it clear that there was a serious split within the organization, and it sparked a desire in me to withdraw from the YLO.

In late September 1970, Puerto Rican activists from Milwaukee picked me up to speak at an event at the Latin American Union for Civil Rights (LAUCR), the leading Latino resistance organization. I was impressed that Mexicans and Puerto Ricans were collaborating closely with the Black community on issues like education, housing, and jobs. Their actions gained media attention and raised awareness of Latinos in the city. They even had a bilingual newspaper, *La Guardia*. The group that brought me to Milwaukee included well-respected Puerto Rican leaders in that city, like Carmen Cabrera, Edwin Quiles, and his brother William, who had just returned from Vietnam and ran Centro Nuestro, a community-based organization. William suggested I could work with *La Guardia* to help with Spanish writing and coverage of Latinx actions, noting that the Chicanx writers had limited Spanish. In late November 1970, Carmen and Edwin helped me move to Milwaukee. The short distance meant I could still see my children and continue my political activism.

Moving to Milwaukee did not stop my collaboration with Cha Cha and the YLO. While underground, Cha Cha kept in regular contact, seeing my move as an opportunity to establish a YLO chapter in Milwaukee. I agreed to help, though I was becoming more involved in the local Latino community. Cha Cha moved his operations to a house near Tomah, Wisconsin, and despite the risks, he often came to Milwaukee. We met to discuss YLO issues and tried to mobilize youth, though the leader of the Latino Youth Federation, Luis Santiago, opposed the idea. Santiago, who had grown from a street gang member to a political force, tried to intimidate me. Others warned me he might've been capable of worse. Despite this, I maintained a small group of YLO sympathizers, and some of the women even joined Cha Cha in Tomah.

During this time, students from Los Angeles reached out to Cha Cha about forming a YLO chapter, and he asked me to meet with them. A representative came to Milwaukee, and we discussed it, but the meetings with YLO representatives from Chicago did not go well. Soon after, the FBI came looking for me in Milwaukee, wanting to talk about my involvement in Puerto Rico, particularly my connection with the Sixto Alvelo Committee and my relationship with Antulio Parrilla Bonilla. On Cha Cha's advice, I went to Los Angeles under another identity. I spoke at UCLA,

San Diego State University, and even visited Ensenada, Mexico. After some time, I returned to Milwaukee and gave Cha Cha the funds we had raised. Civil rights attorney Curry First represented me when we met with the FBI. They admitted they did not have an arrest order from Puerto Rico because the federal judge overseeing Puerto Rico was refusing to sign extradition orders for island youth resisting military service. The FBI warned me they would be watching, but I was not arrested.

In late 1972, Cha Cha came to see me in Milwaukee from his hideout in northern Wisconsin. He told me he could not continue to lead the YLO while underground and had decided to turn himself in, serve time, and return to Chicago. That evening, I drove him to Chicago to turn himself in, as he did not want me involved beyond that. He believed I was doing important community work in Milwaukee. I dropped him off at the designated location and returned to Milwaukee, where I had a meeting the next day about action on bilingual education in Milwaukee Public Schools. Cha Cha served a year in prison. After his release, he ran for alderman and lost, but he remained involved in local politics through his work in the Harold Washington campaign. He continued visiting Milwaukee, pushing for the formation of a YLO chapter, but it never came to fruition. Most of us were deeply involved in other civil rights organizations.

Milwaukee provided something I had not found in Chicago. Though it was a smaller city, racism and discrimination were severe, earning it the reputation of being the "Selma of the North." The city's police chief, Harold Breier, had been appointed for life by the Wisconsin legislature, and he was deeply involved in racist, violent actions against Black people, Latinos, and the Indigenous community. His reputation for suppressing civil rights activism was well known, and I would personally experience his retaliation when he later targeted and arrested me—though the charges did not hold.

In 1972, University of Wisconsin, Milwaukee, received National Teacher Corps funding to develop educators in corrections. I had been doing similar work at the Council for the Education of Latin Americans (CELA), so I was approached to coordinate the program, which involved progressive minds like Mike Murphy and Adrian Chan. Students were trained in the Advocacy Counseling Model, a rigorous approach that documented objections to the Vietnam War while promoting a commitment to peace. The program recruited forty-two students from Black, Latino, and Indigenous communities, and it was overseen by a community board chaired by another Puerto Rican activist, my friend and roomate Loyd Guzoir. I was tasked with coordinating a team of students and developing an alternative school for so-called at-risk Latino youth who had been pushed out of Milwaukee Public Schools. With five, I started the Community Independent Learning Program (CILP). This was my first attempt at implementing a pedagogy of liberation for youth. Our work focused on reading, travel, music, and arts, and we created a welcoming, liberating space centered on Latino identity.

CILP had a profound impact. I worked closely with the students' families, often advocating for them in Juvenile Court. Judge Vel Phillips, a civil rights icon in Milwaukee, once made me personally responsible for a student with a history of violence. Today, that student is a highly respected school counselor. Many of our students also went on to become prominent musicians, playing with salsa legends like Willie Colón, Eddie Palmieri, and Ray Barretto. CILP's musical group became a launching pad for many successful careers in Milwaukee's Latino community.

During my time at CILP, thanks to support of Puerto Rican educational leaders like Dr. Ricardo Fernández, Olga Valcourt, Linda Lopez, and Awilda Rosario, I became deeply engaged in the fight for expanding bilingual education in Milwaukee Public Schools. In 1968, Olga wrote a proposal under Title VII of the Civil Rights Act, which focused on Latinos. By the early 1970s, that program was ending, and I was asked to take a leadership role in securing funding for its expansion. While I served as the public voice for the bilingual activists, the others provided critical information about Latinos in the school district. Together, we negotiated throughout 1973 and 1974, securing a 13-point agreement with Milwaukee Public Schools. This agreement, found in the MPS archives on May 7, 1974, focused on maintaining the Spanish language, developing Latino culture, and creating a more politicized bilingual curriculum. It bears a striking resemblance to the Young Lords' Ten-Point Program and remains in place today.

What made the bilingual program unique in Milwaukee was the leadership of Puerto Ricans in shaping the strategies for bilingual education. While other Latinos in other parts of the country accepted *transitional* bilingual education, where students learned in Spanish only until they became proficient in English, Puerto Ricans in Milwaukee rejected this assimilationist approach. Drawing from experiences with colonial education in Puerto Rico, they argued for a bilingual program that maintained and developed Spanish language and culture, especially for those frequently traveling between Puerto Rico and the mainland. This was a bold, progressive strategy, unlike anything elsewhere in the country. While a similar approach was adopted in Coral Gables, Florida, by anticommunist Cuban exiles dreaming of a return to Castro-free Cuba, Milwaukee's program stood as the only *district-wide* bilingual program that truly prioritized maintaining and developing the Spanish language.

My involvement in this struggle, and the subsequent negotiations with the school district, became an extension of my earlier anticolonial battles in Puerto Rico and within the Young Lords Organization. The program we fought for continues to this day, and it has deeply influenced my approach to pedagogy. Reflecting on this, I realize how these experiences have defined my career. They have prepared me to continue spreading this vision of bilingualism on a national level, advocating for a future where bilingualism is embraced across the country.

Tony, at eighteen, president of La Juventud Independentista de Caguas, with vice president Dalila Aguilú, Che Solá, and mentors Dr. Rubén Berrios and Dr. Guillermo Mulero.

Tony, as provost and vice president at Milwaukee Area Technical College, hosts Cesar Chavez in 1986. Photographer unknown.

Tony with grandson Neiko Terwelp at a rally for school desegregation and funding. Photo by Larry Miller.

IV.
Turning Points: From Repression to Political Strategy

Aldermanic Campaign and YLO Politic

(ca. 1974)
Omar López Zacarias, Minister of Information, YLO
Unpublished essay, personal collection

Introduction

This paper has been written based on concrete research; however, it is a paper where I have not attempted to sound totally objective. Objectivity, besides, could not possibly exist without subjectivity. Reality is approached closer when both, objectivity and subjectivity, maintain a balance. I have not been detached from any of the event described in it. The proximity to all activities and my degree of involvement as Minister of Information for the Young Lords during its most difficult years influence my perception as much as the perception of a detached scientific writer whose detachment creates a myopic condition to significant events. It is, therefore, an analysis of an organization from first-hand experience backed with the documentation available on the organization.

This is also an incomplete description because of the continuity of the group's work. Work that may be seen materialized in the February 25th aldermanic election results, with José "Cha Cha" Jiménez challenging incumbent Chris Cohen in the 46th Ward. A victory for Cha Cha will be a giant step in the main work and organization carried out up to now. A defeat will still be a victory because the very same precinct structure will be maintained to continue the political work and because electoral politics have presented those favorable conditions to do it.

The emergence of the Lords into electoral politics comes at a time when the old machine type politics is entering into its agonizing stage. The Young Lords' politics should never be confused, however, with the Hamburger's politics.

Organizational Strategy and Tactics

Once a problem is defined, the organization can go about developing a strategy to attack the problem and the tactics to accomplish the task. An organization has an additional worry, and it is its own survival, which should be included as part of the strategy; particularly when one has a radical organization.

The survival of an organization should not include a separate strategy but should be closely knit to the fate of the people it serves. At times, if organizations claim to serve, but act separately from the people, it becomes easy for the police or city hall to isolate the "leadership," their actions and the people, and destroy the organization. The Young Lords remained close to the people until the police, not separated the organization from the people, but obstructed the work done for the people to the point where people began to see the Lords as somewhat ineffective. So, in this sense, the Lords had to develop a strategy of survival that seemed, at times, separate from the people.

What was happening to the Lords was not too different from what was happening to the people. It was simply a difference in intensity. Common, everyday people, in a Latin neighborhood get stopped on the streets, searched, abused, punched, and thrown in jail, but it may happen to a particular person once a week, maybe once a month, and at times in interval longer than a month. But, when plain clothes detectives and uniform police stopped cars with Young Lords who were about to do work; perhaps drive a lady to the welfare office, to a speaking engagement, to get someone out of jail, or simply on their way home, and this happens every day of the week.

The work of the organization slows down, its funds are drained with bail money, and services and programs begin to decline. The police, then, shapes the actions of the Lords. More propaganda goes out about police brutality, and the more goes out, the more people read about police injustice, the more powerless they feel. Propaganda about positive programs slows down and the organization and people fall into a constant reaction to the "keepers of the peace." This is seen as two separate strategies: one to serve the people, the other to fight police. Both should be combined but becomes difficult in the everyday work.

The problem, as defined by the Young Lords, was capitalism. What to do about it, defined strategy and tactics. It was obvious the Lords could not solve that type of a problem. It was also obvious that a large percentage of people did not see capitalism as their problem. Their problems were closer to home: Health, welfare, schools, housing. So that the task of the Lords became that of working to help people meet those immediate needs and attempting to make the problems have a direct connection to capitalism. Those programs to meet people's needs were called survival programs. They were: Free Breakfast for Children, Free Health Clinic (Betances Health Center), Free Clothing program. These programs were not only to meet people's needs, but also ways of recruiting workers for the organization. Mothers became active in the Health Program and Breakfast Program. The next step was to have new recruits go through P.E. Classes (Political Education).

Political education was a concern particularly when the North Vietnamese were able to have wide support and troops morale high because their political line helped them interpret both victory and defeat. Through the direct actions against Urban Renewal, the Lords expected to educate people by taking a violent stand against what seemed an impenatrable institution and at the same time stop the powers that left many Latin families out of Lincoln Park. It all boils down to:

> Direct violent stands against institutions followed by explanation of the acts through newspaper or leaflets. Recruitment followed this and an attempt to consolidate the organization.
>
> Service to community people in need while explaining the reason we have the problems doing person to person contact; recruit and add to the organization.

At another level, while in speaking engagements, the idea was to spread the Lords' analysis of the situation urging other street groups to follow the model of the Lords. Having a long-range plan "to create the objective conditions for a revolution."

The Young Lords, because of its analysis and political line, never accepted money from federal or state resources. It functioned with contributions with "no strings attached." Besides, the leadership of the Lords felt that money from the government would place them as a mere social service agency. The strategy called for an organization free from any political ties, or at least political ties that implied conformity or agreement with government agencies.

The direct confrontations, the racial rhetoric, the adamant line and the unchanged analysis began to take its toll; not because they were wrong, simply because the mood of the nation began to change and the organization had half of its leadership underground or tied up in court. Cha Cha Jimenez had left Chicago to avoid incarceration on a charge of stealing $23 worth of lumber that was used to remodel a church basement for a daycare center; the rest of the Central Committee had pending cases to which lawyers from The People's Law Office consistently got continuances and were prolonged for years. These were desperate attempts at saving the organization. But it needed an overhaul. Those members who remained behind lacked the time and the detachment to make an objective revolution and reorganization of the group.

A type of evaluation, a detailed analysis, a self-criticism took place, but away from Chicago, while members of Central Committee met in the different parts of the nation where Cha Cha found himself. The conclusion was that the police had waged an effective campaign of "encirclement and suppression," and it had to be broken. The organization had been separated from its base, the people, and then arrests and convictions delivered the final blow. Once the analysis was completed, the organization went into a period of reflection, study and preparation for a new phase that was to bring the group back in touch with the people.

The new stage began on December 4, 1972, with the surrender of Jose Cha Cha Jimenez to the authorities after 22 months of underground organizing work. Today the organization is at work on electoral politics, working on issues that touch the entire community; issues that are a sound base for a true mass movement. There is continuity to the work done during the radical years in this nation, and the Lords have come back a sophisticated, combat scarred, wise and determined group ready to take issue again with the established institutions in Chicago. This time with the same analysis of society but without the spontaneity of the 60s; with the same courage as before and with as much planning as determination.

From here on, the Young Lords Organization, the former gang, the radical group now involved in unsitting and beating politicians at their own game, is a phenomenon worth following.

4.

COMMUNITY ACTIONS AND PROGRAMS

Poor and Working Class Demands to the Community Conservation Council

(1969)
Lincoln Park Neighborhood Collection
Folder Brochures and Flyers for Various Neighborhood Events
Special Collections and Archives
DePaul University Library, Chicago, Illinois

Representatives of seven Lincoln Park organizations have met and agreed on four demands to the C.C.C. Other organizations are in sympathy with the demands but were unable to be in on the planning process, so their names are not on the list. The groups endorsing the demands are:

- Young Lords Organization
- North Side Cooperative Ministry
- Young Comancheros Organization
- Independent Precinct Organization
- Hermanos
- Lincoln Park Town Meeting
- Concerned Citizens Survival Front

These demands are being presented to the C.C.C. to make our position clear and as a basis for negotiation. We feel that until the question of representation is settled, the CCC should make no decisions.

We demand that there be a legally binding agreement establishing the following points:

1. Since poor and working-class people are the ones who suffer because of urban renewal, the CCC should be composed entirely of poor and working-class people, five Latin, five Black and five white. Rich people should not be allowed to set up an advisory committee to this new CCC.
2. In view of the fact there has been demolition (on Larrabee St. and on North Ave.) and more is being planned (in the Orchard-Vine area) since the old CCC passed a resolution against it, there must be a new and stronger resolution. We demand that there be no

more demolition in Lincoln Park until low rent housing (with rents within welfare ceilings) is built on all vacant urban renewal land in Lincoln Park.

3. Because private speculators have already provided ample upper and upper middle income housing in Lincoln Park, all new housing in the community should be low rent family housing (within welfare ceilings).
4. When demolition and construction is once again approved by poor and working people, the new CCC should resolve that bids for demolition and construction be accepted only from those companies who will hire poor people, of all races and cultures, through the facilities of the Poor People's Coalition.

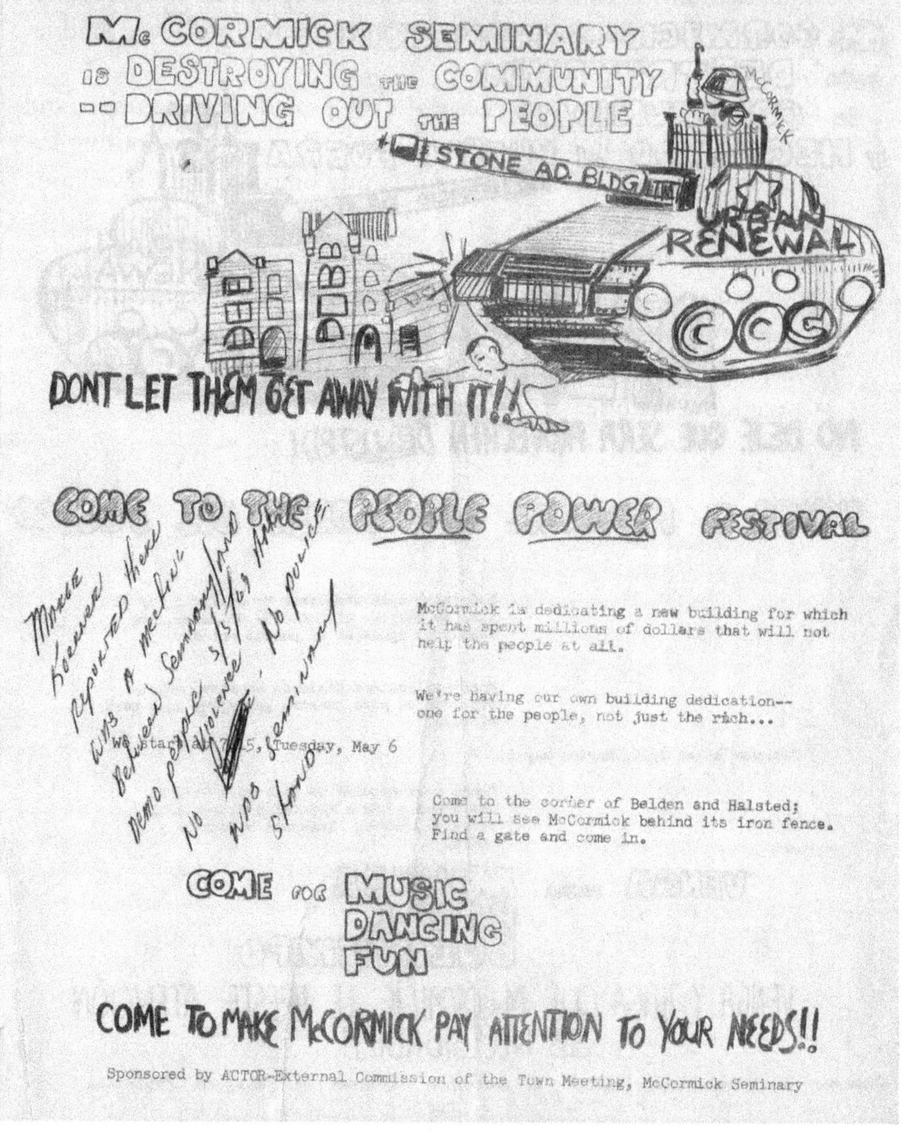

McCormick Seminary Is Destroying the Community /
McCormick Seminario está destruyendo la comunidad (1969)
Collection on McCormick Theological Seminary, Box 2, Folder 19
Special Collections and Archives
DePaul University Library, Chicago, Illinois

NO DEJE QUE SERA PROVECHEN DE USTED!

VENGA AL FESTIVAL DEL PODER DEL PUEBLO

McCormick esta dedicando un edificio poy el cual ha gastado millones de dollares, los cuaies no ayudaran al pueblo entodo.

Nosotros estamos teniendo nuestra propria dediccacion para nuestra gente, no solo para el rico.

Comiensa a las 7:15, Martes May 6.

Venga a la esquina de Halsted y Belden: usted podra ver a McCormick detras de la cerca de hierro. Encuente un porton y entre.

VENGA PARA MUSICA
BAYLE
BUENTIEMPO

VENGA Y HAGA QUE McCORMICK LE PRESTE ATENCIÓN A SUS NECESIDADES!

auspiciado por la organizacion ACTOR lo commision external del Town de McCormick

Join Us Tuesday—March to Police Station /
El martes—Marcha a la estación de policía
Lincoln Park Conservation Association Collection, Box 81, Folder 13
Special Collections and Archives
DePaul University Library, Chicago, Illinois

EL MARTES 13, DE MAYO ALAS
6:30 PM. EN LA ESQUINA DE
HALSTED 2 ARMITAGE, A MARCHAR
ALAESTACION DE POLICIA DISTRITO
18ADEMANDAR QUE EL GOBIERNO
REPRENSENTANDO POREL ABOGADO
HANRAHAN–ARRESTE AL ASESINO,
PUELCO LAMB QUE ES----- CULPABLE
PORLA MUERTE DE NUESTRO HERMANO
Y COLEGA, MANUEL RAMOS

Y.L.O.

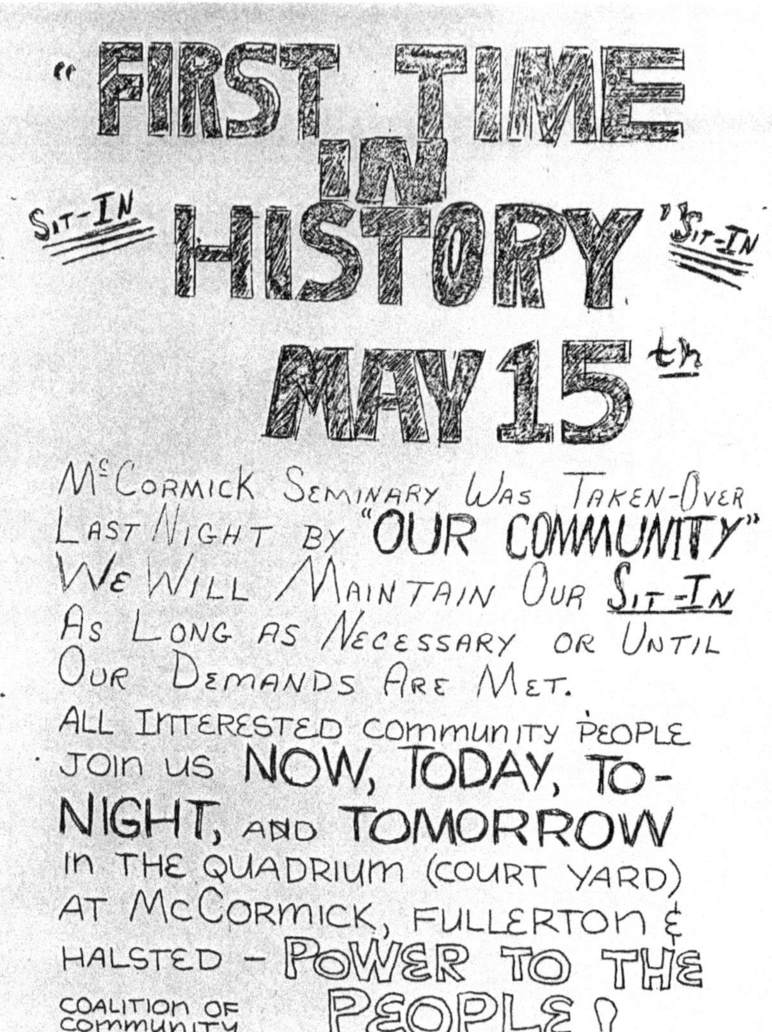

First Time in History, Sit-In May 15th (1969)
McCormick Theological Seminary, Box 1, Folder 18
Special Collections and Archives
Depaul University Library, Chicago, Illinois

Come See About Huey! (1969)

Lincoln Park Conservation Association Collection, Box 78, Folder 3
Special Collections and Archives
DePaul University Library, Chicago, Illinois

HUEY P NEWTON, who set the Black Panther Party in motion, who has given direction to people's movements of all kinds - black, brown and white - is now serving 2 to 15 years in prison on the trumped up charge of "manslaughter". On May 1 Huey has the chance to be liberated from prison and to function on a day to day basis on the streets again. On May 1st Huey goes to court for a bail hearing on an appeal bond and on May 1st we are not going to school, or work or any place else until we have massed at the Federal Building at 12:00 noon to show our support for this great leader of the black liberation struggle and of the whole people's struggle in this country.

Through concrete programs for the people - programs to adequately employ, feed and house, to truly educate and to liberate from the injustice of the courts and prisons - Huey P Newton has shown that true revolutionaries serve the people, while the rich, racist power structure of this country gives only those necessities or bribes to the people which it is forced to give. By taking on the occupying army - the Oakland Pig police force - Huey P Newton raised in practice the right of oppressed people to self-defense. And for these things Huey P Newton has been put in prison.

The meanigless, inadequate education of our schools, the hopelessness of dead-end jobs or unemployment, the state which says that we must fight and die to destroy the colored peoples of the whole world have made so many of us come to one single conclusion. We have no future in this United States the way it is. Huey P. Newton has begun to explain to us the nature of the system behind our situation. He has identified the racist, capitalist power structure as the enemy of the people. And he has shown we must organize and fight against it for whatever changes we need. HUEY MUST BE SET FREE.

On Thursday, May 1st, his lawyers will be asking the federal court, Judge Sirpolli presiding, to set bail for Huey pending an appeal. "This is our relentless demand. We will not let up one day. We will not give up the struggle to liberate the Minister of Defense. And we will continue to exert pressure upon the power structure and constantly bombard them with the people's demand that HUEY NEWTON MUST BE SET FREE!

BE AT THE FEDERAL BUILDING - 12:00 NOON, THURSDAY, MAY 1

People's Demands

(1969)
Poor People's Coalition
The Movement, June 1969, p. 5
Civil Rights Movement Archive

1. That McCormick Seminary immediately turn over to the community $601, 000 for low-cost housing development.
2. That McCormick provide a building and recreational facilities for a badly needed cooperative daycare center. That the seminary provide a bus so that children can be picked up for the center.
3. That all apartments owned by McCormick and rented to people in the community should be rented to poor and working-class families.
4. That the fence around McCormick be torn down so that the seminary can become a part of the community, not a fortress against the community.
5. We demand that the Stone Building be made available to the Puerto Rican community for the creation of a Puerto Rican Cultural Center to preserve and strengthen our cultural and historical heritage and to transmit these values to other peoples in our community and in Chicago. If it is found mutually advantageous to the McCormick Seminary and to the Young Lords Organization, we propose that the seminary make available to the Young Lords Organization sufficient funds to purchase the property of Armitage-Dayton Methodist Church to be made the Puerto Rican Cultural Center.
6. That McCormick extend a grant in the amount of $25,000 to the Young Lords Organization to be used in a community leadership development program and in the continuation and strengthening of a work of protecting and serving our poor community.
7. That McCormick actively support the efforts of the Latin American Defense Organization to end the arbitrariness of the Cook County Department of Public Aid in its dealings with welfare recipients defense groups.

   Specifically, we demand that McCormick publicly support the three demands that LADO, along with the Wicker Park Coalition for Welfare Rights, have submitted to David Daniel, director of the Cook County Department of Public Aid and to George Dunn, President of the Cook County Board of Commissioners,

- Removal of Walter A. Cunningham, District Office Supervisor and James Patterson, Assistant Office Supervisor, for their lack of sensitivity to the needs and the human dignity of welfare recipients at the Wicker Park public aid office.
- Voice of the community served by the Wicker Park office in the selection of a new director of the office.
- Voice in the interpretation and implementation of welfare laws and regulations at the Wicker Park office level.

8. That McCormick extend a grant in the amount of $25,000 to the Latin American Defense Organization to further the aims of creating a strong organization for welfare recipients in our community.
9. That McCormick publicly oppose and condemned the political persecution carried out by the city of Chicago against poor people's organizations such as the Black Panther Party, the Latin American Defense Organization, and the Young Lords Organization. McCormick must demand from their respective authorities that charges arising out of the public arrests be dropped by the complaining institutions namely, Department of Urban Renewal, Cook County Department of Public Aid, Chicago Police Department, the City of Chicago and the State's Attorney Office. The Young Lords Organization and the Wicker Park Welfare Office defendants and, in particular, Jose "Cha Cha" Jimenez and Obed Lopez must not be jailed and punished for their beliefs, injustice, and for their concern with their community's rights.
10. That McCormick Seminary extend a "seed money" grant in the amount of $25,000 to establish a legal Bureau controlled by poor people's organizations, the attorneys to be chosen by the organizations to work full time for them, and to be responsible only to them.

The time limit, decided on by the community to receive a definite answer was seven days from May 3, 1969.

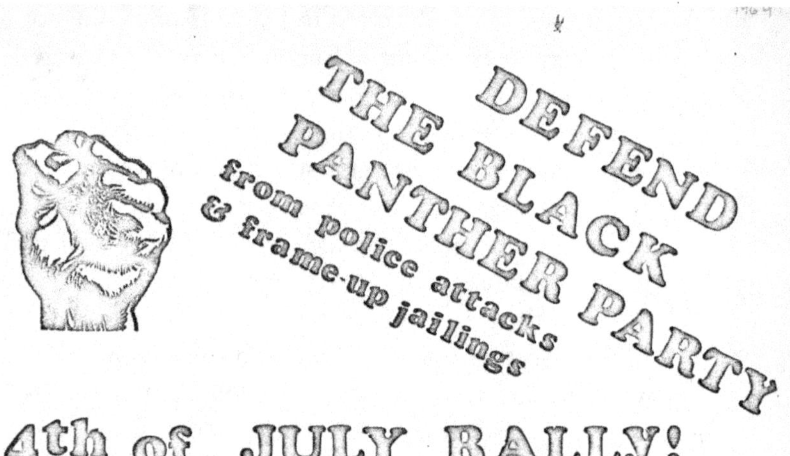

4th of JULY RALLY!

where : in Lincoln Park at North Ave

when : 4 pm, Friday, July 4

SPEAKERS & MUSIC!

DAVID HILLIARD, Chief of Staff, Black Panther Party
Dr. Charles Hurst, Pres. Malcolm X Community Col
Jeff Jones, National Officer, S.D.S.

and representatives from

THIRD WORLD LIBERATION FRONT, San Francisco

YOUNG LORDS ORGANIZATION

YOUNG PATRIOTS ORGANIZATION

THE RED GUARD

FREE THE PANTHER 16! FREE PANTHER CHAIRMAN FRED HAMPTON!

FREE HUEY P. NEWTON! HANDS OFF CHA-CHA JIMENEZ!

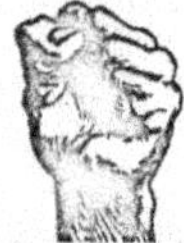

REMEMBER: DEFEND THE STRUGGLE FOR BLACK LIBERATION: COME TO THE RALLY ON THE 4th of JULY, at LINCOLN PARK at NORTH AVENUE; 4:00 p.m. TELL YOUR FAMILY & FRIENDS!

Defend Black Panther Party, 4th of July Rally! (1969)
Lincoln Park Conservation Association Collection, Box 78, Folder 3
Special Collections and Archives
DePaul University Library, Chicago, Illinois

People's Church Response to Alderman McCutcheon

(1969)
Lincoln Park Conservation Association Collection
Box 81, Folder 13
Special Collections and Archives
DePaul University Library, Chicago, Illinois

ARMITAGE PEOPLE'S CHURCH

Sept. 22, 1969

(Armitage Ave. United Methodist Church)
834 W. Armitage

We, the members of Armitage People's Church, expose the intemperance and prejudice in the public accusations of Alderman George Barr McCutcheon of the 43rd ward, in Wednesday's Daily News, concerning our church members and the United Methodist denomination.

To our knowledge that public official has never come to the church board to inquire about our concerns nor to express his own in relation to our work with the Young Lords Organization. We are a part of his constituency, and we have always sought to respond to the needs of this community, which are, in fact, his public responsibility. The church is continuously amazed at Mr. McCutcheon taking the part of resistance to and sabotage of organizations trying to help him do what is his work.

City agencies have frequently exposed the need for daycare facilities, and yet here is Mr. McCutcheon standing in the way of an attempt to meet that need. If his complaint is the methodology or radical style of the Young Lords and the church, doesn't he realize that the escalation of force or pressure is generated by the degree of resistance? The Young Lords and the church and the community and the city agencies—all want daycare developed, so why can't our Alderman aid it, lend his influence and assistance to make it happen for the sake of his community? Mr. McCutcheon's very resistance is a part of the blockade which guarantees the forceful confrontation which he seems to dislike.

His behavior in resisting our simple street festival last month was directly responsible for forcing a violent encounter between the police and the community. The police had to enforce whatever was his decision regarding the granting of a permit for use of the street. His refusal meant the police had to be his muscle, guaranteeing a violent confrontation, ending with guns aimed at the dancers and the church. That decision, which had about it the quality of sabotage, again faced the community with the threat of death.

In the face of all these forces of life and death, Armitage People's Church is a worshipping congregation seeking to do the work of Christ in Lincoln Park, and we have indeed, as Mr. McCutcheon has accused, been "taken in" by the Young Lords if that term means we agree with them that low income housing, daycare, and dignity for the disenfranchised people are the priorities for Lincoln Park.

We challenge Alderman McCutcheon to reconsider the effect of his style upon our community and then to support the movement for daycare. The demonstration of his intention to work for ALL of the people in his ward will be a supporting vote on the City Council to free up the code restrictions upon daycare development in order to make it easier for communities in Chicago to meet their own needs.

The members of Armitage People's Church

Operation Childcare Center

(1969)
Lincoln Park Conservation Association Collection, Box 81, Folder 13
Special Collections and Archives
DePaul University Library, Chicago, Illinois

OPERATION CHILDCARE HAS BEGUN!

EVERYONE CAN BE PART OF OPERATION CHILDCARE

Right now the church is being repaired—and there are still many things to be done. We need help with carpentry, plumbing, painting and cleaning. We need donations and people to collect donations of food, materials, clothes, furniture and money. And most of all, the center needs the advice and help of mothers and fathers—to make this daycare center the best possible for the children.

MAKE OPERATION CHILDCARE AND PEOPLES CHURCH REAL

On Monday, Sept. 29, the Reverend Bruce Johnson, the minister of the People's Church, and his wife, Eugenia, were brutally murdered. On Wednesday, Oct. 1, at 7:30, the Peoples Church and YLO are holding a memorial service for Reverend Johnson and his wife—the man and woman whose dreams were a real people's church and daycare center to serve the community.

Everyone is invited to this memorial.

People who want to work on the day care center or are interested in finding out more about it are welcome to drop in the church any time.

ALL MOTHERS AND FATHERS—
interested in the childcare center
COME TO A MEETING—
SUNDAY, OCT. 5
SAINT THERESA'S 1:30
SHEFFIELD AND ARMITAGE

March to Humboldt Park to Honor Albizu Campos (1969)
Lincoln Park Conservation Association Collection, Box 81, Folder 13
Special Collections and Archives
DePaul University Library, Chicago, Illinois

Demands to DePaul University for Community Controlled Daycare

(1969)
Lincoln Park Conservation Association Collection, Box 81, Folder 13
Special Collections and Archives
DePaul University Library, Chicago, Illinois

TO THE ADMINISTRATION AND TRUSTEES OF DEPAUL UNIVERSITY

Whereas, DePaul University is a Catholic Institution based upon the Judeo-Christian Tradition and Teachings of St. Vincent DePaul.

Whereas, DePaul University is dedicated to "purposeful involvement of this institution with other persons, communities and institutions."

Whereas, DePaul University is the largest single institution in Lincoln Park Area, having over 10,000 students, and intending to add more than ten acres through the "Program for Greatness" within the next four years.

Whereas, the University is not using large segments of its existing and projected facilities, particularly the Academy Building.

Whereas, the Lincoln Park area is a community of over 80,000 people, most of which are poor and working-class people.

Whereas, there are over 20,000 children in the Lincoln Park community.

Whereas, the Lincoln Park area has over 2,500 mothers on welfare, who would be willing to work, if someone were to watch their children.

Whereas, there are few, certainly not enough and no community controlled, free day care centers in all of Lincoln Park.

Whereas, the Rev. John R. Cortelyou has said, "This country needs a day care center every two blocks."

Whereas, NO ONE can deny the crying needs of not only Lincoln Park but all other poor and working-class communities for child or day care centers, as soon as possible.

The following groups and organizations request that DePaul University, immediately consider:

1. Making available to the following community organizations and groups either the Academy basement or a similar facility for a free community controlled day care center.
2. Supporting the Armitage Avenue Day Care Center in whatever way their resources and the Community see fit.

The Community, Student,Faculty Alliance

Students and Faculty for a Day Care Center

The Young Lords Organization

Concerned Citizens Survival Front

The Poor People's Coalition

Students to Defend the Conspiracy Eight

Mothers and Others

DePaul SDS

Presented Nov. 6 at 2:30 P.M.

One year ago, Manuel Ramos, a Puerto Rican brother & member of the Young Lords Organization, was murdered by an off-duty cop - James Lamb (badge #12509). Manuel and some of his brothers and sisters from the Young Lords were at a friend's birthday party. Without warning or provocation, Pig Lamb shot into a group of people standing at the doorway of the party. Manuel Ramos was shot in the head, thrown into a paddy wagon, and died in the emergency room of the hospital. Another Young Lord, Raphael Rivera, was shot in the neck.

Today, four Young Lords are facing charges of aggravated battery!! The pig still picks up his check & packs his gun to "Serve and Protect" the people!

We've seen Ronnie Nelson from Lake View and Chairman Fred Hampton of the Black Panther Party shot down by the pigs and countless numbers of our brothers and sisters tried and convicted on trumped up charges.

THE ONLY JUSTICE IS THE JUSTICE OF THE PEOPLE

If our people fight one tribe at a time, all will be killed. They can cut off our fingers one by one, but if we join together we will make a powerful fist.

Little Turtle
Master General of the
Miami Indians, 1791

AN ATTACK ON ONE OF OUR BROTHERS AND SISTERS IS AN ATTACK ON US ALL!

People's Community Information Center
348-9702

YOUNG LORDS ORGANIZATION
IS CALLING A

MARCH
&
RALLY

SUNDAY
MAY 3
1:30 pm

HUMBOLDT
PARK

CALIFORNIA &
DIVISION

*March for Manuel
*Free the Four Lords
*Free All political Prisoners

March and Rally for Los Cuatro Lords (1970)

Lincoln Park Conservation Association Collection, Box 81, Folder 13
Special Collections and Archives
DePaul University Library, Chicago, Illinois

Lincoln Park Citizen's Committee Meeting

(1970)
Lincoln Park Neighborhood Collection
Folder Brochures and Flyers for Neighborhood Events
Special Collections and Archives
DePaul University Library, Chicago, Illinois

*** Manuel Ramos, Young Lord, murdered by off-duty cop ***
*** 2-year-old child shot in Cabrini Green by "stray bullet" ***
*** People protesting Urban Renewal removal at
CCC meeting indicted for "mob action" ***
*** Fred Hampton, Black Panther leader,
murdered by Chicago cops ***

These acts are no shock to us of Lincoln Park. Every day one of our friends is busted, harassed, shot, or killed by some cop in the name of "LAW AND ORDER."

In the name of "law and order" Waller High School has become an armed camp, patrolled by uniformed and plain clothed cops. All attempts to protest the inferior education students get or the discrimination against Black, Latin, and poor students has been met not with change but with increased police repression.

In the name of "law and order" our streets are unsafe to walk on. Young people can no longer stand around or walk on corners without fear of being busted as "loiterers." "Stop and frisk" laws in our community means that anyone (especially if we are Latin) who is out of place is likely to be stopped and busted at any time.

And at work, how many times have our picket lines for better working or decent wages been broken and many of us arrested in the name of "law and order?"

As the rich try to kick us out of our community through urban renewal, the police are aiding them with increased harassment of the working people of this community especially those who are Latin or Black.

In the name of "law and order," the militant protests to fight against the oppression and removal of the poor people of this community by the Young Lords, Concerned Citizens, and others have met with increased harassment by the cops.

It is clear that the police serve not the people of our community but those who profit from the oppression of Black and Latin people, and who think that property rights are more important than people's rights.

We're tired of this kind of "LAW AND ORDER!!!" We want a law and order that is just and serves the people, not the businesses & politicians.

We'll fight for that justice! The people of Lincoln Park are holding a meeting on February 8th to decide how we can best fight police repression. The meeting is being sponsored by the Lincoln Park Citizens Committee, which is part of a city-wide group moving against police repression in our schools, communities, on our jobs, and in the courts. Meetings like this are being held all over the city. People are fighting back!!!

Some of our demands are:

- Abolish the Gang Intelligence Unit
- Repeal the Stop-and-Frisk Law
- Revamp the Police Recruitment Policies
- Recall the "Shoot to Kill" Order
- Put control of the CHA (Chicago Housing Authority) back into the hands of project residents
- End the use of high bail to keep people in jail

There is no way we can win these demands unless we're all willing to fight for them. We can't rely on the courts, we can't rely on "liberal politicians"!! WE CAN ONLY RELY ON THE PEOPLE!!!

Bring your grievances and ideas to the meeting

Sunday afternoon—2:00
February 8, 1970
People's Church
Armitage and Dayton
For any information call:
*** 348-6042

NDC Housing Pamphlet

(1970)
Lincoln Park Conservation Association Collection, Box 92, Folder 11001
Special Collections and Archives
DePaul University Library, Chicago, Illinois

THE PROBLEM

Lincoln Park is changing, extraordinary amounts of cleared urban renewal land: new projects being planned and under construction: remodeling everywhere: new schools: new businesses: new people.

But what about the people? The people who built the neighborhood. The people, who by virtue of their various cultural, ethnic, and economic backgrounds, make the neighborhood a community. The people who, while providing the community with an element of diversity, contributed the essential element of individuality. Individuality with which people could identify and from which they could derive pride—pride both in themselves and in their community.

These people have been displaced by urban renewal, by the economic reality of real estate development, and by progress. These people have been excluded from the community by the planners and the developers. The housing which is now available, and which is being planned provides predominantly for the monied middle class—for the fashionable townhouse owner or the junior executive who chooses to live in a luxury high rise. It does not provide for the immigrant Yugoslavian family with four children. It does not provide for the young Latins who are forced into the streets from their overcrowded apartments to attempt to establish their identity as individuals. It does not provide for the young artist who is struggling to establish himself and define his art. It does not provide for the Black mother who is fighting to give her son a home of which he can be proud and a sense of personal dignity which the world seems to be denying him.

This then is the problem. People whom this community needs and who need this community are being excluded from it.

THE PLAN

People have become aware of the problem and are trying to do something about it. The Neighborhood Development Corporation was organized on a non-profit basis by a group of concerned residents of the community to research the problem and provide a solution. A solution, a partial one at best, does appear possible utilizing the property on the Northeast corner of Armitage and Halsted—The People's Park. This property is now designated by the Department of Urban Renewal for use as "commercial recreation"—a land use which hardly seems appropriate in light of the recent history of the property and the current desperate need of the community for modestly priced housing. NDC suggests that the property in question be redesignated to accommodate such housing, and that, through the provisions of Section 236 of the Federal Housing Act and/or similar government programs, that NDC in conjunction with Limited Dividend Partners develop the property to provide housing for low- and moderate-income families.

THE PEOPLE

Who are the members of NDC? They are individuals who, in the main, live and work in the Lincoln Park community and who all share the common view that moderate- and low-income housing is desperately needed in Lincoln Park and that it can and should be provided.

Among the more active members have been: Rev. Matthias Hoffman, Pastor of St. Teresa's Church; William Ryan, Neighborhood Development Worker at Christopher House Settlement, Inc., Ron Chew, Research and Statistician at the American Mutual Insurance Alliance; Rev. Larry Deutenhaver, Pastor of the Church of the Three Crosses; John Sweeney, Vice President, J.E.S. Building Corporation; Howard Alan, Architect, Howard Alan and Associates; James Decker, Director, George E. Taylor Youth Center; Rev. Harold Smith, Pastor of the Armitage United Methodist Church; Rev. James Reed, Pastor of the Parish of the Holy Covenant; and Morris Kalish, President of the April Construction Company.

Actively supporting the efforts of the NDC are the following institutions and organizations; Christopher House Settlement, Inc., Church of the Three Crosses; McCormick Theological Seminary; Neighborhood Commons Corporation; Parish of the Holy Covenant; St. Teresa's Parish; and the Taylor Youth Center.

The attorney for NDC is Stuart Glicken of Holleb, Gerstein, Glass and Glicken. Howard Alan of the Firm of Howard Alan & Associates is the architect.

NDC proposes to build 72 units of primarily 3- and 4-bedroom apartments on the Armitage and Halsted site. Each apartment will contain generous living and storage space. Residents will be able to obtain access from bedrooms to kitchens and bathrooms without passing through living and dining areas. Fire-proof construction, building configuration, and plumbing layouts will result in excellent sound proofing between apartments. Each group of apartments will have its own private landscaped yard for children's play area and family activities. Some apartments will have balconies which will serve also as corridors from the totally enclosed stairway to each apartment. The interior finishes will be durable and require minimum maintenance. Parking will be provided on a one car per apartment basis and will be located at the rear of the property adjacent the alley.

By virtue of the pattern of alternate open and filled spaces as well as the variations in the heights of the buildings the possibility of a long monotonous ribbon of buildings will be avoided. The scale of the project is also very much in keeping with surrounding structures as well as the predominantly informal scale of buildings in Lincoln Park.

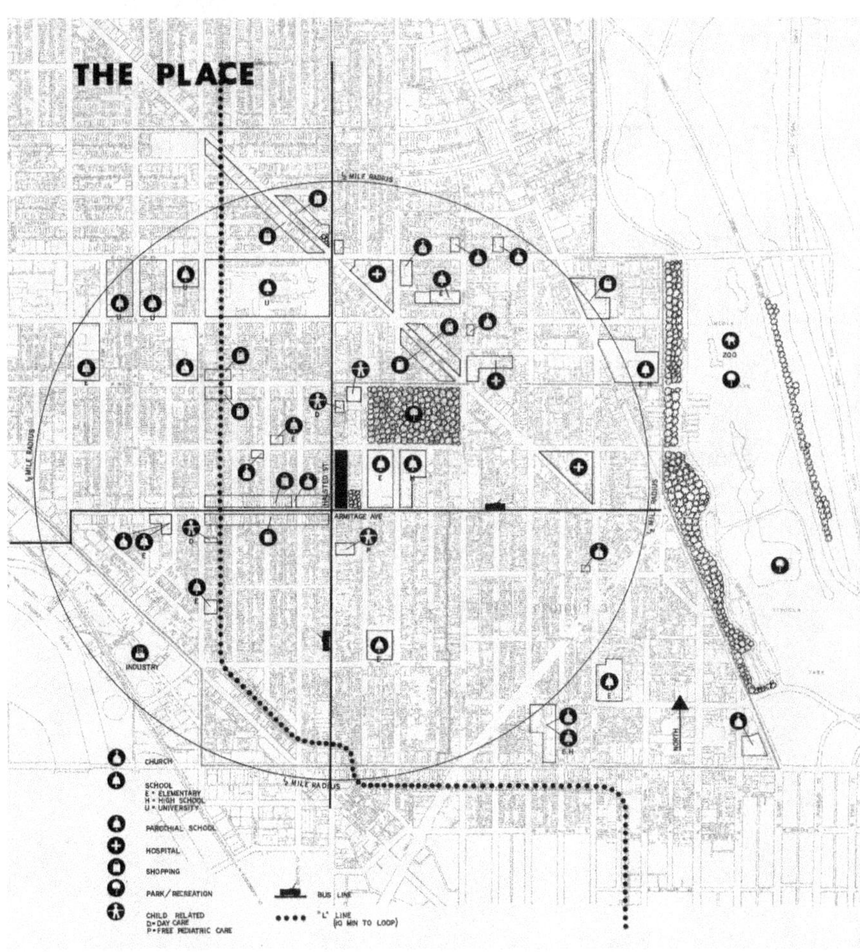

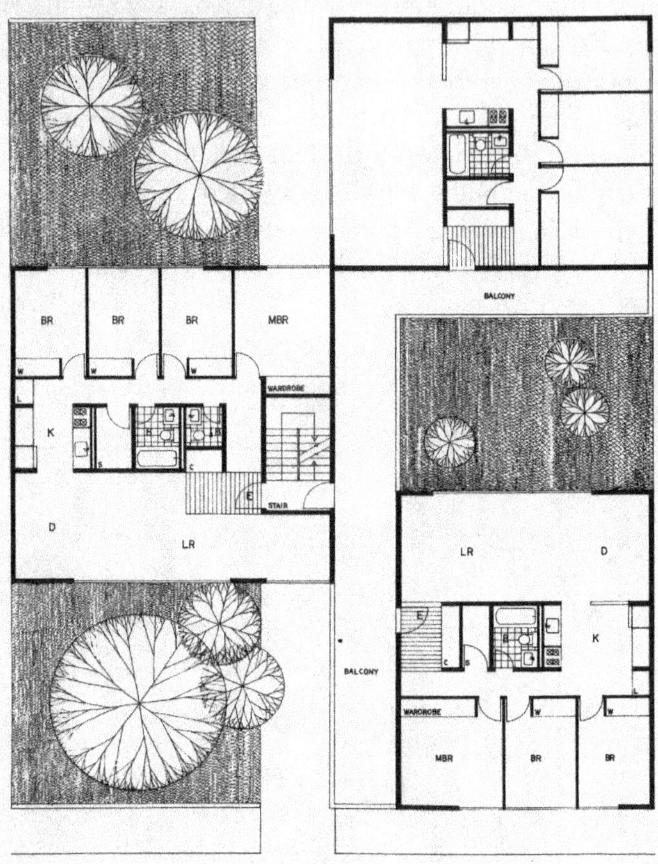
APARTMENT PLAN
BALCONY
BR
BR
BR
MBR
W
W
W
WARDROBE
L
K
S
C
E
STAIR
D
LR
LR
D
E
K
C
S
L
BALCONY
WARDROBE
W
W
MBR
BR
BR

World Renowned Architect Supports Poor People's Housing

Lincoln Park Press vol. 3, no. 2, February 1970
Lincoln Park Conservation Association Collection, Box 131
Special Collections and Archives
DePaul University Library, Chicago, Illinois

[Lincoln Park Press] *editor's note: A few days before the city turned down the Poor People's Coalition proposal for housing, the coalition received a telegram from Buckminster Fuller, a world-renowned architect, supporting their housing plan.*

Feb 8 AM 3 46 1970

THE POOR PEOPLES COALITION
2512 NORTH LINCOLN CHGO

PLEASE ADD MY NAME TO THE MANY ENDORSING YOUR PLAN OF DEVELOPMENT FOR YOUR COMMUNITY REGION OF CHICAGO. IT IS NOT ONLY GOOD AND FEASIBLE BUT IT ALSO HAS EXTRADORDINARY MERIT OF BEING PRODUCED IN YOUR OWN INITIATIVE WHEREAS OTHER DISTRESSED COMMUNITIES TEND TO CONFINE THEIR EFFORTS TO NEGATIVENESS. YOU HAVE BEEN SO THOUGHTFUL, CONSTRUCTIVE AND CONVINCING AS TO WIN SUPPORT OF THE CONSERVATION COMMUNITY COUNCIL WHO FORMERLY OPPOSED YOU AND THIS RENDERS INVALID ANY OPPOSITION TO YOUR PLAN BY THE FEDERALLY SPONSORED REDEVELOPMENT ADMINISTRATION'S LOCAL AUTHORITY. BOTH CONSERVATIVE AND LIBERAL PHILOSOPHIES HAVE URGED COMMUNITY INIATIVE SUBSEQUENTLY FORTIFIED BY GOVERNMENT FUNDS. IN THIS MOMENT OF GREATEST POPULAR AWARENESS OF URBAN EVILS AND STRESS I FIND YOUR INITIATIVE AND COOPERATIVE CONSTRUC-

TIVENESS DEMONSTRATED IN ONE OF THE WORLD'S GREATEST CITIES TO BE TRULY INSPIRING OF THE TOTAL CITIZENSHIP.

BUCKMINSTER FULLER

Buckminster Fuller speaks with José "Cha Cha" Jiménez at the People's Church, ca. 1970. The visionary architect, soon to receive the American Institute of Architects (AIA) Gold Medal, expressed support for the NDC and the Poor People's Coalition's housing plan. Fuller had once lived in the same neighborhood as Jiménez. Photographer unknown. Courtesy of José "Cha Cha" Jiménez personal collection.

Betances Clinic Demands to Grant Hospital

(1970)
Lincoln Park Conversation Association Collection, Box 81, Folder 13
Special Collections and Archives
DePaul University Library, Chicago, Illinois

If Grant Hospital is to exist in our community, it must serve the needs of people in Lincoln Park first. It must begin to treat all of us in our community whether we can pay or not, and it must give the same good quality treatment to poor people that is now reserved to paying patients. It is not the poor people who are to blame for the high cost of health care; it is not our fault that we cannot afford to pay for the inflated profit—for cost of going to a hospital. We did not create the doctor shortage; we did not create a hospital bed shortage; we do not benefit from the profits that the drug companies, equipment companies, and other health businesses make—yet we are expected to be the first ones to go without good health care. Grant Hospital must face up to its responsibility to provide good adequate low-cost health care to the people in our community.

The Dr. Betances Health Program was begun by the Young Lords Organization three months ago to begin to meet the great need for community-oriented, community-controlled health care. We started with very little money ($800.00), but we have made a good start (we described our services in another leaflet that is available at the People's Church, 834 W Armitage). Our health teams give better and more complete care than is available at a doctor's office and we do it for free. However, we will never be able to provide complete health care without hospital backup service, which simply means that there are many tests and procedures that only can be done by a hospital. Therefore, we believe that it is the responsibility of Grant Hospital to provide us with the following service.

We demand that Grant Hospital begin to meet its responsibility to the community specifically by providing the following:

1. We want the licensed doctors which serve the community through the Betances Health Program to be the ones to decide whether our

patients need to be hospitalized or not. (At this time, it is entirely up to the hospital to decide who can or cannot get into a hospital)

2. When one of our patients needs to be seen by a specialist because of a complicated problem; we want the specialists at Grant Hospital to see them for free.
3. We want Grant Hospital to provide whatever is required in order for us to be able to set up an X-ray machine in our Health Center to take routine X-rays (i.e. simple X-rays to check for TB, lumps, broken bones, etc.). We also want Grant to do the more complicated X-rays at their X-ray facilities.
4. Free laboratory work that cannot be done by ourselves, plus free laboratory supplies and equipment so that routine uncomplicated laboratory work can be done by us.
5. Free and prompt emergency care of patients referred to Grant by our doctors.
6. No police questioning of patients in the emergency room. The only thing that should occur in a hospital is the healing of sick people.
7. Any cases of drug overdoses should be treated medically by Grant Hospital without reporting the patients to the police.
8. Absolutely no one is to be turned away from the emergency room before being seen by a doctor. Absolutely no one is to be sent to Cook County.
9. A drug fund of $15,000 per year to be given to the Betances Health Program to provide free medications to our patients.

Grant Hospital has not yet shown that it is willing to be a Community Hospital whose main goal is to serve our community. Where poor people's housing used to be, Grant Hospital has built a parking lot (which is empty much of the time). The amount of money that Grant will have to spend will probably be less than what it costs them to build the parking lot.

Health Care Is a Human Right

(1970)
Lincoln Park Conversation Association Collection, Box 81, Folder 13
Special Collections and Archives
DePaul University Library, Chicago, Illinois

HEALTHCARE IS A HUMAN RIGHT

In a leaflet last week, the YLO stated that Grant Hospital not only neglects its obligation to the poor brown, black, and white people of Lincoln Park but also its obligations to its employees. On Monday we came to meet for the second time with Grants administrators and head doctors and found that not only did Mr. Goschy not want to meet with us, but he didn't even have the courtesy to send a hireling down to tell us that the meeting was called off. Last week the workers at Grant were invited to meet with Mr. Goschy to hear him run down how the hospital doesn't dig workers getting together to fight for their rights. Both of these insulting actions by Goschy and the heads of Grant can only be met by a united action of both workers and community people.

WHEN YLO SAID THAT ALL GRANT WORKERS SHOULD HAVE:

A minimum wage of 125 dollars per week.
Free daycare center at Grant for working mothers.
Paid maternity leave for working women at Grant.
An end to all racist practices in hiring and firing.
Free Hospital care for all employees at Grant Hospital.

To forge the unity necessary to win these demands, the YLO is calling a rally of community people and workers on Sunday, June 21 at 4:00 PM 834 W Armitage.

Ministry of Health
Young Lords Organization

Mothers and Others (MAO)

(1970)
Nina Boal and Angie Lind
Lincoln Park Press vol. 3, no. 1, January 1970
Lincoln Park Conservation Association Collection, Box 131
Special Collections and Archives
DePaul University Library, Chicago, Illinois

Mothers and Others (MAO) is a new women's organization. MAO consists of Black, White and Brown women. The reason we chose MAO as our organization name is because we are not only a group of women, but we are a group of revolutionary women. We believe that the struggle against male supremacy cannot be separated from the class struggle. The ruling class gives men, as well as white people, certain privileges, but these privileges do not really benefit anybody except the ruling class. Because without our really knowing it, the ruling class uses this to divide the working class. We believe that Marxism-Leninism is the ideology of the proletariat revolution, which means that the bourgeois ruling class will be overthrown and the power will come to the working-class people.

Women should stop thinking that their place is only in the home and begin having a revolutionary consciousness.

ALL POWER TO THE PEOPLE!
FREE ALL POLITICAL PRISONERS!
SEIZE THE TIME!

MAO

2 Children Killed, 3 Injured at Broadway & Buena

On Saturday, November 2nd, two young boys were killed in a tragic accident that left three other young people seriously injured. The boys killed were Adrian Espada, 13, and Michael Jimenez, 12, both of Gordon Terrace.

Several youths had been sitting on the steps of the corner building at Broadway and Buena about 7:30 in the evening when a Yellow cab, hit by another car, crashed uncontrollably over the curb, onto the steps of the building, and into the doorway. Loose pillars fell from the building onto the already injured children, killing two.

The hearts of the community united to set up a fund to assist the children's families, most of whom are on welfare and cannot affort the heavy expenses resulting from the accident.

These are not the first children who have been the victims of fast moving cars on Broadway and Buena. In fact the entire community is outraged with the politicians and city agencies who have consistently refused the pleadings and demands of hundreds of parents for safe recreational playgrounds in this area. Public meetings, petitions, trips downtown and to the Alderman's office have all fallen on deaf ears or met with endless delays as large real estate interests and the downtown city planners have blocked the development of an acceptable safe play area for the youth.

The safety of our children is the most important goal this community must work for.

Le Moyne Boycott Successful!

See article page 3

Newsletter for José "Cha Cha" Jiménez for Alderman, 46th Ward
New Day, no. 1, November 1974
Omar López Zacarias personal collection

NEW DAY

Nov., 1974 Newsletter No. 2

JOSE CHA-CHA JIMENEZ FOR ALDERMAN 46TH WARD

Jimenez Calls For Housing Action!

"Jose Jimenez puts forth recommendations for safer, healthier housing and citizen participation in decision making."

Jose Cha-Cha Jimenez testified and presented specific recommendations to the State's Spanish Speaking Peoples Study Commission, Saturday, November 16, at the Illinois Masonic Hospital auditorium.

Mr. Jimenez called for careful monitoring of millions of dollars coming into the city under the new Federal Housing and Community Development Act. He pointed out the city's past practice of relocating slums instead of rehabilitating them and strongly recommended full citizen participation in the planning of how the money will be spent.

The candidate for alderman of the 46th Ward also outlined a new City Council ordinance which would require that landlords place security deposits with the city to be used for emergency repairs of serious health and safety hazards in their own buildings if the landlord fails to make the repairs on his own. Under this ordinance a landlord would deposit $100.00 per unit with the city with a maximum limit of $20,000 per owner. Landlords would receive interest on their deposits. "This," Jimenez said, "will help eliminate health and safety hazards in apartment buildings which the city is all too often powerless to correct." Jimenez urged the Commission to devise comparable legislation at the state level... "We desperately need and want stable communities," concluded Jose Cha-Cha Jimenez.

Be Informed! Take Action!

1. 43.8 Million Dollars in Federal Housing and Community Development Act funds are coming into Chicago in 1975. How will the city spend this money?

2. These funds *can* be used for stabilizing our neighborhoods, providing more low and moderate income housing, and improving existing housing.

3. Citizens *can* have a real voice in deciding how these funds are spent. BUT THIS WILL HAPPEN ONLY if citizens are well informed about this program, demand real citizen control, and elect representatives to the City Council who will keep them informed and take action to see that this and other money is used *for people* not for big real estate interests.

Newsletter for José "Cha Cha" Jiménez for Alderman, 46th Ward
New Day, no. 2, November 1974
Omar López Zacarias personal collection

Family campaign photo
Newsletter for José "Cha Cha" Jiménez for Alderman, 46th Ward
New Day, no. 2, November 1974
Photographer: Eric Futran
Omar López Zacarias personal collection

Statement to the Spanish Speaking People's Study Commission—State of Illinois

(1974)
José "Cha Cha" Jiménez
November 15, 1974
Personal collection

** Fact: Even according to the city of Chicago's own figures 72% of the Spanish speaking population in the city moved at least once in a five-year period. (This is the 2nd highest rate in the country.)*

—Deptartment of Development & Planning, City of Chicago, "Chicago's Spanish Speaking Population," referring to the years 1965–70

I would like to begin by explaining to you from my own experience some of the human reality behind this statistic.

In the 1940s many Puerto Ricans came to this country in search of better economic opportunities. Well over 50,000 arrived here to work as migrant farm workers, in the steel mills, or in hotels and factories of large cities.

In Chicago, there were two concentrations of the Puerto Rican community. They were known to Latinos as "La Clark" and "La Madison." Because I lived in "La Clark," I will attempt to describe the conditions there.

Latinos began to settle in this area because of its closeness to downtown jobs and nearby factories and also because of the cheap rents at the time. Most of the structures were old and were rooming houses converted into one and two-bedroom apartments. They were all rat and roach infested and were in need of repair and code enforcement.

About 1953 some of the buildings were being condemned and Latino families began to move around from one building to the other—never moving, however, more than a block or so at a time. About '55 and '56 the area was declared an "Urban Renewal Area." Families began to get notices or were told to move. And they moved around like a ping pong ball not knowing where to stop until eventually all had to leave "La Clark." Instead they saw the Carl Sandburg Village built (middle- and upper-middle-income housing).

Almost all the Latinos were pushed into a new area—the Lincoln Park community. At first it was hard for the families to relate to their new neighbors who felt invaded. And it was true. The Latinos were invading their community. The Latino community had been totally destroyed, and they were being forced by the Urban Renewal Program to crowd into this new area.

Eventually most of the poor whites who live there moved northward. As the children of these displaced Latinos grew older, social clubs with trophies for swimming and other athletics turned into street gangs. On Clark Street, among the Latino youth, there had been no street gangs.

In Lincoln Park, the Latino community grew larger between '56 and '66. And it was becoming more stable. It was beginning to feel more like a community again. Small shops sprouted. Along with them came church organizations, baseball teams for parents, and bowling leagues—a typical working-class community.

However, in '66 all the Latinos began talking about having to move again. The signs of Urban Renewal began to appear. Although at that time the people did not know what Urban Renewal was.

When the Urban Renewal Program came, the parents were passive. However, not the youth. They did not like being told to move.

By '68 it looked like no hope. Almost everyone would have to move. Hard drugs were more in abundance as more and more land was being cleared. Many families had already been moved out and headed north.

Some community organizations (non-Latino) began to protest Urban Renewal. At this time the Young Lords Organization—a group that had folded as a gang—reorganized itself. They began organizing street demonstrations against Urban Renewal.

In the Taverns, at neighborhood baseball and basketball games, on street corners, and nearby factories, in barber shops, corner candy stores, at bus stops, churches, social clubs, and dances—the Latinos and later it spread to poor white and black families—commenced talking about being pushed out. The poor of Lincoln Park, led by the Young Lords organization, began to attend meetings related to housing. It was difficult to know when hearings were scheduled downtown (notification was published in a small German newspaper and there were very few Germans at that time living in Lincoln Park).

Over 400 persons held an all-week "sit in" on an empty lot (corner of Halsted and Armitage) to protest against the construction of a $1000 a year membership private tennis club that was supposed to have been built on land previously occupied by Latino families. Also, for a week a good 350 persons occupied McCormick Theological Seminary—demanded and got $600,000 for a low-income housing plan for the area designed with the active participation of the community. Then the Poor People's Coalition (made up of at least 10 organizations in Lincoln Park) won the complete agreement of the Community Conservation Council to bid for the land. However, at the City Council Committee hearings it was vetoed. The Community Conservation Council was supposed to be the representatives of the community. A day after the City Council hearing veto, all members of the Community Conservation Council quit at a press conference at which they emphasized that the citizens of Lincoln Park had in reality no power.

The Latinos began to go to all related urban renewal meetings such as those at Waller High School. Because of police repression they also attended the police community workshop meetings where they demanded of the then 18th district Commander Braasch an end to the harassment of the community.

The Young Lords Organization, in order to involve all the poor of Lincoln Park, set up various programs—for example, a free daycare center, free health care program, a clothing and food program, and so on. These programs helped welfare recipients and other struggling families to join in demanding low-income housing and an end to Urban Renewal programs.

The police, however, following orders from "higher up" jailed women and children for ridiculous charges like leafletting too close to a school, upside down license plates, disorderly conduct, etc. Individuals walking down the street with an insignia or button on their person would be thrown against the wall and searched. These would pay visits to the patients of the clinic and ask them not to enter the People's Free Clinic again.

After a couple of years of demonstrating and protesting to deaf ears, some of the youth, demoralized, went to drugs. The Latinos and other poor of Lincoln Park were pushed out again—by Urban Renewal.

This time the same people who were pushed from La Clark to Lincoln Park ended up in the Lakeview-Uptown community. This new area also has plans for an Urban Renewal Program. Now, probably, it will be known as a Community Development Area. The people here are beginning to repeat the same words: "We're going to have to move again." The slum will be relocated again with the same promises from the same politicians.

*<u>1949</u>. "DECLARATION OF NATIONAL HOUSING POLICY. The Congress hereby declares that the general welfare and security of the Nation and the health and living standards of its people require housing production and related community development sufficient to remedy the serious housing shortage, the elimination of substandard and other inadequate housing through the clearance of slums and blighted areas, and the realization as soon as feasible of the goal of a decent home

> and a suitable living environment for every American family, thus contributing to the development and redevelopment of communities and to the advancement of the growth, wealth, and security of the Nation." (Section 2 of the Housing Act of the United States, 1949)

All of the other housing acts of Congress until 1968 state or reaffirmed the ideas of this act of 1949. Then in

*1968. "HOUSING GOAL: DECLARATION OF POLICY. The Congress affirms . . . the national goal of a "decent home and a suitable living environment for every American family."

And it continues:

> "Further the highest priority should be given to meeting the housing needs of those families for which the national goal has not become a reality, and that there should be the fullest practicable utilization, in administration of federal housing programs, of the resources and capabilities of private enterprise and self-help techniques." (Housing and Urban Development Act of 1968, public law 90-448)

* And this year, 1974.

> "The federal assistance provided in this title is for the support of community development activities which are directed toward the following specific objectives—(1) the elimination of slums and blight and the prevention of blighting influences and the deterioration of property and neighborhood and community facilities of importance to the welfare of the community, principally persons of low and moderate income; (2) the elimination of conditions which are detrimental to safety, and public welfare, through code enforcement, demolition," etc. (Public law 93-383; 1974.)

With all the history of these promises of 25 years, perhaps one cold statistic sums up the reality best: JUST LAST YEAR, IN 1973, TWICE AS MANY HOUSING UNITS WERE DESTROYED AS WERE

BUILT HERE IN THE CITY OF CHICAGO. And many of those newly constructed units were luxury apartments.

And not only have these promises not been kept but the rights of Latinos and other poor people continue to be violated. This week, for example, there is a meeting—vaguely described in yesterday's paper—regarding the new Housing and Community Development program here in Chicago. It is the same man, Lewis Hill, running the show; using the same procedure of not letting anyone know what time or place. On this crucial point of citizen participation, the federal law provides that:

The city must provide "satisfactory assurances that . . . citizens (are provided) with adequate information concerning the amount of funds available for proposed community development and housing activities, the range of activities that may be undertaken, and other important program requirements; (hold) public hearings to obtain the views of citizens on community development and housing needs, and . . . (provide) citizens and adequate opportunity to participate in the development of the application . . ." (Section 104, A, 5, 1974 Housing and Community Development Act)

In addition, the Housing and Community Development Act of 1974 does specifically stress aid to low-income families. But it still plays the games of the past with us. And if it's the same individuals playing the same game—it is clear what that means.

Since 1949, we've been "ridding ourselves of slums" in name but instead really creating more and larger slums and blighted areas. The reason being that we do not concern ourselves with people. We only concern ourselves with structures. And when we do concern ourselves with people it seems we get confused with who's who.

Who lives in slums and blighted areas? Is it middle- and upper-income people? Or is it lower-income people? If it's lower-income people, how come we erect buildings for the middle- and upper-income?

That's just like Mrs. Rodriguez taking Mr. Rodriguez to a hospital to cure a disease. The doctor tells her that Mr. Rodriguez is in critical condition and needs an operation. Instead of operating on and curing Mr. Rodriguez, the doctor finds somebody else—Mr. Smith. The doctor takes Mr. Smith to Mrs. Rodriguez and tells her how successful the operation was on her husband and how her husband's disease is now cured. Meanwhile, Mr. Rodriguez is still dying.

If we want to eliminate slums, we must attack the disease. We should not run away from it. Since 1949, that is all we've been doing. Take a look.

—IN "LA CLARK":NO UNITS FOR LOW INCOME FAMILIES
—IN LINCOLN PARK: 18 UNITS—SO FAR
—IN UPTOWN: 24 UNITS—UNDER CONSTRUCTION

Many, many units of low-income housing are gone; and new units are being developed almost exclusively for the middle- and upper-income brackets, when it was the poor who were in need of the emergency housing.

Title 8, section 802 of the 1974 Housing and Community Development Act gives a very good description for state housing agencies on how to eliminate slums:

> "(1) provide housing and related facilities through land acquisition, construction or rehabilitation, for persons and families of low-, moderate-, and middle-income. (2) Promote the sound growth and development of neighborhoods through the revitalization of slum and blighted areas, (3) increase and improve employment opportunities for the unemployed and underemployed through the development and redevelopment of industrial, manufacturing, and commercial facilities."

I would add to that the key importance of citizen participation. One, because it is a basic right of the people. And two, because people will feel more a part of a community and work to improve it if they can participate in making decisions about its development.

We are no longer in pioneer days. Today we live in large metropolitan areas. Present laws and policies must also be updated to serve this new period where many of us are no longer homeowners but rather tenants. We must begin to fight for tenants' rights and for the right of people at the community or neighborhood level to determine their own destiny.

SUGGESTIONS FOR THE COMMISSION'S FURTHER WORK

I would be happy to meet with the Commission's staff to discuss many ideas and proposals we have been working on to help solve some of the housing problems we face in the city. Today I would like specifically to call your attention four points which the Commission could pursue:

1. Efforts at the state level should be made to educate citizens and

mobilize legislative support for attempts at the local level to gain increased citizen control of zoning—or land use. In Chicago, we are mobilizing support for the Community Zoning Board ordinance currently before the City Council. In addition, it is urgent that no "super agencies" be created by the state that would diminish or negate the local community decision-making power that will be won in regard to zoning.

2. A "Landlord-Tenant Bill of Rights" is currently before the state legislature; it is House Bill 1345 introduced by Rep. Joe Lundy and others. I urge support of this measure as an important step in correcting many legal inequities faced by the majority of citizens in urban areas who are renters.
3. All participating state agencies must be totally committed in practical terms to full citizen participation in the new Housing and Community Development Act which will be the main federal source of housing and related funds in the coming decade. This commitment must be joined with a series of concrete steps to ensure that these funds are indeed used for low- and moderate-income housing.
4. And I urge the Commission support at the local level 4 and the development of legislation at the state level comparable to a bill which I will shortly introduce in the City Council to require landlord security deposits with the city that can be used to correct emergency health and safety conditions in multiple dwelling residencies.

In closing, I respectfully ask that you continue your work in this area and look more deeply into the problems that Latinos face with housing. We did not come to this country because we liked to live in slums. We came because we were told that there was a better life here. However, for nearly 30 years a great number of Latinos have lived in the worst conditions—in this city, in this state. We want to help change not only the way that Latinos live, but also the conditions of all the poor and all of the people of this country. However, we must be allowed to contribute ideas and participate actively in the change at every level of government. We cannot be told where to live or pushed from one neighborhood to the other. We are not slaves. We desperately need and want stable communities!

Jose "ChaCha" Jiménez

OUTLINE OF AN ORDINANCE REQUIRING LANDLORD SECURITY DEPOSITS TO ENSURE THAT RESIDENTIAL UNITS ARE NOT A DANGER TO THE LIVES OR SAFETY OF TENANTS. (TO BE SUBMITTED TO THE CITY COUNCIL OF CHICAGO BY JOSÉ "CHA CHA" JIMÉNEZ.)

- Purpose: To help remedy an emergency situation in the city of numerous multiple residential dwelling units which contain significant violations of the sanitary and building code and seriously endanger the health and safety of the occupants. The city has been unable through its various agencies and courts to assure that such conditions be corrected speedily in all too many cases.
- Provisions: Every owner of a multiple dwelling unit shall deposit security funds with the city to be held in escrow; $100 for each unit (except that occupied by the owner) to a maximum of $20,000. The city will deposit these funds in interest bearing accounts and pay the owner the accrued interest, less a small amount for reasonable operating expenses.

These funds are to be used if necessary to correct or alleviate emergency conditions in the dwelling units if the owner does not do so swiftly.

Provides for a simplified complaint, inspection and hearing procedure to ensure prompt action for emergency situations and coordinates the various agencies involved, principally, the Board of Health and City Department of Building Inspections.

Harold Washington Speech

(1983)
José "Cha Cha" Jiménez
June 5, 1983, Cultural Festival, Humboldt Park, Chicago, Illinois
Personal collection

We gave out thirty thousand free buttons the day I introduced the new, first African American mayor, Harold Washington, before a crowd of one hundred thousand (mostly Puerto Ricans) in Humboldt Park—Parade Day, June of 1983. The very first mayor's neighborhood festival in Chicago. Two days later Rudy Lozano was murdered. Rudy Lozano was to organize and present Harold Washington to the Mexican community at the second mayor's neighborhood festival the following month. Harold Washington's campaign theme was "Neighborhoods vs. Downtown." The Puerto Rican Diaspora Coalition (consisting of mostly Young Lords, later) and I were among the first Latinos to support Harold. I started out as a North Side "Hispanic" precinct coordinator with the office located at Fullerton and Western. Later, the Reverend Jorge Morales and the West Town Concerned Citizens Coalition joined in.

The first Puerto Rican rally was held at the Northwest Hall on Western and North Avenue. About 1,000 people attended. Then, I introduced Harold and spoke about getting kicked out of Lincoln Park and Lake Michigan and forced to swim in a lagoon at Humboldt Park.

After Rudy Lozano was murdered, my family and I stayed at Sal del Rivero's house for almost a week until things cleared or were safe. The rally and campaign were victories in 1983. Some don't want it told because they did not work on that campaign or were working with Daley. It was a people's victory—the Young Lords and the community achieved it—and it is a continuation of our protracted struggle. Here is the speech I made on that day (edited by Sal del Rivero and Mario Arcola).

José "Cha Cha" Jiménez

You, the youth of our community, some of whom have been misunderstood, forced to live under inhumane conditions, beaten by police, manipulated by everyone and then, blamed all. You, the youth of our community are our future leaders and you will get us what we want. And what do we want? Auto-determinación para los puertorriqueños—self-determination for the Puerto Rican people. And please, stop treating our freedom fighters who have martyred their lives for our rights as animals. The Puerto Rican Diaspora Coalition will not tolerate it.

If the people of Ireland can ask for self-determination;

If the people of Poland can ask for self-determination;

If the people of El Salvador can ask for self-determination;

If Black people in America can stand up and demand self-determination,

Then Puerto Ricans DEMAND SELF-DETERMINATION.

Y con eso en mente—les presento el major alcalde en toda la historia de Chicago—Mayor Harold Washington.

SATURDAY APRIL 22,95
8:PM

YOUNG LORDS ORG.
IN CONJUNCTION WITH
DE PAUL UNIVERSITY
ANNOUNCES
PRIVATE SHOWING OF
YOUNG LORDS
PHOTO EXHIBIT

2620 West North Avenue
862-3854

$10 DONATION
HORS D'OEUVRES ENTERTAINMENT

ALL PROCEEDS GO TOWARD COMPLETION
OF YOUNG LORDS FILM PROJECT

Young Lords Photo Exhibit with DePaul University at Rico's
April 22, 1995
Personal collection

Tengo Puerto Rico en mi corazón (1995)
Thirty-fifth anniversary poster, featuring Pedro Albizu Campos
Artist: Mario
Personal collection

Young Lord Opens Activists' Camp

Press release, February 18, 2003
Personal collection

JOSE (CHA-CHA) JIMENEZ
LINCOLN PARK CAMP
P.O. BOX 6932
GRAND RAPIDS, Ml 49516-6932
TOLL FREE: 1-888-886-CAMP
AFTER 9 P.M EASTERN
FOR IMMEDIATE RELEASE

YOUNG LORD OPENS ACTIVISTS' CAMP

Grand Rapids, Ml. Feb. 18, 2003—A new camp retreat to enrich the public about the LAND GRAB that continues to Gentrify Latino strongholds, and SEGREGATE Chicago's downtown and the lakefront was announced today. The Lincoln Park Camp will sponsor a camp retreat:

August 8, 9, 10, 2003 near Grand Rapids, MI. in an undisclosed location due to unwarranted past harassment and repression by the Daley Machine via Red Squad, Gang Intelligence, States Attorney's Office, and Patronage Employees.

In announcing the camp, Jose (Cha-Cha) Jimenez founder of the Young Lords, stated that Mayor Richard Daley continues to plunder the poor by recruiting investors that break up Latino and poor neighborhoods and manipulate renters and owners out of PRIME DOWNTOWN and LAKEFRONT REAL ESTATE. Further Jimenez stated, under Daley's Master Plan, Chicago became the # 3 populated city and he is responsible for today's high rents and lost jobs by driving industry out of the city and by promoting SEGREGATION in Chicago. So "he can never fix it" with patronage handouts to individuals and grants to organizations because "he is the one who broke it." Any and all gains made within the Latino Community were made by the sweat and blood of Latino protests and indigenous leaders, not by Mayor Daley.

The main purpose of Lincoln Park Camp will be education and recreation: support thru networking; and the recognition of true community activists, involved in local and world issues such as: Puerto Rican self-determination, world peace, and neighborhood diversity.

Lincoln Park Camp was named after the Lincoln Park Police Riots of the '68 Democratic Convention and the Lincoln Park neighborhood where the first Puerto Rican immigrants to Chicago were completely kicked out via Daley's urban renewal, high rents, building inspectors, and sheriff's police. But this was not before [sit-ins], protests, marches, arrests, and deaths. The Rev. Bruce Johnson and his wife were both stabbed to death.

The Young Lords became part of the first Rainbow Coalition that included Fred Hampton's Black Panthers and Young Patriots. Later In 1975, Jimenez' aldermanic race became the first Latino campaign to challenge the Daley Machine in the 46th ward garnering 39% of the vote. In June 1983, Jimenez introduced Mayor Harold Washington before 100,000 Puerto Ricans in Humboldt Park. And today, DePaul University's Center for Latino Research is archiving this era with the assistance of Young Lords and the Lincoln Park Camp.

The Lincoln Park Camp is not for profit but it is self-reliant. Last years' planning meeting included members of the Young Lords, prominent community leaders, and professors and students. About 70 people attended. This year the goal is 120.

LINCOLN PARK CAMP

To celebrate the
Lincoln Park Movement
within an educational,
social, and recreational
setting; establish lasting
friendships; and commit to
improve ourselves and the
community

STOP

TERRORISM

SUPPORT SELF-RULE

END DALEY'S

RE-SEGREGATION

Stop Terrorism, Support Self-Rule (ca. 2003)
Poster from Lincoln Park Camp
Personal collection

5.

THE ART OF PROTEST

CULTURE AND ARTIVISM

Carlos Flores, Photography (1969–1970)

Carlos Flores began his photography career around 1968 while attending an Argonne National Laboratory job-training program, where he worked and prepared for his GED. The Flores family was one of the first Puerto Rican families to settle in Lincoln Park. A former member of the Continentals gang, he later joined the Young Lords as a rank-and-file "Rally Lord," using his skills to document Puerto Rican Chicago. His work includes the murals on the People's Church, organized by Chicana playwright and activist Felícitas Nuñez, which are considered the first political murals by Latinxs in Chicago. Photograph by Carlos Flores, ca. 1969. Courtesy of Carlos Flores collection.

Young Lords were deeply rooted in Lincoln Park, where they grew up and formed strong ties within the community. Top: Young Lords Judy Pacheco, Margie Figueroa, and Hilda Ortiz greet friend José "Priest" García. Bottom: Young Lords Joe "Cosmo" Torres (standing), Joe Nieves (seated center), and Benny Perez holding baby. Early 1970s. Photographs by Carlos Flores.

Carlos's sisters Carmen and Mirna Flores (left and right, with their friend Chavela in the center) also joined the "Rally Lords," volunteering in YLO survival programs and participating in protests, 1971–1972. Photograph by Carlos Flores.

Carlos, a passionate music enthusiast, also documented the Latin music and social scenes of the era. In this image, Marta Rodríguez, known as "Martita," performs at a Latino Student Movement event wearing a Young Lords beret and buttons at the University of Illinois, ca. 1973, using her music to inspire and energize the crowd. Photograph by Carlos Flores.

Luis Arévalo, Photography (1969–1970)

Luis Arévalo, a Young Lord and unofficial photographer, captured key moments such as the May 1969 takeover of McCormick Seminary. Supported by seminarians, the Young Lords and allies under the Poor People's Coalition occupied the Stone Administration Building, renamed the Manuel Ramos Memorial Building, for nearly a week, demanding funding for low-income housing and community programs. Opposite page: Cha Cha Jiménez and "Loca," a Young Lord from California, led hundreds of protesters calling for the arrest of the police officer who fatally shot Young Lord Manuel Ramos in spring 1969. Photographs by Luis Arévalo. Courtesy of DePaul University, Richardson Library Special Collections.

MANUEL RAMOS

The Manuel Ramos rally, like most YLO marches, began in Lincoln Park, bringing together allies from the Black Panthers, Young Patriots, street organizations like the Latin Kings, and many other community members. Photograph by Luis Arévalo.

Judy Waldman, one of the dedicated medical students who helped form the Health Ministry of the Young Lords Organization, volunteering at the Emeterio Betances Health Center at the People's Church. Photograph by Luis Arévalo.

Compañera Puertorriqueña

Cáno
Y.L.O. vol. 1, no. 5, January 1970, p. 10
Young Lords Newspaper Electronic Collection
Special Collections and Archives
DePaul University, Chicago, Illinois

Y.L.O. QUISIERA DEDICAR SU SECCION
DE VERSOS AL GRAN POETA REVOLUCIONARIO
PUERTORRIQUENO JUAN ANTONIO
CORRETJER Y SU ESPOSA CONSUELO

Quiero dedicar estos versos a todas
Nuestras hermanas que historicamente
Han luchado y siguen luchando por
La Gloriosa Liberación de nuestra
Madre Patria, Borinquen.

Compañera Puertorriqueña

Mi lucha es tuya
Tu lucha es mía
Lo que importa es
Calor
Valor
Mucha camaradería!
Por ahora no podremos vernos.
Tu estaras lejos
También yo.
Sufriras
También yo sufriré.
Amor de Revolucionario!
Veo claramente el amanecer
De un nuevo día!
Yo estaré en ti pensando
Y a veces hasta soñando

Y cuando estés en las calles
O allá en el campo
Por Nuestro Pueblo luchando...
Alcanzaré tus claros pensamientos
Y los uniré
Con los míos de vez en cuando.

Compañeros de Lucha

Habib Tiwoni
Y.L.O. vol. 1, no. 5, January 1970, p. 10
Young Lords Newspaper Electronic Collection
Special Collections and Archives
DePaul University, Chicago, Illinois

(For Don Pedro Albizu Campos)

As a boy of fourteen
Playing Ball on the streets
Of Caparra Tierra, I
First heard your name,
Don Pedro Albizu Campos.

Riding through the streets of
Manatí, our bus was stopped
And searched in your name,
Don Pedro Albizu Campos.

As a man of twenty-seven,
I saw your face just once,
But brief. And now, I see
You again in the faces of
The Young Lords

Wet and Angry with the
Warm massacred blood of
Un revolucionario Manuel Ramos,
They come from todas ciudades
In Estados Unidos.

They come, resuelvemente por
Luchar, and they shout "Presente!"
Yes these sons and daughters of
Las montañas, las sierras, y los llanos
Have not forgotten su sacrificio
Don Pedro.

These sons and daughters of
Lolita Lebron, Oscar Collazo,
Blanca Canales, Torresola and
Octavio Ramos Rosario.
These descendants of Juan Antonio
Corretjer, Ramón Emeterio Betances,
Pelegrin García and Compañero
Ruben Malavé, have not forgotten
El Massacre de Ponce (1937) nor
El Grito de Lares in (1868).

And now, history must reckon
With the poor of America Latina.
And they are here, armed with
Ideología, machetes, pistolas, flags
And banners unfurling in the
Winds, and they say to America
"Abajo los asesinos!"
"Viva la Republica!"
"Viva Puerto Rico Libre!"

Young Lords Song

(ca. 1973–1974)
David Hernández and Bob Gibson
Courtesy of José "Cha Cha" Jiménez personal collection

Chorus:
And together we can change it
Turn it round and rearrange it
Hand in hand . . . hand in hand
There's a new day dawning in our land

Repeat chorus

People have you heard the news
City Hall has got the Blues
People dancing in the streets
United to a mighty beat

Chorus

People in the neighborhood
Working for the common good
No more roaches ni casas frias
Ni abuso de policia

Chorus

A new barrio we will grow
Urban renewal means we must go
But we're free to mold tomorrow
To build hope and end the sorrow

Chorus

People have you heard the news
City Hall has got the Blues
People dancing in the streets
United to a mighty beat

Chorus

The Dawning of a New Day / El amanecer de un nuevo dia

(ca. 1974)
Campaign song
Courtesy of José "Cha Cha" Jiménez personal collection

People have you heard the news?
City hall has got the Blues
Uptown dancing in the street
Cha-Cha to a mighty beat.

And together we can change it

Chorus

Turn it around and rearrange it;
Hand in hand and hand in hand
New Day Dawning in our land.

Families and neighborhoods
Working for the common good;
People stay machines must go
Nightly yes, but Daley no.

Chorus

We the people like the sun
Shining out on everyone
United we are here to stay
The Dawning of a brand new day.

Chorus

They're always taking, never giving
Tearing down the homes we live in
In the shadows in the dimness
Building profits for their business.

Chorus

Vendrá un Nuevo Día
No more roaches en casa fria

Politicians don't you know
Estamos aqui and you gotta go.

Chorus

We won't move and we won't go
City Hall we tell you so
If you don't or won't believe us
We will show you we mean business.

Chorus

We Shall Not Be Moved

(n.d.)
YLO protest song
Courtesy of José "Cha Cha" Jiménez personal collection

Chorus [Repeat 2X]:
We shall not, we shall not be moved
We shall not, we shall not be moved
Just like the tree that's standing by the water
We shall not be moved

We're fighting for our freedom, we shall not be moved
We're fighting for our freedom, we shall not be moved
Just like the tree that's standing by the water we shall not be moved

Chorus

Boricuas y Mejicanos, we shall not be moved
Latino americanos, we shall not be moved
Just like the tree that's standing by the water
We shall not be moved

Chorus

There's power in our barrios, we shall not be moved
There's power in our barrios, we shall not be moved
Just like the tree that's standing by the water we shall not be moved

Chorus

Our barrios know no boundaries, we shall not be moved
Our barrios know no boundaries, we shall not be moved
Just like the tree that's standing by the water
We shall not be moved

Chorus

The people in my heart, we shall not be moved
El pueblo en mi corazon, we shall not be moved
Just like the tree standing that's standing by the water
We shall not be moved

Chorus

Power to the People—In Art

(1969)
John Weber
Excerpt, *The Black Panther Community News Service*
Reprinted from *People's World* vol. 3, no. 28, November 1969, pp. 16–17

The next time you're in this celebrated city, take a look at what used to be a filthy vacant lot next to St. Dominic's Church at the corner of Locust and Sedgwick.

Early in the summer the lot was cleared, a cement playing court made and grass sod laid. We began thinking about the wall. There were also about a dozen boarded-up windows to be painted.

At first people were slow about suggestions: "Anything is all right with me" was the refrain. But as soon as the ice was broken, Black Power was immediately agreed upon as the theme. After a good deal of discussion around the idea of a realistic portrayal of ghetto life, a more symbolic portrayal of the black liberation struggle was chosen. Somebody suggested portraits of black heroes. This idea was accepted right away. There was, curiously, no hesitation about the choice—Malcolm X, Frederick Douglass and Huey P. Newton. Later, Erika Huggins was added. I presented a design proposal, which was modified by Kenney Webster (an art major at a local high school). The content of the mural was entirely based on the ideas of the young people at St. Dominic's.

The teenagers and children of the neighborhood accepted the mural enthusiastically, following its progress day by day. As the work proceeded, more and more of them asked to participate in its execution and they did. In the groups watching the painters, older children would explain the symbols and the heroes to their younger brothers and sisters—pointing out the police (pigs), the black heroes, and reading the "All Power to the People" slogan . . .

I believe the project was significant beyond its obvious value in giving the residents of the neighborhood an artistic representation of their own struggles and in giving a number of young people some enjoyable afternoons and their first chance to participate in making a work of art. It showed that it is not only possible but easy to involve inexperienced teenagers and subteens in a large-scale collective art project. Secondly, public art is rare in today's America and political art is even rarer. Collective art also runs against the grain in our "every man for himself" society. Every such project is significant for this reason alone.

And there is more People's art in Chicago. . . . The Young Lords Organization have decorated their church inside and out and the People's Park is being equipped with the participation of well-known sculptors, such as Mark di Suvero—whose sculpture is popular with the kids.

Art with overt political or social themes is suppressed by the white upper-middle class control of art patronage, by the dominance of commercial art in society as a whole, and by a conspiracy of silence. It has also been hurt among artists by the old, completely false idea that so-called "social realism" is the one style of art which is compatible with social revolutionary themes. But if the connoisseurs disdain "propaganda" art, the youth of the Cabrini-Green area accept this work, modernist, symbolic, and, I hope, fairly high quality, because it expresses their concerns, their own ideas.

Hanging Play Sculpture / People's Park

(1969)
Mark di Suvero

Renowned sculptor Mark di Suvero, celebrated for his monumental steel works and radical politics, joined forces with the Young Lords and local residents to create three large-scale swinging play sculptures for People's Park. Built from salvaged materials, the structures invited children to climb, swing, and reimagine the space as their own. Though the sculptures were eventually destroyed, they remain a powerful example of creative resistance and collective vision. Photographer unknown. Courtesy of the artist and Spacetime C.C. © Mark di Suvero.

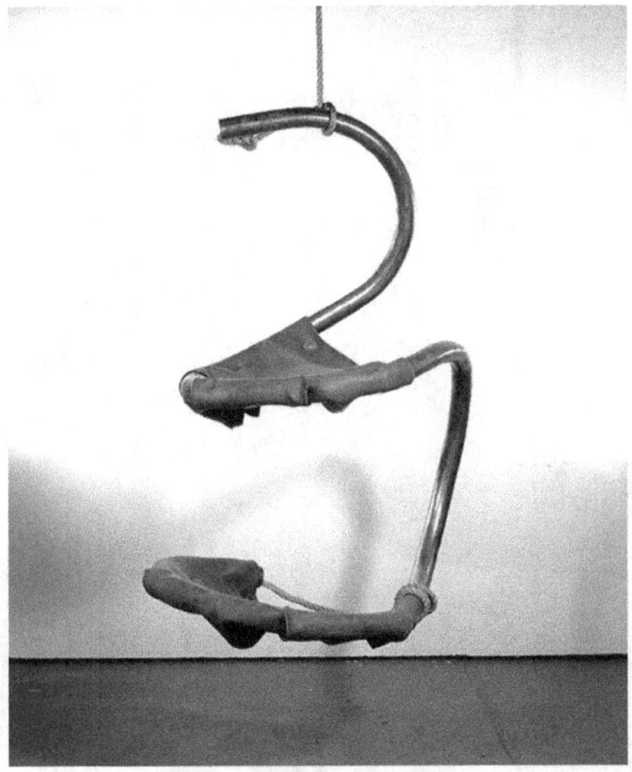

Steel, rope, and painted rubber. Studio reproduction of the work installed in People's Park, Chicago, 1969.

PEOPLES PARK

Children playing on Mark di Suvero's *Hanging Play Sculpture*, 1969 (destroyed).

Fuertes Somos Ya!

(1971)
John Pitman Weber
Courtesy of the Segundo Ruiz Belvis Cultural Center, Chicago, Illinois

Fuertes Somos Ya!, 1971. Created for the Latin American Defense Organization, this mural stands as the first known public artwork to depict the Young Lords. Originally exhibited in *Murals for the People* at the Museum of Contemporary Art Chicago, it is shown here at the exhibition *Tengo Lincoln Park en Mi Corazón: The Young Lords in Chicago*, curated by Jacqueline Lazú. Photo: Bernardo da Costa Soares, DePaul Art Museum, 2025.

People's Church Murals

(1969)

Chicana playwright and Rally Lord Felícitas Nuñez led the project and painted many of the building's historic facade murals, considered the first political murals by a Latinx in Chicago, and depicting Latin American revolutionaries such as Albizu Campos, Betances, Lebrón, and an "Adelita de Aztlán." Other Young Lords and activist artists also contributed to the murals, including Ron Clark, who is cited in some accounts as having participated, and Mark Rogovin, who painted the Che Guevara portrait and the YLO National Headquarters sign. Historical photos: Murals documented by photographer Carlos Flores, ca. 1969.

"No queremos colonia
ni bajo España
ni bajo Los Estados Unidos"
"¿Que hacen los
Puertorriqueños que
no se rebelan?
Ramon Emeterio Betances
PADRE de La PATRIA

simbolo del sacrificio por la
PATRIA LIBRE
LOLITA LEBRON

Felícitas Nuñez in 2018 with a photograph of her iconic murals.

Murals by the members of the Young Lords inside the People's Church childcare center blended culture, politics, and play. *Y.L.O.* vol. 1, no. 4, February–March 1970, p. 4. Courtesy of DePaul University Special Collections and Archives, Richardson Library Digital Collection.

Latin Eagles Mural at Wilton and Grace

(ca. 1972)
Gamaliel Ramírez

Around 1972, the YLO moved their headquarters to Wilton and Grace in Lakeview, home to another Puerto Rican community and gangs like the Latin Eagles, Spanish Lords, and Young Lords. The Latin Eagles enlisted young artist Gamaliel Ramírez to paint a mural after rivals tagged their corner. With the support of the YLO, Gamaliel completed his first large-scale mural on the wall of Plaza Aponte Restaurant, launching his career as a renowned muralist and close Young Lords affiliate. Photos from Cha Cha Jiménez's personal collection. Photographer unknown.

Poetry

Alfredo Matías, YLO Minister of Finance
Courtesy of José "Cha Cha" Jiménez personal collection

Introduction: Characters of My Poetry (undated)

The characters of my poetry originate in my
Anti-this and that.
Poets have the tendency to explore the mind
And *that* makes us psychologists.
We speak of rivers to explain a teardrop,
Out of the ruins of a thought we create a poem,
Just for the hell of it.
That's frequently perceived by others as
The idiom of poets'
Artistic creation out of colloquialism
Configuration, a-la-jo-jo-jo-ha-ha-ha,
Noteworthy to the national book award
Pulitzer Prize.
But you must wait your time, *third-world* thinkers.
In other words, inner city dwellers, take it easy
Don't be so pushy.
After all, have you ever seen a black angel?
So stop the plebian masquerade
And stay in your place among the you know what.
Hollywood doesn't want you
You cannot merge with the
You know what.

Faith in the American System (undated)

Faith in the American system is to cry over 50
Hostages in Iran and meanwhile down at Cook County
Jail, red-blooded, all-American hostages wait for trial
In the so-called "People of the State vs. John Doe."

Big deal if John Doe didn't get no mail for Christmas.
He didn't need it anyway.

Untitled
(1987)

Division Street it divided the very poor the very rich
West and East, North and South
You know what it is all about
Black stand back white alright
And if you speak of Humboldt Park
Humboldt Park is not that humble after all
Division Street, Ho Ho
What a split
It divides the very poor the very rich
A wall to wall concentration camp
You look East and it's heaven without a doubt
You look West and it's depression time
Mother Cabrini's children living in hell
Division Street the dream
Division Street the nightmare
Like I said it divides the very poor the very rich
Division Street, Division Street . . .

Untitled
(1990)

Black writers have a responsibility to set
The record straight
We are not of Cinderella or Snow White
And the Seven Dwarf story
We have got to tie our story
And tales to all the Sojourner truth
The Harriet Tubman of the world
Black writers in South Africa
Puerto Rico, America or any other part of the world
Got one thing in common
We are all products of the master

And slave story
We got responsibility
To set the record straight
Writer has got to keep society
On it's toes
The thorny wheels of history will not
Do you justice
So your quest is the truth
And nothing but the truth so help you God
So sacrifice rhyme
Cast adrift your alliance to the land
Of the fruit and nuts
I mean ally yourself with friends
And neighbors regardless of personal consequences
And the truth should set you free

Untitled
(undated)

The flower children wilted away like all flowers.
They bloomed one spring, they were beautiful, and like all flowers,
they wilted into oblivion or into history.
One summer of love, one summer of life, and that was all.
The flower children wilted, a dead flower.
Generations grew in the American garden,
I was there too, like a bumble bee.
And like the decade of the 60s, they are a thing of the past.
They die from too many parties
Too much drug-filled nights
Too many sunny afternoons in the park doing nothing.
Suddenly it was all over.
The hippies are a "thang" of the past
No more flower children
Just plain thorns
Feeding squirrels in the parks
To hell with the Panthers, the Young Lords and SDS
Rising up angry.

Here squirrel, squirrel, squirrel
Come get your nuts.
And my question is
"What happened to the flower children?"
Did they simply wilt into existence or into oblivion seedless?"
Or did they simply become red-blooded BMW, Mercedes,
Jaguar-driving "Americans?"
Or are they getting ready to bloom into the year 2000 with new buds?
Or will they bloom into plastic memories of flowers?

Décima: Boricuas de Lincoln Park

(2002)
José "Cha Cha" Jiménez
Courtesy of José "Cha Cha" Jiménez personal collection

Para su mamá, Eugenia Rodríguez
Día de las Madres, mayo 12, 2002

1
A FINES DE AÑOS CUARENTAS
A FINES DE AÑOS CUARENTAS
SE ENBARCAN LOS TOMATEROS
Y A CHICAGO DAN UN VUELO
EN BUSCA DE LAS RIQUESAS

EN DOWNTOWN CON SUS MALETAS
SE PARAN A PROCREAR
POR LA MADISON Y POR LA CLARK
PUESTAN A CHINOS Y LOTERIA
A MISA VAN CON FAMILIA
BORICUAS DE LINCOLN PARK

2
BODEGAS DAN RESTAURANTES
BODEGAS DAN RESTAURANTES
BEISBOL DA LOS CLUBS SOCIALES
CON PARADA-REINA Y BAILES
BORINQUEN ECHA PALANTE

RACISMO TARDO SU AVANCE
UN PATRONATO COLONIAL
DESPLAZAN PA'RENOVAR
SU DOWNTOWN Y CERCA EL LAGO
SE REVELAN EN CHICAGO
BORICUAS DE LINCOLN PARK

3
DESAYUNO-CON-MEDICINAS
DESAYUNO-CON-MEDICINAS
PROGRAMAS QUE MARCHAN YOUNG LORDS
PUERTO RICO EN MI CORAZON
POR LAS CALLES MAS PERDIDAS

TRATAN TODAS LAS MEDIDAS
EL BARRIO QUERIAN SALVAR
NO TENIAN MIEDO LUCHAR
Y FUERON INVESTIGADOS
POR LOS GUARDIAS DE CHICAGO
BORICUAS DE LINCOLN PARK

4
SUS VIDAS FUERON OFRENDAS
SUS VIDAS FUERON OFRENDAS
QUE IMPACTO A GRANDES MENTES
INSCRIBIO MILES VOTANTES
Y ABRIO TODAS LAS PUERTAS

ESA BATALLA HONESTA
DALEY LA QUIZO APLASTAR

NO LA DEJA RESPETAR
POR TRASLADAR MAS BORINCANOS
PARA SIEMPRE RECORDAMOS
BORICUAS DE LINCOLN PARK

Madre de Corazón

(2002)
Felícitas Nuñez
Lincoln Park Camp, unpublished play
Courtesy of Felícitas Nuñez

This skit was written for September 21, 2002, and performed at the Lincoln Park Camp. The skeleton of the skit was divided into five scenes and opened for changes. The parts played by youngsters came from Michigan's youth program, community members of Chicago and the women's teatro group from California.

José Jiménez, who was one of the main organizers of the Young Lords in 1968, also planned this Lincoln Park event to pay tribute to the dedication of various leaders who fought and continue to fight with hearts of love.

Scene I, "In the Wild," is about an old woman who seems to live in the forest and four youngsters who decide to go to the forest for a day and get lost.

Scene II, "City Planning," involves four characters shaping society: a politician, media person, landowner and real estate agent. (All wear white hoods and empty heart.)

Scene III, "City Home," begins with a wife and husband at home, talking at the dinner table. They are going into their twenty-fifth year of marriage, but urban renewal seems to be interfering with plans to rejoice in this union. Then come Las Comadres to visit with their friend, the wife. The husband is already on the way out. They all continue the talk on urban renewal. The TV is turned on so the newscaster (who has no heart) reports a couple of events with a commercial in between that advertises credit as a way of life.

Scene IV, "City Streets," shows Las Comadres going on a cruise to see for themselves the history of what urban renewal has done. They end up going to eat ice cream while talking about the future.

Scene V, "Back to Nature," ends with the old woman guiding the youngsters from the wild of nature on their journey toward the home of the heart.

MADRE DE CORAZÓN

FELÍCITAS NUÑEZ

Scene I:

(An old woman is in the forest, sound of a wolf in the distance. Several youngsters who are bewildered approach the gray-haired figure who smokes her pipe. Some branches portray a forest, and a lit candle encircled with twigs represent a campfire.)

Youngster #1: What are you smoking, witch?
(Attitude: smart snob.)

Youngster #2: Don't speak to her like that. She could be your grandma.
(Attitude: compassionate.)

Youngster #1: This bag! No way, she ain't my Nana!
(Attitude: smart snob.)

Old Woman: You tell me who I may be. What is going through your mind and your heart depends on whether I could be or could not be loved like your Nana.

Youngster #3: You sound like, "To be or not to be."
(Attitude: comedian.)

Youngster #4: Yeh, like that guy Cheesecake.
(Attitude: management.)

Youngster #1: You mean, Shakespeare, idiot.
(Attitude: smart snob.)

(Old Woman gets up off the floor to exit.)

Youngster #2: Stop labeling and name calling. Wait! Old lady, where are you going?
(Attitude: compassionate.)

Old Woman: I'm going to see about some business.

Youngster #3: You are coming back?

Old Woman: I may. I may not.

(The Old Woman exits and youngsters focus on each other.)

Youngster #3: There she goes again like . . .

Youngster #4: Shut up. (Gives #3 a nudge to stop talking.)

Youngster #1: (To Youngster #3) Idiot, because of you we don't have any music. Your batteries ran out this morning.

Youngster #3: Oh yeh, you are the biggest idiot because you forgot the compass! And now we are lost!

Youngster #4: Come on, you guys. (Comes between #3 and #1) What we need to do is figure out our direction.

Youngster #3: I agree, maybe that old woman can help us out.

Youngster #1: That bag of bones! If she returns, and then she could also be an idiot.

Youngster #3: Could be. Could be not.

(#1 gives #3 a push; #4 steps between both again).

Youngster #2: We can ask her?

Youngster #1: What! And then we'll look like idiots in front of her!

Youngster #2: So what? It's better to get back on our journey.

Youngster #4: Right! Let's find her. We must journey back to the city and our families.

Scene II:

(Everyone exits and stage is set up with a table and four chairs.)

(Enter: the landowner, real estate, media, and politician. They have a white hood over their head and a heart with a big hole.)

Politician: We are gathered here to determine where we are going next with our plans to make the city of Chicago more prosperous.

Landowner: Yes we have managed to make Lincoln Park, Wicker Park, and all lakefront property attractive to attractive people. In other words, we have taken the scum out and cleaned part of the city.

Media: Yes, and we must continue to clean the streets of scum bags by publicizing the "war against gangs," relaxing the flow of drugs and unpublished crime in the community.

Real Estate: Right, tripling the rents is a great way to start unrest, red lining and most important, discrediting and corrupting honest community leaders.

Politician: We are now focusing on the area of Humboldt Park and its scum. So, let's get ready.

(They tear away more pieces of their heart. All four persons exit leaving table and chairs set up for next scene.)

Scene III:

(The table has a cloth, a vase of flowers, and a TV set with a family picture sitting on top of it. The wife and husband sit together in their home. TV is an empty square, cloth on the bottom and propped to stand.)

Wife: Bueno, corazón, do you think we can afford to celebrate our 25th anniversary at Humboldt Park with friends and family?

Husband: If we sold our home for the high price being offered, we could have a big, classy party.

Wife: Corazón, I don't want to sell our home. This is where all the people we love, and grandchildren can come and be with us.

Husband: Then how are we going to deal with the harassment by city police, fire, and building inspectors? We need money to make our home measure up to the new building codes.

Wife: Haven't we always found a way to make our dreams real with the toil and labor of our hands and our bodies?

Husband: Yes, but how much more hard toil and labor can our hands and our bodies take before our energy and health goes?

Wife: You are being negative!

Husband: And you think you can come up with a solution?
(He is walking out of the room and enter Las Comadres to visit.)

Wife: Maybe together we can work out a solution?

Comadre #1: What's wrong with him?

Wife: Oh, he's not in a good mood and most likely on his way to the local bar with his compadres.

Comadre #4: Have you heard the news? There has been fires and murders in the neighborhood and no one has been caught.

Wife: Turn on the TV.

TV Reporter: (Reporter wears a heart with a hole in it.) Today, this morning, an elderly woman was found stabbed in the heart and died in her residence in front of Humboldt Park. It is said she had been holding a kind of arts and crafts class in her garage for children after hours. She was a retired teacher, and felt youth needed more social programs to keep them out of trouble and out of the streets. It is ironic to think that her actions have been repaid in this manner. We have no suspects as of yet. Her name was Joanna Ellma.

Wife: She means Juanita Alma! This is very sad news, Juana Alma was loved by all of us. Who will take her place? Bless her sacred soul.

(Everyone comments the sad loss and are frozen in sadness while a commercial about credit card comes on. The sound of a heart with a drumbeat in the background is heard.)

Commercial: Ever find yourself in need of money to buy, buy, buy, things, more things, and many desired things? This card called Alma Search, search is the way to live and find yourself at last. This card will buy anything in your soul desires, big cars, faster computers, the latest fashions and more. Call us at 1-800-FOR-Alma, hablamos Español. Call now and the first 50 pendejos will be rewarded an extra $50. Get your ALMA-Search Card today!

TV Reporter: Addressing the war on gangs is one of the main concerns of all public officials. It is a known fact that poverty breeds the kind of gangs that are destructive to a prosperous growing city. Higher officials in government and respectable landowning citizens are working day and night to resolve growing number of gangs in the Humboldt area. The "arson fires" may be the result of vandalism . . .

Wife: Please, turn it off. I can't bear all this negative issues.

Comadre #3: I know what you mean, I have to move my family because my rent has been raised.

Comadre #4: The concept of urban renewal is good. It brings in more hospitals, and universities, and the buildings are greatly improved.

Comadre #3: How can improvement be wrong? My apartment has been with bad plumbing, infested with rodents and insects for years. I would have loved for this renewal, rebuilding, and remodeling to have taken place a long time ago, but with affordable rents. Unfortunately, renovation is dumping me!

Comadre #4: I would love to live close to better and higher education for my children. As a single parent I have labored hard, but it is not enough. I would love to be trained for a good paying job.

Wife: In my heart there has to be a better way for all of us.

Comadre #1: I say, let's take our hearts for a historical ride.

(All four women seem to go along with the idea. They exit. The table and TVs are pulled to the side; four chairs are arranged like a vehicle, center stage.)

Scene IV:

(Wife and comadres re-enter.)

Comadre #3: This is my new car I bought with the Alma card.

Comadre #1: It must be a classic model. (Reacts to unstable chair)

Comadre #3: Well, I'm paying high interest on it, so yes, it is classic.

(Rest of comadres make comments on the car and get in it. #3 is the driver, #1 sits in front and #4 and wife sit in the back. #3 is wild but cautious and #1 sits a bit higher to speak to her comadres. Driver is struggling to get car started then it gets accelerated.)

Comadre #1: Drive towards the Lincoln Park area. Oh no!

(BUMP on the road)

Comadre #3: (yelling) My hemorrhoids!

(All except driver hold their body parts and state them.)

Comadre #1: My cabeza!

Comadre #4: My pansa!

Wife: Mis pulmones!

(The car ride gets smoother; everyone shakes upper body comfortably.)

Comadre #1: As I was saying, this at one time was a Puerto Rican community, full of hard-working people. Industry was in full swing but then as the workers started to get organized for better working and living conditions industry started running away from organized workers.

Wife: What is wrong with industrial work being done by organized workers?

Comadre #1: With organized workers, owners of industry don't make as much profit although conditions are better for the majority. The owners of industry have hearts filled with greed.

Comadre #3: So, where did these hearts of greed go?

(Car makes a right turn. Everyone in car motions to the right.)

Comadre #1: These owners of industry went to locations where the working families were not organized and accepted poor wages and working conditions.

Comadre #4: And with poor working conditions the land is also destroyed because with cheap production there are no conscious measures or laws to preserve the wild land.

Wife: I can see this Lincoln City neighborhood is very nice.

Comadre #3: Yes, but only a small number of the original Puerto Ricans live here. Many working families were evicted and escorted out of their housing by sheriff's police.

Comadre #1: At the time, gang members were involved in the relocation of these evicted families.

Wife: You mean like the delinquent gangs that the news was covering on TV today? How?

Comadre #1: Well, these gang members first started out by trashing the urban renewal. And later they learned nonviolent means to protest against the displacement of the working families. Right here on Halsted and Armitage.

STOP for the ball!

(Driver comes to a screeching stop and everyone goes forward, jamming into the front. All the comadres complain. Ball bounces on the stage. They figure out that a child might be running after the ball.)

Comadre #1: As I was saying right here on Halsted and Armitage tents were pitched in about 400 community residents camped in protest.

Comadre #3: Going back to gangs, I heard these gang members set up a People's Park for the children, converted a church into a People's Clinic that once had the painted mural of Adelita de Aztlán. The roots of our Mexican heritage. Que viva la mujer!

(Driver turns around to face back and everyone freaks out.)

Wife: Watch where you're going!

Comadre #4: Ave Maria Purisima!

(#1 hits #3 on the shoulder.)

Comadre #1: And the other murals were of Emeterio Betances, Don Pedro Albizu Campos, Lolita Lebrón, and Ernesto "Che" Guevara.

Comadre #4: Didn't these youngsters also get the McCormick Seminary to give funding for low-income housing and a west side clinic? They also showed support for a People's Law Office.

(Car makes a left turn. Everyone in car motions to the left.)

Wife: Did you say these were gang members?

Comadre #3: Yes and–

(Driver turns to face the back seaters; comadres react)

Comadres #1, #3, and #4, Wife: (yelling) Mira por donde vas!!!

Comadre #1: They were called Young Lords, and I heard that the women were and still are a symbol of strength. But la FUERZA of this foundation stemmed from working families in the community and members of organizations like LADO—Latin American Defense Organization, PROPA—Puerto Rican Organization for Political Action, SAC—Spanish Action Committee, Casa Central, y Los Caballeros de San Juan. Right here on Division Street.

(THREE SHORT BRAKES for BALL. Driver keeps eyes on the road and does three short breaks before stopping for another ball. Everyone motions jerks of the three small brakes in comments that a kid could be behind the ball.)

Comadre #1: As I was saying right here on Division Street riots broke out when Arcelis Cruz was gunned down by police officers. The community as a whole came out and joined forces to bring PEACE and also demand JUSTICE.

Comadre #4: I heard other groups like the Black Panthers of California, the Young Lords, Young Patriots, Students for a Democratic Society and many community forces joined in a Rainbow Coalition.

Wife: This whole neighborhood has so much history. What history are we going to make in our community?

Comadre #4: Sí, ¿qué historia vamos hacer en nuestra comunidad?

(Sign, Margie's Ice Cream Place, appears on side stage.)

Comadre #3: I am parking here. That's it! The famous ice cream place! I have to have an ice cream!

Comadre #4: Wait aren't most all those Puerto Ricans inside the place?

Wife: They look friendly, maybe we can get to meet some of them.

Comadre #4: Yes, we could get some insights on their lives.

Wife: We could learn from their experience.

Comadre #3: And we can eat lots of ice cream while we mingle.

Comadre #1: All right, let's go so I'll get home to my children at a decent hour.

Wife: Oh, yes, I agree, and I must tell my husband, children and everyone everything we have seen and heard today.

Comadre #4: As parents we must guide and stick close to our children.

Comadre #3: First I will eat my ice cream and later, look for my children and the children of my children.

Comadre #4: They are all, our children!

(All the comrades exit.)

Scene V:

(The vehicle is removed, branches put back onto stage. The old woman enters holding a basket of fruit, hums a tune, adds twigs to the fire and cleans the fruit. Wolf howls in the background. The lost youngsters enter as if afraid. They sigh with relief catching sight of the old woman.)

Old Woman: You're still here?

Youngster #1: Yeh, we are, huh . . . We are . . .

Old Woman: A little lost? Make yourselves comfortable for a while and I will guide you back to what is called civilization.

Youngster #4: Would you be so kind as to offer us some fruit?

Old Woman: Of course, child, here pass the basket.

Youngster #2: I knew or felt that you would take us into consideration.

Youngster #3: You, wouldn't turn us into frogs, would you?

Old Woman: I hear frog legs are pretty tasty. But thank your lucky stars I am a vegetarian.

Youngster #3: What is that?

Old Woman: Respect for nature like our bodies, the land, the howling of the wolf. Desires can be preciously replaced.

Youngster #1: What are those precious replacements?

Old Woman: For example, Harmony which in my case is spiritual survival. Then there's others like Truth, Compassion, and mostly, Love.

Youngster #4: These are feelings.

Youngster #2: In our city we are surrounded by feelings of greed for things.

Old Woman: Greed enters into a heart that bears no Love.

Youngster #3: Maybe, we should stay here in this wild land of love.

Old Woman: Your city was once a wilderness inhabited by the Native American Indians, who had great respect for the spirit of the land.

Youngster #2: We can't afford to live where we are at. My mother cries at night while we pretend to sleep in a land that will be sold for a higher price.

Youngster #1: At least you have a mother that cares for you.

Old Woman: I care for you; my mother cares for you.

(Wolf is heard howling in the background.)

Youngster #3: Call of the wild mother.

Youngster #4: The call of the wild loving mother.

Old Woman: That is indeed the call and the need to return our hearts to the land of our loving mother. Shall we continue on our Journey?

(Everyone gets up, looks around at nature; the wolf howls in the background.)

Youngster #2: (Gives #1 a hug) My mother, our mother, will be glad to know that we are safe. (#1 returns the hug to #2)

Youngster #3: I can't wait to be home and have some ice cream!

(The youngsters start picking up and helping the old woman with her articles.)

Youngster #4: What is your name?

Old Woman: My name is Juana Alma.

(Youngsters stare at her and stop movement.)

Old Woman: Come on, don't be afraid. Follow your hearts.

(Youngsters follow her out and exit. Stage is empty. Ball bounces, actors re-enter, and chant tune for "Who Let the Dogs Out?" with changed lyrics. Youngsters re-enter with drum and beat to the tune.)

Old Woman: Who let the ball go?

(All other actors repeat in chorus)

Old Woman: Who let the hearts down?

(All other actors repeat in chorus)

Old Woman: What can the hearts do?

(All other actors repeat in chorus)

Old Woman: Who wants to play ball?

(All other actors repeat in chorus)

Old Woman: Who wants to save hearts?

(All other actors repeat in chorus)

Old Woman: Come on and join love!

(All other actors repeat in chorus)

Old Woman: Hearts made of love, rise!

(All other actors repeat in chorus)

(Everyone stands and joins in the lively background music dancing of the wife and husband's 25th anniversary at Humboldt Park.)

All: ¡Que Vivan los Corazones!

All: ¡Que Viva el Amor!

All: ¡Que Viva el Pueblo de la Madre Tierra!

All: ¡Que Viva la Madre de Corazon!

Graphic design by Areli Lupercio, originally created around 2010 while she was a student at DePaul University. Developed through her coursework and research on the Young Lords in Lincoln Park, Lupercio's series honored the organization's history. Her reimagined YLO logo, centering women and Afro-Latino identities, was later adopted by Cha Cha Jiménez and the Young Lords in Michigan and used as the organization's logo during its fiftieth anniversary in 2018. Courtesy of the artist.

6.

MAPPING THE MOVEMENT

Latino Civil Rights Tour and Memorial Service Flyer (2013)
Grand Valley State University, September 23, 2013
Courtesy of José "Cha Cha" Jiménez personal collection

The Young Lords in Lincoln Park Tour

(2016)

Derek Potts, Archivist
DePaul University Library
Special Collections and Archives

Since 2016, I have had the honor and privilege of leading walking tours of the Lincoln Park neighborhood for groups of students and others who want to meditate on and engage with the history of the Young Lords Organization in Lincoln Park during the implementation of urban renewal in the late 1960s. DePaul University Special Collections and Archives preserves and provides access to historical materials related to the topic and from the time, including the Collection on the Young Lords, Lincoln Park Conservation Association records, Lincoln Park Community Conservation Council records, DePaul University records, and local newspapers. These primary sources are the basis for the walking tour, providing participants with visual evidence and information about significant activities and events the Young Lords were involved in.

José "Cha Cha" Jiménez, founder of the Young Lords, began the tradition of neighborhood tours in the mid-1990s when the Young Lords Organization partnered with DePaul through the Lincoln Park Project. He included these tours in every program organized with the university, particularly around YLO anniversaries. His tours often involved other Young Lords and allies who had significant roles in the events, sharing their memories and reflections at each stop. These tours were a type of "rally," occupying the streets of what is now a transformed neighborhood. Participants were led through spaces that, in most cases, no longer exist, requiring them to imagine the neighborhood as it was during the height of the Young Lords' activism. The tour I lead blends the original rally-style experience with a contemporary exploration of archival materials, offering reflections on the historical impact of urban renewal and displacement in Lincoln Park. It also emphasizes DePaul University's significant, yet often understated, role in this history—arguably the most impactful force in shaping the neighborhood's long-term development.

As part of DePaul Special Collections and Archives' instruction program, the first tour we developed was for Dr. Susana Martínez's liberal studies first-year class, "Explore Chicago Latino/a Writers." During a planning session with the instruction archivist at the time, Morgen MacIntosh Hodgetts, Martínez expressed a similar interest in students having the ability to "occupy" the same spaces and places that the Young Lords and allied community members chose as sites for demonstration and protest. As an assistant to the instruction session Morgen was leading, it became my task to create such a tour. Essentially, the class would meet with the Archives over two class periods—the first session in the library working hands-on with archives, the second session exploring Lincoln Park sites where the events took place. While elements of the tour have changed somewhat over time, the general history and narrative are largely the same.

SAC Pit / Schmitt Academic Center, DePaul University

We regularly begin the tour on DePaul's campus, with the first stop being the Schmitt Academic Center's "SAC Pit." As a gathering spot for students on the first floor of the Lincoln Park campus building, the Pit was the site where Steve Berry, chairman of DePaul's Black Student Union read the group's demands of the university on May 7, 1969. The brick seating area looks largely the same today, so it is relatively easy to identify from the photograph accompanying the article. Along with demands for Black Studies and increased representation on campus, the manifesto specifically aligned with the objectives of Concerned Citizens of Lincoln Park and other groups calling for a halt to DePaul's physical expansion and subsequent displacement of lower-income residents who were disproportionally people of color. When these demands were not met to the BSU's satisfaction on the following day, DePaul students took over, occupied, and locked down the SAC building in the early morning hours of May 9. When "white students attempted to forcibly gain entrance to SAC," the BSU enlisted the help of the Young Lords to provide security "in case of any further trouble."[19]

On our tour, participants can stand outside the doors of SAC where Cha Cha Jiménez and other Young Lords can be seen talking with students and others. After SAC was eventually reopened at noon that day, members of the Young Lords and Black Panthers, including Fred Hampton, were invited by the BSU to participate in a continued discussion. Tour

Left: BSU lists demands. *DePaulia*, May 19, 1969, p. 2.

Right: Fred Hampton speaks to DePaul BSU students. *DePaulia*, 1970, p. 38. DePaul University Special Collections and Archives, Chicago, Illinois.

participants are again able to interact with this space, a busy place where students continue to gather between a coffee shop and offices offering campus services. This stop ultimately offers an immediate opportunity to make a direct connection between DePaul, the Young Lords, and the coalition of community groups who were active in the Lincoln Park area. These same groups once again supported the BSU and their shared views at another meeting on May 14 with Lincoln Park residents and faculty.[20]

Photo: Young Lords in the crowd outside Schmitt Academic Center by S. Queira, May 9, 1969. DePaul Photographs, Box 12, Folder 13. DePaul University Special Collections and Archives, Chicago, Illinois.

Manuel Ramos Memorial Building / The Stone Academic Administration Building (Music North, DePaul University), 804 W. Belden Ave.

The next walking tour stop, at 804 W. Belden, also offers an opportunity to make direct and indirect connections between DePaul University and the Young Lords. Currently DePaul's Music North building, in 1969 the new Stone Administration Building was part of McCormick Theological Seminary. Much like the SAC Pit, one can still easily identify the location today as compared to a May 1969 photograph by Luis Arévalo showing the occupation of the building by Young Lords and community members (see page 237). On May 14, 1969, just days after supporting the occupation of a building on DePaul's campus, the Young Lords, alongside their allies under the banner of the Poor People's Coalition, seized the Stone Administration Building and held it for five days, pressing McCormick Theological Seminary to invest $601,000 in the Lincoln Park community to address critical needs such as affordable housing, daycare, and legal services. These demands included access to affordable housing, daycare, and legal resources.[21] Another of Arévalo's photographs shows a close-up of Cha Cha Jiménez and other Young Lords in front of a banner by the building entrance, renaming it the "Manuel Ramos Memorial Building" in honor of the Young Lord shot and killed by an off-duty police officer just ten days earlier.[22]

In September 2023, a permanent historical marker was installed at 804 W. Belden, marking the first such recognition in Chicago honoring the Young Lords. This installation was the result of a decades-long effort by members of the Young Lords Organization, along with faculty, staff, students, and alumni, all working to ensure this pivotal history would be officially recognized by DePaul University. The marker commemorates the Young Lords' fight against displacement in Lincoln Park, reflecting their broader struggle for justice, housing, and civil rights within Puerto Rican and Latinx communities. It serves as part of a larger initiative to preserve the memory of their activism and educate the public about their role in shaping the neighborhood's history during urban renewal efforts. The marker stands as a testament to their radical resistance against the forced displacement of working-class Puerto Rican families, a legacy that continues to resonate today.

Photographs of a YLO historical marker placed at the site of the old Stone Administration Building in 2024, now the School of Music, DePaul University. Photographs by Bernardo da Costa Soares, 2025.

Shakespeare Avenue at Orchard Street (Oz Park), 2021 N. Burling Street

Having now visited two sites where the Young Lords confronted higher education institutions for their impact on the Lincoln Park community, the tour continues south on Halsted Street toward Oz Park. Entering by the basketball courts on Webster, the tour pauses near the baseball field to examine an old photograph from the *Chicago Tribune* (1964), showing housing on the now-vanished "Shakespeare Avenue at Orchard Street." The housing and street are of course no longer there, rezoned and replaced by a city park. Reflecting on this image, with buildings and people once visible on the sidewalk, offers a moment to consider the fate of those displaced by urban renewal. The stop invites reflection on the urgency of the Young Lords and other community groups as they sought to prevent further displacement in Lincoln Park.

Residential buildings on Shakespeare Avenue at Orchard Street. Photograph by Alton Kaste, *Chicago Tribune*, April 23, 1964. Chicago and Lincoln Park Ephemera Collection, Box 19, Folder 12, DePaul University Special Collections and Archives, Chicago, Illinois.

Waller High School (Lincoln Park High School), 2001 N. Orchard St.

Continuing down the path toward Lincoln Park High School, the tour stops again to consider the northern corner of the school visible behind the baseball field. Known in 1969 as Waller High School, this part of the building includes an auditorium space. On July 4, 1969, Young Lords and others disrupted a meeting of the Lincoln Park Community Conservation Council over a planned vote on a private tennis club proposal for a nearby vacant lot and issues of representation on the Council charged with making the decision. A photograph on the cover of the *Lincoln Park Conservation Association News* shows the level of disruption that ultimately shut down the meeting with community members taking over the stage, climbing on a table, raising fists, and holding a chair in the air. When the meeting reconvened on September 11, Chicago police lined the room and protected the front of the stage. Engaging with this image offers the opportunity to consider the relationship and history between the Young Lords and Chicago police and imagine the tension that was likely in the room.

Lincoln Park Conservation Association News

Disruption at LPCCC!

Left: *Chicago Today* photograph in *LPCA News* vol. 69, no. 4, July 29, 1969. Lincoln Park Conservation Association Records, Box 1N, Folder 15, DePaul University Special Collections and Archives, Chicago, Illinois. Right: Chicago Police at LPCCC Meeting. Photograph by Larry Nocerino, *Chicago Sun-Times*, September 11, 1969. Chicago and Lincoln Park Ephemera Collection, Box 19, Folder 17, DePaul University Special Collections and Archives, Chicago, Illinois.

People's Park (Halsted St. business district), Armitage Avenue and Halsted Street

Above: People's Park. Photograph by Larry Graff, *Chicago Sun-Times*, August 7, 1969. Chicago and Lincoln Park Ephemera Collection, Box 19, Folder 9, DePaul University Special Collections and Archives, Chicago, Illinois.

Right: Children swing on Mark di Suvero play sculpture. Photograph by Carlos Flores.

Continuing west on Dickens Avenue and then south on Halsted Street, the next tour stop is the actual vacant area under consideration for a private tennis club. A photograph from August 1969 shows a group of young people raking the empty lot near a tent and "People's Park" sign. Standing on the sidewalk on the east side of the street and comparing the image then and now, one can look across the street and see that the same buildings in 2020 and 2024 Halsted are visible in the 1969 photograph as well. A closer look at the photograph reveals a white building spire with a black pointed roof in line with a telephone pole. The building with the spire is still visible today, although repainted white in recent years making it a bit more difficult to identify. Looking at the residential buildings that now fill the space from Dickens to nearly Armitage, one can wonder if these are the affordable units presented by the Neighborhood Development Corporation proposal in 1971—designs commissioned using money obtained from the McCormick Theological Seminary negotiations with the Poor People's Coalition. Tour participants discover that the current condominiums on this site are not part of the People's plan and are not currently considered low-cost or affordable. Fresh off the Oz Park and Waller High School tour stops, the People's Park site offers tour participants the opportunity to consider how spaces were and are currently used, who made those decisions, and ultimately how those decisions align or conflict with the objectives of the Young Lords and Poor People's Coalition.

People's Church, 834 W. Armitage Avenue (Walgreens)

Photograph of José "Cha Cha" Jiménez in front of Armitage Methodist Church. *Chicago Sun-Times*, June 11, 1969. Chicago and Lincoln Park Ephemera Collection, Box 16, Folder 8, DePaul University Special Collections and Archives, Chicago, Illinois.

The final stop on the tour is the People's Church/Armitage Avenue Methodist Church site at 834 West Armitage Avenue. Heading south on Halsted and then west on Armitage Avenue to Dayton Street, one will come upon the same identifying street signs visible in a June 1969 photograph of Cha-Cha Jimenez in front of the church where they staged a sit-in and ultimately occupied as their headquarters. However, you will not find a church. The building has now been converted into a Walgreens. Although there are additional street signs there honoring legends John Prine and Charlie Trotter, you will not find any kind of marker acknowledging the site as the former headquarters of the Young Lords Organization. Fortunately, we do have photographs of the exterior and interior from the 1960s showing YLO activities in and around the space, including a rally featuring a "People's Church, Iglesia de la Gente" sign by the church pulpit. Included in these photographs is an image of the daycare center the Young Lords set up in the church, complete with revolutionary slogans on the wall behind the children.

While we are fortunate to have the archival evidence, we do have to re-create the spaces and activities of the Young Lords, and we can

Photograph of People's Church (Armitage Methodist Church) interior, 1969. Collection on the Young Lords, Box 2, Folder 9.

walk the same sidewalks and (some) streets, the end of the tour provides an opportunity to reflect on the current physical space of Lincoln Park and lack of visual evidence that the Young Lords were/are in the area. The Young Lords Organization was formed in the neighborhood and was part of a social justice movement in the 1960s which was concerned in part with protecting and advocating for the most vulnerable people in the Lincoln Park community, but you would not easily know this by simply walking through and observing the area. With this in mind, we end the tour with a call for participants to document their communities, groups, and experiences to have a more complete and representative historical record—a meaningful record that people in the future can discover, engage with, and be informed by.

Young Lords daycare center. Photograph by Luis Arévalo, 1969. Collection on the Young Lords, Box 2, Folder 3, DePaul University Special Collections and Archives, Chicago, Illinois.

7.

ALLIANCES AND COALITIONS

The Rainbow Coalition: Unity in Action

(2018)
Elaine Brown, Former Chairman and Minister of Information, Black Panther Party, Oakland
Keynote address, Young Lords Fiftieth Anniversary Symposium
September 21–23, 2018
DePaul University, Lincoln Park, Chicago

I see we have my great comrade here, Cha Cha Jiménez. I'm glad to see you. I always say, "Power to the people!" I'm going to attempt this. (You know, the thing about these coalitions between the Young Lords and the Black Panthers is that we understood that we were on common ground. So sadly, I never learned Spanish, especially because I lived in California.) "*¡Todo el poder a la gente!*" Is that all right?

We're here to commemorate the founding of the Young Lords fifty years ago, which we should be honoring and celebrating. We're celebrating the powerful unity of oppressed people, organized by comrades Cha Cha Jiménez and Fred Hampton of the Black Panther Party. United, they launched the Original Rainbow Coalition—the real Rainbow Coalition, not the ripped-off, bastardized version. It was an alliance of revolutionaries, not bootlickers. The Black Panther Party was grounded in the ideals expressed in the first point of our ten-point platform: "We want freedom and power to determine the destinies of our community." Self-determination was our core goal. The Young Lords fostered a similar agenda with their first point: "We want self-determination for Puerto Ricans, liberation on the island and inside the United States."

This is an important theme that unites us. We recognize that we are not free, and we talk about liberation, freedom, and so forth. But as we celebrate this powerful effort of the Lords, their ideological and practical connection with the Black Panther Party and others, we also commemorate the blood that was shed in the name of freedom and liberation. At the same time, we have to ask what Dr. King asked back in 1967: "Where do we go from here?" This was when he launched the Poor People's Campaign, though he was assassinated by the government before it could take off. To answer King's question, we must assess where we are to understand where we go from here.

In 1967, Dr. King noted that even though Black people had seen some "successes" in the movement when he looked around the United States, southern Black people had "half of what is good and double what is bad."

Today, we mark another anniversary: one year after Hurricane Maria struck the island of Puerto Rico. We now know that at least three thousand Puerto Ricans have died due to the US government's ruthless denial of provisions and funds before, during, and after the storm. The $1,800 housing grant the government provided was nothing, and most people couldn't even get it due to qualification hurdles. The impoverished conditions created by US colonialism, both before and after the storm, remain. Most of Puerto Rico is still without power. When we talk about power to the people, Puerto Rico is indeed powerless. We must recognize this because if we don't, we are merely going down memory lane and ignoring the realities of today. As my comrade Cha Cha Jiménez said last night, the struggle is ongoing. You're not a revolutionary for just a moment; we have to commit ourselves for the long haul because it took a long time to put us in this condition. Even though some of us had the hubris to say, "Revolution in our lifetime," we've learned a lot as we've grown older.

Why are we talking about Puerto Rico and the US government? Puerto Rico is not a state; it's a colony and has been for over one hundred years. The people of Puerto Rico are still colonized. You still can't vote for president, there's no investment, and they have no real representation—just a resident commissioner who's a Republican. Forty-five percent of Puerto Ricans live in poverty today, which is higher than any state in the US. It's almost double the poverty rate of Mississippi, the poorest state. So, while not much has changed since the Young Lords were founded fifty years ago, that doesn't mean we should be depressed; it means we recognize that our work is far from finished.

There are 5 million Puerto Ricans in the US, representing less than 2 percent of the population, yet Puerto Ricans have the second-highest poverty rate. Black people have the highest poverty rate in America, but many believe in the "Oprah and Obama factor," thinking if they work hard enough, they can succeed, as though there could be more than one Oprah. We need to recognize that our struggles are far from over. When you combine the poverty rates of Black and Hispanic people, it's almost double that of non-Hispanic whites. In 2018 (or maybe it was 2017), someone could argue with me on the exact number, but we still stand on common ground, don't we? We Black people and we Puerto Ricans. And that common ground is that we still live at the bottom of life in America. Indeed, in the world.

I remember the day in December 1968 when we announced the coalition between the Brown Berets and the Black Panther Party in LA. Bunchy Carter led the drive for that coalition. It was serious, based on ideals and practice. But at the time, many Black people were like, "We ain't got nothing to do with Mexicans. Why are we with these Mexicans?" The good thing about the Black Panther Party was we didn't have democracy, which I call mob rule. If everyone decided to jump on me, I'd be dead after a vote. The point is, we didn't necessarily like each other. There was no cultural common ground, no need to be multiculturally conscious. We recognized that we stood on common ground as oppressed people, including the American Indian Movement. Looking back, we set a standard for change based on a concrete analysis of the US, not on emotions or personal feelings about who liked whom. Even within our own group, we had many internal battles—like how Black people still fight over light skin and dark skin. Am I right?

The United States was born from the blood of all thirty tribes of the Powhatan Confederacy, nearly wiped out when settlers founded Jamestown in 1607. We have to recognize that. When I lived in Georgia, people would ask how we could live there with Confederate flags flying. But I ask, how can we live in America where they still fly the American flag, the flag of slave-owning people? We don't understand the basic founding of this country. Jamestown, named after King James—the same King James of the Bible—was built on the blood of the Powhatan, including Pocahontas' father and the thirty tribes he led. Using the same colonial patterns, we began snatching people from Africa and started the slave trade in the US. This was a hundred years after Columbus "discovered" Puerto Rico, known as "the rich port." How do you think that happened? By enslaving and murdering the native Taino. It's just a memory now—if that—because colonization wiped out nearly everything building slavery, capitalism, and the US empire.

When we recognize that, and we recognize the significance of the vision of Cha Cha Jiménez and Fred Hampton, carried through all these years, we see that they understood how we had been divided. Yet, they stood their ground and boldly moved to unite us—despite all the divisions, both external and internal—recognizing that unity was the singular path to our shared dream of freedom and liberation. The key was understanding that these populations had to unite.

When the Black Panther Party started talking about various oppressed groups, including Latinos and poor whites, we added that other struggles were also part of this. People may not realize it, but we also recognized that gay liberation, women's liberation, environmental racism, and environmental issues were part of our struggle. The fight for independence for disabled people was part of our struggle. The liberation of the African continent was part of our struggle. People fighting for liberation around the world, from North Korea to Vietnam, were part of our struggle, but they got lost along the way.

Jean Genet once said that France was a colony of the US, and people got mad about that. It's important to recognize that, as Huey Newton called it, our "subjective goal" was the liberation of Black people, but to achieve that, we had to recognize the "objective relations." We represented only 13 percent of the population, so how were we going to stand up and fight the rest of the population on our own? We needed more than just allies; we needed others who were in the same fight. And we had them. On both moral and strategic grounds, we had to develop these coalitions. These weren't just alliances or whatever they call it now with terms like *intersectionality*. What does that even mean? I have no idea. The divisions among us were manifested in our own tribal behaviors, in how we treated each other.

You know, when I grew up in Philadelphia, we had a pretty large Puerto Rican population. Black people didn't like Puerto Ricans, and it was mutual. Even though we didn't like each other, Black people would say, "Oh, they don't want to be Black," because some Puerto Ricans would try to pass. Light-skinned Puerto Ricans would try to pass, but not as Black if their hair was too curly, just like how Black people try to pass. But the reality was different.

My mother was a presser in a factory. She was a crazy and very strong woman pressing dresses at a literal sweatshop all day with her head wrapped up, standing over an iron. She used to try to organize other pressers. And she would always say, "Yolanda, the Puerto Rican dropped dead at her board right next to me." Yolanda was twenty-seven years old and died of pneumonia because she was constantly going in and out of heat and cold. It was common back then, and my mom would say so. Black and Puerto Rican women were at the lowest level in clothing manufacturing—pressing was the lowest level. And they couldn't get past that to get to the cutting boards. This is how deep this stuff went. When people talk about workers' rights, Black and Puerto Rican workers in Philadelphia were standing on the same ground—literally, at the same ironing board, if you don't mind the metaphor.

Cha Cha, Fred, and the other coalition members recognized that our divisions were created and maintained by our common oppressors. So, they moved to organize and unite our people around a common agenda—a revolutionary agenda. We read Marx, Mao, and Che, and educated ourselves about the nature of our oppression and how it came to be. We learned that only fundamental revolutionary change in the United States could bring about our collective freedom, which is why we moved the way we did.

We fed our people because if we didn't, nobody else would. We nourished both body and soul, providing free healthcare and education. We fought for decent health and endured and survived COINTELPRO and violent attacks by the FBI, which aimed to discredit, disrupt, or destroy us. We battled the police, went to prison, and were murdered by the United States government. Our enemies understood the danger in our unity.

You know, when I was in the party, I started out in Los Angeles. This thing about the branding fire—if I was bringing the fire, at least I knew I was doing something, because we had to hit the streets to sell newspapers and do everything else. There was no gender division in that, believe me. We were all in the streets. One time, two LAPD undercover cops stopped me and others. They stopped me a lot, but one time this guy put a .44 Magnum in my face. I asked, "Is that standard issue?" Of course, I was asking too many questions with that barrel right in my face. And then he said, "You know, I can't stand n****** and s****. What do you think about that?" I thought to myself, I'm thinking about this bullet right now. I have no comment on your views.

Now, despite this incredible history, we have returned to our old colonized minds, and we have to fix that. This isn't just a minor issue of race, though that's the international question. Think about it—what country hasn't owned or controlled land anywhere else? At this point, we just want to be Americans. And I'm not just talking about Puerto Ricans. I'm talking about both Black people and Puerto Ricans. We just want to be Americans. What do I mean by that? We don't want to challenge the status quo; we just want to be part of it. We want our share. We want our piece of the pie.

You know, there's a film that came out a long time ago called *Rollerball.* It was about a futuristic world where society was united, and basically, there were two classes of people: the executive class and everyone else. But overall, people did well—there was no more poverty or anything like that. The only big entertainment was this Rollerball game. Millions of people would pack into the arena. I guess it started after people got used to things like the internet and all that.

In *Rollerball*, you could literally kill people in the game, and that's how you became famous—by being a killer rollerball player. The game was a mix between basketball, roller skating, hockey, and ice skating. It was crazy. Anyway, the main character, played by James Caan, had a friend who was killed during a game. He was one of the top global players, based in Houston. After his friend's death, he told them he wanted to quit playing. But they said, "You don't seem to understand—you don't get to quit." He had been groomed for this role, and that's just how it was.

So, fast forward, he's running around trying to figure out how he became a rollerball player. He wanted to know how it all started, as if his life had been assigned to him. Then his girlfriend told him, "Don't you understand? Fifty years ago, people had the choice to vote for freedom or comfort, and they chose comfort."

That's where we are today. We don't mind. We've got a leased car, a cell phone, internet service, and a little bit of money in our pocket. We're not thinking too much about homelessness—sure, we're worried about it, but not that much. We just want to be equal in capitalist America. We want to break through the glass ceiling. We want women to be corporate oppressors too, to be equal to men. We want to be Hillary Clinton or something. We want to be the first woman president for something like this. We want queer army generals saying, "I, too, can kill some fat kid," and we want people to know we're queer, gay, transgender—whatever it is, in these roles. We want Black and Latinx CIA operatives. I'm not making this up. You have no idea how many young people I work with are talking like this every day. We want our piece of the American pie.

We're not upset with the state; we just want our lives to matter in America. Everyone thought Black Lives Matter meant something— as if I care what America thinks about Black people. We already know from two hundred and fifty years of slavery what the deal is.

We're mad at Trump for throwing paper towels at Puerto Ricans, but we don't want to talk about Puerto Rican independence. We get mad about paper towels, regardless of the powerful legacy of the Young Lords. Black people walked around calling Trump a hillbilly president, as though Obama had been our president, and as though poor white people were our enemy. We don't want to admit that Obama was no different from Clinton, that racist from Arkansas who gave us the welfare reform bill and, more importantly, the crime bill that criminalized poor women. That bill, which Obama never addressed, led to the largest prison population in the world—over two million people, mostly Black and Brown, right?

This is where we are today. So we have to ask ourselves: Where do we go from here, knowing this legacy? What do we do with the information we have, knowing we haven't made much progress? There's a powerful precedent that's been extremely successful because those in control have all the guns and all the money.

There was a psychologist and revolutionary ideological theoretician in France whose ideas truly changed my life. Frantz Fanon wrote a book called *Wretched of the Earth*, where he said that the greatest fear of the oppressed is to draw the oppressor's blood. He added that only when the oppressed draw the oppressor's blood will they truly be free. Now, I know this might not sound good, but wait—are we talking about violence now? Nonviolence? Because these are big questions. Fanon also said that a gun isn't necessarily revolutionary because reactionaries have guns too. And this is the most armed state in the world—this empire of the United States.

You know, when thinking about the raids on our offices, the Black Panther Party fought back. In 1969, we had a raid where eleven people in our office fought three hundred SWAT team members, and after five and a half hours, they walked out. They were heroic. But at the end of the day, we knew the LAPD could call in the LA sheriff's department, then they could bring in the state police, the highway patrol, the national guard, the coast guard, the FBI, the CIA, the army, the navy, the air force—this country is heavily armed. So we have to understand that at a certain point, when we commit ourselves to life-and-death struggles, it becomes a moment of liberation. That's what touched me about the Young Lords. This wasn't about ego. It was about freedom, about liberation.

As we commemorate the powerful and beautiful Young Lords Organization, we need a new generation to rise up for freedom. You can't sit back and choose comfort over freedom. A new generation must rise up—no more hashtag activism, hip-hop viral videos, or poetry slams as revolutionary acts. That's not enough. People tell me, "I'm a revolutionary poet." Well, Mao was a poet, Che Guevara was a poet, Huey Newton and Bobby Seale were poets, but they were revolutionaries who happened to write poetry. We need to write as revolutionaries, not just as revolutionary poets. When Amiri Baraka (formerly LeRoi Jones) said, "We need to write poems that kill," I thought, "Really? Let's see how that works out."

A new generation has to rise up, unite, and commit itself to freedom. No more struggling to find identity in a country built on the blood of enslaved Africans, Latinos in the sweatshops and fields of California, or poor whites dying to maintain a system that benefits the rich. The disparities aren't just in our imagination—they exist in reality.

If we want a world where no one is hungry, homeless, or imprisoned, where people have access to healthcare and aren't dying early, and where society isn't controlled by greedy, barbarous men, we must fight. If we want to be free, we must lift up the light of the Young Lords, resurrect the spirit of the Panthers, unite, and keep fighting until we are all truly free. Power to the people!

Cha Cha, Fred Hampton, Bob Lee, and others march to the Wicker Park welfare office, March 1969. Photo courtesy of José "Cha Cha" Jiménez personal collection.

Unrepresented Launch New Organization

(1968)
Lincoln Park Press vol. 1, no. 5, June 8, 1968
Lincoln Park Conservation Association Collection, Box 131
Special Collections and Archives
DePaul University Library, Chicago, Illinois

Plans are well underway for a new community organization of poor and moderate-income people, as well as other unrepresented people in Lincoln Park. The early goals of the organization are to attack the major problem of the community: urban renewal, housing, and schools.

The temporary steering committee, and any future board or steering committee of the organization, will be composed of 1/3 Black, 1/3 Latin, and 1/3 Anglo representatives, elected by respective black, latin and anglo caucuses. The policy of equal representation for these sectors of the community was adopted to give extra power and voting strengths to Blacks and Latins who have had no voice or votes in Lincoln Park or in American Society.

The purposes of the new organization are best stated in the preamble to a proposal for funds which was adopted on May 28: the preamble reads:

> We are convinced that the situation in near north has been allowed too long to be out of hand. A community rich in structures and resources has failed to act in the radical sort of way necessary to rest the primary decision making for the community out of the hands of downtown political and business structures.

The time is rapidly approaching when the possibility of a truly diversified community will no longer be available. Since to a great extent those who join in making this proposal represent that diversity, it is plain we operate out of self-interest. We have no objections to better garbage collection, better housing, and more effective street patterns, behold as priority concerns:

- adequate housing for all of the people now living in the community, including especially poverty level or low and moderate income families;

- quality public schools, recognizing that all are poor and some are deplorable;
- the organizing of unrepresented people, particularly those in the Latin and Black communities to secure power to make the decisions that affect their lives.

Newly elected members of the temporary steering committee for the organization: Jim Reed, seated; Ramon Campos and Larry Dutenhaver, center foreground; and left to right, behind them: Ramon Valdes, Pat Creer, A.I. Dunlap, Jos Davidson, Sergio Herrero, Neil Shadle, Maria de Jesus, and Felix Silva. John McDaniel is also on the committee.

We want them to be decisions that make possible—even enlarge—the humanity which we experience. We are prepared to pledge, as we have in the past, our time, our resources . . . and to join with all others in this near north area who share our self-interest in the common battle which lies ahead.

Discussions about a new community organization have been going on for about two months. People participating in the discussions are members of two community groups—concerned citizens of Lincoln Park and Neighborhood Commons, a Black group; representatives of five Lincoln Park churches—Saint Teresa's, Saint Paul's, Armitage Ave. Methodist, Holy Covenant and Church of the Three Crosses; representatives of Christopher House, a settlement house for children in the western section of Lincoln Park, as well as many other people from the community.

New developments in the organization will be reported in the future issues of the PRESS.

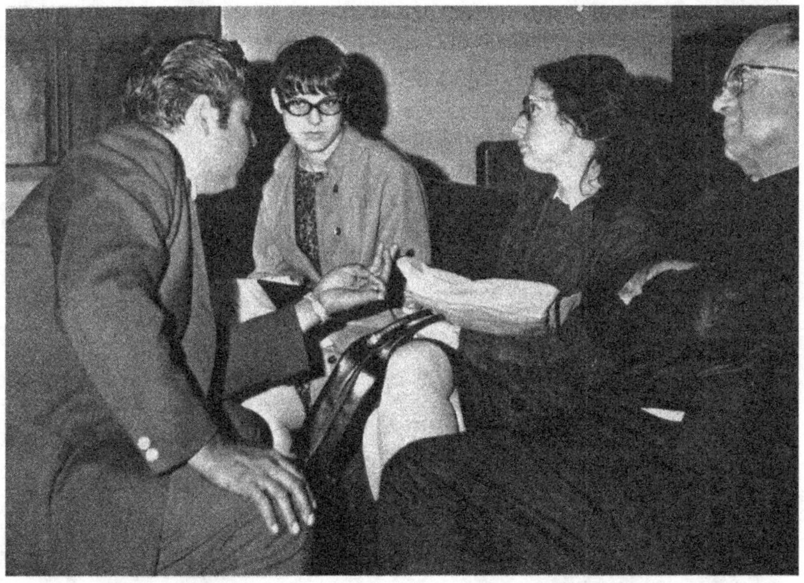

Ramon Campos, Pat Devine, and Mimi Harris discuss representative areas the new "umbrella" organization will cover after meeting dissolved for a "transition break" till next week.

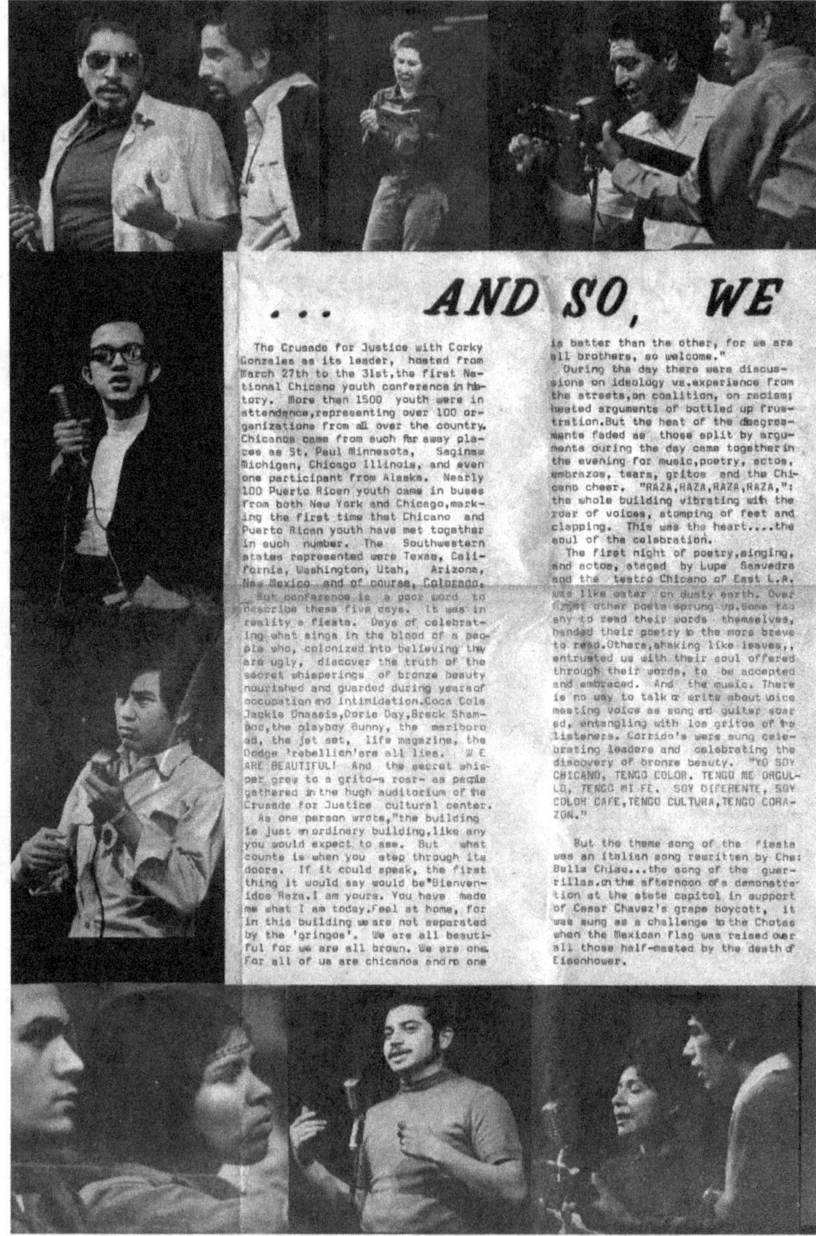

. . . AND SO, WE

The Crusade for Justice with Corky Gonzales as its leader, hosted from March 27th to the 31st, the first National Chicano youth conference in history. More than 1500 youth were in attendance, representing over 100 organizations from all over the country. Chicanos came from such far away places as St. Paul Minnesota, Saginaw Michigan, Chicago Illinois, and even one participant from Alaska. Nearly 100 Puerto Rican youth came in buses from both New York and Chicago, marking the first time that Chicano and Puerto Rican youth have met together in such number. The Southwestern states represented were Texas, California, Washington, Utah, Arizona, New Mexico and of course, Colorado.

But conference is a poor word to describe these five days. It was in reality a fiesta. Days of celebrating what sings in the blood of a people who, colonized into believing they are ugly, discover the truth of the secret whisperings of bronze beauty nourished and guarded during years of occupation and intimidation. Coca Cola Jackie Onassis, Doris Day, Breck Shampoo, the playboy Bunny, the marlboro ad, the jet set, life magazine, the Dodge 'rebellion' are all lies. W E ARE BEAUTIFUL! And the secret whisper grew to a grito—a roar— as people gathered in the hugh auditorium of the Crusade for Justice cultural center.

As one person wrote, "the building is just an ordinary building, like any you would expect to see. But what counts is when you step through its doors. If it could speak, the first thing it would say would be "Bienvenidos Raza. I am yours. You have made me what I am today. Feel at home, for in this building we are not separated by the 'gringos'. We are all beautiful for we are all brown. We are one. For all of us are chicanos and no one is better than the other, for we are all brothers, so welcome."

During the day there were discussions on ideology vs. experience from the streets, on coalition, on racism; heated arguments of bottled up frustration. But the heat of the disagreements faded as those split by arguments during the day came together in the evening for music, poetry, actos, embrazos, tears, gritos and the Chicano cheer. "RAZA, RAZA, RAZA, RAZA,": the whole building vibrating with the roar of voices, stomping of feet and clapping. This was the heart....the soul of the celebration.

The first night of poetry, singing, and actos, staged by Lupe Saavedra and the teatro Chicano of East L.A. was like water on dusty earth. Overnight other poets sprung up. Some too shy to read their words themselves, handed their poetry to the more brave to read. Others, shaking like leaves,, entrusted us with their soul offered through their words, to be accepted and embraced. And the music. There is no way to talk or write about voice meeting voice as song and guitar soared, entangling with los gritos of the listeners. Corrido's were sung celebrating leaders and celebrating the discovery of bronze beauty. "YO SOY CHICANO, TENGO COLOR. TENGO ME ORGULLO, TENGO MI FE. SOY DIFERENTE, SOY COLOR CAFE, TENGO CULTURA, TENGO CORAZON."

But the theme song of the fiesta was an italian song rewritten by Che: Bella Chiao...the song of the guerrillas. On the afternoon of a demonstration at the state capitol in support of Cesar Chavez's grape boycott, it was sung as a challenge to the Chotas when the Mexican flag was raised over all those half-masted by the death of Eisenhower.

. . . And So We Are Again, Aztlán (1969)

El Gallo vol. 2, issue 5, pp. 13–14, April 1969

Image from *El Gallo*, published by the Crusade for Justice, showing the 1969 Denver Youth Conference where Young Lords members participated in the

ARE AGAIN, AZTLÁN

And the poetry was not seperate from the commitment to change....to revolution, which sung through every discussion, every workshop and every speaker's words. As one workshop wrote:"Our culture has been castrated through the various institutions of this system. We have known the profound pain of becoming strangers in our land, of seeing beautiful lands turned into parking lots, of seeing birds disappear, and fish die, and waters become undrinkable, and the sign 'private property' hung on a fence around land that once was held in common, of mountains becoming but vague shadows to our eyes behind a veil of smong. We are being killed in Vietnam,yet our own lands are in the hands of strangers."

The Chutes, of course, did their thing. All the tapes of all the sessions,workshops,speakers,etc. were
The Chutes, of course, did their thing. All the tapes of all the sessions,workshops,speakers,etc. were
stolen from a private home, as was film of every single session. It was a thorough,professional job. Also, the FBI requested the bus drivers on the buses from New York to file full reports on all conversations and activities on the buses as they drove cross-country.

And the final result of the celebration? A realization and dedication to nation-building..the chicano nation. To the bringing about of a nationalistic consciousness that encompasses the total bronze continent of this hemisphere. This commitment was set down in a "PLAN ESPIRITUAL DE AZTLÁN". The first act of our nation is to rename our territory and renounce the boundaries drawn by the thieves who first tore us apart. And so, we are again, AZTLAN.

por M.E. VARELA

I'VE HEARD
BLACK IS BEAUTIFUL
B U T
I WANT
BROWN IS BEAUTIFUL

TO FEEL IS TO BE
TO LIVE
MY FEELINGS ARE BEAUTIFUL
BECAUSE THEY'RE REAL
BECAUSE THEY'RE
ME

AND I'M BEING BRAVE ENOUGH,
LOVING ENOUGH
TO ALLOW MYSELF TO FEEL
TO BE MYSELF...TO GROW.

BUT SHIT
WHO CAN/WILL UNDERSTAND
MY FRUSTRATION,
MY PAIN
WHO CAN I TURN TO
WHO WILL HELP ME UNTWIST MY STOMACH
MY PAIN
WHO CAN I TURN TO
WHO WILL HELP ME UNTWIST MY STOMACH
MY BODY IS SCREWED WITH THIS
PAIN...MI GRITO
ES LOUD AND LONG

CAN'T YOU HEAR IT?
THAT I FEEL UGLY . . .
TO DISCOVER AFTER ALL THESE YEARS..
THAT I DON'T LOVE MYSELF
THAT ALL THESE YEARS I'VE BEEN LOOKING AT MYSELF THROUGH GAVACHO EYES..
JUDGING, CONDEMNING.

DAMN! I WAS A RACIST
AGAINST MYSELF.
I HATED MYSELF BECAUSE I'M ME ? ? ?
NO MORE, WHITE MAN, NO MORE
GAVACHO, GAVACHA. . .

I'M BROWN, I'M BEAUTIFUL
I'M A CHICANA
Y SABES QUE WHITE MAN,PIG,EDUCATOR,
NO CHINGAS CONMIGO MAS ! ! !

por olivia de san diego

first major national gathering of Chicanx youth to address oppression and inequality. Led by Rodolfo "Corky" Gonzales and the Crusade for Justice, the conference produced *El Plan Espiritual de Aztlan* and became a defining moment in the Chicanx movement. Courtesy of Felícitas Nuñez.

People's Demands, 1969

The Movement vol. 5, no. 5, June 1969, p. 5

PEOPLE'S DEMANDS

1. That McCormick Seminary immediately turn over to the community $601,000 for low cost housing development.

2. That McCormick provide a building and recreational facilities for a badly needed cooperative daycare center. That the Seminary provide a bus so that children can be picked up for the center.

3. That all the apartments owned by McCormick and rented to people in the community should be rented to poor and working class families.

4. That the fence around McCormick be torn down so that the Seminary can become a part of the community, not a fortress against the community.

5. We demand that the Stone Building be made available to the Puerto Rican community for the creation of a Puerto Rican cultural center to preserve and strenghten our cultural and historical heritage and to transmit these values to other peoples in our community and in Chicago. If it is found mutually advantageous to the McCormick Seminary and to the Young Lords Organization, we propose that the Seminary make available to the Young Lords Organization sufficient funds to purchase the property of Armitage-Dayton Methodies Church to be made the Puerto Rican cultural center.

6. That McCormick extend a grant in the amount of $25,000 to the Young Lords Organization to be used in a community leadership development program and in the continuation and strenghtening of the work of protecting and serving our poor community.

7. That McCormick actively support the efforts of the Latin American Defense Organization to end the arbitrariness of the Cook County Department of Public Aid in its dealings with Welfare Recipients Defense groups.

Specifically we demand that McCormick publically support the three demands that LADO, along with the Wicker Park Coalition for Welfare Rights, have submitted to David Daniel, Director of the Cook County Department of Public Aid and to George Dunne, President of the Cook County Board of Commissioners,

1. Removal of Walter A. Cunningham, District Office Supervisor and James Patterson, Assistant office Supervisor, for their lack of sensitivity to the needs and the human dignity of welfare recipients at the Wicker Park Public Aid Office.

2. Voice of the community served by the Wicker Park Office in the selection of a new director of the office.

3. Voice in the interpretation and implementation of welfare laws and regulations at the Wicker Park Office level.

We demand that this support be expressed in letters to David Daniel, Director of Cook County Department of Public Aid and to George Dunne, President of the Cook County Board of Commissioners.

8. That McCormick extend a grant in the amount of $25,000 to the Latin American Defense Organization to further the aims of creating a strong organization for welfare recipients in our community.

9. The McCormick publicly oppose and condemn the political persecution carried out by the city of Chicago against poor people's organizations such as the Black Panther Party, the Latin American Defense Organization, and the Young Lords Organization. McCormick must demand from the respective authorities that charges arising out of political arrests be dropped by the complaining institutions, namely, Department of Urban Renewal, Cook County Department of Public Aid, Chicago Police Department, the City of Chicago and the State's Attorney Office. The Young Lords Organization and he Wicker Park Welfare Office Defendants and, in particular, Jose "Cha-Cha" Jimenez and Obed Loped must not be jailed and punished for their beliefs in justice and for their concern with their community's rights.

10. That McCormick Seminary extend a "seed money" grant in the amount of $25,000 to establish a legal bureau controlled by poor people's organizations (the attorneys to be chosen by the organizations to work full-time for them, and to be responsible only to them.)

The Time Limit, decided on by the community to receive a definite answer was

Interview with Cha Cha Jiménez, Chairman—Young Lords Organization

(1969)
The Black Panther, June 7, 1969, p. 17[23]

BM: Cha Cha, how did the Young Lords come into existence and become an organization?

Cha Cha: In 1959 the Young Lords was a gang, a street gang on the near north side of Chicago in the area of Old Town. It got together as probably being more or less for protection because it was primarily a white area and the Young Lords were Puerto Rican. Later on more and more Puerto Ricans came into the area as more and more of the racist whites moved out into another community which was close to Old Town. After a while they became a social club, they had parties for the benefit of raising money for sweaters and T-shirts. They had picnics, they had dinners for the families, and, slowly but surely, they were changing organizationally into helping the people in the community. After a period of time of giving money to the people in the community, and giving donations of food and clothing, the Young Lords tried to sit down to cope with the needs of their environment. So they got together to find out what was the real problem, how could they help their people best. This was the main reason why the Young Lords Organization turned politically, because they found out that just giving gifts wasn't going to help their people, they had to deal with the system that was messing over them.

BM: Cha Cha I see that more and more in different medias that you are associated with different political groups such as the Black Panthers, which is a very political organization, and they have a political line and a political platform and program which they follow. What inspired you to align yourselves with the Black Panther Party?

Cha Cha: Well you see, we're still looking for that way in which we can help our people. Now we're starting to realize who our people really are, who are friends are and who are enemies are. And as we read and studied other organizations that are appearing now in the United States, we see and we recognize the Black Panther Party as a vanguard party, a vanguard revolutionary party. And we feel that as revolutionaries we should follow the vanguard party. This is why we follow them.

BM: Cha Cha, I've seen in the news, and it's been in different medias, where you lost a member of your organization, he was shot down by some of the Chicago police. And in working in a political way as the Black Panthers do and knowing Mayor Daley and the officials or the power structure of Chicago to be, as they've demonstrated in the past, are you prepared and willing to deal with that situation or whatever for existence as a political organization?

Cha Cha: As a political organization, I think we're well prepared to deal with it. I think we've dealt with it already. I think we've showed Chicago our following by coming out in 24 hours bringing 3,000 people to the streets which is something that isn't done very often. Manuel Ramos was a regular guy from the ghettos of Chicago. He was just like most of us are right now. Like we said before earlier, we're still searching for a way to help our people. We're still helping search for a way towards perfection. Manuel Ramos was a regular member in the organization since the beginning. We feel that he was a true revolutionary for changing along with it, because most of us don't really understand all of the basic issues. Most of us are new in the movement but we can see every day, this is a common experience for us, you know, this is a common experience for people in the ghetto. Daley just this past week had a press conference four days out of five days, showing the people of Chicago that he is planning this repression against gangs. Fred Hampton, the Deputy Chairman of the Illinois chapter of the Black Panther Party is in jail right now serving a two to five sentence, the head of the Cobra Stones is in jail doing three to twenty. I have myself been arrested on a fake charge of aggravated kidnapping, the kidnapping of my own child they claimed, but I was released right away when they found out. The reason I say gangs, Fred Hampton, Deputy Chairman of the Illinois chapter of the Black Panther Party and myself is because this is what he means when he talks about getting rid of the gangs, at least most gangs, are changing and are turning politically.

BM: Have you been confronted or had to deal with any situations dealing with agent provocateurs trying to get into the organization or coming into the organization or creating situations that might have charges brought against you by the FBI, the CIA, etc.?

Cha Cha: Just the other day we had our march on the pig station because of the brother Manuel, we demanded the arrest of pig James Lamb and a group calling themselves the Cobra Stones came and threw stones at the demonstrators and we passed through Cabrini housing project which is mostly a black populated area and we felt that the blacks were our brothers and we wanted them to come in. We thought that they would join us, and they did. They joined us except for these provocateurs. I wouldn't say that they were CIA or FBI, but I do say what they told me after the demonstration. They told me that the pigs were saying that we wanted to provoke a fight with them, that we were trying to take over their turf, you know, treating us more like a gang style and we talked to them. A couple of days later we took over McCormick Theological Seminary and there we had a meeting, and we found out that the pigs were trying to pay them to attack us.

BM: Cha Cha since you've been moving in a political fashion as a political organization how many people have been arrested?

Cha Cha: How many people, I say it's hard to count. About five a week (an average) get arrested. This is including all the Lords. Some of the charges that come on us are like mob action, assault and battery on the pigs whether we touch them or not. Just the other day a brother was searched down, because they have this stop and frisk law in Illinois where they just search you any time they want to, he was searched down and all of a sudden, he came out with a bag of marijuana which he never knew he had in his pocket, he couldn't believe it. This is some of the charges that we get charged with. We get stopped for leafletting and they say something about littering the streets you know ridiculous charges, you know, like kidnapping or anything, or just basically disorderly conduct or resisting arrest. Basically, disorderly conduct is usually a \$25 bail, resisting arrest is \$25.00 bail. Most of these bails are \$25 or there are some up to \$50. This is the basic bond for most people who do get arrested. Now when a Young Lord gets arrested it's a special case, sometimes the bails come up to \$1,000, \$10,000 and \$25,000 and even higher than that, a \$100,000. Excessive bails are given to the Black Panthers and the Young

Lords and the Young Patriots, the coalition that we have formed.

BM: Since the Young Lords have become a political organization rather than a street gang how is it accepted in the community? Do the people relate to and support you; how do they feel about the young Lords; about this transition; do you get more support?

Cha Cha: In the beginning when we were just a regular organization, a gifting organization, giving gifts out to the people we didn't get too much support, but we did feel happier when we gave gifts. But now that we've started organizing people, getting them together and starting them to work politically, we've gotten much support in the community. We have given much aid to the Latin community especially in the school committee or any committee where no Latins or even blacks could be found, but now these places are filled with Latins and blacks and poor whites. So the people in the community are for us and every day we get new members.

BM: So then would you say that the people are beginning to recognize, or they do recognize, that the movement is one of a class struggle rather than a race struggle?

Cha Cha: I think our organization just by the people, just by the content, just by being Puerto Rican, you just have to understand it's a class struggle, because we have light skinned people like myself, I'm very light, we have dark skinned people, we have red, we have yellow, we have all kinds of people, a rainbow of people. And this is why we can easily understand it is common sense to us that this is a class struggle. I can't relate to black people hating white people and white people hating black people and Puerto Ricans getting hated by anybody, you know, and people can't relate to that, you know we look to see which is our enemy, which is our common enemy and we just see that the pigs are the bodyguards of the capitalist pigs that are oppressing and exploiting our people. We look to see that this octopus, the United States has been sucking all the resources from Puerto Rico, and we see who our enemy is. We see that the United States is our enemy. And we look out for allies, you know, we look at Cuba, we look at Mao, we look at all these other countries that have liberated themselves from the monsters.

This article is reprinted from a new newspaper from Chicago, RISING UP ANGRY. The first issue contains articles on the Panthers, Young Lords, dealing with the pigs, abortions, music, drag racing and a movie review. Real good to sell on the streets. For bulk orders or subscriptions ($3.00/year) contact: RISING UP ANGRY, Box 3746, Merchandise Mart Chicago, Illinois 60654 (312)472-7090 or 929-0133

GANG BUSTING

For the past month in Chicago we haven't been able to pick up a paper or listen to the T.V. or radio, and get the straight scoop on the gang scene. All this despite a barrage of publicity about the gangs, Black, White and Latin. So what's happening? Let's get into it.

First of all, we have to understand some stuff about ourselves. It's real simple: man is a social animal; we can't make it alone, so we get together in groups. We do this despite attempts to separate us from each other, like they send guys to one school, girls to another, kids from the same neighborhood to different schools; they divide us up with 'specialized jobs' at work, get us to try and out-answer each other in class, get kids to be brown noses (just where does that phrase come from) and tricks, and on and on. One thing is certain about this society we live in: they don't want people to get together.

But people dig each other! They're always getting together in groups. The need to be together is real. It's human. It's natural. And it's a necessity. So we form 'gangs', clubs and political groups (which the Man calls gangs unless he thinks they're respectable and proper). It's happened throughout the history of mankind. Every neighborhood and school in the city has its groups, its gangs.

Let's repeat it: THEY DON'T WANT US TO GET TOGETHER. Why? Because the people who run the show are threatened by any group that they don't control. So they try and either get the gangs on their side (we'll give you this and that if you don't do this and do that -- or else) or smash us. They don't understand how human beings work. They try and split us up to control us.

OK, so a lot of gangs are violent. This can be good, or it can be bad. Sometimes violence has been misdirected. We've been frustrated and pissed off at the world for good reason. So we strike out. We all know that sometimes this isn't cool, like when guys turn in on each other, or vamp on some wino, or lady with a purse who's carrying home bread to feed her kids. But other times violence is ok. When someone is stepping on your neck you don't say 'hey, please cut it out.' So sometimes we're violent 'cause we have to be, we have to survive, we have to protect our people, our members, our turf, our neighborhood, and our families, against cops, tricks, businessmen, urban renewal and other gangs who aren't hip to the real enemy so they hit on us.

OK, we all know that something is happening. We're hip that it's a waste of time to keep jamming, vamping and gang bopping just because there ain't nothing else to do. So a lot of the gangs are becoming political groups and people's organizations, talking about serving and protecting the people from the Neanderthals and Bloodsuckers who run the show. Now this is where the Man, like Daley, Conlisk, State's Attorney Hanrahan, Chief Judge Boyle, and the Gang Intelligence Unit (G.I.U.) creep Buckney get uptight. They're really uptight. And they should be, because as our people get hip to who to hit, the man knows he's in trouble unless he can control us and use us.

But we're getting cool; so it's getting hard for them to use us. So now there's a shift, a difference in the way they deal with us. Right now they're trying to put us all down, smash us, White, Black and Latin.

Here's how they do it. Hanrahan, lover of the big crooks, uses his ties to the bullshit newspapers to get them to blast us. They give Hanrahan, Daley, Buckney, Boyle and Conlisk all the press they want. Big deal front pages 'exposing' somebody or some group. Once in awhile they cover the gang's side, like when the P-Stones (Rangers) and Disciples made their alliance public.

But look what happened. Sengali of the Rangers made it real clear that the gangs would take responsibility for their members as far as possible and that future incidents didn't indicate a breakdown of the alliance. So the next day Hanrahan takes something that happened and gets a big story saying how the alliance is a phoney. If something did happen it might not have even involved Rangers or Disciples. It might have been some dude trying to prove himself, or someone in a gang who just wasn't hip to the changes, to the new spirit growing among Chicago's gangs.

It's clear that the reason the Neanderthals are waging war on gangs in their papers and on their T.V. and radio stations is because they're making a move to get more cops. Check out this connection. When they decided to raise the fares on the CTA (again), they blamed it on workers wanting more money (the politicians and businessmen get more money off us, and when some of us want more money to survive they take it out of our checks, not their's.) But they also made a big deal in the papers for a week about how many robberies and beatings were happening on the CTA. They of course didn't tell us that that stuff does happen all the time (go ahead, check the statistics.) They tried to brainwash the people, and the next week they raised the fare. TOO MUCH!

The same thing is true now. A week after Hanrahan starts shooting off his mouth about gangs, blaming anything that happened anywhere on gangs (especially organizations making peace and serving the people like the P stones and Disciples, Young Lords, Latin Eagles Young Patriots and Black Panther Party), Conlisk came out requesting 1000 more cops for next year to deal with the streets. Of course neither he, the papers, Daley, Buckney, Boyle or Hanrahan said anything about how they were politically threatened and scared, 'cause they couldn't control the gangs anymore.

Hanrahan laid the propaganda groundwork, Conlisk made the move, and now we'll see Daley's mangy dogs (the Aldermen) trot along in agreement. Meanwhile big crime, and bloodsucking businessmen go about their dirty business untouched.

The Gang Intelligence Unit

Now the dudes who do the nitty-gritty dirty work (the ones we have to deal with on our turf) are the punks in the GIU. GIU is part of the police dept. and was formed in 1967. It only had a few people. It replaced the Youth Group Intelligence Unit which had been set up to help gang kids, to keep them from fighting each other. That was when the cops and city were trying to use the gangs, make them like the Conservative Vice Lords. (The Conservative Vice Lords on the west side are now sucks for the Democratic party, and made crook State Senator Bernie Neistein an honorable member.)

Under bootlicker Captain Ed Buckney the policy is one of throwing gang members in jail and keeping 'em there as long as possible (he said it on T.V.) This spring they upped the number of pigs in the GIU from 37 to 200. Quite a jump, and it goes to show they're scared of people in the streets, afraid that White, Black and Latin gang kids will become the people's liberation army that can bring justice back to Chicago and America.

Right now the GIU spends more time with Black and Latin gangs than White. That's because those groups moved sooner and faster than a lot of us Whites. It's obvious that they're tighter, more together, and have a greater spirit of solidarity running among their people because they know they got to be tight to survive. But things are changing in the White gangs. All over the city we're working out alliances with each other, and talking to Black and Latin organizations like the Panthers and the Young Lords. One of the first white groups to make its position clear, in support of the people and against the cops, was the Young Patriots. GIU has stepped up its harassment of our Patriot brothers and is doing likewise with white gangs everywhere in the city.

In the past GIU could be loose with us. Our cats were bought off with stuff like 'we'll let you drink if you keep it cool, if you hassel the Blacks, Latins and hippies.' But a lot of us know that never worked for long. As soon as too many of us were on the corner, blam, blam, under arrest. Don't let the people get together.

Now we know that there are some White gangs that get special treatment because some of their members became cops. (This is true of some duper gangs in particular). But even a lot of these groups who tricked on people and sold other people out, while doing more bad shit than most other gangs, are catching their lunch. So they had better dig what's going on and stop their bullshit, or catch their lunch from a lot of directions.

ALL POWER TO THE GANGS THAT FIGHT THE REAL ENEMY, LOVE THEIR BROTHERS AND SISTERS, AND SERVE THE PEOPLE!!!

AUGUST 1969 THE MOVEMENT PAGE 15

Gang Busting (1969)

The Movement vol. 5. no. 7, August 1969, p. 15

Reprinted from *Rising Up Angry*

US Get Out of Vietnam Now

(1969)
Lincoln Park Conservation Association Collection
Special Collections and Archives
DePaul University Library, Chicago, Illinois

US GET OUT OF

VIETNAM NOW!

Despite the bullshit propoaganda coming from Nixon and his flunkies about "negotiations" and "troop withdrawals", the Vietnam war continues - and the heroic Vietnamese people have won.

How is it possible that the "most powerful" military force in the world can be beaten?

All the Vietnamese people - with the exception of a small group of Saigon militarists - are united under the leadership of the NLF and the Provisional Revolutionary Government (PRG). They are fighting a people's war for national liberation and independence. And just as the 13 colonies could defeat a more powerful British Army in 1780 and a united French resistance could defeat the Nazi's in 1944, so, too, have the Vietnamese defeated the U.S. imperialists. If this war continues, it can only mean tens of thousands more GI's dead. And it will end when the U.S. withdraws all occupation troops and recognizes the Provisional Revolutionary Government - the only true representative of the Vietnamese people.

We in the U.S. must build a movement that can win -- a mass militant anti-imperialist movement; one that can unite all the people opposed to this war - black, Latin, white, men, women, students, street people, GI's, working people. The struggles of the people of this country - for liberation, an end to imperialist wars, against white supremacy and male supremacy - are the same as the struggles of the Vietnamese. UNITED WE BOTH SHALL WIN!

A call has been issued for everyone opposed to this imperialist war to come to Chicago (Oct. 8--11) for a series of actions:

**a hospital action focusing on the oppression of women under imperialism; the struggle of black, Latin, and white women against white supremacy and male supremacy is the same as that of the Vietnamese women for liberation.
FULL EQUALITY FOR WOMEN!

**actions around institutions created by the people themselves such as the Black Panther Party's Breakfast for Children program and the Young Lords Day Care Center.
SERVE THE PEOPLE!

**a rally on Oct. 9 at International Harvester, 26th & California from 3 to 5 pm. TEAR DOWN THE JAIL, KEEP THE PLANT OPEN!

**a mass demonstration on Oct. 11, starting at 12 noon at People's Park (Armitage & Halsted) and marching through black, Latin, and white working class neighborhoods,
demanding: U.S. GET OUT OF VIETNAM NOW!

As successful as the Oct. 8-11 action may be, it is not enough; we must continue the struggle throughout the year carrying it into the schools and all other oppressive anti-people institutions!

If you are interested in working on the National Action call 348-2246.

year of solidarity with the vietnamese

the coordinating center during Oct.8-11 will be :
Church of the Holy Covenant
925 W. Diversey

phone : 348-8578 or 348-2246

power to the people

Revolutionary Youth Movement (sds)

endorsed by:
THE BLACK PANTHER PARTY
THE YOUNG LORDS ORGANIZATIC

Despite the bullshit propaganda coming from Nixon and his flunkies about "negotiations" and "troop withdrawals," the Vietnam war continues—and the heroic Vietnamese people have won.

How is it possible that the "most powerful" military force in the world can be beaten?

All the Vietnamese people—with the exception of a small group of Saigon militarists—are united under the leadership of the NLF and the Provisional Revolutionary Government (PRG). They are fighting a people's war for national liberation and independence. And just as the 13 colonies could defeat a more powerful British Army in 1780 and a united French resistance could defeat the Nazi's in 1944, so, too, have the Vietnamese defeated U.S. imperialists. If this war continues, it can only mean tens of thousands more GI's dead. And it will end when the U.S. withdraws all occupation troops and recognizes the Provisional Revolutionary Government—the only true representative of the Vietnamese people.

We in the U.S. must build a movement that can win—a mass militant anti-imperialist movement; one that can unite all the people opposed to this war—black, Latin, white, men, women, students, street people, GI's, working people. The struggles of the people of this country—for liberation, an end to imperialist wars, against white supremacy and male supremacy—are the same as the struggles of the Vietnamese. UNITED WE BOTH SHALL WIN!

A call has been issued for everyone opposed to this imperialist war to come to Chicago (Oct. 8–11) for a series of actions:

** a hospital action focusing on the oppression of women under imperialism; the struggle of black, Latin, and white women against white supremacy and male supremacy is the same as that of the Vietnamese women for liberation.

FULL EQUALITY FOR WOMEN!

** actions around institutions created by the people themselves such as the Black Panther Party's Breakfast for Children program and the Young Lords Day Care Center.

SERVE THE PEOPLE!

** a rally on Oct. 9 at International Harvester, 26th & California from 3 to 5 pm.

TEAR DOWN THE JAIL, KEEP THE PLANT OPEN!

** a mass demonstration on Oct. 11, starting at 12 noon at People's Park (Armitage & Halsted) and marching through black, Latin, and white working class neighborhoods, demanding: U.S. GET OUT OF VIETNAM NOW!

As successful as the Oct. 8–11 action may be, it is not enough; we must continue the struggle throughout the year carrying it into the schools and all other oppressive anti-people institutions!

If you are interested in working on the National Action call 348-2246.

year of solidarity with the vietnamese
power to the people
the coordinating center during Oct. 8–11 will be:
Church of the Holy Covenant
925 W. Diversey

Endorsed by: Revolutionary Youth
Movement (SDS)
The Black Panther Party
The Young Lords Organization

A Conversation with Cha Cha Jiménez and Oscar López Rivera

(2018)
Moderated by Jacqueline Lazú
Young Lords Fiftieth Anniversary Symposium
September 21–23, 2018
DePaul University, Lincoln Park, Chicago, Illinois

Jacqui Lazú: Cha Cha Jiménez and Oscar López Rivera, welcome home. Speaking of home, I want to start with a question about family and the family members that have shaped your lives. Cha Cha, I know that throughout our conversations, you often mention your parents and the influence they had on your way of thinking and your activism. I think that's something most people don't consider often enough—the disconnect between generations. People tend to think activism emerges out of nowhere, when, in reality, our homes are often where our ideologies first begin to develop, and I know that's been true for you.

And Oscar, I know your granddaughter means so much to you. My opportunity to reflect on your experiences came most deeply when I read your letters to Karina from prison, which of course were published, and I've used them quite a bit in my classes. Would you mind talking to us about your granddaughter as well?

José "Cha Cha" Jiménez: I want to start by saying this is really humbling for me. I'm sitting next to a brother who risked everything for our people and was incarcerated for thirty-six years. I did a little time myself, and I can remember doing a year in jail. After about three or four months, I woke up in the middle of the night, and I was in tears thinking, "When is this going to be over? When can I get out?" Then I'd try to sleep it off. But that was just a few months. This brother was in for thirty-six years—for us. So, I'm deeply honored that he's here to honor the Young Lords. Thank you so much.

The Young Lords are nothing without the people of this community, the people of Lincoln Park. When you leave tonight, I want you to remember that from North Avenue to Addison, from Clybourn to Racine, was once the first major Puerto Rican community in this city. And they evicted all of us from this community. We didn't come back to Lincoln Park because we loved it so much—it's because that was the heart of the Puerto Rican community. Whether we're in Lincoln Park or Humboldt Park, it's about Puerto Ricans being displaced, as they are today in Humboldt Park. The Puerto Rican Cultural Center is doing great work there with the people, and we're proud to work alongside them.

It's still the same struggle we're fighting. It's a protracted struggle. We learned a lot about organizing from many people. Sister Elaine Brown, chairwoman of the Black Panther Party, is here from Oakland, and we're honored to have her supporting us today. We learned so much from the Black Panther Party. But, like Jacqui said, we also learned a lot from our parents, who were just trying to get Spanish mass for a few years. My mother had catechism classes in our living room. I was more religious than the Pope back then! You'd wake up in the morning and see an altar—and sometimes some chicken feet. That was the kind of community we grew up in.

She gave catechism classes to public school students so they could make their first communion, even though she never went to school herself. That's how she earned her status as a community leader. That's the kind of community we had here. I don't want to take too long, but that's what I mean when I say this was a community struggle. The Young Lords are nothing without the community, and we were fighting for our parents too. Even though some of our parents didn't agree with us, they knew we were being discriminated against. They'd say, "You're a little crazy, moving too fast," but they knew we were fighting for something important. Your community is struggling, and we're all in this together.

Oscar López Rivera: Family is crucial—very, very crucial. I want to say this before I go any further: this is a very meaningful and deeply grateful moment for me, to be able to share this experience with Cha Cha and all of you. It's important for us to understand the dynamics—what happened in the past, from a particular moment, and how it continues to happen up to now.

When we look back at the late '60s and the '70s, and when we look at this moment now, we can see how struggles evolve, how people evolve, and how we change. And that's important, because we definitely do not remain the same.

My granddaughter came to me when she was just 14 days old. My daughter brought her to me at the penitentiary where I was being held. It was called "sensory deprivation"—the deprivation system of that time. It was 1986. Amnesty International had defined the conditions in that penitentiary as a human crime—an illegal human crime. That's how we were treated.

My granddaughter kept visiting, and little by little, we developed a relationship. My daughter would bring her to visit, and we started playing a game with our hands. I couldn't touch her. I couldn't touch my granddaughter, my daughter, or any member of my family, because all the visits were no-contact. But we found a way. I would always look at my granddaughter and think that I'd never get to see her grow up, but little by little, our bond grew stronger.

My granddaughter is special in two ways. First, she is the granddaughter of one of my codefendants. Her father is my codefendant's son. So, she would visit her grandmother in California and then visit me. Over the years, we developed a deep connection, even though it was at a distance. It's never the same as having someone next to you, but we made it work, even though we probably only saw each other twice a year.

Yet, I can say this much: my granddaughter is now a young woman who is very sensitive, very conscious, and who wants to fight for a better, more just world. And even now, when we come together, we still play that same game with our hands. The way we transmit our love is the same as it was when we first started. We automatically move together, and that's how we keep our relationship alive.

Jacqui Lazú: Thank you so much for that. You know, I think it's important to acknowledge that even though you've both led incredible political lives, it's easy for people to mystify movements and the individuals behind them. It's important to remember that ideologies, at one point or another, are grounded in your experiences at home, with your family, and within your community. I think it's essential to always return to that.

As I mentioned in my opening, this is a very heavy time to be thinking about Puerto Rican consciousness, and to be reflecting on the future of the island. It's hard not to return to that in our daily lives right now, especially from the perspective of the diaspora. There's no question that on the island, this is an ongoing issue every single day. For those in the audience who are feeling the intense emotions that I am, I can tell you there's no more critical time for this conversation.

So, I want to ask both of you: Can you share your perspectives on why *you* believe this is such an important time to discuss Puerto Rican unity and the need for us to come together as a people?

José "Cha Cha" Jiménez: Well, I think, again, I want to relate it back to where we are here in Lincoln Park. I know people might be tired of us talking about displacement after fifty years, but it's still the same situation. When we first had the independence demonstrations, they were here, in this very community in Chicago, for Puerto Rican independence. That's why this community is important.

Back then, we connected it as a way to push back against colonialism in Puerto Rico, and this was the diaspora. I mean, I'm in school, I'm just a student. In fact, I just did my homework last night! I'm at university right now in May. So, I'm just learning, and I just found out the other day what "diaspora" means. It refers to the scattering of communities, right? We were scattered from Puerto Rico here, after World War II, into places like Parkland, Madison, and Lincoln Park.

When we started fighting, we came into this neighborhood. They called us young gangbangers, but really, we were just youth who were being beaten up. So, we decided to form our own little club and start defending ourselves. Eventually, we realized the guys beating us up were under the same conditions we were. We were fighting the wrong enemy. We should've been fighting the mayor and people like that.

When we figured that out, we started the Young Lords. We chose Grito de Lares because we were trying to learn about our stolen history. We didn't know anything about ourselves, and that's why we picked that name. We still don't fully know what it means, but we know there was a revolution. We know about Betances and the others, and we're learning the meaning every day through our struggle—this protracted struggle against displacement that's happening in Humboldt Park and all these other places.

Our fight against displacement, against them kicking us out of lakefront and downtown areas, isn't just happening in Chicago. It's happening in cities all over the country. Our struggle is for unity, for solidarity, for getting rid of that "diaspora" word. I'm still trying to figure out exactly what it means. But that's what displacement is.

Look at who lives in Lincoln Park today, and look where we live. We're in the suburbs now. The white flight that once fled to the suburbs has returned downtown, and now we're the ones being pushed out. It's just another scattering, another loss for us. That's how they divide and conquer. They keep us divided by race, by color, by class.

Jacqui Lazú: Oscar, I want to ask you why unity is such a challenging concept, especially for Puerto Rico. As hard as it is for us to talk about, time and time again, we're shown just how difficult the notion of unity is—first for ourselves, and then even more so when it comes to coexisting with other groups.

So why is unity such a challenge, and how is it important at this particular moment in time?

Oscar López Rivera: It's crucial. In the case of Puerto Rico, unity has been slow to come. And for Puerto Ricans outside of Puerto Rico, we have to become conscious of one fact: there are 5 million Puerto Ricans living outside of Puerto Rico, and the number of Puerto Ricans remaining on the island is getting smaller every day.

Now, why is it so important to unify? It's important because, no matter where a Puerto Rican lives—whether it's in Hartford, St. Paul, California, or anywhere else—as long as that Puerto Rican identifies as Puerto Rican, there's hope and the possibility of coming together.

We've been displaced historically from Puerto Rico, and it didn't start yesterday. It started in 1901, when the US government began sending Puerto Ricans out of Puerto Rico to places like Hawaii and the southwestern US. They did this for one reason: the US government had an agenda. They claimed Puerto Rico was overpopulated, but that was a lie. There were fewer than a million Puerto Ricans on the island at the time. The real reason they did this was to take over the land for sugarcane and military purposes.

By 1914, 13 percent of Puerto Rico's land was occupied by military bases. Then, the sugarcane industry came in and destroyed Puerto Rico's diversified economy. We have to be careful and aware of all these things. It started in 1901, when Puerto Ricans were sent to Hawaii.

So, why is unity so important? It's crucial. It's of utmost importance that we see ourselves as one. Whenever I talk to Puerto Ricans living outside of Puerto Rico, I remind them that Puerto Rico is the promised land for all Puerto Ricans. If any Puerto Rican wants to come back to Puerto Rico, let them come back—because that is our promised land!

Jacqui Lazú: Your reflections resonate with my work recovering overlooked histories. I'm not from Chicago, yet I'm always struck by how much Puerto Rican history unfolded here and how much remains undocumented.

So many movements, including the Young Lords, emerged from this city. Why? Why did movements like yours, Oscar, take root here? What is it about Chicago that inspires such deep commitment?

José "Cha Cha" Jiménez: I think the reason it happened in Chicago was because we had people like Mayor Daley here, and we faced heavy discrimination. We had no power, and we realized that from the very beginning. If we could get together, one of the ways we could gain power was through the gang structure.

We weren't doing sit-ins at restaurants like you hear about elsewhere. Here, we went to Benny's Pizzeria to order a pizza, and the Italian boys would say, "What do you mean, order? You can't order food here." But we insisted, "We want a pizza. It's a free country." And they'd say, "No, you can't."

At that time, gangs played a very important role. They weren't like the gangs today, which are tied to the drug trade. Back then, we were territorial. All we were trying to do was hang out in our neighborhood, go to North Avenue Beach, Oak Street Beach, Fullerton Beach—but we couldn't go to those places. We couldn't even go to Benny's Pizzeria.

So the way we opened up this neighborhood was through fistfights, rocks, bottles—anything we could get our hands on. That's how we started to make space for ourselves in the beginning. Then, when society told us that was wrong, we decided to go legitimate. We followed the Black Panther Party because they were legitimate. And guess what? We got into even more trouble with them!

Oscar López Rivera: Chicago is a very interesting city, and our environment is very interesting too. I came home from Vietnam in 1967, and that was a very crucial year. In 1966, the Puerto Rican community in Chicago experienced a big riot. It was the first Puerto Rican riot, and it deals with the Chicago Police because they were incredibly brutal toward Puerto Ricans. What Cha Cha mentioned about discrimination is true. But to a great degree, it was young Puerto Ricans who refused to accept that treatment. They called us names like "spic," tried to abuse us, and worked to displace us. The Chicago Police Department was probably our worst enemy.

When I came back in 1967, our Humboldt Park community was a very marginalized community. It was a very invisible community. It was a community without a voice or its own identity because we weren't allowed to express it. There's another element that's important to mention here, from my perspective. That year, 1967, there was a Puerto Rican nationalist. He would come by when we were hanging out on Division Street and ask, "Hey, do you want to come over to my house to listen to a tape of the nationalists?" As we were listening there was a voice—a

Puerto Rican woman who said, "I came to Washington not to kill anyone, but to give my life for Puerto Rico."

I have to be honest, when I was listening to her voice, she had a rhythm, like a "ta ta ta," just like an automatic weapon. Like the weapons that I heard in Vietnam! I asked myself, "What is it that you are going to do?" So, little by little, we started working for the freedom of our five national heroes. At the time, there were five Puerto Ricans in prison. Óscar Collazo from 1950 and the last four, Rafael Cancel Miranda, Andrés Figueroa Cordero, Lolita Lebrón and Irving Flores were imprisoned in March of 1954.

So, we talked and said that we had to do something. Slowly, we got involved in the campaign to excarcerate our five national heroes. Luckily, in 1979, on the 10th of September, those five national heroes were freed because Puerto Ricans in the US and on the island united and worked together. If we could come together back then and make progress, I believe we can continue working for the unity we need today.

Jacqui Lazú: When looking at these movements in Chicago, they can at first seem parallel, contemporary in many ways but developing on separate timelines. Some have even questioned whether they belong in conversation with one another. Yet their histories do intersect in important ways.

Could you talk about why it makes sense for these movements to be in dialogue? Oscar, how did the activities of the Young Lords and your work for Puerto Rican liberation align with the legacy of the Young Lords in Chicago? And then I will ask you the reverse question, Cha Cha.

Oscar López Rivera: I think there was always a connection, not necessarily a personal link, but a link of ideas. The Young Lords had a significant influence, and two things stand out to me: the idea of "Tengo Puerto Rico en mi corazón" and the beautiful mural of the five Puerto Rican nationalists painted at the top of the church on Armitage. The influence of the Young Lords was clear in our communities, especially through their powerful symbol—the raised fist representing political power—and the conflicts they created, particularly with the police. These were things we could all identify with.

Now, the difference between our movements was the target. We chose education as our primary focus—getting Puerto Ricans into universities, pushing schools to respond to the needs of Puerto Rican students, and ensuring Puerto Ricans had access to education. So, I think it was more a matter of target than any real differences. Ideologically, I don't think there were many differences. The Young Lords made it very clear that Puerto Rican independence was crucial, and we also made it clear that independence for Puerto Rico was extremely important. In that sense, we were united in spirit, if not always in the specific issues.

For example, I remember when Cha Cha ran for City Council. He was still in prison at the time when the idea of his candidacy came up. One of the Young Lords sisters asked us if we were willing to help, and we did as much as we could to support his campaign. So, there was definitely solidarity from us in those key moments.

José "Cha Cha" Jiménez: If I could just say that we agree with everything con las Fuerzas Armadas de Liberación Nacional. And we organized too. I remember going to the University of Illinois campus to support what you guys were doing there. He came to the church to support what we were doing.

All we knew at that time was the streets. That's where we started, with the gang and all that. So, of course, that's when we began our organizing efforts. We came out real strong at first, and then we said, "We've got to unite with more people." That's when we started getting involved in civil rights. Then, the police tried to trick us into talking about violence. "Are you for violence or nonviolence?" But no, it's not about violence or nonviolence. It's about whether you're for slavery or nonslavery. That's the issue.

They tried to trick us and everything, but we agreed with everything they were doing. In fact, we went in and supported it. I remember I walked into a demonstration for you and I got booed, and thought, "Why am I being booed? Why am I being booed when we're supporting this 100 percent?" Then, I started thinking about COINTELPRO and the work they were doing to divide us, to make it seem like we weren't all fighting for the same thing. But we are. We're fighting against colonialism, US colonialism. We're fighting to unite our people. For solidarity. That's what we're fighting for. Together.

The struggle in Lincoln Park and in Humboldt Park is the same struggle. And if some of us are organizing with students, that's okay. If some of us are organizing with the gangs, that's okay! Because we're gonna unite all of our people, you know, free Puerto Rico—that's what we're gonna do.

Jacqui Lazú: What are the strengths of Puerto Rican resistance movements? How did you sustain yourself when facing conservative forces within our community, and the fear that comes with state-sponsored terror? I think people often misunderstand the divisions among Puerto Ricans because they don't grasp where they come from.

How have you confronted the forces that make people hesitant to engage with militant or radical organizations, or even with you?

José "Cha Cha" Jiménez: You know, the object of any battle is to preserve yourself and destroy the enemy. We got that from Chairman Mao. We used to read all those things. Our objective was to sustain the movement, and in order to win, to be victorious, we did what we had to do. There are things I can't say, but one of the most significant things we did was the occupation of McCormick Theological Seminary. We took three hundred and fifty community residents and stayed there for a week, winning all of our demands. The Young Lords were victorious there.

When I ran for alderman, a lot of people said, "Este es reformista." We came out of the underground—our central committee was all underground—and I had eighteen felony cases on me within a six-week period. I had one year to serve. So, as he was saying, I was running for alderman from jail, doing that one year while waiting for the other seventeen cases, all while running for alderman.

So, we were never informants, we were just trying to stay alive! If we stayed in the media, maybe we'd stay alive. Running the campaign was a way to do that. I think the Panthers did the same thing when they ran Bobby Seale for mayor—to stay alive and sustain the movement. We did whatever we had to do to stay alive.

I don't know if it was courage. We did what we had to do. There's nothing wrong with retreating if you have to. But we called it "active retreat." If you just retreat and don't do anything, then you're a coward. But if you go into hiding so you can come back and fight again, that's different. And luckily, we're back, right? We haven't gone too far away, and we're not going anywhere.

So, what I'm saying is that sometimes you have to retreat, sometimes you have to be quiet for a while so you can regroup and unite. Sometimes we just needed to get out of jail so we could keep going. We're united like we were then. I believe in everything your organization, the Puerto Rican Cultural Center, and all the other progressive movements are doing in town to free Puerto Rico and unite us as a nation.

Jacqui Lazú: Oscar, how do we unite people across fears, anxieties, and in many cases, ignorance about movements? There are real implications, and sometimes perceived ones, when it comes to being involved and fully committed to this kind of work.

Oscar López Rivera: Number one, we are a colonized people, and the problem is we live under colonial power. This has been part of Puerto Rico's history, and we bring that history because the United States sees us as a colonized people. From the very beginning, when the US entered Puerto Rico, they identified a Puerto Rican elite that would help them maintain control. One fact people don't always understand is that the colonizer cannot control a colony without the help of the colonized.

The US government knew exactly who they would depend on to keep Puerto Rico shackled. For over four hundred years, we've been under the yoke of colonialism, and it's easy to split us apart. With colonization comes dependence. The colonized are always reduced to being dependent subjects.

But historically, we've also had wonderful examples of courage. We mentioned the Grito de Lares. If you look at the Grito de Lares, you'll see how brave those people were in resisting Spanish colonialism. They even demanded the end of slavery. Leaders like Betances, Segundo Ruiz Belvis, Eugenio María de Hostos, and Mariana Bracetti showed incredible courage.* Puerto Rican women were empowered in this struggle too, and we must ensure they're included in our history.

The Grito de Lares sowed a seed of courage that continues to grow in us. For example, the slogan "Tengo Puerto Rico en mi corazón" became central to the Young Lords, and many Puerto Ricans internalized that sentiment. Of course, there's a vested interest in keeping us divided, and the powers that be exploit that.

---

* Eugenio María de Hostos and Mariana Bracetti were key figures in Puerto Rico's nineteenth-century independence movement and collaborators of Ramón Emeterio Betances and Segundo Ruiz Belvis. Hostos advanced their vision through education and reform, while Bracetti, known as "Brazo de Oro," helped lead the 1868 Grito de Lares and sewed the flag designed by Betances.

One example is found in COINTELPRO. In a 1960 memo, J. Edgar Hoover instructed the FBI in Puerto Rico to delve deep into the personal lives of leaders of the independence movement—whether they had extramarital affairs, drank alcohol, or any other detail that could be used against them. The FBI would take photos of Puerto Rican leaders with the wives of other leaders, then send these misleading photos to the spouses to sow division and disrupt the movement.

This tactic was also used in the diaspora to foment hatred and create differences among us, and it was very effective. J. Edgar Hoover's goal was to destroy the nationalist movement in Puerto Rico, and he did everything possible to achieve that. Unfortunately for him, he passed away. Puerto Ricans continue to fight for independence, and we are still here, fighting for a free Puerto Rico.

Jacqui Lazú: I want to turn to something that often gets lost in historical narratives, especially those centered on charismatic leaders. This is about the role of women. How are we going to center women's stories as we begin reconstructing the narrative of the movements in Chicago?

José "Cha Cha" Jiménez: We had a group from the gang days, and it wasn't politically correct—they called them the Young Lordettes. At the same time that we were getting ourselves together, the women in our group were different from what you'd call "middle-income women." They actually wanted us to learn and started organizing. We worked together in the same daycare center at the People's Church.

You had people like Marta Chavira and Judy Cordero, who is mentioned in an article in the *Reader*—make sure you pick up a copy, it came out last night, and it shows Judy Cordero on the cover. The daughter of Angie Lind is here. Angie was the leader of Mothers and Others. She organized the women of the Young Lords. She was a Young Lordette, married to José "Pancho" Lind, who was later killed just because of the color of his skin. She represented us at the Vietnamese Women's Conference in Canada in 1969. When she returned, she found out her husband had been killed by a white, racist mob.

He was walking in a playground, and they beat him with baseball bats. We went to court, but nobody paid attention. It's the same thing we see with Black Lives Matter today. They go to court, and nobody listens. We were doing the same with Manuel Ramos, and Angie Lind became a leader of the women's movement at that time. María Romero, who is here in the audience, was also a key figure.

We had many women activists in our group, and today we are trying to document that and let people know we weren't the only ones. It was a broad-based movement. A lot of people just know my name, but it was the people in this community who got involved. Hilda Ignatin. There were many women involved in the movement, both here and in Puerto Rico.

Oscar López Rivera: I think the fact that quite a few women spent time in prison for the cause of Puerto Rico's independence tells us a lot about the Puerto Rican woman. Olga Jiménez de Wagenheim wrote a book about the Puerto Rican heroines—the women who truly gave their hearts to the Puerto Rican independence movement, particularly in the 1950s.

If we look at history, we can truly appreciate the role of modern Puerto Rican women. Unfortunately, for the Puerto Rican independence movement, including all of us, we've often relegated women to secondary positions. We're still struggling with that and trying to change it. It's not an easy thing to address, but I will say this: last year, the strike at the University of Puerto Rico was led primarily by women, and right now, almost everything happening in Puerto Rico is being led by women.

So, I believe there's a change happening, and I hope that in the future, it will be Puerto Rican women who lead us to victory in the fight for Puerto Rico's independence.

Jacqui Lazú: A question from the audience: What is the name of the book—the one that made the biggest impact on you?

José "Cha Cha" Jiménez: *Military Writings of Chairman Mao.*

Oscar López Rivera: I think that probably the book that had the biggest impact on me was Antonio Corretjer's *The Struggle for Puerto Rican Independence / La lucha por la independencia de Puerto Rico.* If we look at the most complete leader in the Puerto Rican independence movement, I would have to say that Juan Antonio Corretjer was, and still is, the best leader we've had. He transcended so many obstacles and gave us an incredible example that we can truly identify with.

I'd also like to mention Lolita Lebrón. I mentioned that she said, "I came to Washington to give my life, not to take it." I think it's important for people to understand why she did what she did, the twenty-five years she spent behind bars, and how strong she was when she came home. She always spoke about peace, and I think that's something we need to appreciate.

Jacqui Lazú: These are also questions from the audience: How can individuals in rural areas participate in and make their voices heard in movements that are often concentrated in urban centers? Additionally, when the Young Lords expanded into Puerto Rico, how did they engage with indigenous populations and Taíno culture in their revolutionary efforts?

José "Cha Cha" Jiménez: Well, I mean, we had the Puerto Rican Cultural Center in the church, where we learned about Puerto Rican history. You know, we live in a shuttle culture, so we go back and forth to Puerto Rico all the time. My family is in Puerto Rico, and my family is here, and I'm sure it's the same for Oscar. Yo soy del campo. La familia mía es del campo. Cuando tenía quince años, yo estaba jalando bueyes. So I went to Puerto Rico, and my grandfather said, "You'd be a good worker, son," so he had me pushing the cow, you know, the ox.

We all share the same culture. Todos somos jíbaros. It doesn't matter whether we're from an urban area or the countryside. Puerto Ricans are proud to be from rural areas too. I may be going off on a tangent, but the point is that we're indigenous people, and we can't make a revolution without the people. That's why, instead of just jumping out there crazy, we focused on organizing our community. And that takes time. The revolution is a job. La patria es valor y sacrificio, right? As Don Pedro Albizu Campos said.

So, the revolution is a job, and someone has to do it. We were doing it, but all of us can do it. We're not the only ones. It's a collective effort. Everyone here needs to be involved because this is our nation.

Jacqui Lazú: Oscar, you said something critical just before we started this evening, about looking at Native American reservations as a place to begin and end a lot of these conversations.

Oscar López Rivera: Yes. When I was in prison, one of the things I would often ask Puerto Ricans who visited me was whether they had ever been to a Native American reservation. By having a historical appreciation for what the United States government has done to the native population, which is most visible on these reservations, we can better understand their plight. I would ask them if they had ever visited a Native American reservation because we need to appreciate what happens to a people whose land, culture, language, and way of life are taken from them—a reality they continue to face, even today.

If I were to visit a Native American reservation now, say the Navajo reservation, I would see what the US government has done to Native Americans. The same kind of treatment is happening in Puerto Rico, where we are being replaced. There's an article in *The New York Times* that talks about this. The gentrification in Puerto Rico and how land is being purchased and controlled. The colonial administration is complicit. In fact, the governor of Puerto Rico, who is part of the Puerto Rican elite, recently eliminated protections for eight areas that had been preserved, putting them up for sale. So now, beaches and other beautiful areas that were once protected are under threat of being bought by developers. And that's what the future holds for Puerto Rico.

Jacqui Lazú: As we mark the first anniversary of Hurricane María today, it also happens to be International Peace Day. And tomorrow, we observe El Grito de Lares. The idea of peace sits uneasily between these two moments, suspended somewhere between resistance and hope. It raises a difficult question: in a world as divided as ours, can the word *peace* still hold meaningful weight for the future?

And I want to close with a question I hear often as an educator, one tied to the role of youth and the importance of Black and Latino solidarity in Chicago. What guidance would you offer students today, especially those gathered in this historic space? How can young people build on the Young Lords' legacy and their commitments to solidarity while remaining hopeful about what comes next?

José "Cha Cha" Jiménez: This year in Grand Rapids, Michigan, we participated in the International Day of Peace. The Young Lords actually worked with the Institute for Global Education in Grand Rapids, so we were a part of that peace movement. But what you're really asking is, how can we bring peace to our neighborhoods, especially with the youth? And how can we get students involved in that process? Back in May of 1969, we were asking students to come to the community and use their skills to help us organize for the fight.

When you mention Indigenous people, we're automatically thinking about the struggles we're talking about today, right? But how do we help the youth who are killing each other every day? We have to work with them. This is a people's revolution. If we can't work with the gangs, with our own youth—our own children in the community—then what are we about?

These are our brothers involved in the gangs; we should be able to talk to them. That's how you build a peaceful world. We were once substance abusers and had our struggles, but if we don't clean up ourselves, the revolution starts with us first. That was our philosophy back then—bringing the students and everyone to work within our neighborhoods and communities, reclaiming the Puerto Rican nation.

The first step is unity. The first step is solidarity. But that's just the beginning. The next step is building our nation again. So we need to move from solidarity to actually going out and working. I'm a senior substance abuse counselor now, and I've been clean from alcohol and drugs for about thirty years. Yesterday, I was at BUILD Incorporated, which works with twenty-nine different street gangs. I'm trying to stay involved with the youth in this community, but together we can do so much more. That's part of freeing Puerto Rico—educating people, learning our history.

Oscar López Rivera: I think, first of all, the youth represent the future of our society, and we have to do everything possible to help guide them in the right direction. They need to find meaning and purpose in their lives, to become human resources, rather than dysfunctional individuals. We face a lot of dysfunctionalities, but we also need to talk about systemic issues right now.

In Puerto Rico, we are facing the biggest crisis in education. If the educational system in Puerto Rico collapses—and it's collapsing—we won't be able to develop the human resources we need for the future. That's crucial. The system is not allowing Puerto Ricans to really develop.

Here's one example: the Puerto Rican governor is buying mobile units, but they are closing schools. Schools that are in good shape are being closed, while billions of dollars are spent on mobile units. I remember in Chicago, we fought against mobile units. In Puerto Rico, they are spending billions on them. I remember my Humboldt school, which had mobile units throughout the whole yard. It was once a predominantly Jewish school with an 800-student capacity, but when the population became 2,100 students, 80 percent Puerto Rican, they used mobile units for classrooms, and that's when Puerto Ricans started to drop out of school in the early '70s. Every school in District 6 had mobile units because most of the students were now Puerto Rican.

It's important to understand how crucial it is to develop human resources and to ensure young people have access to education. In fact, I believe education should start as early as the fetal stage, with the home being part of the educational system, to ensure a functional school system.

From left to right: Aaron Dixon, former captain of the Seattle chapter of the BPP; José "Cha Cha" Jiménez; Elaine Brown, former chairman of the BPP; and Oscar López Rivera, Puerto Rican independence activist and former political prisoner. Taken at the fiftieth anniversary of the YLO in 2018, one year after López Rivera's release and on the first anniversary of Hurricane María. The event highlighted the importance of solidarity in the struggle for liberation. Courtesy of Jacqueline Lazú.

Young Lords

Conference Program 2018

Friday, September 21st

2323 North Sheffield Ave.

McGrath Arena/ Sullivan Athletic Center

6:00-7:00 pm Registration and Opening Reception (light fare and refreshments)

7:00-7:15 pm Welcome Remarks, **Guillermo Vásquez de Velasco**, Dean of the College of Liberal Arts and Social Sciences

7:15-9:00 pm Keynote Dialogue, **José "Cha Cha" Jiménez**, Founding member and President of the Young Lords and **Óscar López Rivera**, Former political prisoner and Puerto Rican independence activist. Moderator: **Dr. Jacqueline Lazú**, Associate Professor, Dept. of Modern Languages, DePaul University

Co-Sponsors

College of Liberal Arts and Social Sciences
Center for Latino Research and Latin American and Latino Studies
Department Celebración de Nuestra América Series
The Office of Institutional Diversity and Equity Diversity Signature Series
The Steans Center for Community Based Service Learning
The Center for Black Diaspora
Studio Chi
The John T. Richardson Library
Department of Modern Languages
Department of Criminology
Department of Geography
Department of African and Black Diaspora Studies
Community Service Studies Program
Committee on Global Justice of The Society of St. Vincent DePaul Professors
School of Public Service
LAS Faculty Scholarship Support Center

Young Lords Fiftieth Anniversary Symposium, Conference Program (2018)
Courtesy of Jacqueline Lazú

8.

COUNTERINTELLIGENCE, INFILTRATION, AND INDICTMENT

WITCH HUNT

WASHINGTON, D. C.—The Senate Internal Security Subcommittee, under the chairmanship of Sen. James O. Eastland of Mississippi, has launched a new investigation into several radical groups.

The investigation involves at least four groups:

—Liberation News Service, a news distribution agency which sends a packet of articles, photos and drawings twice a week to 500 subscribers in the U. S. and abroad, of which Alliance is a member.

—The SDS New York Regional office, now an independent collective. The office has been used as a meeting center and for printing and propaganda work.

—Cambridge Iron and Steel, Inc., a corporation operated by movement people for the purpose of distributing money donated by a wealthy benefactor. A spokesman for Cambridge Iron and Steel described the organization as a "fluke"—that is, not the ordinary movement funding apparatus—and said the name was a joke. The corporation disbursed nearly $25,000 to about a dozen movement groups, including LNS and the SDS New York regional office. An "expose" in PL Magazine (the Progressive Labor monthly) brought the corporation into the public eye last year. The corporation has since become inactive.

—The Institute for Policy Studies, a well-endowed left-liberal think tank located in Washington, D. C. IPS's fellows and visiting researchers include movement academicians and activists. Its director, Marcus Raskin, was a co-defendant with Dr. Benjamin Spock.

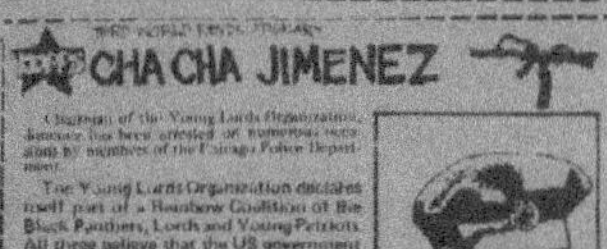

The Eastland subcommittee has so far obtained the bank records of IPS (which offered no resistance) and of Cambride Iron and Steel (whose bank, Cambridge Trust, did not notify the corporation.)

The banks of LNS and SDS were served with subpoenas to produce the records of the accounts for the subcommittee, but the banks notified the movement groups. LNS and SDS went into court together, successfully obtaining a temporary restraining order.

Continuing legal action by the two groups will seek to enjoin the subcommittee from continuing its investigation. So far, a federal judge has postponed making a decision.

No one is sure just what Eastland and his cronies are going after. Presumably, they figure the revolutionary movement would be considerably weaker if it had no research, newspapers, pamphlets or leaflets, the First Amendment notwithstanding. More specifically, it seems that the subcommittee is really after the rich people who give financial support to the New Left movement. The investigation is most likely to be an attempt to intimidate such donors and thereby starve the movement propaganda network.

The only hint as to the direction the Eastland investigators may be going came in a Chicago Tribune article written by Ronald Koziol, a reporter known to have close ties with the FBI and the Chicago cops. Koziol's informants told him that they were concerned about the fact that "some federally tax exempt foundations have supplied funds to LNS."

Koziol wrote, "Senate investigators believe that the Liberation News Service could not have stayed in business without financial contributions .... Investigators who have studied the news service's releases said that they are Marxist-Leninist, anti-capitalist, anti-military, pro-Red Chinese, pro-Viet Cong, pro-Cuban, pro-Black Panther, and anti-police."

A spokes,an for LNS said: "Judging from Koziol's article, senate investigators have a pretty accurate view of where LNS is at politically. But their analysis of our finances is fucked up. LNS survives primarily on subscriptions, and we most definitely would not go out of business even if outside contributions ceased altogether. We have welcomed outside contributions from a variety of sources, including Cambridge Iron and Steel, a handful of wealthy individuals and various Protestant Church demonisations.

"We continue to welcome these contributions, and will vigorously fight any attempt to intimidate these donors. But we will always count on the people who read the underground and radical press as the ultimate source of our political and financial strength."—LNS/CPS

PERIODICALS OF SPECIAL INTEREST

WIN MAGAZINE, 339 Lafayette Street, New York, N.Y. 10012
A sprightly bi-weekly magazine full of news and comment and controversy, poems, photographs, good cheer.
$5 a year, sample copies 25¢

LIBERATION, 339 Lafayette Street, New York, N.Y. 10012
An independent radical monthly. $7 a year, sample copies 50¢

PEACE NEWS, North American office, c/o AFSC, 160 North 15th Street, Philadelphia, Pa. 19102
An international pacifist weekly newspaper, published in London, excellent. $8.50 a year, sample copies free

PAGE FOUR

Witch Hunt (1970)

The Seed/Liberation News Service vol. 1, no. 5, April 1970, p. 4

Independent Voices Archive

Excerpts from Spies' Testimony

(1970)
Second City vol. 3, no. 1, pp. 7–9
Lincoln Park Conservation Association Collection, Box 81, Folder 8
Special Collections and Archives
DePaul University Library, Chicago, Illinois

*(Care has been taken not to reprint the names given by these political informers, and thus increase the damage done to the victims of their treachery and hatred. This is one reason for the many breaks in the record, which are marked with this symbol: ■■■. We enter our comments in parentheses. —Eds. [*Second City*])*

EXTENT OF SUBVERSION IN THE "NEW LEFT"

Monday, August 3, 1970

U.S. Senate Subcommittee to Investigate the Administration of the Internal Security Act and Other Internal Security Laws of the Committee on the Judiciary, Washington, D.C.

The subcommittee met, pursuant to call, at 2:10 p.m., in room 2300, New Senate Office Building, Senator Marlow W. Cook presiding.

Also present: J. G. Sourwine, chief counsel; Samuel Scott, associate counsel; Alfonso W. Tarabochia, chief investigator; and John R. Norpel, director of research.

Senator Cook: We will come to order. Do you have a list of witnesses?

Mr. Sourwine: These two gentlemen are the witnesses.

Senator Cook: Have they been sworn?

Mr. Sourwine: No, sir; they have not.

Senator Cook: Will you please, gentlemen, stand up; raise your right hand. Do you solemnly swear the testimony you are about to give will be the truth, the whole truth, and nothing but the truth, so help you God?

Mr. Port: I do.

Mr. Feely: I do.

TESTIMONY OF HUGH PATRICK FEELY AND HARRY F. PORT JR.

Mr. Sourwine: Would you identify yourself?

Senator Cook: You are going to take one at a time?

Mr. Sourwine: Sir, with the chair's permission, these men have worked rather closely together. I believe we can make better progress if we take them as a team and simply address the questions and let them be answered by the man best qualified to reply.

Senator Cook: All right.

Mr. Sourwine: Please identify yourselves.

Mr. Port: My name is Harry Port, Jr. I live at 839 Webster, Chicago, Ill. I have lived in the area for 3½ years and have been active in the Lincoln Park Conservation Association, my neighborhood association, which is the Sheffield neighborhood. I am currently a board member of the Lincoln Park Conservation Association, and I operate a printing business at the Lincoln Park Arms.

I am married, have two teenage sons, and have done some investigation relative to the various revolutionary factions in the Lincoln Park area in the last 2 1/2 years.

Mr. Feely: My name is Hugh Patrick Feely, I live at 839 Webster, Chicago, Ill. I have lived in the Lincoln Park area for 10 years. I have been a board member of the Lincoln Park conservation association for seven years, a neighborhood association president. I have done quite a lot of research along with other interested parties in the Lincoln Park area. The Lincoln Park Conservation Association is the parent community association in the Lincoln Park area in Chicago. We, along with our seven affiliates or seven neighborhood associations, comprise a membership of about 4,000 families.

Mr. Sourwine: How long have you two gentlemen been working together?

Mr. Feely: On this particular problem, about one year.

Mr. Sourwine: Did you work together on another problem before that?

Mr. Feely: Well, Mr. Port is a member of my board. We have worked on other community projects within Lincoln Park.

Mr. Sourwine: As we understand it, you gentlemen have information in the area of the committee's particular interest in connection with these hearings, that interest being violent and disruptive organizations which are subversive, organizations which are revolutionary. Is this correct?

Mr. Port: That is correct.

Mr. Feely: Yes.

(We are informed by experts on the question that it is the unvarying practice of these witchhunting committees to establish for the record whether or not a witness appears under subpoena even before he is sworn. Feely and Port appeared voluntarily and not under subpoena as their defenders allege.)

Mr. Port: Revolutionary organizations in the Lincoln Park area are as follows:

- Youth gangs
- BAD (Black, Active and Determined); Cobra Stones; La Gente; Latin Kings; Young Lords Organization; Young Patriots.
- Radical community and political organizations
- Concerned Citizens of Lincoln Park; Concerned Citizens Survival Front; Industrial Workers of the World; Latin American Defense Organization.
- Radical information centers
- The Guild Book Shop; People's Information Center.

Mr. Port: I would like to defer to Mr. Feely now to perhaps discuss some of the community organizations and political organization which are behind this movement in the Lincoln Park area, which are perhaps the brains behind this where the youth gangs turn out to be the muscle of the front-line troops.

Mr. Sourwine: Do you want to do that before you discuss who are the members of these various youth gangs?

Mr. Port: No. I will be glad to discuss the members.

Mr. Sourwine: Tell us what you can about the membership of these various youth gangs.

Mr. Port: As far as the youth gangs go, I have a list who, to my knowledge, are now or have been members of the Young Lords Organization in Chicago as well as a list of the New York Young Lords Organization that we know of. Many of these play dual roles. They are in Chicago for one period of time and then again in New York for another period of time.

Mr. Sourwine: They are visitors to Chicago.

Mr. Port: That is right, but they also have been in attendance at meetings representing themselves as Young Lords in Chicago.

Mr. Sourwine: These two restricted lists were prepared by you for this hearing?

Mr. Port: Yes.

(The lists referred to follows:)

(There follows a list of 51 names of persons alleged to be members of the Young Lords. There is no way right now to determine whether the names were supplied by another informer, Robert [Gunner] Colon, or, possibly by some other person who may have infiltrated the Young Lords.)

Mr. Sourwine: All right. Now, before you move into listing community and political organizations, remember, the committee is not interested in an organization just because it is a community organization or because it is a political organization. We are interested in subversive or violent, or subversive and violent organizations. What organizations of that type can you give us information about?

Mr. Port: Concerned Citizens Survival Front.

Mr. Sourwine: Tell us about that organization.

Mr. Port: They operate out of a store front at 2512 Lincoln Avenue, which is leased by the parish of the Holy Covenant, which is a United Methodist Church. They publish a newspaper called the *Lincoln Park Press*. Again, it deals with revolution, features Marxist ideas, and talks about such things as "off the pigs" and the various other violent methods of overthrow.

Mr. Sourwine: And who are the leaders of that organization?

(Port is deliberately lying in his characterization of the Lincoln Park Press *as well as his description of CCSF. The Lincoln Park Press had little or nothing in it that could be called "Marxist." It mainly carried reports on the struggles of poor people against the Urban Renewal conspiracy and the racism practiced by LPCA and DUR.)*

Mr. Sourwine: All right. Now, that is that organization.

Mr. Port: Right.

Mr. Sourwine: You have told us all you know about that?

Mr. Feely: I think you could expand on that. We could expand a great deal on the Concerned Citizens.

Senator Cook: I would like to get something into the record relative to their activities, relative to any association that they may have with your organization so that we could kind of develop this more than just to put the finger on them and kind of let it pass.

Mr. Feely: The Concerned Citizens Survival Front originated in Lincoln Park about 4 years ago out of a need for some members of the Lincoln Park Conservation Association who felt that they were not being actively represented by the association. This was their front or their excuse. They formed the Concerned Citizens of Lincoln Park and tried to take over three or four of the neighborhood associations by cramming ballot boxes at election, getting their people appointed to important committees—planning committees—that dealt with urban renewal and schools and things like that.

In the last 2 years they have stepped up their campaign in Lincoln Park. They have organized disruptions of Conservation Community Council meetings which is the official board that represents the community on all matters having to do with urban renewal. It is a State-constituted board under urban renewal. On many occasions they have violated the civil rights of many in the community.

They have planned and disrupted board of education meetings, community association meetings, and police workshops. In Chicago every district has a workshop that is attached to its police district. They have violently disrupted police workshop meetings. They have conspired and disrupted meetings at which testimony was being given to the city in response to specific developments in the Lincoln Park area. They have been very active in setting up, or their members—the members that Mr. Port just mentioned—the Weatherman faction in Lincoln Park and the SDS center in Lincoln Park.

The Concerned Citizens are funded by the parish of the Holy Covenant Methodist Church which is the mission Methodist Church.

(Feely's lies in this passage are too numerous to deal with adequately. The North Side Cooperative Ministry had nothing at all to do with founding any of these organizations, with the exception of a small subsidy to Concerned Citizens, a group which never got any extortion money at all from anybody and was never the "front organization" for dealing with the Panthers or anyone else. Feely's hatred of the opposition to his Urban Renewal policies has twisted his mind.)

Senator Cook: Let me ask you, you made a statement not too long ago that this society handled the extortion money by the Latin Kings that later went to the Young Lords. Would you explain the activities of the Latin Kings in regard to this extortion?

Mr. Feely: The Latin Kings are basically a street gang. Any politicizing that has been done has been done by the Young Lords in taking the older Latin Kings and educating them in terms of revolution. The Latin Kings are a very large gang in the city of Chicago. They have a North Side section, South Side and West Side. They have their areas divided up.

Any extortion that they take part in or any robberies that they take part in the Lincoln Park area, the cream off the top of that or a percentage of that goes to the Young Lords, their so-called turf. It is the old feudal system that the land baron whose land you steal receives the percentage off the top and they follow the same principle. A certain percentage of everything that is taken by a Latin King in the Lincoln Park area goes to the Young Lords.

Senator Cook: Is this so that there will not be an absolute confrontation between the Latin Kings and the Young Lords?

Mr. Feely: It might be one reason. Another reason is that before they come into the area, they made such agreements with the Young Lords that they would do so.

Senator Cook: Go right ahead, Counsel.

Mr. Sourwine: Well, I do not want to stop you as long as you are giving us new information. If the information is merely cumulative, such as examples of extortion, I see nothing that would be gained.

Mr. Feely: Well, there are other examples of extortion. I might—what we might try and do here is show you perhaps how the organization of the North Side Cooperative Ministry has spawned all of these children such as the Young Lords, Concerned Citizens Survival Front, Young Patriots Organization, and even part of La Gente. The North Side Cooperative Ministry is a group of 26 churches in the Lincoln Park-Lakeview community. The majority of those people, I would say, are either naïve or innocent of actions of the ministry itself.

I am entering into evidence the North Side Cooperative Ministry Agenda for Mission for 1969 and the progress report on their 5-year plan, the current report for 1970. Note should be taken of their 1970 report, under the caption "Education," concerning the 1969 Headstart programs wherein they specify 200 children of low-income families—one-third Spanish, one-third Latin, and one-third black. It is my understanding that this is in direct violation of the Headstart program. Items under the caption "Peace" should be noted, such as the counseling for draft dodgers, Washington Mobilization involvement, Vietnam Moratorium, public hearings on peace, and education and mobilization around the ABM system.

Note should also be taken of the caption "Student Power" regarding such things as working with various SDS factions, Young Lords, Panthers, and Patriots.

(Feely not only did not overburden the Committee with stories of extortion, he failed to mention one single case, much less to prove any connection between some act of extortion and any one of the political groups or religious organizations he is smearing. He can make these allegations without fear because he enjoy's Congressional immunity for his slanders.)

Mr. Sourwine: Are there any other—

Mr. Feely: By the way, Mothers and Others is a branch of the Lincoln Park Welfare Mothers.

Mr. Sourwine: Are there any other subversive or violent—

Mr. Feely: The Industrial Workers of the World is an old Communist organization which has its Chicago headquarters in the Lincoln Park area. It has lent support recently to the North Side Cooperative Ministry and their groups and the Concerned Citizens Survival Front.

Mr. Sourwine: Is this the same old IWW they used to call the "Wobblies?"

Mr. Feely: Yes, sir; it is.

Mr. Sourwine: It has had a continuous existence ever since the first or second decade of this century?

Mr. Feely: The 1920s, I believe. How they exist I do not know, but they now have many new volunteers from the Concerned Citizens and the *SEED* office, the newsreel office in Lincoln Park. The newsreel offices where all the motion pictures are produced for the leftist movement in the city and I believe supply most of the motion pictures for the leftist movement throughout the country.

Senator Cook: Could we recess long enough for me to vote and I will be right back.
(A recess was taken.)

Senator Cook: We can proceed.

Mr. Sourwine: Are there any organizations you have not yet named that you consider subversive or violent?

Mr. Feely: Yes; I would say that the Student Health Organization has been active in Lincoln Park. They are also part of the Concerned Citizens-SDS movement. They have moved their main office out of the community and to my knowledge, are not now present in any large numbers in the Lincoln Park area.

Mr. Sourwine: Student Health Organization?

Mr. Feely: Yes; SHO.

Mr. Port: They were originally on Halsted Street some time last November. Many of the people who worked with them, including ******** are gone now.

Mr. Sourwine: Who are the leaders of that organization?

Mr. Port: It was at that time—

Mr. Feely: ************

Mr. Port (continuing): Was the main coordinator in our area.

Mr. Sourwine: In what was is it a subversive organization or a violent one?

Mr. Port: They were active at the same time in organizing rampage in Chicago last October. Shortly before they left there was a burglary and they were frightened. A friend of mine owned the building that they were renting space from. We were in the building shortly afterward and picked up a number of things out of there, including a supply of these posters which were distributed in Chicago before the October riots. This was found in the Student Health Organization, posters of this nature and smaller sizes of the same thing, found in the offices of the Student Health Organization, as well as a collection of a number of books of the writings of Mao, and also another book written by Mao on military tactics was picked up there. There are also a number of things which I have in our files such as a children's grammar book printed in China, in Peking, and there were several other revolutionary types of things.

Mr. Sourwine: Are you offering this for the record?

Mr. Port: Yes.

Mr. Sourwine: I might say, Mr. Chairman, I cannot positively identify this, but this appears to be identical with similar samples that the committee has seen which came from Cuba, were printed in Cuba. It might be helpful if the order would be that the committee staff take steps to ascertain if this was in fact printed in Cuba and let the record so show.*

(The foregoing display of ignorance linking together in sinister combination entirely separate and distinct groups within the movement in Lincoln Park demonstrates the fascistic character of the witnesses. Blindly ignorant of the diversity of impulses and ideologies which motivates the various groups, having doubtless avoided knowledge of these matters through conscious decisions, Feely and Port are in fact filled with hatred of all knowledge and all dissent. The humanoids make fine agents of reaction and repression.)

Mr. Port: Under Media we have the various press that is published in or adjacent to the Lincoln Park area. FRED, which now acts as a press service and is not printing a newspaper per se but contributes to the *SEED* magazines. LADO, the newspaper of the Latin American Defense Organization, the *Lincoln Park Press*, which is the publication put out by the Concerned Citizens Survival Front in both English and Spanish. Rising Up Angry, which is a revolutionary paper for what is known as the "grease" element. These are basically the whites of motorcycle type gangs, and so forth, telling them, you know, do not pick on the other brothers, the hippies and the Puerto Ricans, and so forth. Get united and fight the real enemy, which is the pig power structure, et cetera. That is being printed or at least distributed and written in the area.

The *Second City*, which is published by the Guild Book Shop, which is another underground newspaper. The *SEED* magazine, which is the most widely circulated underground newspaper in the Chicago area, is actually composed and written in the Lincoln Park area. The *Y.L.O.*, which is the newspaper of the Young Lords Organization.

I have two comments on that. The LADO, or Latin American Defense Organization newspaper, uses the address at 1509 North Maplewood, Chicago, which in checking is the address of the ******************
**********************.

Mr. Sourwine: What kind of building is it at that address?

---

* The committee staff subsequently was advised the poster had been identified by agents as having been printed in Cuba.

Mr. Port: It is a home.

Mr. Sourwine: A private home?

Mr. Port: Yes. An apartment building where they live.

Mr. Sourwine: How many apartments are there at that address?

Mr. Port: I do not know. It is a residential area. I am not familiar with the building.

Mr. Sourwine: Are there six, four, 10? Is it a high rise?

Mr. Port: No, not a high rise. It is a lower—

Mr. Sourwine: Is it conceivable that there might be *********living in one apartment and another apartment on another floor or a basement would be used for the newspaper?

Mr. Port: Yes. That is possible. This I do not know, never having been in the building. They list that address but they also list their address at that 1509. So, it is coincidental, then, in that case.

The early publications of the Young Lords newspaper or *Y.L.O.* listed the address at 2512 Lincoln Avenue, which was the address of the Concerned Citizens Survival Front. The later issues listed 834 West Armitage Avenue, which is the address of the Armitage Avenue Methodist Church. This address was listed after their take over.

Mr. Sourwine: May I go off the record for a moment?

Senator Cook: Off the record.
(Discussion off the record).

(The fascistic committee and the extreme right in general are especially interested in the suppression of the "underground" and radical press. The revolutionary developments in printing offset have broken the mass media control held by the monopolies before this cheap new process became common. Now almost any group, no matter how small, can speak to the public directly and regularly. The First Amendment to the Constitution protects our right to publish. The reactionaries will stop at nothing to destroy this right.)

Mr. Sourwine: This is a practicing law firm in Chicago?

Mr. Feely: The "law office" is the name of a store front that was set up with funds from McCormick Seminary which purports to defend the poor in Lincoln Park, particularly those of minority backgrounds.

Mr. Sourwine: All right.

Mr. Port: I would like to elaborate on that a little bit. There is some doubt as to exactly if this is where the funds from McCormick were sent. There may be a possibility that those funds to establish a law clinic may have gone to the Latin American Defense Organization. I have a copy of the report issues from McCormick Theological Seminary and in my own checking with them, they were sketchy as to where the funds were used and they indicated at one time one thing and at another time another. We are not really sure. We have no methods of determining outside of the fact that they did make a grant and the law office started shortly after.

The other thing, what I call radical information centers which handle not only the underground newspapers from Chicago but material, which is Communist material, which is printed in China, and so forth, which are the Guild Book Shop, and the People's Information Center, located in the Lincoln Park area.

Mr. Sourwine: Tell us a little about each one.

Mr. Port: The Guild Book Shop as well as acting as a bookshop also is the publisher of the *Second City Newspaper*, which is an underground newspaper purporting to deal in matters of revolutionary activities.

Mr. Sourwine: Is the Guild Book Shop in fact a book shop?

Mr. Port: It acts as a bookshop, yes.

Mr. Sourwine: Where is it located?

Mr. Port: It is located on Halsted Street, 2136 North Halsted, three doors away from the law office.

Mr. Sourwine: What is the Guild, so-called, in connection with the Guild Book Shop?

Mr. Port: I have no idea.

Mr. Sourwine: Do you know who owns the Guild Book Shop or runs it?

Mr. Port: I do not.

Mr. Sourwine: What goes on there that is subversive, or violent, or that contributes to subversion or violence?

Mr. Port: I would say it is the distribution point of most of the radical literature in the area.

Mr. Sourwine: You understand, I am not arguing, either with you or for you.

Mr. Port: No.

Mr. Sourwine: I am just trying to keep the record clear.

Mr. Port: Right. In other words, their ad would read, you know, "Open 7 days a week, Marxists and other radical literature."

Mr. Sourwine: Are you in fact reading from one of their ads?

Mr. Port: Right.

Mr. Sourwine: From what publication?

Mr. Port: From the *Second City Newspaper*.

Mr. Sourwine: Which they publish?

Mr. Port: Which they publish.

Mr. Sourwine: Should the text of that ad go in the record, in your opinion?

Mr. Port: I would say that, since they mention Marxist and other radical literature, Lenin, Mao, underground press, et cetera.

Mr. Sourwine: May it go in?

Senator Cook: Yes.

Mr. Sourwine: Thank you.
(The document referred to follows:)

Mr. Port: I would also at this time like to—here again we have this situation of overlaps. A coffeehouse called Alice's which caters to—you can read this part, revolutionary, Maoist, Leninist, et cetera, and a little bit later in the article—

Mr. Sourwine: This is an article in the same publication?

Mr. Port: Right.

Mr. Sourwine: Do you offer that for the record?

Mr. Port: Yes, sir.

Mr. Sourwine: May it be received, Mr. Chairman?

Senator Cook: Yes.

(Yippee! Just what we needed. National publicity. However, we must add that Second City *doesn't "purport to deal in matters of revolutionary activities," but rather tries to provide some honest coverage to the glorious and historic struggles being waged by the broadcast strata of the American people against war, racism and repression, on the one hand, and on the other to exposing the predatory, racist and belligerent policies of America's ruling class. The activities of "revolutionaries" is considered important only insofar as they are part of and contribute to the former.)*

Mr. Port: In addition, you will notice that the article states that once more Alice's Restaurant's major patron will be the North Side Cooperative Ministry.

Mr. Sourwine: Let us go back to the other information center you mentioned, People's Information Center. Tell us where it is and who runs it and what they do.

Mr. Port: The People's Information Center is new within the last 2 months. They are located again two doors from the Guild Book Shop on Halsted Street. They are a—well, excuse me. Let me defer this to Pat, and Pat can probably aptly describe that a little bit better.

Mr. Feely: The People's Information Center is a store front that has been established in the last 2 months purportedly by the SDS RYM II faction in Lincoln Park. The purpose of the information center is to disseminate information on revolution, on the violent overthrow of the government, on stick the pigs, on Rising Up Angry, many other items that have been previously mentioned. It seems to be staffed by members of the Concerned Citizens Survival Front and the Young Lords Organization. It is directly next door to the law office previously referred to and seems to have the legal protection of the members of the law office.

Mr. Port: Do you want me to go back to this grant from McCormick Seminary? You may have this for the record. It is their Summer Journal of 1969. It was a report on the relations of McCormick Seminary with the Poor People's Coalition.

On page 2, under legal aid, it says:

> The Board of Directors agreed to present this need to appropriate agencies of the mission of the United Presbyterian Church and other communions. It has done so. On June 20, it was possible to transmit $5000 to the Poor People's Legal Bureau, an organization formed by the Coalition. The Seminary and the Presbytery of Chicago have joined in a further request to the United Presbyterian Board of National Missions. That is where the matter presently stands.

This was signed by Arthur McKay, dated September 29, 1969.

Mr. Sourwine: May this be received, Mr. Chairman?

Senator Cook: Yes; it will be accepted.

Mr. Sourwine: Thank you.

(It appears that these informers see some terrible plot in several religious organizations providing, or helping to provide, legal advice for people without much money. Apparently, the right to legal counsel is another right these LPCA officials would like to destroy.)

Mr. Sourwine: I have no more names to check. Mr. Tarabochia, do you have any questions you wish to ask?

Mr. Tarabochia: Yes. With regard to the color of berets worn by the various gangs, you mentioned that the Young Lords wear a purple—

Mr. Feely: The Young Lords wear a purple beret with a black rim, and they also wear a badge that goes on their beret. The Cobra Stones wear a red beret with a black rim or black band. The Young Patriots wear a tan beret. The Latin Kings wear a yellow beret with black trim.

Mr. Tarabochia: How about the red and black? Has anybody tried to explain that one?

Mr. Feely: Supposedly the red beret of the Cobra Stones has some connection with the Black P. Stone Nation. I am not quite sure.

Mr. Tarabochia: No connection with the colors used by Castro's 26th of July Movement?

Mr. Feely: I understand that they are the same colors.

(On the question of symbolism, we suggest that the people running LPCA either expel these fascist spies or, themselves, take to wearing swastika armbands so the decent people of our community will know what they're into.)

Mr. Sourwine: Mr. Norpel, do you have any questions?

Mr. Norpel: No, sir.

Mr. Sourwine: Mr. Scott?

Mr. Scott: No, sir.

Mr. Sourwine: I think we have concluded, Mr. Chairman.

Senator Cook: We will conclude these hearings, and they will be renewed subject to the wish of the Chairman.

Mr. Sourwine: Thank you, Senator.

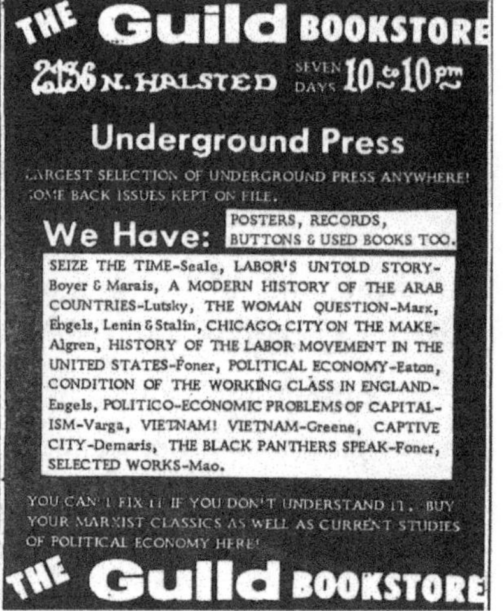

Letter to Senator Eastland from the We Love America Committee

Eugenie Adams, Secretary
August 14, 1970
Omar López Zacarias personal collection

MISS EUGENIE ADAMS
Secretary

"In God We Trust"

WE LOVE AMERICA COMMITTEE

We Are Proud of Our Flag and Think You Should Be Too

POST OFFICE BOX 1451
CHICAGO, ILLINOIS 60690
U. S. A.

August 14, 1970

The Honorable James O. Eastland, U.S. Senator
Chairman, Committee on the Judiciary
Chairman, Subcommittee to Investigate the Administration of the Internal Security Act and other Internal Security Laws.
2226 Senate Office Building
Washington, D.C. 20510

Re: Armitage Avenue Methodist Church
834 West Armitage, Chicago, Ill.
(National Headquarters YLO Gang)

Dear Senator Eastland:

The original copies of some of the subversive material the Young Lords Gang had been receiving are in a safe place (you have photocopies of some of these in your files).

I am enclosing some additional material in printed form which indicates the master "War Plan" to take over the country, incredible as it may seem, in the YLO own handwriting, a list of those who attended an educational meeting on 4/1970 including Latin Kings, a gang which the YLO is trying to indocrinate (handwritten proof is in the hands of the Gang Intelligence Unit in Chicago) in their own subversive activities.

To prove that thismaterial is authentic, there is a printed copy of a letter to Cha Cha Jimenez (who jumped bail this Tuesday and did not show up for sentencing on a criminal charge) from a female, apparently his wife (the first and last pages).

There are also some printed photos showing some of the damage on property inflicted by the gangs in the area; the building with all the posters on it was the key in last years "Pig Roast Festival" at the church disturbance.

Again, the originals of the above are in a safe place; Gang Intelligence has many others along the same line.

One person had been personally threatened with death orviolence at least eight diffeet times; another had been the subject of constant intimidation and harrassment by the gang because of disagreement with their Communist activities; another was also threatened with death and violence; the homes of two others were the subjects of fire bomb threats.

These "threatened" people would like to testify before your Subcommittee on Internal Security; the Police are protecting them, but that is not enough; they feel that our Constitution did not anticipate thissituation, and they also feel that the Courts are also not geared to this continuous "continuance" type of Justice allowing criminals to apparently defeat justice.

Sincerely, Eugenie Adams

It is necessary to use a post office box number because members of the above-mentioned committee have been threatened with violence, death, and building burning on numerous occasions.

August 14, 1970

The Honorable James O. Eastland, U.S. Senator
Chairman, Committee on the Judiciary
Chairman, Subcommittee to Investigate the Administration of the Internal Security Act and Other Internal Security Laws
2226 Senate Office Building
Washington, D.C. 20510

Re: Armitage Avenue Methodist Church
834 West Armitage, Chicago, Ill
(National Headquarters YLO Gang)

Dear Senator Eastland:

The original copies of some of the subversive material the Young Lords Gang had been receiving are in a safe place (you have photocopies of some of these in your files).

I am enclosing some additional material in printed form which indicates the master "War Plan" to take over the country, incredible as it may seem, in the YLO own handwriting, a list of those who attended an educational meeting on 4/1970 including Latin Kings, a gang which the YLO is trying to indoctrinate (handwritten proof is in the hands of the Gang Intelligence Unit in Chicago) in their own subversive activities.

To prove that this material is authentic, there is a printed copy of a letter to Cha Cha Jimenez (who jumped bail this Tuesday and did not show up for sentencing on a criminal charge) from a female, apparently his wife (the first and last pages).

There are also some printed photos showing some of the damage on property inflicted by the gangs in the area; the building with all the posters on it was the key in last years "Pig Roast Festival" at the church disturbance.

Again, the originals of the above are in a safe place; Gang Intelligence has many others along the same line.

One person had been personally threatened with death or violence at least eight different times; another had been the subject of constant intimidation and harrassment [*sic*] by the gang because of disagreement with their Communist activities; another was also threatened with death and violence; the homes of two others were the subjects of fire bomb threats.

These "threatened" people would like to testify before your Subcommittee on Internal Security; the Police are protecting them, but that is not enough; they feel that our Constitution did not anticipate this situation, and they also feel that the Courts are also not geared to this continuous "continuance" type of Justice allowing criminals to apparently defeat justice.

Sincerely,
Eugenie Adams

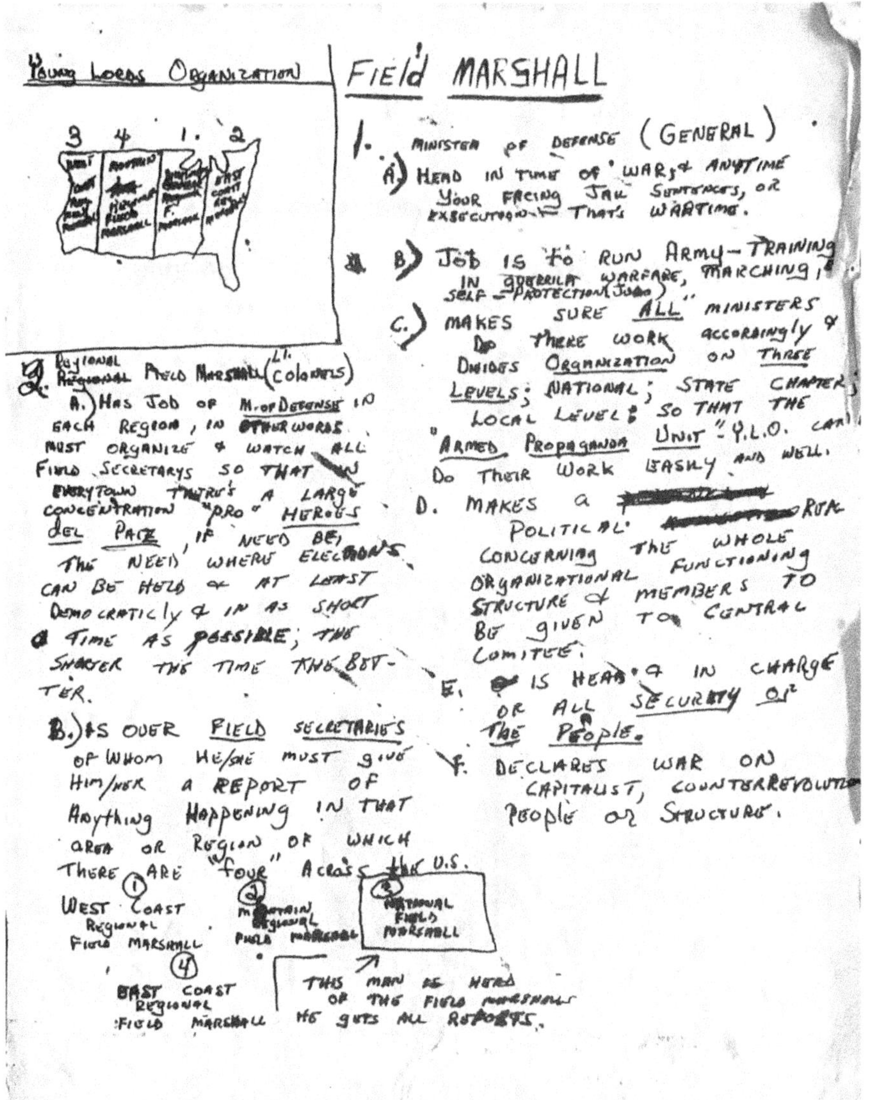

Young Lords Organization

3 4 1. 2

FIELd MARSHALL

1. MINISTER OF DEFENSE (GENERAL)

A) HEAD IN TIME OF WAR; & ANYTIME YOUR FACING JAIL SENTENCES, OR EXECUTION — THAT'S WARTIME.

B) JOB IS TO RUN ARMY—TRAINING IN GUERRILA WARFARE, MARCHING, SELF—PROTECTION (JUDO).

C.) MAKES SURE ALL MINISTERS DO THERE WORK ACCORDINGLY & DIVIDES ORGANIZATION ON THREE LEVELS; NATIONAL; STATE CHAPTER; LOCAL LEVEL; SO THAT THE "ARMED PROPAGANDA UNIT" Y.L.O. CAN DO THEIR WORK EASILY AND WELL.

D. MAKES A POLITICAL RUL[E] CONCERNING THE WHOLE FUNCTIONING ORGANIZATIONAL STRUCTURE & MEMBERS TO BE GIVEN TO CENTRAL COMITEE.

E. IS HEAD & IN CHARGE OR ALL SECURITY OF THE PEOPLE.

F. DECLARES WAR ON CAPITALIST, COUNTERREVOLUTI[ONARY] PEOPLE OR STRUCTURE.

2. Regional Field Marshall (Lt. Colonels)

A.) HAS JOB OF M. OF DEFENSE IN EACH REGION, IN OTHER WORDS MUST ORGANIZE & WATCH ALL FIELD SECRETARYS SO THAT IN EVERYTOWN THERE'S A LARGE CONCENTRATION "PRO" HEROES DEL PAIZ, IF NEED BE, THE NEED WHERE ELECTIONS CAN BE HELD & AT LEAST DEMOCRATICLY & IN AS SHORT A TIME AS POSSIBLE; THE SHORTER THE TIME THE BETTER.

B.) IS OVER FIELD SECRETARIES OF WHOM HE/SHE MUST GIVE HIM/HER A REPORT OF ANYTHING HAPPENING IN THAT AREA OR REGION OF WHICH THERE ARE "FOUR" ACROSS THE U.S.

(1) WEST COAST REGIONAL FIELD MARSHALL

(2) MOUNTAIN REGIONAL FIELD MARSHALL

(3) NATIONAL FIELD MARSHALL

(4) EAST COAST REGIONAL FIELD MARSHALL

THIS MAN IS HEAD OF THE FIELD MARSHALLS HE GETS ALL REPORTS.

Regional Field Marshal Draft Plans (ca. 1970)
Young Lords Organization
Omar López Zacarias personal collection

3. COLONEL (NATIONAL FIELD MARSHALL)

A. DIVISIONS

1. (4) Reg. Field Marshalls
(LT. COLONEL)

2. FIELD SECRETARIES — 2nd LEVEL STATE CHAPTERS
(CAPTAIN)

Job: To Organize in said states! They report to Regional Field marshall & collect reports from other city or local Field marshall who are (Lieutenants)

3. FIELD SECRETARIES (LIEUTENANTS)

A. Divide city or town in sections & sub-sections & platoons
Every member is known as a "cadre"

E.

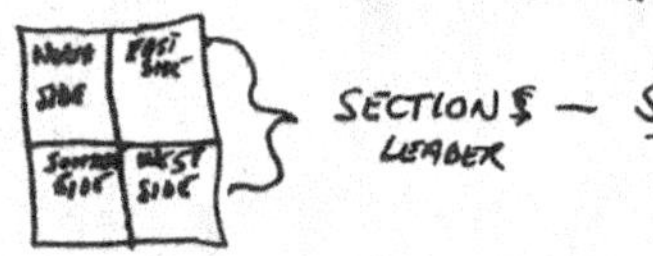

4. SUB-SECTION LEADER — PRIVATES

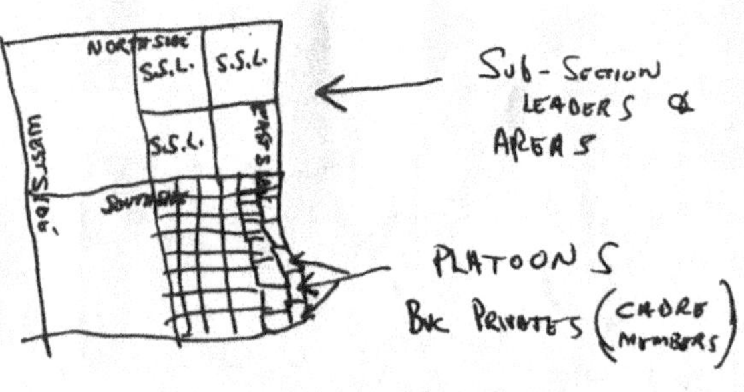

"Battle Plan"

(ca. 1970)
Transcription of discarded materials by the We Love America Committee
Omar López Zacarias personal collection

Minster of Defense

(Page One of "Battle Plan" in detail put out by the YLO Gang)

National Field Marshall (Colonel)

The National Field Marshall will be responsible to the organization for the organizing and development of Y.L.O. chapters, and branches across the country.

These chapters are to follow the structure by the Central Committee and to spread it's political ideology in their areas.

Since their an armed-propaganda unit, they must be well discipline and always eager to help people. They are the people who set the example, that the people must follow u in order to make revolutions.

"Wherever death may surprise us let it be welcome if our battle cry has reached even one receptive ear, and another hand reaches out to take up our arms, and new men come forward to join in our funeral procession with the chattering of machine guns and new calls for battle and victory."

Che

Regional Field Marshalls

The country will be divided into four regions and one regional director will be a member of the central committee. The Field Marshall in the Midwest Region will be the National Field Marshall. Because the National Office is in the Midwest Region and he must

Minister of Defense

(Page One of "Battle Plan" in detail put out by the YLO Gang)
National Field Marshall (Colonel)

The National Field Marshall will be responsible to the organization for the organizing and development of Y.L.O. chapters, and branches across the country.

These chapters are to follow the structure by the Central Committee and to spread it's political ideology in their areas.

Since their an armed-propaganda unit, they must be well discipline and always eager to help people. They are the people who set the example, that the people must follow u in order to make revolution.

> "Wherever death may surprise us let it be welcome if our battle cry has reached even one receptive ear, and another hand reaches out to take up our arms, and new men come forward to join in our funeral procession with the chattering of machine guns and new calls for battle and victory."
>
> Che

The country will be divided into four regions and one regional director will be a member of the Central Committee. The Field Marshall in the Midwest Region will be the National Field Marshall. Because the National Office is in the Midwest Region and he must

. . .

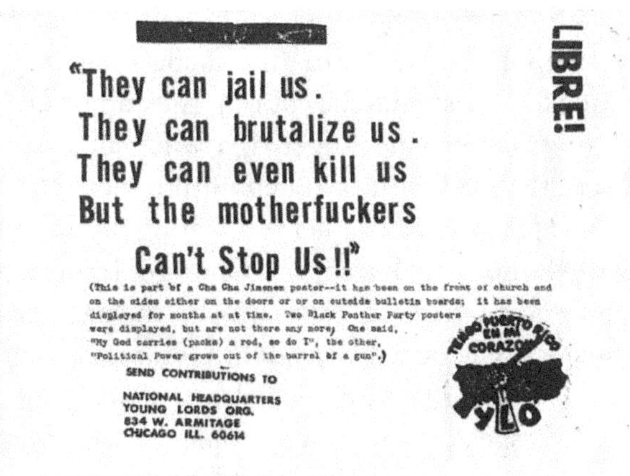

Can't Stop Us (ca. 1970)
YLO poster with comments by We Love America Committee
Omar López Zacarias personal collection

Uptight

(1970)

Pat Devine and Dick Vission

Lincoln Park Press vol. 1, no. 1, January 1970. p. 12
Lincoln Park Conservation Association Collection Box 131
Special Collections and Archives
DePaul University Library, Chicago, Illinois

A group of wealthy white property owners and real estate speculators from the Lincoln Park neighborhood have joined together for the purpose of destroying the Young Lords Organization. They call themselves UPTIGHT—United People To Inform Good-doers Here and There. Despite the name, UPTIGHT is not a people organization and makes no attempt to recruit average neighborhood people.

The organization uses tactics only rich people can use. It uses money and influence to apply pressure. The first tactic the group used was to leaflet suburban Methodist churches during the end of October and the beginning of November, trying to get rightwing suburbanites to withhold money from the Methodist Church until it kicks the Young Lords out of the People's Church. It also held a meeting on Sunday, December 7 at downtown Methodist Church, the Chicago Temple. Here a panel made many vague accusations of "terrorism" on the part of the Lords but refused to name a single specific incident. The reason why is obvious: there were none. At this meeting, they also refused to let other people from Lincoln Park speak. (The other people present from the neighborhood were members of the People's Church and other Methodist churches in the area.) These residents of Lincoln Park wanted to defend the Lords and to point out the lies in the presentation of the people from UPTIGHT. Bishop Prior of the United Methodist Church is not fooled by UPTIGHT. He has taken a strong stand against this kind of blackmail.

UPTIGHT got the TRIBUNE, December 9 to print a scare story on page one. The story's headline is "Charge Gang Uses Church as Crime Base." The story makes vague accusations of "terrorism" and "vandalism" but again fails to give a single example. Again the story is directed mainly to people who don't live in Lincoln Park and so have no way of knowing the truth.

When members of the People's Church proposed a public debate in the community, UPTIGHT people stalled, then suggested (through Alderman McCutcheon) a private meeting, again avoiding allowing people in Lincoln Park to hear their story.

In addition to trying to undermine the work of the Lords by false and vague accusations, UPTIGHT (according to Harry Port who is a member of the group) recently gave money to another group of Puerto Ricans known as Concerned Puerto Rican Youth, who have opened a store front at 1021 West Armitage. Although the purpose for giving funds has not been stated, it seems clear that the money was given to start antagonism between Puerto Rican youth in the community. If Puerto Ricans are fighting amongst themselves, they cannot fight the real enemies—such as the people in UPTIGHT and others who are exploiting Puerto Rican people and pushing them out of the neighborhood. Regardless of whether the Concerned Puerto Rican Youth are aware of it they are being used by wealthy white speculators against their own people.

UPTIGHT has never made its membership public. At first it maintained only an answering service on Lake Shore Drive, but has even discontinued that. With the cooperation of ministers in the neighborhood, the *Lincoln Park Press* has learned the names of 10 people in UPTIGHT. These men are: Harry Port, 839 West Webster, a property owner and nominee for the Board of Directors of Lincoln Park Conservation Association (LPCA), (Mr. Port seems to put out all of the group's propaganda, he runs an advertising agency and has all kinds of facilities and contacts that poor people do not have); Peter Bauer, 545 West Belden, a property owner and a member of the Conservation Community Council (CCC), LPCA Board member and the only nominee for LPCA president; James Moburg, 1950 North Dayton, a property owner, CCC member, and Board member of LPCA; Paul Johnson, 832 Altgeld, a property owner, CCC member, and LPCA Board member; Hans Schmidt, 1954 Fremont, a property owner and LPCA Board member; Don Lebold, 2118 Cleveland, a property owner and LPCA Board member; Carolyn Barrett, 1947 Lincoln, a property owner and LPCA Board nominee; George Thrush, 351 Belden, a property owner and real estate speculator; Roy and Sally Payment, 1955 Fremont, property owners, Roy, a LPCA Board nominee; and Rita Johnson, 840 West Armitage, a property owner. Of course, Alderman McCutcheon works closely with the group.

The fact that almost all of these people are high-ranking officials of LPCA is no coincidence. It is also no coincidence that all are property owners and that most are real estate speculators in Lincoln Park. These are people who are making money by pushing poor people out of the neighborhood and by raising rents. The real reason why they want to destroy the Young Lords is because the Lords defend poor people and try to keep them in the neighborhood. If the poor people stay the speculators can't make nearly as much money.

COMMUNITY MEETING **FRIDAY, FEBRUARY 12, 1971 7:30 P.M.**

Hear

RICHARD CRILEY

EXECUTIVE SECRETARY OF THE CHICAGO COMMITTEE TO DEFEND THE BILL OF RIGHTS

DISCUSS THE ROLE OF THE SENATE INTERNAL SECURITY SUBCOMMITTEE
AND THE MEANING OF ITS MEDDLING IN LINCOLN PARK.

Coffee and informal discussion will follow Mr. Criley's presentation and general discussion

PEOPLES CHURCH **ARMITAGE AND DAYTON**

WHY HAS THE LINCOLN PARK CONSERVATION ASSOCIATION LEADERSHIP GONE TO A SENATE COMMITTEE TO SMEAR PEOPLE WHO OPPOSE THEIR POLICIES?

The people of Lincoln Park need low-cost housing for working-class people, Black, White and Latin. They need better schools, jobs, day care centers, health care, tenants' unions, etc.

There have been many community organizations fighting for these things, among them, The Concerned Citizens, The Young Lords Organization, Neighborhood Commons Corporation, the Lincoln Park Town Meeting, La Gente, and a few newspapers that have supported them, like Y.L.O., The Lincoln Park Press, and Second City.

HOW HAVE THESE DEMANDS BEEN MET?
THEY HAVE BEEN IGNORED...
AND THE ORGANIZATIONS HAVE BEEN PILLORIED BEFORE CONGRESS AND THE NATION!

Leading this effort to smear them are Hugh Patrick Feely, Executive Director of LPCA, and Harry Port, Jr., LPCA Board Member.

WHY?

Because the LPCA membership is largely upper middle class property owners who are easily manipulated by the powerful real estate speculators and the big financial interests behind them.
Because the Regular Democratic Organization, the corrupt, cynical patronage apparatus that sucks the blood of Chicago tax-payers, runs the city and serves the real estate profiteers and promotes their racist schemes for Lincoln Park and Near North.
Because City Hall and the Department of Urban Renewal has the arrogance to treat this totally unrepresentative handful of manipulators in LPCA as the authentic spokesmen for Lincoln Park.
Because they want to save themselves from being exposed and to prevent the people from getting together to work out their problems. That is why feely and Port spilled their venom before the witch-hunting, red-baiting, racist Senate Internal Security Subcommittee, headed by Sen. James Eastland of Mississippi.

SO FAR THEY SEEM TO BE GETTING AWAY WITH IT!

The insiders are stealing millions in federal money by buying land cleared of poor people with public funds at rock-bottom prices, and monoplizing federal programs for themselves and their favored friends. They want to build nothing but luxury high-rises and expensive townhouses on this land, houses they can sell at a fantastic profit. They are not only driving out the poor and working-class people, but they intend to keep them out forever.

Come to the meeting and discuss with your neighbors how we can fight back against these conspirators.

We must hold meetings all over the community, in churches, in homes, anywhere we can get together and talk things over without the manipulators and fast buck artists breathing down our backs.

LINCOLN PARK RIGHTS COALITION

1874 N. FREMONT Tel. 642-2624
Public Meetings Held Each Wed. At 7:30 P.M.

Community Meeting—Hear Richard Criley (1971)
Lincoln Park Conservation Association Collection, Box 81, Folder 13
Special Collections and Archives
DePaul University, Chicago, Illinois

Block Party: Standoff with the Alderman Communiqué

May 4, 1974
Angela Lind, Communications Secretary, YLO
Courtesy of José "Cha Cha" Jiménez personal collection

1. April 10, 1974, Cha-Cha Jimenez and Slim Coleman went with a letter to the Alderman to ask for a permit for this event. They also asked if we needed petitions or letters, the Alderman said "No." The Alderman had Cha-Cha and Slim wait and then changed the subject to the RTA. He finally said that "They should write up the purpose so he could go to the City Council to pass it, and it could then be sent to the Bureau of Streets and Sanitation." Cha-Cha and Slim responded that the purpose was a block party, and it was already stated as such in the letter. The Alderman said, "It wasn't enough." So, Cha-Cha and Slim explained in depth that it was a memorial for Manuel Ramos and Pancho Lind, and also to observe the deaths of other poor people. They would be talking about the urban removal of Latinos and other poor people, the police harassment, and the drug situation on Wilton and Grace. Cha-Cha and Slim said they had already explained the purpose, and they had understood that the Alderman, and not the Bureau of Sanitation, was responsible for giving the permit. The Alderman then gave them back the letter and said he "didn't want it." But as they walked out the door, they gave the letter to his secretary.
2. April 15, 1974 Cha-Cha and Slim went to the alderman's office for a meeting on another subject. They spoke to the ward committeeman, Axelrod. He said "The Alderman reacted a little bit that night and not to worry. The permit is going through and go ahead with the event." That is when we started putting out extensive advertisement, contacted the bands, began making literally thousands of phone calls to groups and individuals. We also began collecting petitions for the support of the event. We invited clergy to give invocations for Manuel and Pancho and arranged speakers representing various community groups.

3. April 17, 1974 Cha-Cha and Slim wanted to make sure that we would get the permit, so they went to the Uptown states attorney's office and spoke to Francis Baumgart and asked to please call the Alderman to help us get the permit. The Alderman told him "It's up to the Alderman—not the state's attorney—to issue permits and maybe he would or maybe he wouldn't."
4. April 18, 1974 at a community meeting at Saint Mary's of the Lake church, they spoke to the Alderman again. He changed the subject by saying that we had been disagreeing with him over the college site. When we took the position that we didn't want any more low-income housing torn down and we wanted the families that had been moved out to be relocated. He said, "we shouldn't do that" and walked away without giving us an answer. That same night we also spoke to Sgt. Bullerman, public relations for the 19th police district, informed him of the problems we were having with the permit, and said that we wanted a meeting with Commander Hanley.
5. April 19, 1974 Cha-Cha and Slim went to Sgt. Bullerman's office. He said he felt the police were being used and he didn't like it. He said that we could go on with the events without the permit, but if he got an anonymous phone call informing him we didn't have a permit he would have to come and arrest everyone at the block party. He told Cha-Cha and Slim to go back and make an agenda for a meeting with Commander Hanley. We made an agenda and brought it back. He said he would call us back for an appointment, which he did.

   In the meantime,

6. April 24, 1974, an article came out in the Lerner *Booster* announcing the block party.

   Also, in the meantime,

7. April 24, 1974, Cha-Cha and Slim went to see the Alderman, this time in front of a college student, who was doing an interview with him about how he conducts his office work, he told them, "he didn't see any reason why we couldn't get the permit for the block party." He said many people told him they didn't want the block party, but he was sure that we knew many people who wanted it, but we had to show him something. We asked him again what

he wanted. Did he want petitions? He said "Yes, that would be a good idea." We told him we would bring him back petitions that night. That night we came back with the petitions, his secretary accidentally brought out the fact that the Alderman had already sent out a letter asking for the permit. (She said it says 2:00 to 10:00 PM on the petition but on the letter I sent out I wrote 2 to 9:00 PM.) The Alderman then nudged her with his elbow letting her know to be silent.

We came to the conclusion that he just wanted names to find out who would potentially oppose in the future. It would seem that the Alderman would use his political office for his own personal gains.

We cannot understand why the Alderman would go to such lengths to prevent a social event sponsored by Latinos and for Latinos and other poor of this ward. We did not inform you of this sooner because we did not want to fall into the trap the Alderman wanted us to.—To scare people away from this block party.

Angela Lind
Communications Secretary
Young Lords Organization

9.

A NEW ERA

Los Gritos de Mañana: Revolutionary Pasts and Futures

Dr. Wilson Valentín-Escobar
Keynote address delivered September 23, 2018
Young Lords Fiftieth Anniversary Symposium
September 21–23, 2018
DePaul University, Lincoln Park, Chicago, Illinois

On September 23, 1968, the Chicago Young Lords took bold actions and articulated a vision of freedom and social justice, under the leadership of José "Cha Cha" Jiménez and others. They were building on a long, rich legacy of resistance spearheaded by the likes of abolitionists and freedom fighters like Dr. Ramón Emeterio Betances (1827–1898), Segundo Ruiz Belvis (1829–1867), Ana María (Mariana) Bracetti Cuevas (1825–1903), and others who had organized and rebelled against the Spanish Crown exactly one hundred and fifty years today, on September 23, 1868. This new generation of visionaries and activists hoped to establish a system that opposed internal and transnational colonialism, classism, racism, gentrification, and gender inequality. This is the legacy that underlies this historic gathering convened in September 2018 at DePaul University, recognizing the fiftieth anniversary of the founding of the Chicago Young Lords in 1968.

Today, I want us to reflect on the symbolism of the Young Lords' choice to initiate a civil and human rights movement on the hundredth anniversary of El Grito de Lares in Puerto Rico, and what that reveals. I believe that "El Grito de los Lords," birthed on September 23, 1968, invoked not a static nostalgia for a revolutionary 1868 but rather an active projection of an equitable and decolonial future for boricuas on the island and in the US diaspora. The Young Lords unabashedly inserted themselves as active agents and history-makers that otherwise ignored and devalued their history and their physical presence. They awakened an anticipatory sense of what is and what could be, expressing a vision of a self-determined community where memory sparked a desire for change.

Memory and Resistance: El Grito de Lares

On September 23, 1868, revolutionary forces in Puerto Rico, with assistance from their Caribbean neighbors who were committed to abolishing transatlantic slavery and to ending Spanish colonial rule, planned an armed uprising. Organized in the western Puerto Rican town of Lares, this revolt for political independence known as "El Grito de Lares" was led by Dr. Ramón Emeterio Betances, Segundo Ruiz Belvis, and Mariana Bracetti. The short-lived rebellion remains an inspiration for like-minded activists and revolutionaries, demonstrating the oppositional potential of direct action against a colonial government that ignored, dishonored, and aimed to diminish Puerto Rican humanity. Boricuas of many political stripes admire the goals, courage, and the strategizing approaches undertaken by Betances, Ruiz Belvis, and Bracetti.

Having survived a hurricane in October 1867, in which thousands had lost their lives, crops, and livestock, with no recovery assistance from the Spanish Crown, Puerto Rican agricultural workers and creole elites felt snubbed by the disinterested Spanish colonists. They were angry at the exploitative economic system and enraged by the continuous disregard shown by colonial authorities in Madrid for the plight of the people. The abusive and obligatory tax system compelled Puerto Ricans to subsidize the military regime as well as the colonial forces fighting rebels in Cuba and elsewhere. Determined to undertake a decolonial future, they organized the military rebellion. Betances authored a series of proclamations that described the history of their oppression and insisted that Boricuas revolt against the tyrannical system writing his famous "Los Diez Mandamientos de Hombres Libres" ("Ten Commandments of Free Men"):

1. Abolition of slavery
2. The right to fix taxes
3. Freedom of worship
4. Freedom of speech
5. Freedom of the press
6. Freedom of trade
7. Freedom of assembly
8. The right to bear arms
9. Inviolability of the citizen
10. The right to elect one's officials

From exile, Betances authored another proclamation that stated:

> We must conspire, because of the 5,000,000 pesos that we pay in taxes annually, more than half finds its way to Spain, to never return, under the pretext of surplus, or savings belonging to the peninsula employees. The other half is squandered in an unnecessary military force, in a ravenous public treasury, in an immoral administration, in faulty public works, and in secret police [that spreads terror everywhere].[24]

Rebel cells were organized throughout the island, and they first believed that the town of Camuy was the best location for the armed rebellion. Originally planned for September 29, an informer tipped off the occupiers about the planned attack. The leaders of the various cells regrouped and relocated the rebellion to the town of Lares and moved the attack to September 23, 1868. With ammunition funneled into Puerto Rico from St. Thomas and Santo Domingo, the members of the Lares cell marched to the center of town while clamoring, "Death to Spain, Long Live Liberty, Long Live Free Puerto Rico, Liberty or Death." The rebels arrested close to two dozen Spaniards and raided their properties. The mayor and his assistant were also arrested, and City Hall was occupied. Images of the queen were removed, and rebel troops declared Puerto Rico a free republic.

The neighboring town of San Sebastian was next on the list. On their way to take over Pepino, rebels decided to celebrate Mass. Doing so allowed the mayor of San Sebastian to organize a counter offensive and secure additional support from Aguadilla. Rebel soldiers were now short of firearms and ammunition. Betances was also on the run and hiding, and thus unable to send additional arsenal support. Rebel soldiers retreated, the Spanish regained control, and 545 rebel soldiers were incarcerated; three were women. Eventually, all sentences were commuted.

Betances, Ruiz Belvis, and others were not alone in their anticolonial organizing. During the late-nineteenth century, there were anticolonial movements and uprisings across the Caribbean and Latin America. The Caribbean islands of Cuba, the Dominican Republic, Haiti, and Puerto Rico collectively looked to each other for resolutions to their colonial subordination. The Caribbean uprisings were made possible due to collaborations with other fellow revolutionaries. A decolonial, transnational, Antillean-based Caribbean imaginary was permeating the region; in it, revolutionaries consulted and collaborated with one another to exert their will against an exploitative colonial system.

Decolonial Education and Memory Without Nostalgia

The decolonial freedom fighting efforts led by those who orchestrated El Grito de Lares would serve as a historical marker of the radical potential of the Puerto Rican nation, including the US diaspora community. Often portrayed as obedient and subservient to US colonialism, a new generation of Puerto Ricans—including post–World War II migrants and their descendants—rejected these stereotypes. They critically questioned Western colonialism and imperialism, the Eurocentric canon, and actively explored an alternative body of knowledge from their own underappreciated history, and those of socially adjacent communities—particularly African Americans, Indigenous peoples, Chicanx/Mexican, and Asian Americans. Diaspora-based boricuas understood how media and political officials constructed their community, which informed their everyday marginalized experiences as colonized US citizens.

Between the post–World War II moments and the emergence of the US ethnic studies programs, with little to no Puerto Rican studies history taught in public schools or university curricula, Young Lords members drew from a history of resistance to inform their current actions. They led political education classes in their homes and in the community and taught each other about the radical history of resistance in Puerto Rico relaying it to their struggles in Chicago. This decolonial civic engagement served as a model for the growing boricua community. The Young Lords shared their growing knowledge of Puerto Rican, Caribbean, and Latin American histories, to inform political activism among the youth. Announcing themselves as a human rights organization in 1968, they demonstrated their effort to teach an alternative history that offered self-dignity and pride, transforming their history into "resources of hope."[25]

By understanding their history as transnational, the Young Lords came to understand the significance of both building on *and* linking with other (de)colonial systems, movements, and solidarities across the

Afro-Caribbean, Latin America, and the United States. These shared experiences of language barriers and racial exclusion, akin to those faced by African Americans and Native Americans, underscored the congruent histories of misery and struggle that served as a foundation for forging revolutionary networks. This solidarity mirrored the relationships that revolutionaries like Betances and Ruiz Belvis built with Antillean and Latin American counterparts a century earlier.

The Young Lords practiced a form of decolonial civic engagement, using their history of resistance to inform current actions without invoking nostalgia. By looking back at El Grito de Lares, they understood colonialism as an unjust racial, economic, and gendered system and drew inspiration to challenge contemporary conditions. This *nostalgia for the future* enabled them to imagine new decolonial worlds and engage in political action to both decodify and codify significant memories into present-day realities. They recognized that politics involves defining one's own history and resisting political domination through historical redefinition. The Young Lords critically engaged with the past to construct themselves as successors of a radical activist tradition, understanding that social power dictates which historical narratives are valued, and which are silenced.

Drawing on the past can help nurture a commitment to social justice organizing in the present. Karl Marx reminded us that "[people] make their own history, but they do not make it under circumstances chosen by themselves, but under circumstances directly encountered, given and transmitted from the past." It is those "circumstances directly encountered" that allowed the Young Lords to connect the internal colonialism in the present to the colonialism of the past and thus invoke a decolonial "nostalgia for the future." This is important because all too often, nationalist mythmaking obfuscates an opportunity for a current generation of activists to critically interrogate and ask questions, and thus, they never challenge the past. The Young Lords were not swooned by the myths, but fiercely and critically engaged the past and constructed themselves as successors of a radical activist tradition through their praxis.[26]

Just as social power can define which historical narratives are deemed important and treated as official, it can similarly determine which stories and types of knowledge are socially valuable and worth public consideration. And within the power-history-community triad, the knowledge of a marginalized community is often constructed as having no value, and they have minimal power to challenge such constructions. Collective memory relies on access to material resources. Within this invisible underground of dismissed knowledge, acts of resistance and cultural actions also go unnoticed. This invisibility is a double-edged sword: it keeps you unrecognizable to the white mainstream and marginal to some in your community, yet it also makes you harder to detect, offering potential as a weapon of resistance. Thus, colonial invisibility is repurposed to organize political intervention.

When the Chicago Young Lords transitioned to a grassroots political organization on September 23, 1968, they brought this history before a community that had been unfamiliar with it and emancipated the information about this uprising from its marginality. In other words, the Young Lords brought this lesser-known history to everyday people, and to boricuas who were denied access to it, mostly through their social action and political organizing. Their militant action and the popular education they provided liberated an alternative archive of knowledge as a source of decolonial praxis. This insurrection of rejected and dejected knowledge—found in our homes, churches, bodegas, kitchen tables, social clubs, and street parks—was relocated into the political sphere through their voices, their bodies, and their grassroots organizing.

To achieve this, they rejected passive resignation and linked their 1968 struggle with the one initiated a hundred years earlier. Believing in their capacity, agency, and wherewithal to bring about social transformation was historic; it revealed a decolonial consciousness with the competence and commitment to undertake the challenging task of effecting social change and shaping their future. By rejecting negative portrayals of Puerto Rican history and identities and reclaiming that history as a source of empowerment, they refused to view themselves or their community as passive or fatalistic. They legitimized Puerto Rican history, initiated change without waiting for elite approval, and responded to dire community conditions with immediate action. Alienated by institutional racism, sexism, and classism, and tired of false political promises, the Young Lords committed to advocating for social change, community redevelopment, and reclaiming public space as a show of power.

Political Collaboration and Solidarity

A major component of the success of the Young Lords was their commitment to intersectional coalition building. DePaul University professor and key organizer of this symposium, Dr. Jacqueline Lazú, observed that as the Young Lords grew and engaged in activism throughout Chicago and circulated their own newspaper, so did their solidarity networks. They understood the significance of forging coalitions that both celebrated their Latinidad while also transcending it.[27] Because the Young Lords were racially and ethnically diverse, and included non-Latinx members, the emergence of a Latinx identity coalesced with a cross-ethnic and transracial vision of liberation.

Segregated circumstances call for collaboration and support networks among sidelined and disregarded individuals to create community. The second-class status of the working poor and people of color have brought these communities together in institutions like prisons, churches, housing projects, and schools. In this context, as Cha Cha's story shows, second-class citizens used their status to connect, fostering important conversations and relationships across oppressed communities. The collaboration between the Young Lords, the Panthers, and the Young Patriots, known as the Rainbow Coalition, responded to multiple forms of oppression affecting African American, Indigenous, Latinx, and poor white communities. This solidarity and collaboration embodied the spirit and strategy of the '60s and '70s, culminating in a shared vision of liberation and survival, advancing intersectional alliances into the shared, everyday worlds of marginality.

The Young Lords transformed their collaborations into public action, using shared oppressions to stage public theatrics of solidarity, such as the 1969 McCormick Theological Seminary occupation. These dramatic housing battles challenged Richard Daley's urban renewal program, renaming it "urban removal." During the 1960s and '70s, they used public spaces and institutions as domains of struggle, inspiring the community into social action. Their approach was intentional, emotional, and symbolic, such as renaming a building on the McCormick campus the "Manuel Ramos Memorial Building" after a victim of police brutality. Their public displays of power and resistance became focal points for enacting self-representation and community.

Within these public gatherings, protests became collective expressions that allowed for a sense of community to develop amidst the drama of demonstration. By going out in public to communicate their ideas, enact cultural practices, partake in communal celebrations, and contribute to political discourses and activities, community members and activists also created a space in which to celebrate their marginalized identities and cultural practices. They created a space *where a solidarity of difference* directly confronted issues of racism and classism. And because public space is a contested terrain, the takeover of the streets or of city-sponsored policy discussions around housing and policing, were interpreted as political acts and as an affront to routine political practices. Thus, the public displays of power and resistance foregrounded by the Young Lords became a focal point for enacting a radical acclamation of self-representation and community despite the state-imposed limits on their secondary citizenship. Public expressions allowed for a sense of community to develop and allowed them to celebrate their identities in a manner resembling theatrical political drama.

The Young Lords built alliances across movements and organizations, forming partnerships based on "chains of equivalence"[28]—a network of creative and political strategies by allied groups working to challenge hegemony. These groups united around shared struggles, though not all faced identical oppression. What linked them was the shared experience of powerlessness under a dominant system. These alliances often sparked fear in authorities. The strategic use of a revolutionary history promoting an international, transethnic, and transracial vision of change alarmed figures like J. Edgar Hoover and Richard J. Daley. Organizing within one's community was one thing, but when the Lords expanded to form alliances in *struggles of equivalence,* they created a broader platform to challenge hegemony. This coalitional organizing drew too much attention, as their decolonial and ideological strategy became a visible threat to those monitoring them.

In the theater of struggle, where the state upholds its hegemony and suppresses social movements, it considers "place, content, audience, time, and the goal—the end" as key elements of its actions.[29] These factors guide the state's strategies against movements or individuals it sees as threats. One key element—time—involves reflecting on history and its implications for the future. It considers the memories tied to a space, person, or community and the longings these might inspire. A striking example is the FBI's assassination of Filiberto Ojeda Rios, alleged leader of the underground organization Los Macheteros on September 23, 2005—the very same date so symbolically tied to rebellion and cultural pride. This act served as a display of state power, asserting hegemony over memory and aiming to sever the connection between the date and visions of independence. The state's choice of timing was a deliberate effort to reframe historical and cultural markers of counter-memory as tools of control.

Place is also a crucial factor in the enactment of power. Ojeda Rios was assassinated in Hormigueros, Puerto Rico, the birthplace of Segundo Ruiz Belvis. While the FBI and Puerto Rican authorities did not choose Ojeda Rios's hiding place, their actions sent a clear message: all locations within the nation are under state control and susceptible to intervention. In this context, location became a stage where histories are performed and collective memories are created, lived, and recounted. The assassination in Hormigueros now redefines the town, shifting its meaning from the birthplace of Belvis to a symbol of state authority. Hormigueros has since become a focal point for debates about the legitimacy of the Puerto Rican state, the power of memory in a transnational struggle for survival, and the counter-memories of resistance that endure.

Places are not just symbols; they are spaces where people live and where history is made and remade. Space is never empty; it holds memory and history. Chicago is the place where a younger generation of proud boricua activists and visionaries dared to dream a new world into being. Despite facing numerous institutional obstacles, injustices, and acts of hatred, the Young Lords audaciously declared their presence and sense of belonging. Cha Cha and his comrades, like Betances and others before them, became new *diasporican* symbols of resistance. Their "gritos" were visions and urgent calls for justice, looking backward to move forward toward a better mañana.

The significance of the Young Lords cannot be overstated. Their gritos de mañana (cries of tomorrow) rippled across the Puerto Rican diaspora, helping us find our voice, remove "ay bendito" from our vocabulary, and foster civic action and pride. They cultivated an assertive collective self, free from despondence, and showed us how to break the mental bonds that had been used to define the diaspora boricua community. Through their praxis, the Young Lords taught us that history is made through social action, education, and a fierce commitment to listening to community. Their gritos de mañana continue to inspire us to see ourselves as historical agents of change, creating a decolonial present and tomorrow.

Building Revolutionary Ideology in a New Era

(2024)

Paul Mireles, Chairman, Chicago Chapter, New Era Young Lords
MA Candidate, Critical Ethnic Studies Program
DePaul University, Chicago, Illinois

Over fifty years ago, the Young Lords Organization became a pivotal movement in Chicago, fighting against police brutality, gentrification, and the deprivation of basic human needs. Fast forward to 2021, following the George Floyd uprisings and amidst a global pandemic, a new generation has revived the YLO's legacy, continuing the fight against enduring systems of oppression. My path into the New Era Young Lords has been shaped by my Mexican and Puerto Rican heritage, my upbringing in Chicago, and my experiences with street tribes, which all contributed to my political awareness and commitment to the movement. These experiences not only drew me to the Young Lords but also gave me the tools to help revitalize their revolutionary spirit in present-day Chicago, bridging the legacy of past movements with today's struggles.

Growing up in Chicago, I spent most of my early years in Belmont Cragin, a Northwest Side neighborhood on the border of Austin. Family situations often had us staying temporarily with relatives in Pilsen, Little Village, and Bridgeport. Initially, we were among the few Latinx families in a predominantly Polish and Italian area, but by the time I was six or seven, more Latinx and a few Filipino families had moved in. Visiting Pilsen and Little Village gave me glimpses of rich Mexican culture, but as a non-Spanish-speaking Latino, I sometimes felt out of place, and the kids called me "Pauly from the North Side." My pops had introduced me to Chicanx history, the Zoot Suit Riots, and the Brown Berets. During an argument one day, I learned he wasn't my biological father, revealing my Puerto Rican heritage and adding layers to my identity.

I started school at St. Genovese, a Catholic school in Belmont Cragin, but financial challenges led my mom to enroll me at Abraham Lincoln School in Lincoln Park. Every morning, I took a long bus ride from our neighborhood to this new world, one that demanded resilience and adaptation. At Lincoln, the environment was markedly different, with a clear divide among students based on academic tracks. The school had three distinct programs: the American Program, the Gifted Program, and the International Baccalaureate (IB) Program. The American Program, where I was placed, was seen as the "standard" track and was mainly composed of Black, Muslim, and Latinx students. By contrast, the gifted and IB programs were predominantly white and considered elite, with greater resources and higher academic expectations. Being in the American Program left me with a lingering sense of inadequacy, yet it also fueled my determination to prove myself in an environment that didn't expect much from students like me.

My childhood in Lincoln Park is marked by mixed emotions including sadness and a touch of resentment. As a student at Abraham Lincoln, our school helped design part of the new Oz Park, likely between 1990 and 1995, without understanding its historical significance. I now realize I was standing in what was once a vibrant Puerto Rican community, unaware of the legacy my people had left. In seventh and eighth grade, I stepped off the bus each morning carrying a Mexican or Puerto Rican flag, a deliberate assertion of identity in a school that often overlooked us. Many of my peers did the same, creating a shared expression of Latinx pride. Knowing now what I didn't know then about Lincoln Park's history, I would have been more vocal. Today, as I reconnect with this community, I bring both my experience and a deeper understanding of its past.

Domestic violence from a nonbiological grandfather occasionally forced my mom, sister, and me to relocate from our North Side home.

In second grade, we stayed with Pops in Bridgeport. My parents taught me how to recognize gang symbols for safety. When I was caught adding gang notes to a notebook, Pops and my mom were furious, even though they had taught me! After that, I became more discreet. Later, we moved in with my grandmother's sister on Damen and 18th, where bussing issues led me to be homeschooled for a year. During that time, I witnessed my first shootings, including seeing a young girl my age hit by a stray bullet. By fifth grade, we returned to our North Side home.

Reflecting on my academic journey, I'm surprised to still be in academia. My early school experiences were rough; many teachers seemed indifferent, which opened my eyes to deep inequalities in the city's school system. Even private schools couldn't match the resources of public schools in wealthier neighborhoods. Though I was in the basic tier at Lincoln, I still had more advantages than my peers in Belmont Cragin. High school magnified these issues with limited resources, stratified programs, and teachers' apathy, all set against a backdrop of gangs, drugs, and constant pressure. I briefly attended Weber High, a Catholic school, where I struggled as an outsider. My cousin, newly out of prison and affiliated with the Latin Kings, moved in with us, bringing gang culture closer to home. Despite family warnings, I felt its pull, trying to carve out my own space amid constant threats.

I remember the day my cousin marked my schoolbooks with gang symbols and a rival gang noticed. Threats followed, and I had to find new routes and friends to stay safe. By the end of freshman year, my group had grown into a tight-knit crew blending gang politics, graffiti, and chulo culture. Our numbers swelled to about sixty, with connections to the Latin Kings, Unknown Vice Lords, and Pachucos. That chaotic summer, filled with fights and near-misses, dragged down my grades, and my family couldn't keep up with Weber's tuition. I transferred to Taft, hoping for a fresh start.

At Taft, students clustered by race, with Latinos with Latinos and Black students with each other, except when gang alliances like the GDs crossed those lines. I joined the Maniac Latin Disciples but left after a year, questioning the legitimacy of the affiliation while staying connected to various networks. Amidst the chaos, I held onto an ideology rooted in unity and self-preservation. Latinx youth at Taft were marginalized, as

Vice Lords, predominantly African American, held power in numbers. This imbalance drove me to create an alternative for those seeking refuge from both Vice Lords and other Latinx factions. While we aimed to protect the vulnerable, the path we took often left scars, a bittersweet irony in our search for safety and belonging.

Taft, located in a predominantly white area with many police officers nearby, became a battleground where Black and Latinx students confronted hate and violence. Hate graffiti reminded us daily of racial tensions, but facing these threats together created temporary alliances. Bussing only worsened divisions. Intended to integrate us, it disrupted social bonds and led to prison-like gang affiliations. Racial lines were stark: Latinx and Black students found their spaces, while white students held theirs. Gangs served as a protective barrier in our community. Conflicts among minorities were painful, but there were moments of adversity that brought us together, like when skinheads targeted our school. GDs and Latino Folks joined forces leading to truces that temporarily bridged our differences. These experiences shaped my understanding of our community's challenges and fueled my passion for change.

My educational journey took a turbulent turn after my expulsion from Taft, which had become suffocating. A brief stint at Cosmopolitan, an alternative school, confirmed that the traditional system wasn't for me. I saw how systemic inequities marginalized Black and Brown students. Disparities in teacher attention fueled higher dropout rates and gang affiliations, and despite excelling on tests, I was often treated as inconsequential. One teacher gave me a barely passing grade for poor attendance, which pushed me further away. After being expelled again, I cut ties with formal schooling and pursued my GED, skipping prep courses and passing with a strong score. After dropping out, I worked an overnight job to support myself. One morning, after finishing a shift, I returned to Taft to drop off a friend and was confronted by a police officer called Taz. He accused me of wielding a knife, actually a work tool, and arrested me despite witnesses supporting my innocence. The incident pulled me into the criminal legal system and showed how easily unfounded accusations are used against young people in our communities. My employer testified, and the judge dismissed the case, but I was still placed on probation with a warning.

In my search for historical knowledge, I looked to figures like Pancho Villa, Emiliano Zapata, and Malcolm X, seeking narratives beyond the typical focus on Martin Luther King Jr. Finding resources on the Puerto Rican community was difficult, but the internet in my late teens offered some hope. Financial responsibilities weighed heavily. I had been working since I was fifteen, and by twenty-one, my mother gave me an ultimatum to get a job or leave, forcing me to balance education with economic necessity. Tensions at home often drove me to seek shelter elsewhere, and I relied on train rides for rest and creative expression. Determined to reengage with school, I enrolled at a for-profit university and initially excelled. However, personal tragedies and the violent loss of close friends led to deep depression and eventual withdrawal. I moved through various jobs until I landed at Northwestern University, where its libraries and resources sparked a turning point in my political awakening. With renewed determination, I was admitted and completed my BA, achieving a goal that once felt impossible.

I returned to my art, inspired by the ethos of the Young Lords and my stepfather's connection to the Brown Berets. Incorporating imagery from the Young Lords, Black Panthers, and Brown Berets into my work caught the attention of the New Era Young Lords (NEYL) on social media in 2019, just before the George Floyd uprisings. My art, blending Puerto Rican nationalism with these symbols, sparked mutual support online. While researching the Young Lords, I found an NEYL chapter in New York and reached out, learning there wasn't a Chicago chapter yet, though interest was growing. By early 2020, as NEYL chapters formed in other states, I observed from the sidelines, focusing on Hurricane Maria recovery efforts until COVID-19 halted most community activities.

In 2021, my stepfather's death deeply affected me. His life reflected both pride and struggle, shaped by gang involvement, addiction, and homelessness. Despite his service in Vietnam, he died unrecognized, his medals and honor still unclaimed. This loss strengthened my resolve to address injustices, particularly for Black and Brown communities. Knowing it was time to act, I reached out to Edgar "Suby" Toro, NEYL's national chairman, and told him, "We need to do something." Suby connected me with Alfredo, another Illinois-based organizer, and Charlene "Que Mala," as we worked to launch the Chicago chapter, inspired by Cha Cha and the original Young Lords.

In March 2021, I was interviewed by original Young Lords Omar López Zacarias and David Rivera, who tested my political knowledge and historical understanding. Soon after, I was officially appointed as Cacique, later deputy chairman, for the Chicago chapter, which, unlike other chapters organized by state, is rooted in the city as a tribute to the movement's origins. Alongside Alfredo and Charlene "Que Mala," we solidified our leadership team. Later that year, NEYL merged with the Young Lords Organization, bringing structural changes and adopting titles like deputy chairman and minister of defense to strengthen our mission. Suby's vision aligned with mine: to provide Puerto Rican youth with role models and challenge the negative narratives imposed on marginalized communities, a need amplified by the events of 2020.

I spent a lot of time observing NEYL's values and inclusivity before fully committing. I wanted to make sure they truly upheld equity across all identities and were serious about antiracism. Seeing that commitment was what convinced me to get involved because I've always believed in fighting oppression through cross-community solidarity. That sense of inclusivity is still at the heart of our movement. Our focus is on Puerto Rican independence, and we've rejected statehood as a solution. Looking at examples like Flint, Michigan, where people went years without clean water, it's hard to imagine what guarantees Puerto Rico would have within the US when even basic needs aren't met on the mainland. We've put our energy into independence and grassroots efforts, like hurricane relief, raising awareness about the Jones Act, debt issues, and gentrification that pushes Puerto Ricans out of their communities. Advocacy has always been about fighting for policies that put Puerto Rican rights and self-determination first.

Chicago has also played such a huge role in shaping global social justice. Movements like the Young Lords and Black Panthers, led by people like Chairman Fred Hampton Sr., left a lasting legacy. Even today, Chicago's influence shows up in things like the Latin Kings and Vice Lords, which, for better or worse, have reached far beyond the city. Despite all the segregation that still exists in 2022, Chicago's history of both division and solidarity offers powerful lessons for building resistance. Looking at US interventions in Central America, the Cuba embargo, and selective wars in the Middle East raises some big questions about our national priorities. It shows how connected oppression is, both at home and abroad, and reminds us why we have to fight for justice everywhere—whether it's in our neighborhoods or across the world.

As a master's student in the Critical Ethnic Studies Program at DePaul University, I've been focused on how social movements and street organizations protect vulnerable communities. I don't see society as "broken"—I believe it's intentionally designed to favor straight white male power structures rooted in religious ideologies. Chicago's Division Street Riots and the way the Young Lords transformed from a gang into a political force are clear examples of how street organizations push back against systemic oppression. I saw this same dynamic during the George Floyd uprisings, where gangs stepped up as protectors in communities that had been abandoned by the state. The media often gets it wrong, but I've witnessed real solidarity, like in Little Village, where the Latin Kings and Black communities came together to fight shared struggles. This kind of unity isn't just a Chicago thing; in Los Angeles, the Bloods, Crips, and Latinx groups have teamed up with the Panthers to take on systemic violence.

These examples inspire me to rethink how we talk about "gangs." I prefer to call them "street tribes" because it highlights their resilience, resourcefulness, and deep sense of community. Just like the Black Panthers, the Young Lords showed how groups that start as gangs can evolve into revolutionaries, building alliances that demand real change. I saw this kind of unity in action at a peace summit in Garfield Park on September 3, 2022. Minister Rico of the Vice Lords brought together groups like the Black P Stone Rangers, GDs, New Breeds, Black Panthers, and Brown Berets. They all came together to focus on community protection and building connections across divides. It was a powerful moment that showed how alliances like these can pave the way for real and lasting change.

The Young Lords Organization has always been rooted in a deep sense of kinship, carried over from gang loyalty, which filled personal voids and kept the group strong across generations. As someone from a later chapter, I've always respected this legacy, even as modern street tribes face divisions that didn't exist when the Young Lords were united. On June 4, 2022, we came together for the Passing of the Torch event, honoring Cha Cha in a way that doesn't often happen while people are still with us. It was more than a tribute; it was a chance to reflect on his legacy, recognize a generational shift, and recommit to the collective action that defined him and the Young Lords.

We spent months preparing for the event, which brought people from all over to Chicago, from Uptown to Lawndale, Humboldt Park to Lincoln Park. It felt like a historic moment, with so many voices coming together to embody the spirit of the Young Lords. Humboldt Park was the perfect setting, symbolic, powerful, and deeply connected to our community. Groups like the Black Panthers and Brown Berets stood with us, showing how solidarity across movements can create lasting strength. But this event wasn't just about celebration; it was about confronting the erasure of our history. We are now partnering with DePaul University to continue the reparative work started by the Young Lords, uncovering and sharing the stories of our communities. We honor the past by ensuring that the legacy of the Young Lords remains a guiding light, inspiring future generations to carry the torch forward and continue the fight for justice.

Tray Weathersby and Paul Mireles, New Era Young Lords at a rally protesting the murder of Anthony Alvarez in the Portage Park neighborhood of Chicago, March 16, 2022. Photograph by Eduardo Rodriguez.

Liz and Charlene Reynoso, New Era Young Lords. Photograph by Suby Toro.

Megan Galarza at DePaul rally, *The DePaulia*. Photograph by Amber Stoutenborough.

Young Lords and New Era Young Lords at Siguiendo Pa'lante event, Little Cubs Field, Chicago, June 4, 2022. Photograph by Jacqueline Lazú.

Intergenerational Dialogue

(2024)
Omar López Zacarias, Minister of Information, YLO
Paul Mireles, Chairman, Chicago Chapter, New Era Young Lords
Dolores Huerta Annual Symposium
October 16, 2024
DePaul University, Chicago, Illinois

Omar: My parents came to Chicago in the late 1950s to Humboldt Park, which was a predominantly white community. When I was twelve years old, I started looking for places where other Latinos were congregated. I came from San Luis Potosí, where I was part of a group of young boys and girls, and we had a very nice community. So when I got here, I was looking for that. I started venturing into other areas beyond Humboldt Park. I ended up hanging around Maplewood and Division. There was a hot dog stand there. I was going to Tuley High School, and I was hired at the hot dog stand. So that was sort of like my corner with all the other guys that came around there.

My connection with the Young Lords—there was a friend. His name is Kenny Smith, Appalachian white from Uptown. He used to come around all the time. And of course, you know, we're always looking for fights. One day, he invited me and said, "Let's go pick a fight with Chi-West." Chi-West was the gang that was on Chicago and Western. It was primarily Italian. Of course, there was already a history of conflict between the groups on Damen and Division, Maplewood and Division, California and Division with the Italian gangs, and then the Polish gangs. So that's why, when he invited me, I said, "Yes, naturally, let's go." When we got to Chicago and Western, it was too many of them. We had to go. And he said, "Well, let's go get my friends." So I said, "Let's go get your friends."

We went over to the playground at Burling and Armitage, but we didn't find anyone there at the time. Later, we found out that this spot was a hangout for the Young Lords. So, my first encounter with the Young Lords was when they were still considered a gang. Later on, many, many years afterward, I re-established contact with José "Cha Cha" Jiménez, when he was already starting to try to convince the other members to become more active in community politics. So, you know, we reconnected at that point, and from then on, I just became very active with the Young Lords.

Just before that, I was with the Latin American Defense Organization, which was one of the organizations that emerged from the Puerto Rican rebellion of June 1966. LADO was the very first organization that believed in direct action. They had four principles, but one of them was: if institutions do not respond to your needs, then it's okay to take direct action. So for me, it was sort of a natural progression—going from the gang environment to LADO, which became a direct-action organization, and then to the Young Lords. That was my transition into the Young Lords. And, of course, Cha Cha asked me to become the Minister of Information. Most of the guys used to joke around, saying, "Well, yeah, you became Minister of Information because you were the only one with a high school diploma." All the other guys had dropped out of Waller High School, now known as Lincoln Park High School. But that's how I became part of the Young Lords.

Paul: How did that work—your progression from the gangs to LADO and then eventually into the Young Lords? What lessons did you learn that helped you keep growing in activism? Because, you know, a lot of people look at unpoliticized street tribes, or what most would call gangs, as problematic. But there was something you learned there that eventually helped build into your direct actions with LADO, and then eventually into becoming the Minister of Information with the Young Lords.

Omar: No, I don't know how many people would share the kind of background I had. I came from a Protestant family in San Luis Potosí, which was extremely conservative. So, from the beginning, I would tell people that when I came to Chicago, if I experienced discrimination, I didn't even realize it because I was already used to it in San Luis. Being Protestant in a predominantly Catholic area meant we had to learn how to navigate those situations. We developed a sense of justice even as kids because the church instilled certain principles and a strong sense of community and helping each other. I think that had a lot to do with my progression from one thing to another. The Christian principles were very strong, and we truly believed in them.

Whenever we felt the need to take direct action, we remembered how Jesus drove the moneylenders out of the temple by force. He wasn't always just turning the other cheek. So, it was easy to hold on to those principles. With the Young Lords and with LADO, our main motivation for organizing was to help people. That was central to LADO's mission. One of our first organizing efforts was around welfare. Many young families coming from Puerto Rico needed assistance, but the system was blocking them from receiving the benefits they were entitled to. So, one of the very first things we did was make sure the Department of Public Welfare, which eventually became DCFS, started coming through with those benefits.

It felt natural to confront an institution like the welfare department because we believed in helping people. I think this was mentioned in the documentary about Cha Cha, too, that he initially wanted to be a priest and was active in catechism with his mother. I believe strongly that Cha Cha was also motivated by those same Christian values, which gave him the vision to organize and help people.

Paul: I want to learn a bit more about the direct actions that were happening with LADO, especially when we start talking about the Division Street Uprising and the roles LADO played there. And then, how did the Young Lords get involved? We can also go into the takeovers of both the People's Church and the Stone Academic Building.

Omar: You know, I mentioned that LADO was really the first Latino organization where we engaged in direct action. When we started organizing young Puerto Rican families, we had to overcome all the barriers the bureaucracy put in place to prevent families from receiving benefits. One major barrier was that if you were married, had a husband, or a partner, you'd be disqualified. So, one of the first things people learned was that you had to get around that obstacle—you had to say, "There's no man in the house. I'm not married." This approach led to LADO becoming a women-led organization. Not that men weren't involved, but it was the women who were really out front, setting the tone for change. They instilled that kind of determination in their sons and daughters, who also started to take action.

LADO wasn't alone in this. In addition to the active women leaders, their kids, their sons and daughters, were influenced by this environment. And because LADO operated in Latin King territory, even the Latin Kings started wanting to become more active as a community organization. They wanted to model themselves after the Young Lords. I think the direct influence came from watching their own mothers and fathers take action. So, these were some of the things that shaped the paths of both LADO and the Young Lords.

In Lincoln Park, it wasn't welfare but housing that became the primary issue. Still, for the sons and daughters of those families, this kind of activism felt natural. It took time, but eventually, most of the Young Lords members came to understand and embrace that philosophy.

Paul: As Minister of Information, what kinds of roles did you play, and what did you learn from that experience? What were some of the key aspects of organizing in your role, and what were some of your main responsibilities?

Omar: Minister of Information—that sounds really nice, but it was basically about propaganda within the Ministry of Information. Our responsibilities included the newspaper and all the leaflets that came out from the ministry, as well as creating slogans, graphics, and everything related to how we projected the image of the Young Lords. We always tried to come up with something catchy that would make an impact. That was essentially the role of the Ministry of Information.

But the members of that committee, the Ministry of Information, were involved in all the other programs, too. We helped with the breakfast for children, worked in the daycare centers, and supported the clinic. So, yes, we had specific departments and roles, but we were active across the whole operation of the Young Lords. Our main responsibility, though, was putting out the propaganda. We used to say we were an "armed propaganda unit"—that's what we were.

Paul: Is there a slogan we might all recognize that you helped create, or some kind of propaganda about the Young Lords that we might have seen?

Omar: Well, we won't go too far: "Tengo Puerto Rico en mi corazón." That came out of a conversation with Cha Cha and Spaghetti (Ralph Rivera). It's interesting because Spaghetti had just returned from Puerto Rico, where he'd experienced some of the political campaigns. Those campaigns are very theatrical, really unlike the ones here in the United

States. There's a lot of drama. So, he came back excited about doing something similar and involving the group. Around the same time, Cha Cha was getting out of jail and already had the idea of turning the Young Lords into a political organization.

At one point, we met at the Presbyterian Church on Washington and Ashland for an organizer's meeting. The three of us—me, Cha Cha, and Spaghetti—started talking about what needed to be done to shape the organization. Of course, one thing we decided was that we needed a logo and slogan. In that meeting, I ended up designing the button we still have. And from that conversation came our first slogan with the map of Puerto Rico, the fist with a rifle, and the phrase *Tengo Puerto Rico en mi corazon*. That was probably the first slogan from the Ministry of Information.

After that, we developed more slogans, like "Los Cuatro Lords," because we wanted people to know that it was Latinos, specifically, who were facing the courts in the Manuel Ramos case. We used Spanish in the slogan to make it clear that it was Latinos involved. Then, when students were killed at Kent State, we came up with slogans calling it a "state crime." Our aim was always to use slogans that would teach something.

Paul: I remember having that conversation with you as we sat down, looking at the New Era Young Lords flag. The original Young Lords slogan and emblem are right there at the center, and I found it really interesting that as we looked at the flag, we also got a bit of a history lesson on how it all came about. So, let's talk a little about the emergence of the New Era Young Lords and how you felt about that. I know you played a pivotal role in our development and continue to do so. Can you tell us a bit about how you were first introduced to the New Era and what your thoughts were?

Omar: I think it was Cha Cha who first talked to me about a group that wanted to organize again. I believe they were from New York and wanted to call themselves the New Era Young Lords. There was some conversation about whether they should use the name. After some discussions, Cha Cha was convinced that, yes, the new group would also be faithful to the principles of the Young Lords. So, he gave his blessing to go ahead and form it.

It started in New York, but we felt that Chicago was really the Young Lords' home and that we needed to establish the group here too. I think that's when I got in contact with you. Someone had given us your name. At first, I thought it would be a little difficult because we knew the kind of history that street tribes, or gangs, have. And for another group to rise up in Humboldt Park, I thought it might be challenging. I felt I needed to talk to you to make sure you understood what you were getting into.

When we spoke, I realized you had a parallel kind of history to the original Young Lords. You weren't an angel. And we needed that. I felt more comfortable knowing that your background was also rooted in the streets, so I knew you understood what you were stepping into and the challenges you'd likely face. That's how I first heard about the group. We met, and you all just took off from there.

I've been able to contribute whatever I can, mainly in sharing history, because I realized in talking with you that, while we have a parallel history, you all are much younger. We could probably share some lessons. And I think it's important that you share your own history and the path you've taken because those things helped us support the New Era Young Lords. Your history is worth sharing too.

Paul: I was born and raised here in Chicago and come from an intergenerational family of street tribe members, from Latin Kings to SDs (Satan Disciples) and Ambrose. Street politics ran deep in my family, and that was instilled in me from birth. I remember almost getting expelled from Abraham Lincoln Elementary, right down the street. In second grade, I got caught with a notebook where I'd listed every street corner I passed, noting the gang symbols I saw. Everywhere we drove, I'd stare out the window and mark down territories. So, while other kids were learning their ABCs, I was learning how to navigate the streets. By second grade, I could look at graffiti on a wall, recognize it as Latin King territory, know which colors to avoid, and understand what words not to say. These small but crucial details helped me as I grew older.

Eventually, I became affiliated with a street tribe for a short period in high school, around junior or senior year at Taft. I became a Maniac Latin Disciple for about a year before getting kicked out of Taft. But I never liked being confined to one group. With my knowledge of street affiliations, I could navigate different areas. One day I'd be in Little Village with Latin

Kings, the next day in Pilsen with Satan Disciples, or at the Cabrini-Green towers with some of the GDs I knew. I could move through all these areas, which gave me a unique respect and understanding.

When our national chairman, Suby Toro, reached out to me about developing a Chicago chapter, he felt confident in my ability to enter different neighborhoods, command respect, and keep people safe. In Chicago, *YLO* has different meanings across the city. There's the political Young Lords Organization, but there's also the gang aspect—Young Latino Organization, or YLO Cobras and YLO Ds. In places like Humboldt Park, this difference is significant; YLO Cobras and YLO Ds represented something entirely opposite to the Young Lords' values.

I remember talking to Chairman Suby about just becoming a member. I was interested in becoming a Young Lord and wanted to know what that entailed. After our conversation, he told me, "I'm going to have someone call you. Answer in a few minutes." Then, I got a call from you. You introduced yourself, and I recognized your name from studying Young Lords' history. I thought, "Oh damn, I'm getting a call from you!" It threw me off, but it also confirmed my decision to join. I didn't want to be part of an organization that didn't have the respect and support of its elders. That call played a big role in my decision to become a Young Lord.

Omar: There's a parallel I was talking about—a parallel between your experiences and what we all went through in the original Young Lords. At what point did you realize that being a Young Lord was more than just the name, that there were real responsibilities and actions to take? You had to develop an analysis of your environment to start organizing and acting. How did you go about doing that?

Paul: Like I said, I grew up in low-income areas, just a block away from the Austin neighborhood, which was, and still is, full of food deserts that remain unaddressed. I understood issues around food scarcity and price gouging because, if you could even find a place to buy food, the prices varied depending on the neighborhood. Access to healthy foods was drastically different based on where you were.

Growing up with a single mother and a stepfather who was in and out of jail—he was involved with gangs, drugs, and other things—taught me a lot. Despite that, he played a big role in my life, both good and bad.

As a young man, he had been a Brown Beret, and he taught me about the Brown Berets, Young Lords, Black Panthers, and the Chicanx movement, as well as the Zoot Suit Riots. So, I had all this knowledge, but I was still trapped in systems that limited me. I couldn't walk down certain streets wearing certain colors, like a purple scarf, because I lived in a Cobras neighborhood and needed to understand the codes of each area.

I also understood what many call police brutality, but which I call police terrorism. Brutality suggests just physical violence, but police terrorism includes controlling minds and creating fear. For me, it wasn't just theoretical. At twelve years old, I had a police officer point a gun at me simply because I was in the wrong place at the wrong time and fit a description. To this day, I feel PTSD; even now, if a police car is behind me, I start to feel anxious.

Those experiences shaped me, and while I channeled some of it into art, it didn't give me answers. Around 2012 or 2013, and especially once Trump started running for office, I saw all these things I'd been taught didn't exist anymore, systemic racism, injustice, were still very real. In school, they teach the Civil Rights Movement like it happened so long ago, with no real connection to the present, but seeing all of this resurface, I kept thinking, "What would I do if I were in that situation?" And then I realized I didn't have to wonder. I was in it, seeing people like me, from neighborhoods like mine, being brutalized, with military forces used against students, and the police targeting people on college campuses.

I saw parallels between what we'd read in the Young Lords' papers and what we're living through today. That's when I started asking myself, "What do I do with all this?" and began building an ideology. I eventually found the Young Lords and focused on their work. For example, they had a food program; we started a food program too. It wasn't because we said, "Oh, the Young Lords did it, so we should too." It happened naturally. I tried to set up a table in Humboldt Park just to talk about the Young Lords, but an art group I was working with said, "We have a free food distribution down the street. The organizer at Casa Hernandez was shot, so we need someone to distribute the food." That's what the community needed, so we stepped in.

The same struggles you faced then are still here today. Different names, different faces, different organizations, but the same systems remain.

Omar: I wonder how you're dealing with the issue of youth today, especially in terms of police brutality—or terrorism, as you call it. One thing I feel we contributed to with the original Young Lords was changing the mentality of the youth. Back then, in relation to law enforcement, we felt like victims. You'd get harassed, brutalized, jailed, and there was no recourse, so we were left feeling powerless.

But in the Young Lords, we changed that attitude. We taught the youth to say, "No, wait a minute. We're not victims anymore. We're part of the struggle, and we're equals in this fight." We made it clear that the police were there to protect corporations and the power structure, while we, as the Young Lords, were there to protect the community. It wasn't like before; the police understood that, and our confrontations became something different. Yes, it was still a David-and-Goliath situation, but we weren't victims anymore.

That shift gave the youth a new attitude toward law enforcement, especially when they were being abusive. So I wonder now, with your members, what kind of attitude they have toward that type of abuse.

Paul: A lot of our members already understand that dynamic, and some come from backgrounds similar to mine. Others, though, come from different life struggles—not necessarily a level of privilege, but different experiences. One thing I love about organizing as an older Young Lord is talking with the younger generations. When we look at the Young Lords or the Black Panthers, we see they were young. I remember people saying, "You're too young to make a difference." But Chairman Fred Hampton was only fourteen when the FBI started surveilling him. Cha Cha and all of you were also young when you got involved in the Young Lords, right? Some members were a little older, some younger, but they were all told they were "too young to make a difference." I think that's complete BS.

I have younger members in the organization now, barely eighteen, and they bring some of the best ideas. We nurture that by saying, "Okay, run with this. This is your project; build it up." We're also finding different ways to engage youth in political education. One program we had was "Hip-Hop, Pizza, and Political Education," where we'd bring people in from different neighborhoods—Englewood, Austin, Pilsen, Little Village, Humboldt Park—and we'd break down music lyrics, tying them to systemic issues. If we were talking about gender-based violence, we'd analyze a song that spoke to that issue and then discuss it. We did the same for police terrorism, capitalism, drugs, and substance abuse.

One song we used addressed PTSD. Now we hear about PTSD in Black and Brown communities, but ten or fifteen years ago, people would say, "We don't have that." I grew up thinking that, but now I recognize that, yeah, I do suffer from it because of what I've been through—the losses, the violence I've seen. Another program we had was an open mic at Casa Hernandez. We'd have about thirty-five people from all walks of life, even different gangs, coming together without issues—just creativity and collaboration. People who might be rivals on the street were making music together outside of the open mic.

Then one night, the police raided it. About fifteen cop cars pulled up and demanded to enter. Luckily, there were steel doors, so we locked everyone inside while I went out to negotiate with the cops. After thirty or forty minutes, I got them to agree that only the building inspector and one officer could come in, and they weren't allowed to talk to anyone except me. They came in, saw that everything was free—food, clothing, everything for the community—and then left. Still, I got hit with a cease-and-desist and was threatened with jail time. Eventually, we beat the case, but these confrontations keep happening.

All we were doing was challenging a narrative. I told the cops, "All you want to do is criminalize the youth. You have no places for them to go; the community centers are shut down in Black and Brown neighborhoods, yet you come here and cause terror. We're giving them a free place to be creative, and you're here to intimidate." People inside were terrified because of the aggressive police presence, but we stood our ground.

Omar: I want you to share some thoughts on a couple of things. First, in the Young Lords, we had an ideology. We were socialists. We read philosophical essays by Mao Tse Tung, like *On Practice* and *Serve the People*. That was the kind of literature we'd have our cadre read. Of course, we weren't always successful with it. I remember asking a young guy, maybe sixteen or seventeen, to start reading *On Practice* by Mao, and he said, "I don't have to read Mao. I'm not Chinese!" No, I told him, you read Mao anyway. So, we had that kind of political education. We were extreme left. We took strong positions on issues: we opposed the war in Vietnam, supported draft dodgers, and backed Palestine back when Yasser Arafat was the leader. Those were the kinds of ideological stances we had, and I'd like to hear a bit about how that looks in your organization today.

The second thing is this: I don't know if your members are aware, but when the power structure starts seeing real organization, that's when they come down on you. If you're just hanging around the corner, it's fine. But as soon as you start organizing, they get concerned. You might bring people together to talk about things, and they'll tolerate it. But when you begin to politicize and develop an ideology, that's when you become a real threat, especially if you're bringing people from different neighborhoods to coexist peacefully. That's dangerous to them because gangs, as we know, are very disciplined organizations. They've been easy to manipulate because they don't have an ideology, so they can be pulled in any direction—left, right, wherever someone guides them. But once there's an ideology, it becomes a threat.

I wonder if your members are aware of this; that when you become a Young Lord, it's a commitment.

Paul: One of the things we talk about when people come in and want to learn about becoming a Young Lord today is political education. We study Mao, Marx, Lenin, and Huey—breaking down these ideas. The one issue I sometimes see, though, is how we can turn these figures into dogma, treating ideology as something set in stone rather than a flexible foundation to build from. I believe our current ideologies should serve as a base, something to expand upon, critique, and evolve.

We need to acknowledge that these revolutionary ideologies, while powerful, still contain elements of patriarchy, white supremacy, genderism, and class bias. They're not perfect. When we start treating them as if they are, we run into problems. You see this in groups that Chairman Fred referred to as "opportunistic" and "individualistic" in his comments about the Weathermen and SDS—they acted as though they knew what was best without considering what the people needed. Even within the YLP, there was a moment of disconnect when they went to Puerto Rico with the mindset of Puerto Ricans who hadn't grown up on the island, assuming they knew what the island needed for liberation without respecting the decades of struggle led by people on the ground.

So, we need to take ideology for what it is: a foundation, not a limit. If we get stuck debating ideology alone, without action, we lose relevance. It's about asking, "How does this connect to what we need to do now?" For example, we still hold the same stance on Palestine as the Young Lords did back then; we believe in a free and independent Palestine. We also believe that if escalation is necessary, it can be justified, especially when institutions remain complicit in the ongoing genocide.

We've discussed the recent encampments and condemned actions taken by universities like DePaul, Northwestern, and UIC against students standing up for justice. If further action is needed, then it should happen, with institutions standing behind students rather than oppressing them. These are places of higher education, supposedly built on freedom of speech and thought, yet we're seeing students brutalized by police. On campus, it often feels like we're institutionalized and surveilled, with security guards on every corner enforcing this suppression.

We, as Young Lords, recognize this and ensure our members understand these points. We are building on what past generations realized and fought against, carrying that knowledge forward.

Omar: I'm really happy to hear that, because the conditions we worked in during the '60s and '70s were entirely different from those today. Back then, we believed in dialectical materialism. It was a valuable tool for analysis, and I think it still is. But now, from what you're saying, you understand it's not set in stone; other things need consideration. I can see, for example, that there's a spiritual aspect to the New Era Young Lords that we didn't have. And that's important. It's something that needs to be acknowledged. There's a mysticism about the movement that, if absent, makes it hard to sustain. There must be spiritual beliefs in the work; it can't just be black and white.

For us, though, the conditions of our time were more black and white. We didn't have Latinx aldermen, state reps, congressmen, or judges. We didn't see ourselves in those spaces, so it was easier for us to target the structures we opposed. Today, it's different. You have Latinos in those positions, which is significant for our community. But I think the Young Lords have a big task in clarifying what it means to have these elected officials and helping the community understand that this isn't the end goal. They serve a specific purpose, and accountability is still essential. Not many organizations are willing to hold elected officials accountable, but I believe the New Era Young Lords have a role in that—helping to clear the smoke and showing the youth what needs to be done moving forward.

It's a new stage now. We operated under certain conditions, but yours are entirely different, and in many ways, more challenging. You face more "booby traps" than we did. So, I'm glad to hear that's how you're looking at things. And again, I think the spiritual aspect of the movement is essential. Without it, it's easy to knock down.

Paul: I find it interesting, with your religious background and Cha Cha once wanting to be a priest. Now, fast forward to the New Era, and I have people in the organization about to become santeros and santeras, others about to undergo voodoo head-washing ceremonies, and even myself, I'm about to have a ceremony in Cuba in a month or two. That spirituality, or even the religious aspect, plays a role in our organizing both then and now. As we continue to expand and look at decolonizing, we also focus on spiritual and religious decolonization, pushing back against the mainstream demonization of our practices. I have members who practice Native American traditions, and it wasn't until the late '70s or early '80s that some of these practices even became legal again, free from criminal repression.

We're also mindful of how we need to organize now. You're right; we do face a lot of "booby traps." One thing I remind our members is that we don't always have to jump into militant action right away. If there's a need to escalate, we will, but there are other ways to organize. We have tools and connections at our fingertips that your generation didn't have. When you mention politicians, state reps, and aldermen, we do have a few who are close allies. For example, that's how I got my own charges dropped. I reached out to people on police accountability forums and said, "This was completely unjustified." They brought it to the alderman in Humboldt Park, discussed it, and eventually got the police captains to drop the charges.

So, if our main goal is liberation, we have to recognize that it's not a one-size-fits-all approach. The system is so deeply embedded that we need multiple strategies and ways to address it, while still holding onto the same mission and core values.

Questions from the Audience

Did the Young Lords and the Black Panthers ever work together? If so, what were some of the things that came out of that collaboration?

Omar: The relationship between the Young Lords and the Black Panthers was very close, especially because Chairman Cha Cha and Chairman Fred were tight. There was a lot of cross-pollination, so to speak. The Young Lords really mirrored the structure of the Black Panthers. That's how we organized ourselves. There was a lot of influence there, and we collaborated on many things. For example, when the Latin American Defense Organization held demonstrations at the welfare department, the Black Panthers and the Young Lords provided security for the welfare women. That type of collaboration was already in place.

Later, this collaboration developed into the Rainbow Coalition. It grew because of the shared experiences we had as we progressed, but it started with the Lords and Panthers providing security with the welfare union at LADO. So, the relationship was very tight, and I believe the influence went both ways. Chairman Fred was already an internationalist, but the Young Lords, even as a gang, were also internationalist. The original group included African Americans, Mexicans, Puerto Ricans, and Appalachian whites, so there was already an attitude of inclusivity. I think there was significant influence and contributions on both sides.

Paul: I'll say that even to this day, we still work with the Black Panthers. Chairman Fred Hampton Jr., the Black Panther Cubs, and the New Era Young Lords have joint programs. We're actually starting a new program at Oakley Square, a housing center on Western and Jackson, where we're bringing the breakfast program, along with self-defense and political education classes. So, the work that began between our organizations back in the '60s is still alive and well today.

My question is mainly for Paul: What are you and the New Era Young Lords working on right now to combat issues in the Lincoln Park and Humboldt Park areas, like the housing crisis? And, on a global level, how are you addressing the genocide in Gaza and Palestine? What inspiration do you take from the original Young Lords as you work to fight these issues and bring about justice?

Paul: In Lincoln Park, unfortunately there is not much organizing happening except for some of the work we are doing to support student organizations, like during the encampment, or as we begin to address food disparity among DePaul students. Access to food is not always easy for many of our students here, and that is one of the issues we are currently focused on.

In Humboldt Park, we have taken more direct action. We have been involved in housing takeovers and in working with the growing houseless community in the park. We have launched several programs there and are now reloading those efforts to continue the work.

We have always stood in full solidarity with the people of Palestine. We advocate for Palestine in every context we appear in because it is a state of emergency, and we cannot stop talking about Palestine in any space. When we organize in solidarity, we follow the example of the Young Lords by refusing to center ourselves. We do not come in telling people what to do. Instead, we show up and ask what they need from us. It is their voice, their movement, their time. Whether that means being present, helping with security, or simply standing with them, we are there to support in whatever way they ask.

We are also continuing our work in Puerto Rico. A recent delegation just returned, and some members are still there helping to rebuild infrastructure damaged by Hurricane María. Years later, we are still only scratching the surface, and more hurricanes have hit the island since. Every six months, we send another group, collect donations, raise funds through grassroots efforts like art sales, and return to do the work. Right now, we are rebuilding a destroyed school in Yabucoa that is being converted into a hurricane shelter.

Like the original Young Lords, we do not wait for permission. We fight because our survival is on the line and because we owe it to each other to keep going.

Siguiendo Pa'lante (2022)
Collage design by Charlene Reynoso, New Era Young Lords
Courtesy of the artist

Notes

1 J. De Diego, "Pitirre," *Cantos de pitirre* (San Juan, Puerto Rico: Instituto de Literatura Puertorriqueña, 1949).

2 Arnold R. Hirsch, *Making the Second Ghetto: Race and Housing in Chicago, 1940–1960* (University of Chicago Press, 1983).

3 Gina Pérez, *The Near Northwest Side Story: Migration, Displacement, and Puerto Rican Families* (University of California Press, 2004).

4 Martha M. Arguello, "We Joined Others Who Were Poor: The Young Lords, the Black Freedom Struggle, and the 'Original' Rainbow Coalition," *Journal of African American Studies* 23, no. 4 (2019): 436.

5 Friedrich Engels, *The Peasant War in Germany*, trans. Moissaye J. Olgin (International Publishers, 1926), http://www.marxists.org/archive/marx/works/download/pdf/peasant-war-germany.pdf.

6 See Jeffrey O. G. Ogbar, "Puerto Rico en mi corazón: The Young Lords, Black Power, and Puerto Rican Nationalism in the U.S., 1966–1972," *Centro Journal* 18, no. 1 (Spring 2006): 148–69.

7 Felipe Hinojosa, *Apostles of Change: Latino Radical Politics, Church Occupations, and the Fight to Save the Barrio* (University of Texas Press, 2020), 118–20.

8 Marisol V. Rivera, and Judson L. Jeffries, "From Radicalism to Representation: José 'Cha Cha' Jiménez's Journey into Electoral Politics," *Journal of African American Studies* 23, no. 4 (December 2019): 299–319.

9 Johanna Fernández, *The Young Lords: A Radical History* (University of North Carolina Press, 2020), 229–31.

10 See Adam Cohen and Elizabeth Taylor, *American Pharaoh: Mayor Richard J. Daley—His Battle for Chicago and the Nation* (Boston: Little, Brown, 2000), chap. X; Mike Royko, *Boss: Richard J. Daley of Chicago* (New York: Dutton, 1971).

11 "Interview with Jose 'Cha Cha' Jimenez on Original Rainbow Coalition," *Fight Back! News*, July 1, 2019, https://fightbacknews.org/articles/interview-jose-cha-cha-jimenez-original-rainbow-coalition.

12 Yarimar Bonilla and Marisol LeBrón, eds., *Aftershocks of Disaster: Puerto Rico Before and After the Storm* (Haymarket Books, 2019).

13 Briddenson quoted in *The Black Panthers Speak*, ed. Philip S. Foner (J.B. Lippincott, 1970; repr. Haymarket Books, 2014), xxxiv.

14 Diana Taylor, *The Archive and the Repertoire: Performing Cultural Memory in the*

Americas (Duke University Press, 2003).

15 Jacqueline Lazú, *The Block/El Bloque: A Young Lords Story*, DePaul Humanities Center Faculty Fellow (VHS tape and Dialogo article), Young Lords Records, Box 3, Folder 24, Special Collections and Archives, DePaul University, Chicago, Illinois.

16 Saidiya Hartman, "Venus in Two Acts," *Small Axe* 12, no. 2 (June 2008): 1–14.

17 Jonathan Rosa, *Looking Like a Language, Sounding Like a Race: Raciolinguistic Ideologies and the Learning of Latinidad* (Oxford: Oxford University Press, 2019).

18 José "Cha Cha" Jiménez interviewed by Jacqueline Lazú, August 15, 2018.

19 *DePaulia*, May 19, 1969, page 2, DePaul University Special Collections and Archives, Chicago, Illinois.

20 Joann Makal, "People Power Comes to the Campus," *Aletheia*, May 23, 1969, page 4, DePaul University Special Collections and Archives, Chicago, Illinois.

21 "Five-Day Sit-In at McCormick Seminary Ends," *Chicago Tribune*, May 19, 1969, page 7, Collection on McCormick Theological Seminary, Box 1, DePaul University Special Collections and Archives, Chicago, Illinois.

22 *Y.L.O.* 1, no. 2 (May 1969): 3, Collection on the Young Lords, Box 5, DePaul University Special Collections and Archives, Chicago, Illinois.

23 Also republished in *The Young Lords: A Reader*, ed. Darrel Enck-Wanzer (New York University Press, 2010), pp. 27–29. Both the original and republished versions identify the interviewer only as "BM." Most accounts attribute the interview to Bobby Rush, a leader in the Illinois Chapter of the Black Panther Party who later served as a US congressman from Illinois.

24 Olga Jimenez de Wagenheim, *Puerto Rico: An Interpretive History from Pre-Columbian Times to 1900* (Princeton, Markus Weiner, 2014), 166.

25 Agustín Laó, "Resources of Hope: Imagining the Young Lords and the Politics of Memory," *Centro Journal* 7, no. 1 (1995): 34–49.

26 I am indebted to Roberto Rodríguez-Morazzani's important essay, "Political Cultures of the Puerto Rican Left," in *The Puerto Rican Movement: Voices from the Diaspora*, ed. Andrés Torres and José Velázquez (Temple University Press, 1998), 25–47, for showcasing the important ways boricua activists have long honored past revolutionary figures while simultaneously engaging in current-day social justice organizing.

27 Jacqueline Lazú, "The Chicago Young Lords: (Re)constructing Knowledge and Revolution," *Centro Journal* 25, no. 2 (2013): 32.

28 Ernesto Laclau and Chantal Mouffe, *Hegemony and Socialist Strategy* (New York: Verso Books, 2001).

29 Ngugi wa Thiong'o, "Enactments of Power: The Politics of Performance Space," *Drama Review* 41, no. 3 (Fall 1997): 12.

Index

Page numbers in italics indicate images

About the Authors

Jacqueline Lazú is a professor of Spanish at DePaul University and a recognized scholar of the Chicago Young Lords whose work examines historical and political contexts through cultural analysis, history, and Puerto Rican diaspora politics.

José "Cha Cha" Jiménez (1948–2025) was the founder and Chairman of the Young Lords Organization. Born in Puerto Rico, he moved with his family to the United States as an infant and became a political leader in Chicago, committed to Puerto Rican self-determination and revolutionary grassroots struggle. After being forced underground by state repression, he emerged to serve a one-year prison sentence. In 1975, he ran for alderman in Chicago's 46th Ward as the first Latino to do so and continued his lifelong work in organizing, political education, and preserving Young Lords history.